All by Myself

All by Myself

The Unmaking of a Presidential Campaign

by
Christine M. Black and
Thomas Oliphant

The Globe Pequot Press

Chester, Connecticut

Library of Congress Cataloging-in-Publication Data

Black, Chris.
    All by myself : the unmaking of a presidential campaign / by Chris Black and Thomas Oliphant. — 1st ed.
        p.   cm.
    ISBN 0-87106-547-9
    1. Presidents—United States—Election—1988. 2. Dukakis, Michael S. (Michael Stanely), 1933- . 3. United States—Politics and government—1981-1989. I. Oliphant, Thomas II. Title
E880.B57   1989   89-11929
324.973'0927—dc20   CIP

Manufactured in the United States of America
First Edition/First Printing

Contents

Preface

Just as political history smiles upon the winners of economic struggles, wars, and elections, the act of winning an American election carries with it an air of inevitability and, sometimes, even virtue. History and electorates tend to forget losers. Yet sometimes the loser is as central to the story of a presidential election as is the winner. Thomas Dewey's collapse in 1948 and Richard Nixon's photo-finish failure twelve years later contributed as much to the outcome of those two pivotal elections as did the campaigns of the victors, Harry S. Truman and John F. Kennedy respectively.

The 1988 defeat of Michael S. Dukakis fits into this category of significant loser. Despite an election year of relative peace and prosperity in a conservative era, the liberal governor of Massachusetts made a remarkable ascent from nowhere to the brink of dominance. Ultimately, however, he failed. And that failure had as much to do with his deficiencies as a candidate and potential national leader as it did with the skills and wiles of his rivals. That is why we thought it important to explore this star-crossed campaign in depth. A Dukakis victory was possible in 1988 because most Americans were receptive to a call for change in national direction. His defeat—its roots, its development, and its culmination in an abyss of pain for its champion—is a case study in how to lose a presidential campaign.

Governor Dukakis chose not to discuss the campaign with us in depth after the election. Defeat is a particularly bitter experience for a consistently high achiever; and Dukakis, distracted by state fiscal difficulties and his wife's gutsy confrontation with alcoholism, seemed to delay the process of coming to grips with his loss. But he graciously spoke to us on many occasions during his twenty-month marathon. We also benefited from the assistance of the entire senior leadership of his campaign as well as that of scores of vineyard workers around the United States who generously shared their memories, their analysis, and their contemporary memoranda with us.

Our *Globe* colleagues Curtis Wilkie and Ben Bradlee, Jr., opened their notebooks to us to share their reporting and insights of the final days on the Dukakis plane.

We could not have undertaken this project without the support of our *Boston Globe* superiors, editor Jack Driscoll and executive editor Ben Taylor, which we gratefully acknowledge. But the idea for it could never have taken root without the encouragement of deputy managing editor Helen Donovan, who directed the *Globe*'s campaign coverage. In a political season dominated by talk of leadership, she demonstrated daily what it is. Portions of chapters two through five appeared in the *Globe* from May 8 to 11, 1988, and in similar form in a series called "The Road to the Nomination," which we wrote with *Globe* reporters Andrew Blake, Joan Vennochi, and John Aloysius Farrell.

At The Globe Pequot Press, the willingness and enthusiasm of President Charles B. Everitt to tackle a tough topic were inspirational, and the ability of managing editor Bruce Markot to make us think beyond our factual information was deeply appreciated.

Thanks to Sean Mullin and Charles Liftman of the *Globe*'s computer department, who vastly simplified the production of our manuscript, and to the *Globe*'s talented photographers whose work enhances this project.

Two of our profession's best experts at getting to the point helped us edit the original manuscript—CBS producer Janet Leissner and CBS correspondent Susan Spencer (Mrs. Oliphant, in real life).

We should like to address a final point to future students of the 1988 campaign. This volume is an account of the Dukakis campaign, a case study of defeat. We would urge those doing detailed work to study two books by *Globe* colleagues: *Dukakis*, a biography by Charles Kenney and Robert L. Turner; and *The Duke*, a profile and account of his nomination by David Nyhan.

1

Monos Mou

"Liberal, liberal."

The Republican demonstrators chanted defiantly from the other side of the chain-link fence.

"Lib-raaal, lib-raaal."

They dragged out the word until it became a drone that filled the crisp night air.

It was 3:30 A.M. on election day, November 8, 1988, and a sharp wind whipped fine sheets of snow across the tarmac at the Des Moines Flying Service. A few dozen people jostled together for warmth against the terminal building. As a chartered Gulfstream taxied to a stop, a flood of more than 3,000 people, supporters of the Democratic presidential nominee and almost-certain loser that day, poured from behind the building across the blacktop toward a makeshift stage.

Guido Fenu from the Savery Hotel, the Democrats' favored joint in downtown Des Moines, set up a rickety courtesy bar on the tarmac. The press corps from the zoo plane, already off balance from fatigue, the flight from California, and an unexpected 100-foot bounce upon landing, stumbled toward the iced beer. Jim Steinberg, an issues adviser to the candidate, took nostalgic "happy snaps" with his automatic camera. The crowd murmured in anticipation.

The crowd danced with delight on the tarmac at the Des Moines Flying Service at the pre-dawn election day rally. (Photo by James Steinberg)

On cue, the campaign anthem for Michael Dukakis—Neil Diamond's "America"—thundered into the darkness from the sound system one last time, nearly four months after its national debut on a steamy night in Atlanta. The music raised the murmurs to a roar. *"Far, we've been traveling far/Without a home, but not without a star."* The man they had come to see was gray with exhaustion. He hadn't slept in a bed in two days in order to embark upon a final, fifty-three-hour, nonstop, cross-country, round-the-clock frenzy of last-minute campaigning. He borrowed a taupe suede jacket from trip director Jack Weeks of South Boston. A few weeks earlier, the campaign staff had discovered that Weeks's sporty jacket made the button-down, straightlaced governor look more like a regular guy. Not being a slave to fashion or the image-makers, Dukakis zipped the jacket to the top, nerd style, as protection from the chill wind. By the time he spoke, it was nearly 4:00 A.M.

The crowd danced with delight at being out so late, at the historic moment. They waved their hands high in greeting and brandished signs. One homemade message in Magic Marker on posterboard said, "We're proud of you."

The wind whipped at ten large American and Iowa state flags posted on the podium. Kitty Dukakis, wrapped warmly in a black wool coat, introduced "my passionate partner of the last twenty-five years, the next president of the United States."

"We had to take the red-eye to the Hawkeye state to be with all of you," he cried, his voice raspy from overuse and fatigue. The day before in Cleveland, after another all-night flight from the West Coast, he had tried another version, "We had to take the red-eye to the Buckeye state to be with all of you."

"Libraaal, lib-raaal."

The demonstrators' taunt almost drowned out his words for the bleary-eyed press corps huddled next to a riser behind the crowd. The Republicans began to recite the Pledge of Allegiance. *"I pledge allegiance to the flag of the United States of America and to the Republic for which it stands. . . ."*

One more time, he spoke to a crowd of thousands with simple intimacy, as if talking to his neighbors across a hedge on Perry Street in Brookline. It was not his way to sketch lofty, sparkly visions in the dark night air. Kitty has to leave to make an appearance in Philadelphia before going home to Massachusetts, he said. Our daughters, Andrea and Kara, are here. Our son John and John's wife Lisa send their best wishes. Lisa, he reminds them, will be having a baby in January.

As he hunched over the bank of microphones, memories of worried young mothers, sleepy small towns, and peaceful farmhouses pushed through the numbing fatigue. In turn he pushed out the words into the incandescent artificial light, his breath making small puffs of steam.

He spoke of seven mothers in Sioux City, Iowa, who had no medical care after their babies were delivered, and of the farm families who had opened their homes to him and talked to this would-be president late into the night about the joy and frustration of earning a living from the land. He talked about the Iowa tradition of commitment to excellence in education.

"America is not just another place, not just another piece of land, just another country. It's the noblest experiment ever undertaken on the face of this earth." Heartfelt words came from the weary fifty-five-year-old son of Greek immigrants. His father and mother had come to America in 1912 and 1913 in search of opportunity. Before this day was over, their son would fall 6.8 million votes short of being elected the forty-first president of the United States. So often tarred for lacking any vision, he spoke of "one nation, one community, one family. That is the type of president I want to be, a president who brings us together and unites us."

Then, before he left, the Democratic Party's best hope remembered a promise made when his marathon began. "Our first regional development conference will be at the Adler Theater in Davenport," he said. "You can depend on it."

How characteristic of Dukakis to recall his pledge to hold the first (reporters feared they would be many) regional economic-development conference in Davenport, Iowa at this last moment in the campaign. No gossamer clouds of gauzy dreams and wistful hopes came from this politician. His visions were sturdy, achievable, sensible, and practical— just like Michael Dukakis himself.

Why couldn't the federal government revitalize Davenport as he had revitalized Lowell, Massachusetts? Regional development, now that was a dream!

It was also no surprise that the Republican taunt of "liberal"—the word used as an expletive by his opponents—would dog him right down the home stretch. Strategists for Vice President George Bush had figured out long ago that their man could not beat this Massachusetts governor by debating issues like health care for the uninsured, college loans for the middle class or the budget deficit. Dukakis's own internal polls showed that his greatest strength was what his pollster, Tubby Harrison, described as his "personal-quality advantages" over Bush. First impressions recorded in early summer polls showed that voters considered Dukakis qualified to be president: independent-minded, his own man, someone they could trust, and a person who exhibited strong leadership ability. Bush, a sitting vice president with plenty of baggage, could beat Dukakis only by destroying him and making sure that the name Michael Dukakis became a synonym for big taxer, big spender, polluter, weak on defense, soft on crime, and unacceptable risk.

The strategy had worked better than the Bush-handlers ever dreamed, with amazing, if unintended cooperation from the governor. By the end of the campaign, national polls showed Dukakis was less popular than the hapless J. Danforth Quayle, the Indiana senator whom Bush had plucked from relative obscurity to be his running mate. The yearning for change registered by so many public-opinion polls had dissipated, or at least been diverted, by a greater uneasiness over putting the federal government in the hands of this risky liberal.

Nine days earlier, Dukakis's campaign had chartered an Amtrak train for a trip into the verdant California Central Valley, where farmland stretches to the horizon. From Bakersfield up to Stockton, Dukakis was vibrant. The working-class Democrats chuckled as he mocked the Republicans for prematurely "popping those champagne corks in their penthouses," and they cheered whenever he shouted the simple phrase that had eluded him and scores of hangers-on and advisers for twenty months: "I'm on *your* side."

At sundown, the train pulled into Merced, stopping just short of an old brick train station, now abandoned but spruced up for that evening, and bathed in the flattering sunset's soft light and expertly arranged klieg lights. It was the fourth speech on the tour, and so we wandered away from the cheering crowd back toward the train. In the window of the first car, a lone man's face stared out at the scene—partly somber, partly content, but mostly just watching. We reached up and banged on the window, shaking John Sasso out of his reverie, and shortly he came out to chat.

"This message fits him," he said, as "I'm on your side" drew another roar from the train-station crowd. It had been nearly four years since Sasso had sown and nurtured the seeds that flowered into Dukakis's presidential candidacy. "He is totally comfortable."

It was a strikingly bittersweet observation at that special, if belated moment when the presidential nominee was connecting with voters.

Another such moment came on the Saturday night before the election. At the close of a punishing campaign day including eight hours in the air, Dukakis spoke at a rally in South Texas. Representative Kika de la Garza, a congressman for twenty-four years and an institution in the border-area Hispanic community, introduced him to his constituents. "Oh gentle friend of the sad face and the tender smile," he said, alternating between Spanish and English as Dukakis would do himself. "No matter what happens, we shall always be with you. Here are your people." Saucer-shaped silver, red, and blue balloons sped into the air. A few of the national political reporters were moved to wistful prose about the balloons' carrying Democratic dreams into the Texas night.

In the end, it was Michael Dukakis who tossed away those Democratic dreams.

Time after time, the presidency lay on the ground before him, within his reach. Picking it up was within his power and ability. But something ingrained and visceral kept him from reaching out to let people know him and kept him from reaching in to offer them a loftier vision of the nation's potential. His mother said that his first words were *"monos mou,"* Greek for "all by myself." Even as a toddler he exhibited fierce independence, a strong sense of self, and a willfulness seen later in his political persona. His strength of will had a flip side, stubbornness. He followed his inner voice even when everyone around him said the opposite, even when he was wrong.

That Dukakis blew it makes his campaign far more than just another chapter in the long tale of his party's slide from presidential grace. For the issue in summer and fall 1988 was no longer memories of the last Democratic president's dismal legacy—virulent inflation, lines at gasoline stations, weak leadership, high tax rates, intrusive government. Ronald Reagan, the man who in many ways restored the presidency in the 1980s but left festering problems unaddressed, was not the issue. The widening gulf between the haves and have-nots in society wasn't the issue, either.

The issue for the general election was this modest-looking man standing on a platform in front of the abandoned Merced train station.

Once George Bush made Dukakis the main issue in the campaign, he never let up. A few days after Dukakis took that train trip in California, the vice president started following him around the country, showing up within a day of Dukakis's departure and shouting, "I'm on your side," to confuse the Democratic message. Every night, Bush's campaign kept up a barrage of television commercials hammering at the same themes and images that voters had been hearing and seeing for more than two months: Dukakis is a criminal-coddler, he's a polluter, he's opposed to the weapons the country must have to be strong, he's a *liberal*. See the prison turnstile with all the convicts walking through it; see the mug shot of a menacing black man; see the dirty Boston Harbor water; see the silly little man in the funny-looking helmet and the foolish smile riding in that tank?

For Michael Dukakis, defeat was not inevitable. Victory was more than possible on the day of his first debate with Bush in late September. Victory was not yet completely improbable just before the second debate in mid-October. In fact, the final result was much closer than the popular and electoral-vote margins indicated.

The route to failure, though, was a long one and clearly marked with signs forming a map to defeat in modern presidential politics. These are signs that future candidates, their advisers, and students of the process should not ignore.

Beware of candidates who spend most of their time deciding *whether* to run, instead of *why* and *how*; beware of nomination-fixated strategies; beware of inner circles around candidates tied by their close-knit insularity; beware of buttoned-up candidates who instinctively distrust rhetoric, television, and other politicians; beware of candidates who coast or are smug when they seem strong; beware of candidates who seek to dominate the detail in their campaigns, a species that ironically includes the chronically indecisive and insecure; and beware of candidates who stress means over ends, trees over forests, detailed content over thematic style.

Dukakis's failings, though major, are not unique. Nearly all of modern America's presidential losers who could have won share some of his flaws—including the never-nominated Robert Alphonso Taft, Nelson Rockefeller, Edward Kennedy, Gary Hart, and Bob Dole, and defeated nominees Thomas Dewey, Richard Nixon (in 1960), Gerald Ford, and Jimmy Carter (in 1980). Each of them, in the end, could not honestly look anywhere for an explanation except in the mirror.

The dangers inherent in Dukakis's approach to the campaign were apparent in the very earliest moments of his candidacy. More than three months before Dukakis decided to run for president, and three days after his reelection as governor in 1986, John Sasso wrote him a memorandum to persuade him to consider running; in it he posed two pointed questions. First, he would have to decide before embarking on a quest for the presidency whether he really believed he had something to offer his country that no other candidate had. And second, he asked Dukakis if he would be willing (Sasso's phraseology was intentionally bland) to draw stark differences between himself and his opponents to help make his case, and whether he was prepared to use heightened rhetoric. Heightened rhetoric meant hyperbole, exaggeration, language that identified the bad guys, as well as words arranged and delivered to make a visceral, emotional connection with voters. Sasso wrote that memorandum and posed those questions fifteen months before the Iowa precinct caucuses ushered in the 1988 voting season.

Five months later, just three weeks before his official announcement, Sasso reminded him of something else in a second memorandum. It was all well and good to be cautious and careful, he wrote, to see a presidential campaign as a marathon and to almost sneak up on the public's consciousness as a candidate who would grow on people. Sasso told him bluntly, however, that he would eventually have to be something other than good, solid, *competent* Michael Dukakis; he would have to become a compelling personality who communicated an understanding of the challenges facing the country and forcefully articulated a response to those challenges.

In early July 1987, Sasso wrote again to his boss about the need to put all his views and positions in an overriding framework showing that Dukakis represented significant change. Pointedly, he said that this high note had not yet been hit and that it was critical for Dukakis to become more broadly thematic as he moved into fall 1987. He had to convey a reassuring sense that the future would be safe and secure as long as the country had the right leadership.

Sasso, who had been giving Dukakis memoranda like these every three months for five years, was gone from the campaign before he could write another, the agent in a silly episode that helped drive another Democratic candidate from the race. The Joseph Biden videotape affair raged out of political control because Sasso made a rare error in judgment by not telling Dukakis facts the governor had a right to know, and because Dukakis was unable to go to the wall for a guy who needed a slap in the face, not a bullet in the back.

Dukakis bottled up his deep pain at losing his chief strategist and political confidant and also stifled his prospects for growth on the

national stage. His ambivalence over his political guide's banishment
was so great that he listened and wavered unpresidentially while top
advisers proposed ways of bringing him back. Sasso finally returned to
the campaign at a time of crisis eleven months later.

Dukakis's inability to act decisively also cruelly undercut Susan
Estrich, the Harvard Law School professor and political veteran who
took Sasso's place, held the shattered campaign together after his departure, and coolly managed Dukakis's ascent to the highest position his
party offers. Estrich shared Sasso's view that breadth and depth at the
presidential level of politics were imperative. Long before the public
heard of William Horton, Boston Harbor, or Pledge-of-Allegiance legislation, she tried to persuade Dukakis of another imperative—response
and counterattack. In the end, she fought too hard to keep her position
to be seen as completely selfless; Estrich's behavior, however, is a lot
more understandable in a political campaign than is Governor
Dukakis's.

If three early memos from John Sasso were all we had, one could
argue that Dukakis had been told by an expert very early what he needed
to do, but didn't understand. But we have far more. In an unending
stream from fall 1987 almost until Election Day in 1988, strategists,
pollsters, communications experts, his running mate, debate planners,
insiders, and outsiders alike proposed ideas for grand themes and messages that could have carried Dukakis to the higher plane on which
voters like their presidents.

On the morning he won the nomination in Atlanta, we had breakfast with him in his suite, and while he ate his favorite cereal, bran flakes,
we asked if he felt ready to offer the uplifting vision we suggested voters
want from nominees, which would make people see him in a shape
grander than the skillful governor who had slogged through fifty-six
primaries and caucuses to victory.

Dukakis shook his head vigorously.

"The presidency is less a bully pulpit than it is the center of the
action," he insisted. "It is not necessary to harangue and cajole the
American people. People want their president to have the skill and
energy to reach out and bring people in and build support for the things
they want. The challenges, the needs are out there."

He had a point. But the next evening, for about ninety minutes, he
got our point as he accepted his party's nomination for the presidency.
As the frenzied emotions at the center ring of American political life
washed away his instinctive inhibitions, he—whether he realized it or
not—reached back to people on the same wavelength. Dukakis read a
speech whose content was pedestrian at best, but communication at

a moment like that is not through words; it is through feeling that transmits a sense that the speaker is ready, able, and willing to lead the nation.

He was never able, though, to replicate that performance until the final days. He rejected advice that as a new face on the national scene he should keep pressing in August and begin counterattacking vigorously; he left in his dressing room both of his plans for his two debates with George Bush, frustrating his best chances to climb back into contention.

By the time the nation voted, many Democratic officials and activists and many of his closest advisers and friends were furious with Dukakis. When he attended the farewell campaign party two days after the election, longtime supporters and aides there avoided him because they could not put their deep disappointment into words that did not condemn him.

And yet, after a little more time had passed, some anger began to flow from Dukakis's immediate family (political and personal) back toward his campaign staff for letting *him* down. Where was the plan for the election that the guy started clamoring for after the primaries? If the ideas in the memos were so good, where were the speeches and schedules and political moves that would give them more meaningful form? If you got no for an answer one day and you were so sure no was the wrong answer, why didn't you break down his door? There was more than a strong case, in other words, for the proposition that the campaign did not do its job. "None of us knew how to run a general election," said one Massachusetts operative. "It was David versus Goliath. They had people from Walt Disney doing events. We had a bunch of kids." An advertising consultant said, "They really thought it was a primary. He was running for governor of America."

Some months after the election, Sasso spoke of the lessons to be drawn from the 1988 campaign in a luncheon speech at the Boston World Trade Center. They had all drawn the wrong lessons from 1984, he confessed. The lessons from 1984 were to stay upbeat and optimistic, like Ronald Reagan, and not, under any circumstances, to discuss taxes.

He and his colleagues had failed in 1988 to make a convincing case for change, he said. "Every winning campaign, in my view, must be rooted firmly and fundamentally in a unifying and recognizable theme. Establishing a theme—a theme that rallies people—is the essence of leadership. . . . Reagan's optimism and cheer, his images of Morning in America, we decided, was mostly what voters wanted to hear. Don't offer too much bad news. Don't take the risk of blaming America, of running down America. I think a lot of us reasoned badly. We were too timid. We wore 1984 on our sleeves.

"Looking back, our own lack of a central and sustained theme created the vacuum—a playing field . . . that allowed flags and furloughs to dominate."

Sasso's point is extremely important. In his analysis, if a presidential candidate has established that grand theme, he has erected his best defense against the kinds of attacks George Bush launched, which lowered the tenor of the 1988 general election to a vicious city-council fight. Although any reasonably skillful campaign would be expected to respond like tigers to attacks, if that big theme is there, the attacks will look petty by comparison.

Sasso also said that the Dukakis campaign had taken for granted the proposition that voters would automatically assume the Democratic candidate held dear the nation's basic values: God, patriotism, family, and freedom. "The plain fact is that Democrats must be more sensitive to and have even more political respect for the idea that certain issues pack more weight than only the substance of the issues themselves," he said. "Those same issues also carry messages about personal values, of deep belief and strength, of character, and even the aura of leadership. Our campaign was hurt badly on the subject of values, no matter that our candidate had a long and unbroken history that was strong on personal values."

A modern presidential campaign is a multimillion-dollar coast-to-coast enterprise fabricated almost overnight and operated under stressful conditions. Any postmortem can find shortcomings, mistakes in judgment, and tactical errors. But ultimately every political campaign reflects the candidate.

Bush succeeded in raising questions about this candidate's patriotism though his immigrant father used to weep for love of his adopted country. He questioned the "values" of a man whose devotion to family and public service were beyond reproach for thirty years. He picked apart the aura of accomplishment surrounding a man whose gubernatorial colleagues, Democrat and Republican alike, voted him "most effective" governor in the nation. It was a vicious mugging, beneath the dignity and honor of the office Bush now holds, and that the mugger's victim almost invited the attack by symbolically walking alone down a dark street waving fistfuls of cash in the air does not excuse the mugging.

Throughout the record hot summer of 1988, many of Dukakis's oldest supporters in Massachusetts experienced a queasy feeling of déjà vu about this Dukakis campaign. It was all so familiar: the rat-ta-tat-tat of accusations, repeated over and over again on hot social issues. They recognized the uncanny similarities to 1978, when conservative Democrat Edward J. King, a disgruntled bureaucrat furious with Dukakis for ousting him from his job as head of the Massachusetts Port Authority, ran a gubernatorial campaign that the smart boys shrugged off as trite. King, a stubborn bulldog of a candidate, gnawed away at the death penalty, mandatory jail sentences, tax cutting, higher drinking age, and abortion, excluding other issues. Angelo Berlandi, a King operative, described it as a "hate campaign. . . . We put all the hate groups in one big pot and let it boil." Dukakis had scoffed at the King tactics. Those aren't the important issues, he would say. On that primary election night, he was proven wrong. He squandered a forty-four-point lead and lost the Democratic nomination to King by nine points.

Now ten years later, Vice President Bush was doing essentially the same thing. Bush attacked him on the Pledge of Allegiance, prison furloughs, the death penalty, mandatory jail sentences, and "values." Bush avoided a campaign in areas where he himself was vulnerable—his few accomplishments in public life, his failure to articulate where he wanted to lead the country (a deficiency that made Dukakis's failings seem puny), and his inability to recognize corruption around him from Watergate through the Iran-Contra scandal—by successfully marketing Michael Dukakis, with the governor's unwitting assistance, as a freak from the fringes of discredited liberalism.

Paul Brountas, chairman of that 1978 campaign just as he was chairman of the 1988 presidential effort, was struck by the similarities. Even Dukakis noticed it was the same. "It's Ed King all over again," he explained to the traveling band of national political reporters.

Why didn't he do something about it? Was it hubris, the fatal flaw of self-contained self-confidence that exposed so many heroes in Greek legend and tragedy to their demise, an excessive pride and certainty that his own intellectual abilities were sufficient? No one will fall for this type of campaign, he would say of Bush in private. These aren't the important issues, scoffed the governor, as a seventeen-point lead dissolved into an eight-point deficit. He always vowed that he would never again be caught unaware by that sort of attack. But Dukakis ignored his pollster's oracular warnings, refused entreaties and advice from his staff to broaden his message, and watched Bush systematically destroy his record for competence, the too-fragile foundation beneath his presidential campaign.

After the ignominious Dukakis 1978 election defeat in Massachusetts, Peter McCarthy, a Democratic state representative from Peabody, presented to Dukakis a book with biographical sketches of great leaders in antiquity. McCarthy had lost his own bid for the state senate on the same day Dukakis lost the Democratic gubernatorial nomination to King. The losses caused both of these men great personal pain. One of the figures described in the book was Aristides the Just, an Athenian political leader and general in about 500 B.C. known for his honor and high principles. He had done everything that was right: he had rehabilitated the harbor and instituted duties on imports and exports to raise revenue. But the people wearied of his rectitude and turned him out. He went into exile. Six years later, after his successor proved to be corrupt, the people called Aristides the Just back from exile. They now appreciated his goodness. Dukakis loved the story—perhaps too much.

He also loved one facet of politics with a passion that almost certainly was misplaced and excessive in his worsening predicament. In 1988, he and many of his aides (though not all) clung to a hope that the Democratic ticket could move close enough to Bush—within striking distance—so that a truly massive field organization might haul enough extra voters to the polls to make up the difference. Dukakis believed almost religiously in the potency of a campaign field organization. He felt he owed his electoral success in Massachusetts to old-fashioned grassroots organizing. From the time he ran for Brookline town meeting to the bitter gubernatorial rematch against King in 1982, personal contact with voters by himself and legions of supporters had made the critical difference.

The commitment to field organizing reflected Dukakis's precision, rationality, and thoroughness. It also reflected a basic understanding of Dukakis's appeal as a political commodity. Dukakis was not Mario Cuomo, capable of persuading masses of voters solely by rhetorical skill. James Tierney, attorney general of Maine, said that Dukakis was a candidate you "thought" your way to. Grassroots organizing not only established a favorable first impression, but gentle persuasion by intimate contact fostered commitment among supporters that would bubble into a frothy head of enthusiasm on election day.

Because Dukakis put a high priority on organization, many of his top political lieutenants were organizers—weaned in northeastern urban or labor-union trenches. From the start of his presidential campaign, field organization got a significant share of time and resources; Dukakis always wanted to hear the daily and weekly canvass figures.

Traditional field organization is a Democratic bias and one reason that Democrats dominate the Congress and the nation's state and court houses. The field organization was put together following the teamwork and balance principles that had worked so well in staffing the 1982 Dukakis campaign and the Dukakis state government. After the Democratic National Convention, Operations Director Jack Corrigan and his deputy, Charlie Baker, recruited the party's best and brightest organizers to be state directors.

Each director constructed an enormous voter-contact program. The get-out-the-vote effort was the largest in history. On election day, more than 300,000 volunteers and staff people had specific assignments in contacting and hauling voters to the polls. Throughout the day, as network exit-poll results filtered into campaign headquarters at 105 Chauncy Street in downtown Boston, the field staff reacted to the numbers. Lists of voters' names and telephone numbers were sent by facsimile machine throughout the country. Every phone at Chauncy Street was in use. Even high-level staffers in Boston were calling voters in Connecticut and Missouri.

The plans they executed covered minute details. Representative Richard Gephardt, Dukakis's rival in the primary season, had previously identified 20,000 residents in his Missouri congressional district who intended to vote for Bush as well as Gephardt, but he agreed not to contact those voters on election day, possibly sacrificing his own personal goal of breaking 60 percent in his reelection campaign. (He won anyway with 64 percent of the vote.)

The Democratic vice presidential candidate, Senator Lloyd M. Bentsen, Jr., of Texas sat with his aides, Joseph O'Neill, Victoria Radd, and Michael McCurry, and placed phone calls to key big-city mayors like Detroit's Coleman Young and county officials and labor leaders, from his Four Seasons Hotel suite in Austin. He told them that the race was close, encouraged them to do all they could to get voters to the polls, and to keep the polls open until everyone had voted. We won't forget this effort, he promised.

All this painstaking work can and does produce wondrous results in a primary campaign; indeed, it produced the Democratic nomination for Dukakis in 1988. After months of patient precinct work a candidate can accumulate a critical mass of support that makes him a force throughout a state's political network in ways that television advertising cannot match.

But when Dukakis exceeded his own expectations and became the Democratic Party presidential nominee, he and his lieutenants failed to anticipate the quantum difference between primary campaigning and general-election campaigning. It has far less to do with phone banks or voter lists; the difference has everything to do with message. "I don't want to be . . . the great communicator," Dukakis said in Wisconsin late in March, "I want to be the great builder." That was a big part of the problem, and something in excess of $20 million may have gone down the drain satisfying Dukakis's notions of what a general election is all about.

Dukakis viewed himself as the marathon man—a long distance runner who by constancy and determination would make it to victory

Dukakis, Francis O'Brien, and Jack Weeks confer on Sky Pig, the campaign plane. (Photo by James Steinberg)

and the finish line. Now, on the final, frenetic weekend, the terminus of the longest course in electoral politics was in sight. The polls would open on the East Coast in just hours. He was heading home to Massachusetts. Since Sunday morning, he had logged more than 8,000 air miles in a fierce demonstration of will that carried him through nine states and eleven cities. In twenty-two months, he had traveled nearly 600,000 miles from Texas barrios to Wall Street boardrooms. It had been an extraordinary experience for him. For Dukakis, the presidential campaign was an unexpected adventure rather than the fulfillment of a secret dream. For this bright and curious man from the most parochial of places, the campaign meant new people, new places, new experiences. He found it intoxicating and fascinating.

Throughout September, as his campaign struggled to regain the offensive, his performance was erratic. His staff sank into depression as he plummeted in the polls after his second debate with Bush on October 13, when, fluish and frustrated by conflicting advice, he delivered a flat, perfunctory performance. He did the same thing twelve days later during a live ninety-minute interview by ABC's Ted Koppel on *Nightline*.

But suddenly as the election approached he became energized. Much was at stake. The verdict of history began to weigh on his mind, along with political respectability and the fate of the Democratic Party, and all those down-ballot Democratic office seekers. It was time to reach deep into himself to make the supreme effort. Time for the kick. It was now or never.

He rose to the challenge. He was hot. He finally agreed to an economic message that connected with voters. It was so simple: "I'm on your side." It was the oldest Democratic appeal, the working people versus the elite, powerful rich guys, us against them; the white hats against the black hats; the people versus privilege. It was a version of economic nationalism that did not trash the Japanese people. He resisted many versions of this message for months, insisting he would rather lose with his character and integrity intact than stoke any of the public's latent jingoistic impulses. At long last, he seemed to have found a voice (many back home suspected it wasn't really *his* voice) and a feisty underdog style that played well with crowds.

The end game began Sunday morning, November 6, in Denver with departure from the Radisson Hotel, and just never stopped. It was as if Mindy Lubber's scheduling shop in Boston had gone beserk and produced a campaign nightmare of endless rallies—a mind numbing blur of red, white, and blue.

"They're slipping and sliding. We're rocking and rolling," he called out in Denver. His young daughters pulled him aside after the rally, "No Dad, it's *rockin'* and *rollin'*." Dukakis, using the precise diction his schoolteacher mother Euterpe had always insisted upon, had pronounced the "g."

The Bush entourage had begun to shadow Dukakis into the same media market just hours after he left, to step on his message. "He's following me around the country," he yelled to thousands who spilled across a meadow on Sunday morning before the town hall in Westminster, Colorado. "I'll tell you one place he's not following me. He's not following me and Lloyd Bentsen to the White House." The crowd shrieked with glee.

"He says he's on your side. Who's he kidding?" It took a long time, but at last, Michael Dukakis was speaking in the vernacular. He used words that people understood. He was crisp and clear and concise. No chatter about Urban Development Action Grants or government-program alphabet soup. No one could mangle a poetic turn of phrase as quickly as the pedantic Dukakis, who had a literal mind and recoiled from the deft one-liner, trademark of the television age. "I can't say that. That's not me." He made his speechwriters mad with frustration. Finally, at the end, he began to use the quips and the memorable rejoinders laboriously crafted by a one-liner shop back in Boston run by a young lawyer, Andy Savitz. The crowds loved it.

The smartest kid on the block seemed to have finally figured it out, but in a way that made his earlier failures all the more maddening. After twenty-two months of prolonged campaign days in every section of the nation, he learned that public service is more than sturdy on-the-job performance. He had always been suspicious of overblown rhetoric and emotional appeals. It sounded to this principled politician too much like pandering. It reminded him too much of rantings by Wisconsin Senator Joe McCarthy, whose red-baiting horrified the idealistic Dukakis in the 1950s. But he finally began to interact with his audiences, to touch them, appreciating that the president is not only first bureaucrat in the United States of America but a symbol for American hopes and aspirations.

He realized now that you had to say the same thing over and over to make it register. He had thought that if he said something once that was enough. Early in October, Bush's endless assault on the Massachusetts prison-furlough program and the aberrational case of an inmate who escaped while on furlough and later attacked a Maryland couple so infuriated Dukakis and his feisty eighty-five-year-old mother that they let loose with a double-barreled response. In an angry speech at Bates College in Maine that he wrote himself in longhand the night before, Dukakis accused Bush of "exploiting human tragedy" for political gain. When Francis O'Brien, a campaign adviser, suggested he repeat that performance a week later, Dukakis looked up in surprise: "But we did that."

Dukakis has an orderly mind and makes decisions quickly once he has mastered the subject and digested the information. The learning curve for a national campaign, his first, was far steeper than he had anticipated and beyond his experience as a reform-minded governor in a one-party liberal state. He did not anticipate the physical and mental price for hurtling around the country in a steel capsule for almost two years. At critical junctures—especially while he was losing his polling lead in August and in his two disappointing debates—friends felt he had simply been so overwhelmed by the tough general election that he briefly lost his bearings and his nerve.

But once he connected in the final days, he pushed to the limit. It was still far from perfect. He abandoned his economic-populism message for three straight days at a critical time in the campaign's last month to talk about being a liberal in the FDR and JFK tradition and about abortion rights. But he was definitely performing better than before. He knew that defeat and disappointment were hovering by the finish line, but he hadn't yet given up hope. Sasso, his top political aide and vice chairman of his campaign, often brooding darkly in these final days, compared their chances of victory to drawing a thread through the eye of a needle. It was possible but very, very tough; indeed his final strategy

Dukakis; Bill Woodward, the speech writer; and John Sasso hurry by plane to another campaign event in the final days. (Photo by James Steinberg)

for the Electoral College made allowance for Dukakis possibly losing the popular vote. He had no margin for error. Bush's lock on the South was absolute, and the Democrats had nothing approaching that solid base. They had been forced to concede much of the nation to Bush in September in order to concentrate resources, time, and energy on the battleground East and West coast states and in the industrial Midwest. They needed every conceivable break.

Fighting back put him on the offensive. His Illinois state coordinator, Steve Murphy, collected scathing leaflets being mailed to voters by the Illinois Republican Party. He made sure they were handed to Dukakis the next time the governor appeared in Illinois.

Dukakis was enraged. He read the leaflets and silently shook his head back and forth. He looked up and quietly said, "This is garbage." One leaflet said, "All the murderers and rapists and drug pushers and child molesters in Massachusetts vote for Michael Dukakis." The other claimed that John Wayne Gacy, a notorious mass murderer in Illinois, would be eligible for weekend passes if he were incarcerated in a Massachusetts prison. The day after the Bush campaign had aired a new attack advertisement that showed him looking silly in an Army helmet and riding around in a tank, Dukakis struck back. In Quincy, Illinois, wearing a checked shirt and chinos with work boots as he began a bus tour through rural Illinois, he brandished the leaflets and shouted, "This is garbage." On the way to the event, however, senior aide Kirk O'Donnell almost begged him to get much tougher and call them "lies." He refused.

Nonetheless, the combative Dukakis made himself felt. Veteran political reporters were struck by the enthusiasm in the huge crowds that gathered for the final days in his campaign. These were different from the big crowds that gathered for Walter F. Mondale in his unsuccessful 1984 effort. These people believed Dukakis could win. During those final two days, many stood in the cold and rain. Their throaty roars transferred energy to him in a symbiosis that kept him going and them believing.

At every stop, he discarded his suitcoat regardless of the temperature, rolled back his shirtsleeves to expose his wrists and forearms and leaned into the lectern punching out lines that he once would have dismissed out of hand. He wanted to visit as many states as possible for a last-minute personal appeal. If it would make a difference, he wanted to do it. He would forego sleep. The schedulers complied.

From Denver, the hardy entourage headed west to Portland, Oregon, and Seattle and Tacoma, Washington. November 6 was the eighth birthday of traveling aide Jack Weeks's son, Christopher, and Weeks felt badly that he was missing it. On the flight west Dukakis and everyone else in the traveling party filled a reporter's notebook with birthday notes to the kid. But instead of stopping for the night, they headed back to the Midwest once again, encouraged by late-breaking public-opinion polls suggesting some movement toward him. When Sky Pig, his chartered airplane, wouldn't move fast enough, they booked a speedy little Gulfstream and hurtled straight through Sunday night to Cleveland and St. Louis. Bill Woodward, the bone-thin speechwriter, continued to write as Dukakis stretched out on the sofa for two hours' sleep, about all he would get in three days. Weeks slept on the floor. Dozing fitfully and living out a modern political analogy to Henry V's notion of camaraderie before Agincourt (we hardy few, we band of brothers) were some of his most loyal henchmen: Nick Mitropoulos, the body man who walked every step of the way with him for twenty months; Sasso, his most trusted political aide; Paul Brountas, the campaign chairman and Harvard Law School classmate; Robert Farmer, the Midas who spun Democratic gold by raising almost $100 million for his campaign; and Kirk O'Donnell, a Boston-bred lawyer who had worked as a top aide to former House Speaker Thomas P. O'Neill, Jr.

On Monday, they Ping Ponged back to the West Coast and San Francisco and Los Angeles for rallies before some of the largest and most enthusiastic crowds in the campaign. Dukakis left Los Angeles at 10:10 P.M. election eve and still wasn't done. On the way home, he stopped at Des Moines, where it had all begun, and then in Detroit, where more than 500 supporters waited in a driving rain.

Despite the frenzied reactions the Democratic ticket drew in these final hours, they felt intimations of an unhappy conclusion. In the last airport rally at dawn in Detroit before returning to Massachusetts on election day, Mitropoulos and Weeks glanced at each other in dismay, sharing an instinctive reaction when they noticed the small crowd. "Hamtramck," said Weeks. Mitropoulos nodded. They had had the same sinking feeling at a campaign event in Hamtramck, an ethnic-dominated city west of Detroit, the night before the Michigan caucuses that Dukakis lost to Reverend Jesse L. Jackson.

Only then did Dukakis return home, where he voted at a public housing project in Brookline and at 5:00 P.M. after a power walk, still sleepless, headed to the nearby studios of WGBH-TV to do fourteen more interviews beamed by satellite to key states.

His running mate's schedule was also abruptly changed on Sunday to add two late-night stops on Monday in Kansas City, Missouri and Little Rock, Arkansas. Bentsen, a candidate for reelection to the Senate from Texas as well as a vice presidential candidate, insisted upon returning to his home state after the last stop even though it meant he would not get back to Texas until nearly 3:00 A.M.

As Dukakis began his day in Cleveland, Bentsen was heading for a rally in Dallas. The sixty-seven-year-old Texan would campaign nonstop for twenty hours. He went from Dallas to Shreveport, Louisiana; to Houston, Beaumont, and San Antonio before springing to Little Rock at 9:00 P.M. and then Kansas City at 11:00 P.M. He left Missouri at midnight and headed home to Texas.

By the final day, the courtly Texan was discarding his well-tailored suit jacket to expose carefully pressed monogrammed shirts. He traveled to four states that day: Texas, Louisiana, Arkansas, and Missouri. The last Austin—Boston ticket, John F. Kennedy and Lyndon B. Johnson, had carried those states with just 50 percent of the vote in 1960. He tried to outpace the clock to pull off a repeat of history.

"The Republicans are dropping like a rock in those polls," he said. "The momentum is with us. It's going our way." By the final stops, Bentsen was quoting that Democratic philosopher, Bruce Springsteen. In an old airport hangar in Beaumont, Texas, he ended his stump speech with the words, "*We swore / We made a promise / No retreat, baby / No*

surrender." The accompanying press corps shrieked at the incongruity as
the dignified Senate Finance Chairman quoted the Boss.

Then finally in Austin, a spotlight directed by Mike Pohl, a veteran
advance man, played over the Lone Star Express, Bentsen's chartered
airplane, at the darkened airport. As his wife, Beryl Ann (known as
B.A.), introduced him as the next vice president of the United States,
his campaign theme song, "Highway to the Danger Zone," came up on
the public-address system and Bentsen stepped into the spotlight. Tears
came to his eyes as he accepted the cheers of a few hundred campaign
workers who waved flashlights and sparklers.

In the end, the Democrats' desperate effort—possibly a form of
penance for three months of behavior that deeply disappointed
friends—came up substantially short. In a sparsely furnished holding
room upstairs from where the crowd waited for the concession at the
World Trade Center in Boston, Dukakis stood by himself. His wife
chain-smoked with furious intensity. The others in the room, Mitropoulos, Sasso, and Edward F. Jesser, a political consultant and close
friend of Mitropoulos, knew Dukakis was upset although he masked his
feelings.

After the polls closed on the West Coast, Dukakis went downstairs
to concede the race. A youthful crowd greeted him, chanting "92, 92,
92." Kitty, her face mirroring their shared pain, stood by his side and
kept her eyes fixed on him. His family stood a few steps behind him in
a protective circle.

"Just eighteen months ago, on what some of you will recall was a
cold and snowy April day, I asked you for your support in running what
I called a marathon for the highest honor that the American people can
bestow on anyone," he said.

"I said there'd be good days, and we had a lot of good days, didn't
we?" a smile almost crossed a face ravaged by fatigue and aching
disappointment. "And I said there'd be some not-so-good days, and we
had a few of those, too. And I talked about another marathon that I had
to run in April of 1951, when I found myself struggling up a hill or two,
and people saying to me, 'Looking good Duke, go to it.' That is what
you have done and I'm very grateful to you. We had those good and not
so good days. We reached Heartbreak Hill and overcame it, and then
we found the strength to make that final kick."

On April 19, 1951, the year he graduated from Brookline High
School, he lied about his age and ran in the Boston Marathon, a 26-mile
385-yard course that runs from rural Hopkinton to downtown Boston.
He finished in 3 hours and 31 minutes, fifty-seventh out of 191 runners,
not at all bad for a skinny seventeen-year-old high school boy. Finishing
a campaign but coming up short of first place, however, doesn't count

for anything in politics, no matter how severe the pace at the end. In his remarks that night, Dukakis was unable to say anything to the forty-one million people who voted for him that might help them understand what had happened.

The day after the election on November 9, 1988, he was back at his desk by 8:30 A.M., an appearance widely viewed as almost inhuman after such a punishing ordeal. Within hours he was talking about litter on Route 24 south of Boston. While he worked, he hummed softly. Armchair psychoanalysts immediately decided that he was happy to be free of a campaign he had never really wanted to wage in the first place, but friends later said Dukakis was simply trying to keep his hurt from showing.

Later that day, he held a final press conference at a hotel near his campaign headquarters. Did he blow it? asked Sam Donaldson of ABC News.

Dukakis ducked the question, pleading that it was "too early to try to go into a detailed analysis." But he struggled to reconcile his own loss with Democratic gains in the House and Senate. Clearly that meant the people had spoken in favor of the very things that he proposed. Hadn't they?

Ultimately, he said it was Bush's negative campaigning that frustrated his efforts to communicate a positive message. He said he had tried to campaign on unifying issues like good jobs at good wages, and good, drug-free schools for children. "Now for whatever reason, I think in part because of the nature of the Republican campaign, I wasn't able to do that as effectively as I should have," he said.

> But I think it's important to remember that all over this country yesterday, Democratic candidates for the United States Senate, Democratic candidates for governor, Democratic candidates for the Congress did that, and did it in a way which has now produced even greater Democratic majorities in the face of a very decisive Republican victory for the presidency. What does that tell you?
>
> Well, I think it tells you two things. That if you are able to get that agenda and deliver your message directly to the people that you're seeking to represent, that they will respond in a very broad and very strong way. I've had that experience here in this state.
>
> It's obviously a lot more difficult when you're running as a national candidate. And that may be one of the reasons why we continue to win and win solidly at the state level all over the country, and yet have had such a difficult time winning nationally. Now, the fact that I did get the vote that I did, the fact that

the margin of defeat was a lot smaller this time than the last time—all of those things, I think, are signs of hope for the future, but it is clear, I think, that in these national campaigns, we'll have to do a better job of making the point that these are issues which bring us together as a country, and do the kind of job that candidates for the Senate and governor are doing in states all over America.

It was a very poor answer, worthy perhaps of Aristides the Just, but not of Michael Dukakis.

Eight days later in Boston, a man walked to the subway unnoticed except by a watchful MBTA security guard. The slight man in a raincoat, a muffler wound snugly around his neck, briefcase in hand, descended the steep stairs from Boston Common into the Park Street "T" station. He used his prepaid monthly pass to go through the turnstile, walked to the Riverside sign and waited for a Green Line car to take him home to Brookline. The 1988 Democratic presidential nominee, Michael S. Dukakis, had reverted to his routine. His work day at the State House over, he was heading home to Kitty. But it wasn't exactly the same. He wasn't the same. And it wasn't the way Kika de la Garza had said it would be. Eight days earlier he had lost the presidency, the ultimate political prize. He seemed lost in his own thoughts. On this Thursday night, there were no Secret Service agents or campaign aides, no senior advisers or fevered supporters. He was alone.

2

A Brand New Stage

Michael Dukakis had just ushered *Boston Globe* columnist Ellen Goodman out the front door of his red-brick duplex on Perry Street in Brookline, Massachusetts. She lives nearby and had stopped in for coffee and cornbread on this Saturday morning, March 14, 1987, to quiz him on his political future. As usual, he had been guarded; perhaps he wasn't certain until she had left. On the porch he picked up the mail, shut the door, turned to his wife Kitty, and matter-of-factly said, "It looks like I'm going to do it."

She was pleased and proud but hardly surprised—not at her husband's decision, nor at his anticlimactic way of announcing that he had decided to seek the nation's highest office, to put his record, reputation, and life-style on the line and under white lights and microscopes. By then his decision to run for president had acquired an air of inevitability. A careful, partly public exploration had subtly drawn to a logical, but far from preordained conclusion.

In making his decision, however, Dukakis sped past a very clear road sign: A successful presidential candidacy needs a powerful theme that is suitable to the times, readily comprehensible to the voting public, powerful enough to convince millions of minds, and constantly emphasized.

For Dukakis, the decision had less to do with convictions about the country's needs and how he wanted to meet them, than with the pros and cons of whether he had a realistic chance at winning the Democratic nomination, and whether he could run and still be an effective governor. More than seven years before, another son of Massachusetts, Edward Kennedy, had also wrestled with himself amid public clamor for him to challenge Jimmy Carter; Kennedy's preoccupation with his decision at the expense of deeper thoughts about his road ahead was his first step toward failure in the primaries, dramatized one night on national television when he could not answer broadcaster Roger Mudd's famous question: Why do you want to be president?

For Dukakis, it was a first step toward ultimate failure to define for the voters what the election was all about, a task Bush performed by default. Dukakis's failure was perhaps less dramatic than Kennedy's, but, like a slowly metastasizing cancer, the result was just as fatal.

Michael Dukakis is not a whimsical man and nothing was whimsical about his decision to run for president; but neither was it the last in a linear progression of events, the product of burning ambition, or the natural outgrowth of beliefs about how or where America should be led after the Ronald Reagan era. Dukakis's candidacy didn't just burst into flower like a summer weed, and yet his role in it all was sometimes passive. Without others' wishes, ambitions, and maneuverings, Dukakis would never have sought the presidency.

"As the Reagan administration was winding down," he told us in an airplane somewhere over the Midwest after he'd clinched the nomination the following May, "I thought that people might be looking for something different. After I won the New York primary, Al Gore said something gracious as he was withdrawing from the race, that perhaps in this campaign year competence *is* charisma; it was beautifully and nicely put."

Dukakis also ran because he thought it made sense, that he had the same qualifications for the starting line as everyone else seeking the Democratic Party nomination, and that although he faced stiff odds his chances were legitimate.

These are not unique factors. In modern times, presidential candidacies have not always been the simple product of driving ambition, fueled either by lust for national leadership or burning desire to effect change as they were for such diverse canidates as John F. Kennedy, Nelson Rockefeller, Ronald Reagan, Jimmy Carter, and George Bush.

Candidacies have also grown from fortuitous combinations of men and times. Dwight D. Eisenhower, Eugene McCarthy, and Gerald Ford did not spend years getting ready to run; they responded to opportunities that came their way. For Dukakis, that opportunity to seriously consider the presidency came after Senator Edward M.

Kennedy decided not to run, and as it became clear Dukakis was a cinch to win a third term as governor of Massachusetts in November 1986. But though his taste for the office was acquired from others it was no less real. When his campaign faltered in summer and fall 1988, some speculated that he had never really wanted it badly enough, that his wife and political guru had dragged him in over his head. That analysis was not only false but missed the point. The point was that this methodical man had an iron-hard determination to run as himself, in his way. It was his greatest strength, the root of his success in winning the nomination, and his greatest weakness, the root of his inability to perform a nominee's functions—being decisive when times are tough, reaching out to others, listening, and changing when required—that are most frequently judged in presidential candidacies.

The story of his candidacy has one leading and at least three supporting characters. Above all else, the Dukakis candidacy would never have happened without John Sasso, his chief political aide, and Sasso's alter ego, an intense young politician named Jack Corrigan. Dukakis also drew personal and political sustenance, and no small amount of ambition, from his wife, Kitty, and his stepson, John.

Throughout his three decades in public life, Dukakis was at his best when supported by a trusted accomplice who took natural and joyful delight in the rough and tumble of politics and the inside game of alliance-making, hardball, and maneuvering. Sasso was a natural politician in a way Dukakis never was. For Dukakis, the raw side of politics was neither easy nor fun.

He is, after all, a product of Brookline, an affluent town that hugs Boston's western border. The town is dominated by well-educated lawyers, doctors, and other professionals. In Brookline, political life is clean and liberal. The public schools rank among the best in the state. Dukakis's Greek immigrant parents taught him the principles: duty, honor, and the intrinsic value of hard work. His environment channeled those values into a political career as a progressive reformer. The progressive impulse runs deep in post-Civil War American history. The movement sought to make government, business, and politics fair and accessible to all citizens, and to reduce dominance over the public's business by special and powerful interests. But at its worst the progressive impulse and tradition have sometimes been marred by a tendency toward elitism and moral superiority. Dukakis was also motivated by a specific ambition: from the time he was a college undergraduate he told his friends that his only real goal was to become governor of his state.

Progress toward this ambitious goal was facilitated by two men: his original political mentor, Alan Sidd, a legendary figure in Brookline politics who died in 1978; and Francis X. Meany, a Boston lawyer and deal-maker who led his successful gubernatorial campaign in 1974. Dukakis and Meany became estranged after that election when Dukakis insisted—in a burst of characteristic but unreasonable rectitude—that Meany's Boston law firm refuse a contract to handle state bond issues because of their personal relationship.

After Sidd's death and his split with Meany, Dukakis had no intimate political friend until, wandering in the wilderness following his crushing defeat for renomination in 1978 at the hands of conservative Democrat Edward J. King, he turned to Sasso in 1981 and asked him to manage his rematch campaign in the following year. After he won, he asked Sasso to be his top assistant, a position traditionally called chief secretary: to make his deals, plot his strategy, and fight his fights. Sasso did it all. The governor himself best described the relationship: Sasso was like a brother.

Sasso, a native of New Jersey, came to Massachusetts to attend Boston University, and then, like many other students, stayed. He had vigorously opposed the war in Vietnam. After graduating from college, he worked for a time in construction and volunteered in the campaign of a liberal Democratic congressman from Cape Cod, Gerry E. Studds. Eventually, he became manager of Studds's district office in Massachusetts, and made his first major foray into politics at the state level as manager of a property-tax classification-referendum campaign in 1978. That is when he first met Dukakis, who was supporting the issue and had shown up as promised for a media event on the Saturday after his humiliating primary defeat. Sasso was impressed that the vanquished governor kept his commitment despite his painful loss, and always kept the photograph of their first meeting in his offices.

Since 1980, Jack Corrigan had been Sasso's junior partner, but outsiders rarely realized how close their partnership was. A working-class kid from Somerville, a blue-collar community next to the more highbrow Cambridge, eight years younger than Sasso (all of thirty-one when Dukakis decided to run), he evolved over the years into a mature political strategist. Fanatically loyal to Sasso and Dukakis, his were very sharp political elbows. His street smarts almost masked a brilliant mind (Harvard College and Harvard Law School) and a passionate liberalism that at times gave him an eerie resemblance to John Kennedy's right arm, the late Kenneth P. O'Donnell.

Sasso and Corrigan met as field organizers in Senator Edward Kennedy's ill-fated crusade against Jimmy Carter in 1980—first in Iowa and then in later primary states. It was their introduction to national politics and both drew rave rookie reviews. They became fast friends and inseparable political allies back home in Massachusetts.

Jack Corrigan, Sasso's chief lieutenant, had sharp elbows and a passionate liberal philosophy. (Photo by Bill Brett)

They returned to the national scene to help manage Geraldine Ferraro's vice-presidential campaign in 1984. That frustrating experience, watching Vice President Mondale carry the Democratic Party's tattered ensign against Ronald Reagan, produced the seeds that germinated into the Dukakis candidacy.

After the final primaries in June of that year, John Reilly—a well-connected Washington attorney and political veteran who had been Mondale's friend for more than twenty years—was asked to handle the search for a running mate. His first list, and his last one, included Dukakis.

Dukakis made the list because he had backed Mondale through tough and good times in that year, and because Massachusetts was already rolling on waves of economic prosperity that had carried to national prominence the governor's reputation as a policy innovator and steady chief executive. But Dukakis's name was also on the list for a special reason: Mondale concluded that to have even a remote chance of winning he needed to make a dramatic choice of running mate. That meant either a woman or a member of a minority group. Because it would be tough to make a historic pick, someone who might not meet traditional standards of experience and accomplishment, Mondale had to be prepared in case Reilly's search failed to turn up a suitable candidate. That meant Mondale needed a solid white male to play the ego-suppressing role of standby. He needed someone whose credentials would not be suspect, to whom he could turn at the last minute if necessary. Playing this role required an act of selflessness rarely committed willingly by politicians, but Dukakis carried it off. Sasso handled the details for him in a way that made the Mondale campaign extremely grateful while steering Dukakis away from the supplicant behavior endured by other candidates.

Dukakis had not wanted the second spot on the Mondale ticket. "Tell me it's not me," he pleaded, when his chief secretary reached him in the hospital room where his daughter, Andrea, was recovering from surgery, to let him know a call from Mondale was imminent. He was openly relieved when Mondale chose Representative Ferraro of New York instead.

After Mondale made his historic pick, the Mondale campaign came back to Sasso and asked him to serve as Ferraro's manager and top traveling adviser. Corrigan went along to be his eyes and ears on the ground and to help manage Ferraro's helter-skelter, controversy-dominated national tour from Washington.

Throughout the campaign by the first woman nominated to run on a major party's national ticket, Sasso and Corrigan sensed another imminent Democratic disaster and began talking about the future. They felt the party's crucial handicap involved economic issues, and specifically that first Jimmy Carter and then Walter Mondale had been unable to persuade middle-class voters to trust them with their tax dollars, to trust in their ability to run the government prudently, and to trust them to look out for their best interests without meddling in their lives. The causes may have been complex and were perhaps not all the Democrats' fault, but double-digit inflation and interest rates remained intense memories in the mid-1980s, and too many voters still blamed the Democratic Party.

As Sasso and Corrigan talked, they shared a belief that their party would need a different kind of candidate to succeed after Reagan completed his second term. Other Democratic political operatives across the nation were reaching the same conclusions about the need for a transitional figure, something or someone a little bit different—perhaps someone who was less a performer, monarch, and ideologue, and more a diligent chief executive. To these two men, it seemed obvious that from the nation's state houses might rise the next nominee as the symbol of innovative, even activist government that had strongly progressive goals but used conservative fiscal means and was more partner than antagonist to the business community.

Why not Dukakis? they wondered. On the plus side, the Massachusetts economy was booming, Dukakis's entire record as governor involved using government more as a prod than an agent of change, he was not at all a typical tax-and-spend Democrat, and his political roots and electoral strengths were in the suburbs, among people with independent voting habits. His ties to more traditional Democratic voting blocs like city dwellers and labor-union members had also become strong. They also thought that his personal and political steadiness would be assets in navigating the twists and turns in an increasingly lengthy national campaign season.

On the other hand, they had no illusions about their boss. His broad appeal in Massachusetts could easily mask both intellectual and ideological fuzziness, perhaps even inability to craft a comprehensive and readily comprehensible national campaign message; and his somewhat stiff persona and reformer's emphasis on process and programs could be seen as cold and boring. He was also a foreign-policy nonentity, with no background or reputation at all in a vital field that voters explore for clues to a potential president's readiness.

Like hundreds of other Democratic activists, Sasso and Corrigan returned to their regular lives following Reagan's sweep of forty-nine states with almost 60 percent of the popular vote. Sasso had been back at his desk in the Massachusetts State House only one day when Dukakis called him into his office to talk about the election and the causes behind the disaster. The American people don't trust us on the big economic and budget issues, Sasso told his boss, and until they do the Democrats will not win a presidential election. And then, a bit self-consciously, he shared a more personal appraisal. He told Dukakis that he had many of the qualities the Democrats would need next time out, and that the policies and programs that were making Dukakis better known in Democratic circles could be offered as models for the nation.

Sasso's words took about fifteen seconds to utter. Dukakis dismissed them out of hand. But he did not dismiss, indeed he readily agreed to recommendations by Sasso that were designed to raise his national profile, though to Dukakis a higher national profile was primarily important for enhancing his stature inside Massachusetts.

That Dukakis dismissed Sasso's first mention of the presidency is no surprise. In November 1984 he was the happiest, most satisfied of men. He had avenged his 1978 defeat, the state economy was robust, his new term was going swimmingly, he was in the twenty-first year of a happy marriage to a stunning woman, and he had three almost-grown, remarkable children.

"He had always wanted to be governor," his law-school classmate and longtime friend Paul Brountas later said. "He talked about it, planned for it, worked toward it for years. But he never talked about the presidency, ever; he never even wanted to go to Washington."

Whatever flicker of ambition deep within Dukakis Sasso evoked, it would ordinarily have been quickly snuffed for a very practical reason: in Massachusetts, the franchise on presidential ambition belonged exclusively to Edward Moore Kennedy. Ever since John Fitzgerald Kennedy started his campaign for the White House after winning a second term as senator in 1958, only Kennedys among the Massachusetts-born had run for the Democratic presidential nomination.

Beaten badly when he finally went for the Democratic nomination in 1980, Kennedy had planned a second candidacy for 1984, only to pull back at the end of 1982—with his advance planning already well under way—because of opposition from his children. After the Reagan landslide in 1984, Kennedy's top aide, Laurence Horowitz, began all over again in 1985, and had a plan in hand by that fall. Kennedy had begun to make initial political moves, when on December 15 he abruptly called it all off again after another long talk with his family. This time, he acknowledged that the presidency was not likely to ever be his goal again.

Kennedy's announcement removed the most imposing obstacle to a Dukakis candidacy, but Sasso—now encouraged to believe that the governor might eventually consider running—made no move to raise the

Sen. Ted Kennedy held the franchise on presidential ambition in Massachusetts politics. When he decided not to run in December 1986, he passed the franchise to Dukakis. (Photo by Keith Jenkins)

subject with him again, certain that it would be rejected. Instead, he simply stuck with the plan for stepped-up national activity that Dukakis had approved months before on condition that it not interfere with his State House work or his campaign for reelection in 1986.

Most of Dukakis's limited national time was spent trying to bring three elements in his gubernatorial administration to national attention: an aggressive program to collect unpaid income and sales taxes; an ambitious effort to focus job-training assistance on welfare mothers, and to offer them good jobs in the state's prosperous economy with enough benefits to make work more attractive than welfare; and his continuing work to use the tools of government to encourage economic growth in sections of the state that weren't enjoying the overall prosperity amid ordinary business-cycle events.

Dukakis has never been a puppet on a string. The year 1988 may have been, as *Time* called it, the Year of the Handler, but if George Bush came to represent one extreme—a genial but hyperambitious Dr. Faustus ready to sign away a large chunk of himself to more than one political and media Mephistopheles—Michael Dukakis represented the other. He depended on John Sasso enormously, but he had always insisted upon knowing the essence of the political goings-on around him, and on reserving the right of general approval and disapproval. He was, in business parlance, a hands-on politician.

By 1986 he had some basic limits in mind and he wanted them strictly observed, precisely because he knew he would at least consider running for president. The first, second, and third political priorities were winning reelection that year. His obsession with reelection seemed excessive even to close aides, because he enjoyed extremely high approval ratings and it was not yet clear whether the Republicans—their Massachusetts ranks now including a still-bitter former Reagan Democrat named Edward J. King—could field a credible challenger.

Dukakis was fully aware that Sasso's plans included a presidential campaign. That was fine with him, but his ground rule was that the public focus be entirely on issues, that there be no precampaign organizing activity of any kind, and that any talk behind the scenes among his political henchmen be completely secret.

"He was thinking about it, but he didn't want people generally to be talking about it," Paul Brountas told us after the 1988 election. "We talked more than once, and I would tell him he was now a national figure with a great record and that he should definitely think about it. But his idea was that if he let anything get started in a visible way, that would become the sole focus where he was concerned and obscure everything else."

Dukakis also knew that Sasso was ready to return to national politics in 1988. Sasso told him he would supervise Dukakis's reelection in 1986 and stay with him for a presidential campaign, but not stay to manage a third Dukakis administration in the State House. He had helped the governor win his job back in 1982 and then, as chief secretary, had helped him perform it well. But Sasso had developed a taste for national combat in 1980 and 1984, and he was ready for another presidential campaign in 1988, this time at the top.

If Dukakis ruled out a presidential candidacy for himself, there was little doubt where Sasso would go. The 1988 campaign for the Democratic nomination had room for a Northeast governor; it did not have room for two Northeast governors. The other possibility was Mario Cuomo of New York. The two governors had mutual respect and admiration but they were not personally close and were as different as night and day. Cuomo was rhetorical fire to Dukakis's programmatic ice; he believed in using governmental leadership to shape society, but Dukakis stressed good works. Cuomo was Saint Paul to Dukakis' Peter:

Peter, the pragmatic, down-to-earth builder, versus Paul, the writer, the theoretician. Cuomo could stir an audience like few in American politics. He became nationally known after delivering the keynote address at the 1984 Democratic convention in San Francisco. Dukakis, in contrast, communicated with an audience like a political Phil Dono- hue, speaking directly in conversational tones to a television camera.

Long before there was a Dukakis presidential candidacy, Sasso and his trusted lieutenants had decided that former Colorado Senator Gary Hart was a far from invincible front-runner, despite his domination of all the early national opinion polls. They knew from experience that such polls were meaningless.

Corrigan said, "Unlike Mondale in 1984, Hart was a front-runner without a solid base. He was a creation of Mondale antimatter. Hart was missing compassion for people, he could not communicate with the traditional base of the Democratic Party and he had no record of accomplishment."

But Cuomo had all those characteristics and more, despite a mer- curial personality and thin skin that might keep him from wearing well during the long, grinding primary season. Nevertheless, to Sasso, Cuomo's intentions were the most critical missing ingredient in the precampaign period. Even as he wondered whether he might end up working for the presidential candidacy of Mario Cuomo (who thought the world of his abilities), Sasso realized that Dukakis would be unable to make a fully informed decision himself without first learning Cuomo's intentions.

It was not only possible but probable that Dukakis would not run if Cuomo did, but in the unlikely event both decided to run, Sasso also had to think of how the low-key Dukakis could make himself heard above the cacophony in a Cuomo—Gary Hart fight, with Reverend Jesse Jackson in the ring as well.

But the first task was slowly persuading Dukakis to go for it. Sasso (with Jack Corrigan's assistance) and Kitty Dukakis were the main coconspirators, but as 1986 wore on, they were assisted by another master of the political backstage, Nick Mitropoulos.

Despite a nineteen-year age difference, Dukakis and Mitropoulos were very close, and during the presidential campaign when they were inseparable for eighteen to twenty hours a day they became even closer. Mitropoulos was Dukakis's "body man." He was the governor's closest personal aide on the road. He was the first to see him in the morning and the last to see him at night. He not only accompanied the governor while he exercised on power walks but took care of the most sensitive political tasks for him on the road—always observing the body man's first rule: discretion.

Both were sons of Greek immigrants who came to Massachusetts searching for a better life. The cultural bond was very deep: They spoke Greek to each other when they didn't want anyone else to understand what they were saying. Mitropoulos had been associate director at the Institute of Politics in the Kennedy School of Government at Harvard when Dukakis repaired there to lick his wounds after being ousted from office at the beginning of 1979. They spent a lot of time together while Dukakis figured out, during a rare period of introspection, where he had gone wrong and planned his comeback campaign. When Dukakis returned triumphant to the State House in 1983, Mitropoulos joined him in the sensitive position of director of personnel, running the governor's patronage operation.

Although no member of the troika would push Dukakis too hard, Mitropoulos mentioned running for president about fifteen times to him during the 1986 gubernatorial campaign. "You gotta run for president," he would say before his boss waved him to silence. But the constant badgering gave Dukakis a useful line that kept his own thoughts masked; he told anyone who asked him if he would run for president that Mitropoulos and others were telling him he should.

Corrigan had less direct contact with Dukakis because in the governor's political hierarchy he was Sasso's second. But a presidential campaign made so much sense to him that he acted as if it were predestined. At a dinner party celebrating his twenty-ninth birthday in September 1985, he bluntly predicted that Dukakis would be the 1988 Democratic presidential nominee. Sasso was far less certain, because he could sense the hesitation in Dukakis. But all three trusted aides were leery of raising the presidential profile too soon. Dukakis was so obsessed with the 1986 reelection that it would be totally in character for him to publicly rule himself out of contention for the presidency to quell any excessive spurt of speculation. Indeed, in September, while riding to the State House with Fred Salvucci, long his Secretary of Transportation, Dukakis dismissed a presidential candidacy as a "ridiculous concept."

Despite the strictures against overt activity, as 1986 unfolded a private forum enabled Sasso and his friends to talk politics in confidence. Ever since Dukakis's grudge match with Ed King in 1982, Sasso had met informally nearly every Thursday evening with a small, rotating group of political strategists and tacticians in his office. After the governor had left his own lair for his storied trolley-car ride home to Brookline, the Sasso group would assemble for political chatter and planning over Chinese food or pizza. The conversation was freewheeling, but usually led by Sasso, puffing on a toxic cigar in defiance of Dukakis's no-smoking rule. State Revenue Commissioner Ira Jackson, architect of Dukakis's highly successful effort to collect unpaid state taxes, called the meetings "poker games without cards." The group was a vehicle for Sasso to solicit, measure, and test ideas. Corrigan wryly referred to the meetings as "Sasso's little focus groups."

The Thursday-night discussion group also had an operational adjunct that proved useful as 1986 unfolded. Using the talk as raw material along with polling data, Sasso and chief policy aide John DeVillars drafted memoranda (for the governor's eyes only) every three months, setting forth a handful of his most important policy and political objectives for the period, and how they might be achieved, step by step. This procedure was vital to the more successful operations in the second Dukakis administration. For all his fabled mastery of detail and substance, Dukakis is not a conceptual thinker; he does not read for pleasure, nor does he spend long hours discussing big issues with big thinkers to broaden his mind and develop new ideas—a major personal deficiency for a national leader.

Instead, Dukakis is a shopper. Pushing his idea cart down the aisles of government and politics, much as he likes to do at the Stop & Shop near his Brookline home, the governor takes a notion here, a program there.

Back in office with Sasso at his side in 1983, he benefited from brainstorming by the others, and the quarterly plans gave him not only a sense of direction that made it easy for him to trudge through the steps in implementation, but also a gradually revived confidence in his ability to achieve. It is a subject of endless debate in Massachusetts whether Dukakis had really changed from his first-term persona (the majority view was that he was better, not different).

Despite his relentless focus on reelection, Dukakis was aware of the presidential speculation around him. He even joked about it in spring 1986 at the Democratic State Convention, a pro forma endorsement coronation, with a joke about Sam Adams, his favorite former governor, the Revolutionary War firebrand whose picture hung over his desk at the State House. He could hear old Sam talking to him, he teased the activist Democrats who even then were buzzing about 1988. "I can hear him say to me, 'Dukakis, if you win this election in November and if you play your cards right, maybe, just maybe, someday . . . they'll name a beer after you.' "

As fate would have it, however, the elaborate mechanism supporting Dukakis's reelection campaign in 1986—of which the Thursday-night discussion group was but one part—proved unnecessary in an atmosphere of laughable Republican disarray. Not only did nemesis Ed King pass up a rubber match, but first one and then a second Republican hopeful had to quit the race because of bizarre revelations about appearing nude in a business office and falsifying a résumé to include elite combat service in Vietnam. The result was a lame Republican nominee who gave Dukakis as much trouble as a batting-practice pitcher. Ironically, another successful incumbent who had a chance to run up the score against token Republican opposition was New York's Mario Cuomo, and amid the good-natured but real competition between Boston and Albany, it was a backstage game to see who could get the highest vote percentage (in the end it was Dukakis by 69 percent to Cuomo's 65 percent).

Nonetheless, despite guaranteed reelection by spring 1986, the single-minded Dukakis would not tolerate a detour by his advisers into presidential politics and refused to discuss the subject in any depth with anyone who brought it up. But his conduct belied his dismissive rhetoric during this formative period.

"Sure he was seriously considering it," John Sasso told us later. "He would have called me off if he wasn't. I found him intrigued by the idea and by all the speculation. Obviously he had read everything that was being written and had thought about it all. Every so often he would say things like, this is pretty interesting. The distinction was that he was never expansive about it."

There was, of course, no need for him to be expansive. The reelection campaign in Massachusetts was a legitimate focus, the published speculation and the political chatter in the state and around the country covered all the obvious angles; and interest in Dukakis and his record was being carefully cultivated by Sasso and his lieutenants with the governor's knowledge and approval. Within the National Governors Association, the Democratic Party, and Congress, Dukakis was a peripatetic salesman for his ideas about activist but frugal government.

One of the most telling events had occurred back in February 1986 when the governor journeyed to Washington to publicize his successful job-training program for welfare recipients. The night before a Capitol Hill press conference, House Speaker Thomas P. O'Neill, Jr.—in the final year of his half-century in politics—threw a cocktail party for Dukakis that drew a large crowd from official Washington because of the Speaker's clout. And the next day, Dukakis's press conference drew an unusually heavy assemblage of national reporters—and produced a highly favorable column from the *Washington Post*'s oracular liberal, Mary McGrory. The positive coverage was a pleasant surprise, but the turnout was no accident; for several days previously, members of the Thursday night group had made phone calls to a list of Washington journalists and issued personal invitations.

Although these kinds of events were occasional occurrences in 1986, the Dukakis national clipping file slowly fattened. But at that time his candidacy was in no way assumed or even expected; Gary Hart, Mario Cuomo (disavowals notwithstanding), and Jesse Jackson got most of the publicity. But Dukakis was in the national mix, part of any informed discussion about the alternatives available to the Democratic Party as it prepared to attempt a comeback after eight years in the presidential wilderness. He was several steps behind three men with long-shot candidacies: Governor Bruce Babbitt of Arizona, Senator Joseph Biden of Delaware, and Missouri Representative Richard Gephardt. Being in the group but not necessarily of the group, though, made him like several prominent Democrats who were thinking but not overtly acting presidential in 1986: Senator Sam Nunn of Georgia, Governor Bill Clinton and Senator Dale Bumpers of Arkansas, and Senator Bill Bradley of New Jersey.

For the most part, Dukakis himself was a guarded, visible, though issue-oriented mystery, but in summer he took one halting step that showed how fast his upstairs wheels were spinning. Just before Labor Day, he called his chief fund-raiser, Robert Farmer, a whirling dervish who had made his fortune in educational publishing and now dabbled in politics. He invited Farmer to his home in Brookline, and over the not-yet-famous Dukakis kitchen table asked him directly, "If I go for president I have one basic question: Will the money be there to wage a credible campaign?"

A glib conversationalist, the effusive Farmer immediately said he could put together $6.5 million, including federal matching funds, by the time of the Iowa caucuses in February 1988. That night, though, he thought about his answer in more depth and was bothered by his initially buoyant response.

"I called him the next morning," Farmer later recalled, "and I had had a sleepless night, and I said, 'Mike, I'm troubled about one thing.' And he said, 'What's that?' And I said, 'I've never raised money for a guy who's at 1 percent (in the polls) before, and I don't know how it translates.' "

Dukakis told Farmer his uneasiness was legitimate, another sign that his doubts were as real as his interest.

Just a few weeks later—Dukakis's landslide reelection now assured—Sasso quietly broke off all but perfunctory supervision of the campaign to concentrate on preparing for its aftermath, which he was certain would at least entail serious consideration by Dukakis of a presidential candidacy.

Sasso decided to prepare in private, with only Jack Corrigan as sounding board. His Thursday group had initially greeted presidential speculation with disbelief but had gradually warmed to the idea, though Sasso had originally told the members that he doubted Dukakis would become a candidate. But we can't tell until after the election, he would say, and so let's see what happens.

As November neared, Sasso began drafting a memorandum for the governor that he felt would give Dukakis what he needed to begin thinking about a presidential candidacy. Sasso wrote it himself, helped by his meticulous assistant, Marie Murphy, organizing and typing it. Three days after Dukakis's landslide, Sasso had it delivered by a messenger to Dukakis's home so that the governor could take it with him as he and his wife left for a Florida vacation.

The memo began with a disavowal of advocacy, which Sasso told us much later he tried to suppress. His feelings, however, were evident as he sized up the strengths and weaknesses in a Dukakis candidacy, and told the governor that he should not want to look back a year or so later and wish he had at least given serious consideration to running. The 1988 election, Sasso reasoned, would be a genuine watershed, and a Republican victory would make coming back even more difficult in 1992. On the plus side, Sasso wrote that he saw an opening in the Democratic field for a sitting governor who could add a record of accomplishment to the new ideas he could bring to a campaign; in effect, he said Dukakis could run on a pledge to nationalize the Massachusetts model of government. He also described Dukakis as the right kind of person for a long race—cool, disciplined, and instinctively optimistic about the country's future. And, finally, he said the money for a serious candidacy would be available, and outlined a $6-million budget for an effort through the New Hampshire primary.

He also tried, however, to be blunt about his boss's weaknesses and the criticisms he was likely to encounter, including: geography (a northeastern ethnic in a Sunbelt era); ideology (inclined toward liberalism in the Age of Reagan); style (bland and issue-oriented—specifically referring to Jimmy Carter, another former governor with a reputation as a hands-on administrator); and background (domestic policy strength clashing with a foreign-policy blank slate in an unstable world).

For the political outlook, Sasso was upbeat but he ended with a large question mark. He said Dukakis's strengths could match those of Gary Hart, that if he at least came out of Iowa as a credible force he could hold a natural base in New Hampshire, and then, with money in the bank, challenge Hart in the twenty contests on Super Tuesday (March 8), assuming that the field would include a southern candidate, but not one so powerful he could lock up the entire South.

Clearly, nothing in Sasso's thinking precluded a run against Gary Hart, notwithstanding the long odds against success. Instead, Sasso's major political question was about the other Northeast governor, Mario

Cuomo. He proposed later that he talk to the New York governor, with whom he had rapport, on Dukakis's behalf.

Finally, Sasso's memo included pointed questions designed to help the governor confront the reality that what he was considering was serious business requiring total commitment. He asked whether Dukakis really believed he had something to offer the country that no one else did; if he was willing to draw stark differences with his opponents as required and to use the heightened rhetoric that the media culture has come to require not just of presidential candidates, but of presidents; if he was prepared to entrust major portions of gubernatorial duties to others; and he asked Dukakis to consider how an unsuccessful candidacy might affect a possible fall-back goal, like getting the vice presidential nomination or becoming attorney general in a Democratic administration.

Sasso's memo was not the only strategic document reaching the eyes of would-be candidates in this period. At least a few associates of Dukakis's henchman, soon to be competitors, were developing somewhat different theories. Two of them were friends in Senator Kennedy's office: a South Carolina-spawned operative named William Carrick, and the Yale-educated son of a Bronx plumber, Paul Tully. Each was as aware as Sasso of Walter Mondale's deficiencies, but with no Ronald Reagan on the horizon and therefore a wide-open race shaping up, they believed that the 1988 election would be a watershed and the key to success would not be avoiding statements about tax increases, but coming up with a theme and campaign message that emphasized change over the status quo. Carrick eventually decided to manage Missouri Congressman Richard Gephardt's candidacy, and Paul Tully headed for Denver and Gary Hart.

By the time Dukakis returned from his Key Largo vacation, Sasso had a second memorandum ready for him, this one taking the proceedings a step further. He recommended an elaborate, multiweek consultation with prominent Democrats around the country—and some initial travel to expose Dukakis to something resembling presidential campaign lifestyle—prior to his making a final decision.

To his henchmen's chagrin and frustration, however, Dukakis brusquely put Sasso off, saying he wanted to wait until after Christmas. For those who can see only a hapless governor completely under an adviser's domination, this episode is an instructive reminder that although he relied upon Sasso, there was never any doubt that Dukakis called his own shots. Sasso could move the governor with carefully marshaled facts, and Dukakis would hear him out, but Sasso never operated on the premise that he could "make" Dukakis do anything he clearly didn't want to do, or do anything before he was ready. In fact, in this period Dukakis was rejecting for the moment the option of taking his exploration public because he wanted to do some private exploration and consult with his family, as well as a handful of close friends and political associates.

The governor harbored some real reservations. Just after Thanksgiving, Dukakis got a rare jolt when he stopped by Harvard one afternoon with Mitropoulos to visit that year's group of visiting journalists on Nieman Fellowships. During a desultory discussion of government and politics, Dukakis was asked what he would do as president if he were called to the White House Situation Room in the middle of the night and told that Soviet nuclear missiles had been launched.

The question—a staple on the campaign trail for which any serious candidate must be prepared—caught Dukakis off guard, and he evaded an answer and extracted himself with difficulty by talking about what an important question it was. For Mitropoulos—who told friends about it—the incident was a reminder that the consultation being urged on Dukakis was not just for show, and that indeed Dukakis had to make a transition from the state to the national and international stage. The governor was not well-read, well-traveled, or well-connected, not just in the rarefied foreign-affairs atmosphere but also in the United States.

Paul Brountas and his wife, Lynn, went to the Dukakis duplex during the first week in December, where the frugal governor prepared turkey tetrazzini from holiday leftovers and the two couples settled down for a long, and long-delayed talk. From the vantage point of close personal friendship, as well as long political intimacy, Brountas hoped the governor would run for president but, like the others who were close to him, had been sensitive to his desire to steer clear of the subject earlier in the year. He also understood, as he put it much later, that Dukakis "had no great, burning desire to be President of the United States."

But aware that Dukakis's interest was very strong, Brountas told him he ought to take special cognizance of three major hurdles ahead: having enough campaign money on hand to survive the inevitable bumps in the nomination road; doing well enough in the Iowa caucuses to avoid threatening his position in New Hampshire; and being comfortable as a more than occasionally absentee governor.

That last point was critical for Dukakis. The day after he won reelection in 1986 and the day before Sasso's memo arrived by messenger, he called in Frank T. Keefe, his Secretary of Administration and Finance, whom State House wags dubbed the Al Haig of state government because he had once declared he was in charge of the state. (It was true in a sense, but tacky to say so.) Keefe told the governor that he wanted to leave for a business career but would stay until January to prepare the budget for the coming fiscal year. Dukakis was disturbed by that and told Keefe he needed stability in state government while he considered a run for the presidency. Keefe, wanting to be helpful and eager to see his boss run, agreed to stay through July. Dukakis was openly relieved, pleased, and thankful.

The governor made similar, private overtures to the state legislature's Democratic leadership. Senate President William M. Bulger of South Boston and House Speaker George Keverian of Everett were intrigued by the idea that someone they had started out with in the state legislature would run for president. They promised to be supportive.

Assured of enough money to run, comfortable that the state would be left in experienced hands, he still faced a huge personal hurdle: how a campaign would affect his private life, his wife, and his three children.

"I think emotionally he had made up his mind, but he wanted to be extremely fair to his family, to his children, and to his mother. He wanted to think about it in a careful, deliberate way," said Keefe. "[But] There was no question in my mind that the mere launching of the exercise meant he wanted to do it."

According to his son John, the governor repeatedly postponed a family summit during December, to avoid a cheerleading session. He knew that his family wanted him to run, but when the moment of truth arrived and the family gathered just before Christmas, all were surprised by the gush of anxiety that dominated their discussion.

"There was a lot of struggle within all of us as to whether this was in everybody's best interest," John Dukakis recalled of the gathering that also included his new wife, Lisa; his mother and his two sisters, Andrea (just out of Princeton) and Kara (just into Brown). "We were concerned about security, his safety, and about living in a much larger fishbowl."

The act of airing these questions, however, coupled with their unshaken conviction that he should run, helped Dukakis clear the last hurdle to becoming a quasi-candidate. He and Sasso met again right after Christmas, and Dukakis asked him for one more assessment of the Democratic field and his position in it, some advice on how to run and still be a diligent governor, and an opinion on the likely effect on his and his family's life. Sasso quickly provided the first two, but reminded the governor that the final subject was uniquely his to ponder.

It is typical of Dukakis that he never actually announced that he would take a formal look at the race and make a decision on whether to enter it. Instead, just before New Year's, leaving Boston's political hostelry, the Parker House, one night after a meeting with national party chairman Paul Kirk, he was corraled by a local television interviewer, and told her on camera that he would announce his decision by mid-March.

An excited Jack Corrigan raced for a telephone and placed a call to Florida where Sasso was vacationing to tell him the news: the toes were finally in the water.

Throughout the deliberations, Dukakis was more likely to say no than yes, as he wavered through his staff-planned paces. But after each waver, he stopped short of saying no and moved noncommittally to the next stage. By January the political team of Sasso, Corrigan, and Mitropoulos was practically living at the State House, an elegant Bulfinch building with a striking gold dome atop Beacon Hill, planning meetings, designing a campaign, putting out feelers to possible campaign workers.

Shortly after New Year's, Dukakis put his constituents on notice by making it clear in his inaugural address that something might be coming.

Without letting anyone know the extent of his thinking so far or his staff's preparatory work, Dukakis raised the subject. At the end of his twenty-three-minute address, he pulled out notes he had typed at home. "I've got some awesome decisions to make in the next few months. And they are decisions that I intend to make only after much thought and much reflection," he said. "Whatever decision I make, I want you to know that being the governor of Massachusetts has been the richest, the most fulfilling, the most enjoyable experience anyone in public life could ask for." That he had referred to his tenure as governor in the past tense set the State House to buzzing.

Five days into 1987, we talked to John Sasso, who was typically cautious even as he stage-managed an incipient presidential campaign.

"He's warming to it," Sasso said, adding that the timetable was fixed so that the governor would come to a public decision by the end of February or the beginning of March. The major change that was in store, he made clear, would be a less secretive atmosphere; there would be regular meetings with Washington insiders and national politicians, and there would be at least a few brief out-of-state trips to give Dukakis an introduction to life on the road.

Sasso emphasized that Dukakis's judgment about whether he could simultaneously serve as governor and campaign for president was critical.

"Leaving aside George Wallace, no one has really done this from a state house since Nelson Rockefeller," Sasso went on. "But today we have a much more complex political environment. For six years in a row, the Massachusetts legislature has been in session for the full twelve months. But he also has the option of doing this precisely because the state is now in good shape; and he comes to the presidential table with real assets, including his record, his access to campaign money, and the fact that the New Hampshire primary is where it is in the process. This is possibly a unique opportunity in his life."

But to many national Democrats thinking about the impending campaign in depth as 1987 began, the governor appeared to bring nothing to the race besides his regional base. Said consultant Greg Schneiders, soon to become a top adviser to former Arizona Governor Bruce Babbitt, "Dukakis is a candidate whose plausibility rests largely on his geographical location." And to Robert Beckel, Walter Mondale's campaign manager, who would become a media fixture as a commentator in the 1988 campaign, Dukakis was a potential candidate who could be very helpful to Gary Hart, primarily by providing him with cover for a close race in New Hampshire, and lessening Hart's need to win big there or even to win at all.

Sasso was also assessing his horse against the leading names then in the Democratic picture. Compared to Mario Cuomo, he said Dukakis could be a candidate who offered clear, specific proposals for new policies; and compared to Gary Hart, he could offer his record as a "doer," both competing with Hart for the younger, less partisan voters in Democratic primaries as well as attracting traditional elements in the Democratic coalition who were still suspicious of the now-former Colorado senator.

Sasso, however, was still worried about Mario Cuomo's intentions. Securing his boss's permission, he placed a telephone call to the New York governor on January 18. Machination is second nature to Sasso and Cuomo, and for about twenty minutes they fenced, remarking on the close-knit Dukakis and Cuomo families, their shared wish for privacy, their shared feeling about mixing a presidential candidacy with gubernatorial responsibilities, and the major defeats each had suffered in the past (Dukakis for governor in 1978, and Cuomo for mayor of New York City a year before).

Cuomo then asked Sasso when Dukakis would announce his decision; when Sasso said the announcement would come by mid-March, Cuomo pressed him, "Are you sure, John?"

When Sasso said he was, Cuomo abruptly said, "Well that's good, John, thank you very much," and hung up.

Reading Mario Cuomo is a delicate business, but Sasso had not a shadow of a doubt about what he'd been meant to hear, and he told Dukakis that he thought Cuomo would make up his own mind before Dukakis's deadline; in short, that Dukakis would know Cuomo's plans before he reached his fail-safe point. Sasso was correct: by late February, Cuomo announced that he would not run. Cuomo's decision did not surprise Sasso, for Cuomo was then in his fifth year as governor and Dukakis was in his ninth, because Cuomo faced a Republican state senate and Dukakis did not, and because Cuomo had explicitly pledged to serve a full term while campaigning for reelection the year before and Dukakis conspicuously had not. Still, after the 1988 campaign was history, Sasso said it was his educated guess that had Cuomo decided that January to join the race, Dukakis would not have run; it was a long shot with Gary Hart, but with Gary Hart *and* Mario Cuomo a Dukakis campaign would have been quixotic. Quixotism is not a Dukakis character trait. Despite Cuomo's announcement, Mario scenarios, some fanciful in the extreme, detailing how Cuomo might become the nominee persisted throughout the presidential primary season.

The governor's acclimatization period in January and February consisted of private meetings and a small dose of public travel. For most evenings during those two months while he was in Boston, a steady parade of Democratic Party big shots and gurus beat paths to Dukakis's door at either the State House or his Brookline house to talk politics, issues, and government. At every session, Sasso, Corrigan, or Mitropoulos joined as notetakers. The parade included media mogul Norman Lear, former Iowa Senator John Culver; savvy organizer Willie Velasquez from the Texas Southwest Voter Education Project; and, when Dukakis was in Washington, former Vice President Walter Mondale and his party's top Senate and House leaders.

The sessions were devoted far more to how-to questions about campaigning and government than to major current issues or major themes for the coming decade. Dukakis wanted to know how an outsider could reach Iowa Democrats, how a president could make sure he controlled the Central Intelligence Agency, how an activist president could make a major reduction in the federal budget deficit, how the grass-roots campaigning in his formative years might be transplanted into the mass media—dominated world of presidential campaigns, how a Northeast governor like himself might succeed in the South.

Sasso also exposed Dukakis to life on the road, a three-day trip to Iowa in early February being the principal event. The journey was notable at the time for the horde of Boston print and television reporters who followed along, to the Iowans' bemusement and the chagrin of Dukakis's staffers who worried how he might effectively perform the political "retailing" rituals before small groups around the state during the year-long campaign leading up to the precinct caucuses.

The trip also showed what a rookie Dukakis was in the presidential league, symbolized by an incident that would later subject him to ridicule. While talking to Iowa farmers overwhelmed by corn and hog surpluses, he suggested that they diversify their production. In his home state of Massachusetts, he said, the tiny farming community had taken to growing vegetables for specialty markets, vegetables like Belgian endive, a staple of nouvelle cuisine.

On the plane back to Boston, Dukakis grilled Sasso about the complicated caucus process. He also expressed amazement at the hovering news media, with microphones and cameras recording his every utterance. This is the way it is; this is something you have to get used to, Sasso explained.

But even as Dukakis sat through the scores of meetings with national political operatives and important figures from key states, and felt the rush of attention following Cuomo's announcement on February 19 that he would not seek the Democratic presidential nomination, he still held a large chunk of himself back from a final commitment.

"He is deeply ambivalent," Sasso told us at the end of February, while in Washington with Dukakis for the National Governors Association winter meeting.

"There is no question at all about the plausibility of a candidacy," Sasso said. "We have received all the good mentions since the Cuomo announcement we could have hoped for. He is completely in the mix, but do not assume anything at this point. He's not there yet."

Dukakis's ambivalence had nothing to do with fear of ending up with 1 percent in Iowa, Sasso said. Instead, it stemmed from his commitment to his job as governor, not governor as caretaker but governor as innovator; he was worried that a presidential candidacy would harm the opportunities and challenges he saw still ahead in Massachusetts. Sasso said that shortly before the trip to Washington, Dukakis had gathered local officials from around the state to discuss his priorities for the third term he had just begun; no longer was the health of the Massachusetts economy in question, Dukakis had told them, but what now remained was the extraordinary opportunity to take advantage of that prosperity to improve the quality and distribution of human-services programs by making major advances in child care, availability of health insurance, and all the other efforts that had been on hold while the state's economic and fiscal house was being rebuilt.

Pointedly, Sasso recalled that the day after his testing-the-water trip to Iowa early in February, he had been in his State House office at 7:15 A.M., in effect overcompensating for his presidential activity by making a totally unnecessary effort to display his dedication to being a diligent governor.

Dukakis often seemed curiously disconnected from this highly political enterprise. His ability to divide his mind into compartments was displayed throughout his three days at the governors' conference in Washington during the last week in February. He may have been in the middle of deadly earnest political meetings to help him make up his mind about becoming the political leader of his party, and a speech to a New Hampshire Democratic Party dinner trying out possible campaign themes was barely two weeks away; but while he was Michael Dukakis, chairman of the Human Services Committee of the National Governors Association, his demeanor was scrupulously nonpartisan, even antipartisan.

At the New Hampshire dinner, though, signs of an incipient candidacy were everywhere: in the sizable contingent of national political reporters, the equally large collection of operatives from past Democratic campaigns who were already being recruited for contingency service by Sasso, and in the group of well-dressed, well-heeled white men whom Bob Farmer would ask to fan out around the country to raise money.

With state Democratic stalwarts Mary Chambers and Paul McEachern doing the introductions, the governor was brought to the stage with an appropriate number of references to the statement that was now almost certainly ahead. A custom-printed tee-shirt from Chambers said "Go for It Duke." McEachern, the party's unsuccessful nominee for governor the year before, called Dukakis "a man who should be running for President . . . Michael Dukakis offers what America needs, courage and competence." He called the long primary campaign a crucible and said, as he called Dukakis to the microphone, "From what we've seen, you'll stand the fire."

The man who accepted the ovation from the audience had a lot to learn about big-time speaking. As the crowd cheered, Dukakis's first words as a quasi-candidate for president were: "Thank you, thank you, thank you very much, thank you, thank you very much, thank you, thank you, thank you, thank you very much, thank you."

It would be months before he would learn that saying thank you into a live microphone dampens the effect of applause both for the live audience and for those watching television.

And as he began to speak, another old Dukakis bad habit flared. His hands were clasped at first, but as he spoke they would rhythmically pull apart and then come back together, making it look on the television monitors as if Dukakis were accompanying himself on an invisible accordion. This habit had survived countless attempts by aides and family members to make him understand how distracting it was; on this evening, his stepson, John (a former movie and television actor) had affixed tape to the sides of the lectern, with the sticky sides exposed, to remind his father to keep his hands still, but in the excitement Dukakis paid his props no heed.

The speech was way too long, but the evening was a success, and the governor's words at least served as a rare opportunity to test some themes (most important, the son of immigrants offering a renewal, not of Democratic liberalism but of the American Dream itself) on a friendly, near-home audience (swelled by hundreds of Massachusetts supporters as well) that would have cheered him in reading the Yellow Pages.

The next morning, speaking as an informed source, an ebullient Sasso for the first time outlined for publication the route Dukakis could now be expected to take once he made his final decision to announce.

"We could go a lot of different ways," he said, "but my sense is that it would be a mistake to formally declare right off the bat. I would expect instead that he would announce the formation of a campaign committee, begin traveling more regularly, and then do a formal announcement within sixty days."

"I would like to milk it a little bit, arrange for a big sendoff on Boston Common and put on a big fund-raising dinner, the things you can't put together in a couple of weeks. Besides, we need a little more time to get set up. I feel very, very good about these last two months; we're getting there, but we need practice."

It didn't take long for the milking to begin. The next evening, NBC News broadcast a long report by political correspondent Ken Bode about a candidacy in the making that just happened to be Dukakis's, showing him riding the trolley, getting his hair cut, and being loved in New Hampshire. It was now time for Dukakis to take the next big step himself.

He was about to take that step, however, without spending much time thinking about the office of president as the locus of national leadership. Despite the quantum difference between being governor of Massachusetts and being president of the United States, Dukakis's decision making had focused more on logistics and tactics than substance. This pitfall is common for Democratic presidential candidates obsessed with winning the party's nomination. Although the failing is partly caused by having been the out party for so many years, this lack of vision is also one reason the Democrats have remained the out party.

During one of his meetings with Democratic graybeards, Harvard Professor Richard Neustadt and Kennedy School Executive Dean C. Hale Champion spoke to him about what the job would be like if he won. Neustadt, a prominent historian who specialized in the presidency and who had advised John F. Kennedy, among other presidents, told him he could do anything he wanted once he won, a prospect that seemed to pique the governor's imagination. When Dukakis asked him to name the common characteristic held by each president he had known, the professor paused and thought for a long time: "They were all a little strange," he replied. Dukakis laughed.

Two days after the New Hampshire speech, a Sunday, Dukakis and Sasso slipped out of Boston secretly on the shuttle to New York for two final bits of pre-announcement diplomacy. They chatted about southern politics with Jimmy Carter, up from Georgia in Manhattan that day. The former president emphasized that he would support fellow Georgian Sam Nunn if he ran, but urged Dukakis to study the successful 1986 Senate campaign of Wyche Fowler to learn how a person with liberal leanings can campaign successfully in the South. The two men from Massachusetts then hopped an Amtrak train and headed for Albany, where Mario Cuomo was waiting.

He was very warm and supportive, and offered the first drops of private advice that over the next twenty months would become a steady stream. His major point was that after the Reagan era, there would be an opening for a national leader who was *not* telegenic, who did *not* emphasize symbols or ideology, but who worked hard to solve problems with a minimum of ideological thunder. And to emphasize his point about Dukakis's need to stress his record, Cuomo pointed to the fat New York state budget on his desk and told Dukakis he should always be certain to remind people that he had already balanced nine of those budgets as governor.

The countdown to announcement began March 12, after a Dukakis speech in Washington to the liberal Children's Defense Fund. As Dukakis and Sasso walked down a hotel corridor to return to their rooms late at night, the governor asked his trusted aide if he had thought about how an announcement of his decision would be made.

"I've given it a little thought," replied Sasso. He smiled to himself: obviously an announcement that Dukakis was not running required no special planning; a green light, however, did.

Dukakis then told Sasso he was ready to announce his decision, and while the governor journeyed on to Louisiana for another speech, Sasso returned to Boston to get ready.

Meanwhile, in Los Angeles, a close friend of Sasso's—they met during Edward Kennedy's presidential campaign and became close later in Boston—was asked for help in the rhetoric department for a Dukakis candidacy announcement she was certain he would make. Susan Estrich did not know Dukakis very well, certainly not as she knew Sasso and Corrigan, but she had acted as his parliamentarian at state Democratic conventions, and the governor had graced her November wedding with his presence. The brilliant Harvard Law School professor was then on leave from her teaching post so she could live in Los Angeles with her husband, former Mondale speechwriter Martin Kaplan, who was a rising star in movie production. She was excited about a Dukakis candidacy and her background in the politics of issues was a critical void

Sasso wanted to fill by making her a top campaign official. Estrich took charge of producing a draft for an announcement speech. An initial product written by a friend left her cold, and so she turned to her husband for the one Dukakis would use.

After Dukakis told his wife that he would run, he called Sasso to his home and told him he would announce his intention to run on Monday. They reviewed Sasso's plans for a State House press conference and a speech to a joint session of the state legislature. Sasso told Mitropoulos (who was not surprised), and he began to list people who should be called Monday morning.

The secret held even through Senate President Bulger's traditional St. Patrick's Day breakfast in South Boston on Sunday morning. The irrepressible Bulger spotted Lieutenant Governor Evelyn F. Murphy in the crowd. "Here's Evelyn Murphy. You and I will be governor soon, kid," he wisecracked. "Don't forget, when he gets here, to give him a lot of encouragement."

The Massachusetts State House is a byzantine place with tribal rituals that date back decades. Michael Dukakis had always been regarded as a bit of a prig by most of this building's denizens. He was so holier-than-thou; he thought he was smarter than everyone else and let you know it; he had been sobered by his defeat by that walking accident of a politician Eddie King in 1978 and had returned to office a more political and approachable person in 1983. It wasn't that people didn't respect him. Nearly everyone respected Mike Dukakis, but that wasn't the same as liking him. As bricklayer labor boss Tom McIntyre would say in a television commercial in the following year, he wasn't exactly a shot-and-a-beer kind of guy. But his candidacy seemed to thrill even the most cynical. "Even his enemies are excited," sighed former state representative Peter McCarthy of Peabody.

He made his announcement on Monday morning at the State House. At his press conference he firmly declared, "I am certainly going to run to win." He said other things that were repeated many times throughout the campaign. He said, "I am going to run for this office, not against people"; he said the two most important issues were peace and economic growth; he said that the time had come to stop labeling people and look instead at their records.

His supporters felt that the stars were lining up for this campaign. It felt so right, somehow. Dukakis, the Mr. Competence, the Mr. Integrity of Massachusetts to follow Mr. Glitz, Mr. Hollywood. There was a symmetry to it all. His top aides felt Dukakis needed no special preparation for campaigning. He was a natural at press conferences and loved the intimate campaigning in people's living rooms that characterized Iowa and New Hampshire. But his stiff speechmaking style

needed work, and he needed briefings on foreign policy, defense programs, and agriculture. The demands made by his job as governor and
life on the road left little time for brainstorming ideas with great thinkers
or practice sessions with speech and media coaches. He was, in short,
a rookie.

Indeed, not until the next morning did Dukakis sit down for the
first time with Harvard Law School Professor Christopher Edley, Jr.,
an Estrich recruit, whom he was interviewing for issues director of his
fledgling campaign. Instead of questions and answers, an unusually
crisp Dukakis used the interview to deliver a monologue to his adviser-
to-be, summarizing why he was running and what he wanted a Dukakis
presidency to entail.

Being a sensible prod for economic growth in all parts of the
country was foremost, Dukakis said, and he wanted his campaign to
emphasize expanding economic opportunity and creating "good jobs at
good wages." Dukakis said he wanted to advance new ideas that min-
imized new federal spending, avoided new taxes, and needed no large
new federal bureaucracies. In foreign policy, he would accentuate basic
American values, and cited the Reagan administration's sometimes
illegal assistance to the guerrilla army inside Nicaragua as a policy that
did not.

Early in April, the second of Sasso's ninety-day plans for Dukakis's
eyes only arrived on his desk. The overriding theme for the campaign,
Sasso wrote, was to be providing economic opportunity for all Americans, though that theme was specifically for that stage in the campaign,
a clear hint that something more would be required later.

Sasso also described a campaign that would lean on the governor's
personal attributes: Dukakis's reputation for competence, accomplishment, and integrity would offer a hoped-for contrast to Washington-
based candidacies featuring proposals for legislation. Nonetheless,
Dukakis's image in foreign policy troubled him still, and he urged
Dukakis to consider making a trip abroad, possibly even to the Soviet
Union.

Sasso also stressed Dukakis's need to become a more inspiring and
effective public speaker and urged him to continue his work with a
speech coach, Professor Frances LaShoto of Emerson College.

But above all, Sasso suggested that the governor progress from a
good, solid Mike Dukakis image to a genuinely compelling personality
clearly understanding the challenges facing the country and able to
forcefully articulate responses to them.

Nor did Sasso neglect affairs of state: the governor's Cabinet must
understand it was imperative to push his agenda in the legislature, and
he was very firm on watching the state budget. Massachusetts, Sasso

On April 29, 1987, the day after a surprise spring snowstorm, Dukakis made his candidacy official: "Ask more than what we are going to do. Ask what we have already done." (Photo by Tom Landers)

warned, must end the coming fiscal year in the black, and he urged Dukakis to tell his staff and department heads that he didn't need any budget surprises and that they must be constantly on guard.

The formal announcement—a new ritual for the 1988 race was that publicity-crazed candidates first announced their intention to run and then staged official announcements later—came on April 29, the day after a surprise spring snow had turned historic Boston Common into a giant mud puddle. The already efficient Dukakis organization used truckloads of straw to soak up the muck, and Dukakis became a presidential candidate, first in the oldest public park in America just yards from his State House office, and then in New Hampshire, Georgia, and Iowa.

At each stop, he told Democrats in Massachusetts and New Hampshire and curious Democrats in Georgia and Iowa that they should judge the field of candidates by "what we have already done . . . whether we have already made new ideas work . . . what kind of people we are and what kind of people we have around us."

His rhetoric threw down an unmistakable gauntlet for Gary Hart. Hart was the candidate of "new ideas"; new ideas that work was Dukakis's counter.

The speech made it clear that in a Gary Hart—-dominated field, the Dukakis pitch was Dukakis, not some view of the country and its future; the message was the messenger. It was calculated carefully: Gary Hart could conceivably be taken on by a candidate who subtly reminded people that Hart had never really accomplished anything, and might be seen, in Boston political slang, as "all sizzle and no burger"; by inviting scrutiny of his character, Dukakis was also inviting comparison with Hart, who for all his brilliance still had a weird streak, along with a rootless, rolling-stone persona and more than a whiff of philandering habits. His own candidacy was (Dukakis's words were now famous) a "very, very long shot," but it was nonetheless plausible.

And then the most amazing thing happened. Four days after his formal announcement, a team of *Miami Herald* reporters staked out Hart's Capitol Hill townhouse in Washington and spotted a woman who would soon be identified as not his wife but Donna Rice entering and leaving the premises in the former senator's company. Nine days into Dukakis's official candidacy, the scandalous firestorm consumed Hart's candidacy, and the man who had theretofore dominated analyses of the Democratic race was gone.

In Boston, Sasso received the news with mixed exhilaration and worry. His very, very long shot now had just as much of a chance of becoming his party's presidential nominee as anybody else, but he wasn't close to being prepared for the white-hot scrutiny serious candidates receive. To all who called, Sasso kept muttering, "We're not ready for this."

The day after Hart's withdrawal, a sunny spring Saturday in Des Moines, the remaining candidates had gathered for brief appearances at a Polk County party picnic, a steak fry. Some candidates brought wives, a not-so-subtle acknowledgment of the indiscretion that drove Hart from the race. Although the drill included no major political speeches, the air was electric as the previously underestimated figures made their brief appearances. In a makeshift holding room, Dukakis spent extra moments before the mirror, fixing his tie and straightening his hair; he paused at the door, closed his eyes, took a deep breath, and walked out onto a brand-new stage.

3

Winnowing

Gary Hart's candidacy had been dead less than a month when Will Robinson, a portly, bearded political organizer, arrived in Des Moines to begin drafting a detailed plan for Michael Dukakis in the Iowa precinct caucuses, then more than eight months away. His rumpled appearance masked a keen and creative political mind, and, while still shy of thirty, he had honed his political skills working with the labor unions whose support shored up Walter F. Mondale's candidacy in 1984.

To Robinson and others in the governor's fledgling campaign, withdrawal by Hart, the putative front-runner, was a potential curse as well as a blessing because it increased the pressure on Dukakis to do well in the caucuses. The governor now had to cope with higher expectations even though he was still an outsider in this region, had no credentials in agriculture, and faced competition from two neighboring state candidates (Gephardt, and Illinois Senator Paul Simon, who had entered the race late in the spring after his Senate friend, Dale Bumpers of Arkansas, had decided against running).

In spring 1987, the word in the Dukakis campaign was "winnow." John Sasso's high command viewed the Iowa caucuses as an event that would either winnow the governor into the ranks of leading candidates, or winnow him out and label him a loser. The loser tag could be disastrous in the subsequent contests, above all in New Hampshire, whose first-in-the-nation primary took place just eight days after the caucuses. For all his alleged advantage in his neighboring state, Dukakis did not appear capable of getting more than 40 percent of the vote in a multi-candidate field, and New Hampshire's Democratic voters were notoriously fickle. If the governor from next door failed to make the national grade in the Midwest, they would be the first to spurn him.

In making their plans during that quiet spring, Dukakis and his most important aides were all but unaware of a fact of presidential campaign life: Regardless of plans, the unexpected always happens both to disrupt a campaign and test its standard-bearer's mettle. For the most part, campaigns before and even during the primaries labor in a light-pressure environment to which most Americans pay scant attention; but with almost no warning, an event always occurs that fixes the candidate in a white-hot glare, and his performance at that moment reveals more about him than a thousand pages of campaign plans. Being ever-ready to perform decisively under extreme duress is a requirement for both candidates and presidents.

Four months after Robinson's arrival in Iowa, such a moment arrived for Dukakis, when he learned that his campaign manager had helped make public information that did in another candidate— Delaware Senator Joseph Biden. In late September, with the entire political world watching, Dukakis decided to reject John Sasso's resignation, then changed his mind four hours later, yielding to intense pressure from Washington. He slumped into a brooding, three-month funk that cut off his growth as a national figure.

But in those first June days when excitement and hopes were high, the Dukakis staff was transfixed by its methodical planning for an achievable Iowa goal. The Iowa plan, embellished by Mark Gearan, Teresa Vilmain, and Joe Ricca, stressed the difference between shooting for what Dukakis needed in Iowa (respectability) and going beyond that to what he wanted (victory). The campaign must ignore the ever-changing press speculation about who would finish first. Dukakis, as a candidate from outside the Midwest, needed to move forward gradually, building a base of support carefully and with little hype. At the same time, he could not allow any rival to acquire the momentum that would rocket him to victory in Iowa in a way that would make him a credible threat in New Hampshire. That meant using as much of the governor's roughly four available campaign days a week to get him to all corners in the diverse state. In politics, this is known as "retailing"— seeking support almost voter by voter—in contrast to the wholesale approach with speech themes and television advertising.

Dukakis capitalized upon his reputation as an effective government executive to recruit elected officials at the state legislative and local government levels. At his campaign headquarters in a small office building on the edge of downtown Des Moines, one floor below state Democratic party headquarters and next to the local chapter of the American Red Cross, the first crew of organizers focused on a list of 65,000 party activists that the state party made available to each presidential campaign for a $10,000 fee that all the campaigns considered friendly extortion.

Robinson's initial draft plan analyzed each of Iowa's ninety-nine counties and showed how a well-organized campaign with adequate money and a solid candidate could find and convert 20 to 30 percent of the caucus participants. His plan assumed about 90,000 people would attend the caucuses on February 8, a turnout roughly equal to the one in 1984. Robinson hoped that Hart's absence would create the opening for Dukakis to win, but Dukakis's lack of prominent local support, his unfamiliarity with agriculture, and his bland issue profile left no objective evidence that expecting a first-place victory was realistic.

The candidate who showed most movement in Iowa after Hart's departure from the race was Richard A. Gephardt, the congressman from south St. Louis. He had been campaigning in Iowa longest and hardest and had raised his profile by being first to directly take on Hart. Their difference was foreign trade. Hart's views were relatively liberal, but Gephardt's emphasized tough retaliatory measures against countries that refused to remove restrictions on imports of American products while running large trade surpluses with the United States.

Like Hart, Dukakis adopted a more internationalist position. He argued that America's problems in the international economy were caused not by foreign protectionism but primarily by our own financial and competitive weaknesses. He believed automatic restrictions on imports could depress world trade, and thus retard domestic economic growth. Like Hart, however, he favored temporary protection from import competition for industries that agreed to put substantial investments into making themselves competitive again.

Though Gephardt's stock rose in the meaningless early Iowa polls, no one had filled the Hart void, but that summer brought an early opportunity for someone to make a good national impression, a joint appearance by the candidates on July 1 on "Firing Line," the long-running public-affairs show hosted by conservative columnist William F. Buckley, Jr. The evening was uneventful except for one brief and sharp exchange between Dukakis and Gephardt on their differences over trade policy.

After the broadcast at the Texas-sized George R. Brown Convention Center in Houston, Gephardt headed straight for the press room and attacked Dukakis by accusing him of holding views on trade just like those of Ronald Reagan.

The next day, the aggressive Missourian continued his tough line, saying that the views of people like the governor amounted to blaming America for its trade woes. For Democrats, the crack was particularly nasty. Blame America First was a direct steal from an anti-Democratic Republican line.

Back in Boston, Sasso and Paul Tully (who had joined his old friend Sasso in the Dukakis campaign after Hart's withdrawal) at first counseled Dukakis against making a sharp retort, but over the weekend they talked a lot about Gephardt. According to Sasso, they noticed that Gephardt's language away from the debate had been far sharper than anything he had to say during it. In other words, he was presenting a more positive persona to the voters at large on the television broadcast but mixing it up for the press. Sasso thought this type of "long-range bombing" could be a campaign constant unless disrupted. He, Corrigan, and Tully decided to recommend that Dukakis challenge Gephardt to a debate, and Dukakis quickly agreed. The risks were obvious this early in the game, but considering Gephardt's advantage in Iowa, they figured Dukakis had little to lose and a major opportunity to make gains at Gephardt's expense. They also believed that unless Dukakis took him on, Gephardt was likely to continue his attacks, because his populist message needed a foil, a "villain."

This debate plotting was interrupted by a long-planned revelation about Kitty Dukakis and her twenty-six-year dependence on prescription diet pills. On July 8 she announced that she had taken diet pills until entering a drug-treatment facility in Minnesota in the midst of her husband's 1982 gubernatorial campaign. At the time, Governor Dukakis had said she was recovering from hepatitis contracted by eating raw seafood in Europe, a falsehood he candidly said he would tell again to protect his wife's privacy. Even John Sasso knew nothing of the drug dependency until shortly before Dukakis's presidential announcement when Mrs. Dukakis told him. The disclosure made a one-day story, a tribute to the manner in which it was disclosed.

For a week before the August 15 debate in Des Moines, Dukakis crammed on issues and practiced answers to possible questions. As part of his own preparation, Sasso telephoned several of Gephardt's House colleagues, trying to get a feel for Dukakis's opponent. From these conversations he learned that although the Gephardt trade message might be tough, the messenger himself was universally regarded on Capitol Hill as an nice person, who rarely played rough in the close quarters of congressional debate. To Sasso, that meant the Dukakis plan for the debate should be simple: be very aggressive, and challenge

Gephardt throughout. The governor did both, not only on the merits of trade and economic policy, but on the much more basic question: the two men's different approaches to national issues. Dukakis painted Gephardt as someone who proposed legislation. He, by contrast, was a chief executive who was used to getting results instead of making debating points. The aggressive Dukakis had Gephardt on the defensive throughout. The favorable reviews his performance won in Iowa helped fuel a Dukakis surge as summer drew to a close.

Gary Hart's self-destruction provided visibility and a financial boost to the little-known governor. But that summer Dukakis began to move beyond his meager beginnings in Iowa to become by Labor Day something no one—not Will Robinson, and no one in the political press—had imagined he might be, a genuine challenger for first place and not only mere respectability in Iowa. The summer's events also displayed Dukakis's intimate, trusting relationship to his own campaign and, above all, to Sasso: his ready acceptance of the recommendation to challenge Gephardt, his enthusiastic plunge into exhaustive preparations for their meeting, and his adherence to the recommended tactic of aggressiveness in the event. The evening before the debate, Dukakis and his top aides had spread papers and other campaign detritus all over the floor in his hotel suite, and the governor showed no signs of stopping the rehearsals as midnight neared. Finally, sensing that enough was enough, Sasso quietly told the governor that he thought he was ready and that he ought to go to bed; Dukakis agreed, and he did.

Dukakis's performance against Gephardt and then against the field in debate at the Iowa State Fair at the end of August, however, provided a misleading sense of optimism.

Above all, most analysts failed to notice the definite, possibly explosive potential of Joe Biden. Irwin Harrison, the Boston-based pollster known by his nickname "Tubby," was probing the Iowa electorate regularly for the Dukakis campaign. In his August poll, Biden was only at 5 percent, but his detectable capacity to shoot far beyond that impressed not just Harrison, but the Gephardt campaign as well.

Biden's potential strengths mirrored the potential weakness in Dukakis's young campaign.

> In his poll memo, Harrison said that Biden has the strongest issue profile of any candidate in terms of issues making a difference to trial-heat results. Concern about the following issues helps Biden: jobs, pocketbook, protectionism, fear of war, defense . . . he threatens to fill the foreign-policy gap. His strength in this area matches Dukakis's weaknesses. He is also well regarded among those who cite toughness. Those who cite him for leadership,

[being] able to deal with problems and hands-on competence are
strong supporters. Here is the area where he has the potential to
intersect with Dukakis. . . . With his tough-liberal image, his
perceived foreign-policy expertise and his opportunity to demonstrate social issue liberalism with the Bork appointment, Biden
may be well positioned.

Committed to his marathon metaphor, Dukakis by definition was
always vulnerable to a sprinter. In dramatic contrast to all the other
candidates, but particularly to Dukakis, Biden could deliver speeches
that soared in their challenging rhetoric, cleverly designed to pluck
generational heartstrings and stir America to renewal in the face of
international economic threats. Biden was moving slowly, but his pace
quickened in August; moreover, in September he would have the
national spotlight to himself as he chaired the Senate Judiciary Committee's hearings into President Reagan's controversial nomination of
conservative jurist Robert Bork to the Supreme Court.

The scene was set for the most damaging event for the Dukakis
campaign in the primary season, and more important, the event that
may have cost him the presidency by depriving him of his campaign
manager and political guide. In police patois, Biden's potential in Iowa
constituted motive; Biden's foolish use of another politician's words
without attribution in a debate at the Iowa State Fair constituted
opportunity; and the wonders of videotape provided method. The
difference, however, is that what John Sasso did never came close to any
reasonable definition of a political misdemeanor, much less a crime. In
presidential politics, though, a bad error in judgment can always become
a high-visibility crisis, and this one provided a textbook case.

Pollster Tubby Harrison summarized Dukakis's situation as good,
but not that good on September 9, 1987, just three days before the first
damaging story about Biden appeared in the press. "Dukakis supporters
on virtually every item except foreign policy are in the average position
of all voters," he wrote. "Issue by issue they are the most centrist of all
the [likely] caucus attenders. With the exception of the foreign policy
item they almost represent a random distribution of the voters."

"Although Dukakis is found among the leading candidates, his
position is a precarious one," wrote Harrison. "It is based on a gener-
alized, positive opinion of him, supported to some extent by his reputation for having performed well in Massachusetts and vaguely focused
around a concept of leadership."

"The worry is that his could add up to a candidacy without a
constituency, people liking Dukakis but not willing to stand with him
when the going gets rough," he wrote. "We might characterize the

situation thus: people have taken a look at Dukakis as the result of his favorable publicity nationally and locally and they like him. He has not yet, however, given them strong reasons for doing so, but unless he bonds this relationship of support much more strongly and soon, people could begin to look elsewhere."

John Sasso shared Harrison's view and had already begun to address the shortcomings by having Dukakis take more specific positions that summer; and as the end of September arrived he had begun to take the first steps to fill Dukakis's foreign-policy void. His fourth and final ninety-day plan for 1987 was set to begin October 1, which turned out to be the day after he was let go. From more than six years of intimate experience with Dukakis, Sasso had learned how essential it was to develop a plan for the governor that showed how he could take a political journey from point A to point B, with extensive details on the specific steps required to get there; once Dukakis had discussed these plans with Sasso and agreed to them, it was never much of a problem getting him to do his share by taking the specific steps. Sasso understood that Dukakis could best be managed if presented with a logical procedure. Dukakis was in his handler's embrace far more than he realized, but he maintained some control and involvement, especially in his schedule and speeches, that a George Bush, for one, never did.

Together, Dukakis and Sasso were ready to begin making a move both in Iowa and the nation. Each felt the governor had taken his Massachusetts reputation about as far as prudent and that it was time to move beyond it. Dukakis's record of achievement in Massachusetts allowed him to present in outline an image of a strong leader who could get things done; his task now, he and Sasso had both agreed, was to make the outline much clearer.

"By building in this direction," Harrison had written in summation, "we will head Biden off at the pass, so to speak."

But John Sasso tried to take a short-cut.

On August 23, eight days after Dukakis's tussle with Gephardt, all the Democratic candidates gathered for a spirited debate at the Iowa State Fair. At its conclusion, Biden nearly stole the show after a desultory performance by delivering a moving two-minute closing statement about his family's working-class roots. To a few trained ears, Biden's close was a repeat of some lines he had been using in a recently freshened campaign speech, borrowed word for word from, and heretofore carefully attributed to, British Labor Party leader Neil Kinnock. But on this day, the attribution was missing. Biden's senior aides, immediately aware of his oversight and worried about possible criticism, discussed issuing a clarifying statement on the spot to set the record straight, but in the post-debate rush they had no time for a chat with their candidate. The error did not pass unnoticed by John Sasso or members of other candidates' staffs.

Unlike his competitors, Sasso acted. He saw in the affair, knowing nothing else about Biden's past, a minor embarassment to the senator. Sasso first tried to persuade friendly Democratic politicians to say something that would produce news stories about the gaffe; he was unsuccessful. By the week's end, he had in his office both the videotape of the Iowa debate and a tape of Kinnock using the same words in a famous campaign video earlier that year. Kinnock's powerful rhetoric was credited for a brief surge in the polls in his abortive effort to unseat Tory Prime Minister Margaret Thatcher. When Sasso played one after the other for other campaign officials, the tapes caused heads to shake in wonderment, because Biden's copycat performance of Kinnock was eerily accurate down to emotional tenor and gestures. He also showed the two recordings to *Boston Globe* reporter Thomas Oliphant, who stopped by for a visit on September 1 after a two-month, precampaign-year fellowship in Japan. Oliphant informed *Globe* national editor Royal Ford that day and was told that the *Globe* had already covered the fresh Biden speech, including the attributed mention of Kinnock's words; a late-August *Globe* story had also erroneously said Biden attributed the words at the Iowa State Fair. With that background it didn't seem to be a story.

Just before Labor Day, Sasso took the step that made it become a very big story. *New York Times* reporter Maureen Dowd had called him as she researched an unrelated story about Biden. As all good reporters do, she was fishing for potentially damaging information from an opponent's camp. During their conversation, Sasso told her about the Iowa State Fair incident, not mentioning anything except that Biden's language had been identical to Kinnock's. It was clear from his comments that videotape was available. Dowd, her interest piqued, pressed Sasso for a copy of the tapes he had, and Sasso eventually agreed to send her one, on the understanding that the Dukakis campaign not be identified as the source.

With the aid of a young campaign worker in the Dukakis press office, just outside his office door, Sasso had two copies made of the taped material he had, splicing the Biden and Kinnock performances together.

Later in the week, acting on his own but with Sasso's knowledge, Tully took another copy of the spliced tape to the *Des Moines Register*. Jack Corrigan, meanwhile, sent a third copy to New York for NBC News, mindful of the sharp visual power in juxtaposing Biden's and Kinnock's nearly identical words.

Officials at *NBC News* decided not to do a story after looking at the tape. To their knowledge, it was the only time Biden had failed to attribute his remarks, and they reasoned that to put something on the air would blow a possibly accidental failure out of proportion.

But Dowd and David Yepsen, leading political reporter for the *Des Moines Register*—the only statewide newspaper in Iowa—both wrote stories that were published Saturday, September 12. The stories were very different.

Dowd's story screamed scandal. The front-page article juxtaposed Biden and Kinnock quotes, recorded convulsions in the Biden camp about the story, and mentioned only in passing and far down in the account that Biden had used the material on other occasions with full attribution.

By contrast, Yepsen's story on page 2 of the *Register* focused on the fact that another, unnamed campaign was taking a shot at Biden with "an attack video," and then summarized its content with less journalistic hyperbole.

Because of the *Times* story, NBC switched gears that evening and aired a report showing Biden and Kinnock emotionally uttering the same phrases.

At first, nothing very significant happened, but beneath the seemingly placid surface as Biden made his final preparations to open the Judiciary Committee's hearings on the Bork nomination, journalistic wheels were spinning all over the country. Three days after the first accounts, a tidal wave of negative stories washed over Biden. The stories reported that he cribbed words in a paper at law school, cribbed words in a California speech early in 1987, and used Kinnock's words in a taped interview for a teachers' union meet-the-candidates series without attribution. The final blow came with reports of a taped outburst with a New Hampshire voter months previously in which Biden was not only unacceptably nasty, but also misrepresented his academic record.

Dukakis was campaigning in Birmingham, Alabama on the day that Dowd's story on Biden ran in the *New York Times*. His press secretary, Patricia O'Brien, was emphatic about its significance. This is an issue; this is character, she said. Dukakis was inclined to agree.

Like many fiascos, the one that may have cost Michael Dukakis his best chance to become president did not start big, but neither did it start small. Arguments about the Biden tapes affair rage to this day. The September 1987 events raise difficult political and ethical questions. The loss to Dukakis, however, was obvious and very large. The affair cost him his campaign manager, his top strategist, his alter ego; less obviously at the time and since, it also cost him the services of the senior aide who was working hardest on shaping a Dukakis campaign message for the post-Reagan era—Paul Tully. Even more than people, though, the affair drained Dukakis's self-confidence as a presidential candidate when he was just beginning to acquire it; his substantive development as a national figure was arrested, a development that probably cost him a chance at victory in the Iowa caucuses four months later.

The revelation, moreover, came when sensitivity in the national press corps to character issues was heightened because of their Gary Hart experience. This deluge, however, was far more than Biden's campaign could withstand. On September 23, with grace and almost no bitterness, a forthright Biden withdrew and went on to a key role in Bork's demise, mixing partisan fairness with diligence.

Still, a lingering question inspired constant gossip: Who had cast the first stone?

The first suspect was the then-struggling Gephardt campaign. Even Nick Mitropoulos, completely unaware of Sasso's act from his post in the traveling cocoon with his boss, assumed that the Gephardt people had done it. Gephardt's media consultant and chief speechwriter, Democratic veteran Robert Shrum, had had a well-publicized falling out with Biden's guru, the equally veteran Democratic consultant Patrick Caddell. Indeed, the vitriolic Caddell had publicly fingered his former friend and the Gephardt camp. In the genteel, cleaner-than-clean world of Iowa politics, the rumor hurt Gephardt almost at once. Responding to urgent pleas from the Gephardt high command, Craig Whitney, then the *Times* Washington editor, took the unheard-of step of saying publicly that the Gephardt campaign had not been the source of its story. The denial convinced few people in the political world.

Within forty-eight hours of Biden's withdrawal, however, a *Register* employee told *Time* magazine that its version of the story had come from the Dukakis campaign. Still three days from publication, the magazine went directly to the alleged culprit, Tully, who flatly denied the allegation.

The inquiry did not surprise Sasso when Tully told him about it. He had dreaded something similar from the moment it first became apparent that the torrent of disclosures was certain to sweep Biden from the race. Almost from the instant he sent the copied videotape to Washington, he had feared a very bad result, and once Biden left the race he assumed that his own days as campaign manager were numbered. His reasoning was not complicated. It did not matter that the disclosures were all accurate and showed an unformed Biden whose persona in the campaign was part artifice. What mattered was that someone had helped do him in just as he was embarking on almost a Democratic political Jihad—preventing Robert Bork's ascension to the Supreme Court. Along with the ultimate price paid by Biden, Sasso believed that as first stone-caster he too would probably pay the political price.

As the controversy over the source of the original stories built, Sasso, Corrigan, and Tully, along with a few other operatives had discussed whether to inform Dukakis, which they knew would mean a full, public disclosure. As a matter of simple good sense as well as ethics, informing the candidate was an imperative; the governor was, after all, entitled to know about something his top aides had done that could cause him embarrassment or harm. Although Sasso and his compatriots were not in the business of helping other candidates, an additional ethical issue was that Gephardt was taking on water for something he hadn't done—could silence from the Dukakis campaign be said to constitute complicity?

These questions were seen as valid, but Dukakis's aides never came close to offering the truth. After all, they reasoned, Sasso had not told any public lies, and it was almost unheard of for a confidential news source to voluntarily come forward and reveal himself. It was not his fault that the initial act set in motion events that had spun out of control.

But pressure to get to the bottom of the Biden affair persisted. The young woman working as a Dukakis intern who had spliced the Biden and Kinnock tapes at Sasso's request deduced that her campaign was behind it all when the *New York Times* story broke. At her gym one day she bragged to a young male acquaintance that she knew all about the Biden episode because she had made the videotape. Her acquaintance turned out to be a former *Boston Globe* copy assistant in the paper's State House bureau who wanted to be a news reporter himself one day. He carried his explosive intelligence—leaving out only the intern's name—to *Globe* reporter Andrew Blake on September 16; he in turn told assistant metropolitan editor Peter Mancusi. As often happens in the newspaper world, however, the left hand (local desk) did not pass on the details to the right hand (national desk) for further checking, and nothing happened.

Shaken by her knowledge, the intern had also confided in a Dukakis press-office assistant, who in turn told campaign press secretary Patricia O'Brien. A highly regarded former Knight-Ridder correspondent who was trying political life on the inside, O'Brien went straight to Sasso. She was angry that her staff had been used without her knowledge. She told him that she would have no part of lying or cover-ups. Sasso at first denied any involvement but then told O'Brien that he had sent the tape to the *Times*; he continued, however, to deny any involvement with the *Register* and NBC, asked her to trust him, and included her in discussions with a close friend and media adviser, Francis O'Brien (no relation) about what the campaign should do. He also periodically sent her news clippings discussing possible complicity by Gephardt campaign officials, and according to O'Brien argued that public disclosure about the

New York Times story would wreck the Dukakis campaign while letting the others off the hook for the leaks to NBC and the *Register*. O'Brien remained suspicious enough, though, to ask Sasso and Corrigan directly if they had anything to do with those acts; Sasso denied it, and Corrigan obfuscated.

On Sunday September 27, 1987, Nick Mitropoulos dropped off the campaign trail long enough to get married to Nayla Sahyoun in the Holy Cross Chapel at the Hellenic College in Brookline. Dukakis couldn't miss a debate that day on foreign-policy issues in Iowa, and so his wife represented him at the wedding. Sasso and Corrigan were also among the wedding guests who celebrated afterward at the Wellesley Country Club. By then, the senior campaign staff were buzzing about the *Time* story that was scheduled to hit the newsstands the next day, identifying the Dukakis campaign as the source of the videotape comparing the Biden and Kinnock speeches.

In Des Moines, meanwhile, during the post-debate mingling, the other candidates' staffs were also talking about the *Time* story. A relieved but still-angry Gephardt campaign manager William Carrick approached us to whisper word that the *Time* story was on its way out. We quickly pulled first Tully, and then Patricia O'Brien aside, seeking more information. Each of them said there would be no formal comment.

Back in Boston, Sasso sensed that the end for him might be very near. Dukakis too had heard about the *Time* story, but had to leave Iowa almost immediately after the debate for a fund-raiser in Kansas; he spoke with Sasso briefly from a Wichita airport pay phone, and in their short conversation his campaign manager simply told him he was looking into it. Dukakis boarded his chartered business jet for a late-evening flight home.

Next morning, Dukakis went to the State House to work at gubernatorial duties. Just before a morning press conference, his State House spokesman, James Dorsey, briefed the governor and told him to expect questions on the *Time* article. Dorsey told him he had checked that morning with Pat O'Brien, who told him the campaign response was the Tully denial. Thus assured his campaign had nothing to do with the videotape, Dukakis went out and said there was a "strong possibility" he would fire anyone in his employ who engaged in "unacceptable campaign tactics."

Meanwhile, Francis O'Brien, a Sasso friend and colleague from Geraldine Ferraro's 1984 campaign, had flown up from Washington the day before to counsel Sasso. Shortly after the press conference, a somber Francis O'Brien placed a tape recording of Dukakis's comments on Sasso's desk and watched his friend turn white as he heard the governor's words. They immediately left Sasso's campaign-headquarters office in an old building on the fringe of Boston's financial district, and took refuge in a private office five floors higher. O'Brien had also known, via Patricia O'Brien, of Sasso's admission about the *New York Times* story; however, he said Sasso had consistently denied involvement with the other leaks, which left Francis O'Brien with the impression that other campaigns too were involved. Had he known the full story, he said he would have immediately pressed his friend to make a full, fast disclosure, following the classic public-relations theory that the longer negative information is suppressed, the worse the damage upon inevitable disclosure. That would have been Patricia O'Brien's recommendation as well (she resigned from the campaign late in November).

Before joining Francis O'Brien and Sasso in the upstairs meeting at which the only conclusion could be that it was time for Sasso to make a personal confession to Dukakis, Tully stopped off at a campaign contributors' luncheon to deny again that anyone in the campaign had provided the videotapes to the press. But the outside pressure was building. *Boston Globe* reporter Joan Vennochi was suspicious about the denials as the newspaper resurrected the tip about the campaign intern following the *Time* disclosure. She visited the intern at her apartment in Winthrop on Monday night. The frightened intern refused to tell her anything. Vennochi spoke to Sasso the next morning by telephone, and he put her off by promising to see her later in the day. That afternoon Sasso eluded her as she waited outside his office, but he also knew that calls had come into the campaign from the *Washington Post*. Emotionally spent, he trudged up to the State House at about 4:00 P.M. to confess alone to his boss. Dukakis was severely shaken. A $1-million fund-raising party was taking place that night at the World Trade Center on the waterfront. The governor told Sasso he would obviously have to make a full disclosure the next day, but wanted to think about what to say. That evening, while Sasso's absence was noticed by more and more reporters clamoring to see him, Dukakis's public demeanor betrayed not a trace of unease. He even displayed his modest skill on the trumpet.

Very late that night, back home, he told the story to his wife Kitty, Sasso's most important ally in the long effort to nudge Dukakis toward a presidential race. His private face was substantially different from the cool one he showed at the fund-raiser.

"He was devastated," she told us later. "John had never meant for this to get out of hand, but I think Michael was disappointed that he wasn't told."

He also placed a late phone call to Paul Brountas, aware that his campaign chairman might have to take a more direct role in the campaign. Brountas immediately placed a call to Sasso, but couldn't reach him.

The next morning, while Dukakis prepared to make his public statement, a crestfallen Sasso formally told the campaign's senior staff about his involvement. Most had suspected or already knew the truth. He left the glum gathering and retreated to his hideaway office upstairs. Shortly before the governor's announcement, he made several phone calls to friends and a few reporters; to us, he said that the entire affair had been his idea, that the reason he didn't tell Dukakis was that he knew the governor would never have approved, and that he had submitted his resignation.

But to Sasso's complete surprise, Dukakis didn't accept it. He went to his press-conference room on the first floor of the State House, announced that Sasso had told him he was the source of the videotapes, apologized to Biden (though not to Gephardt), and said Sasso would take a two-week leave of absence.

Dukakis looked as upset as he had ever appeared in public during his years in office. His face was grim. "I know something about the pain of defeat, the pain of loss. What it means to one's family and friends," he said. "I regret very much that my campaign contributed to that pain and loss."

"John offered to resign. I considered it seriously but rejected it. I did so even though what he did was a very serious error in judgment and a very serious mistake," he said. Sasso's friends sagged in relief at those words. "He is somebody who has served with me for seven years, a person of extraordinary competence and ability." He called Sasso "one of the most extraordinary public servants I know" during the question-and-answer period that followed.

"Although I had no knowledge of this," he said, "as a candidate I assume full responsibility for it. I'm accountable, and I expect to be held accountable."

Just before the press conference, Dukakis informed Brountas of his decision, and his longtime friend—who was forming the opinion that Sasso had to resign—questioned him sharply about it on the telephone and did not come to the governor's press conference. Instead he began to receive a barrage of telephoned advice from around the country saying that Sasso's mistake had been fatal.

As the news spread, Dukakis found himself almost at once caught in an excruciatingly tight vise. From one side, prominent politicians called him to say that Sasso had to go. The executioners included Biden's Senate colleagues, Edward M. Kennedy and John F. Kerry, as well as Paul Sarbanes of Maryland, another Dukakis classmate at Harvard Law School and fellow Greek-American; of particular importance was Brountas's recommendation that Sasso be jettisoned because he had let his boss hang in public the day before and, in effect, ever since the Biden plagiarism story broke, without sharing the truth he had a right to know.

But from inside the campaign, Dukakis sought and received an anguished torrent of opposite advice: that however wrong Sasso was to have essentially lied by omission, punishment by banishment did not fit the sin of giving three news organizations an accurate story. Susan Estrich left her office at Harvard Law School and rode the subway to the campaign office in Boston. She arrived to find a despondent Sasso insisting he had to resign. She placed what she later said was the first direct phone call she had ever made to Dukakis to tell him that he should stick to his leave-of-absence decision.

Tormented and close to tears, Dukakis placed a call to Nick Mitropoulos. Married for only two days, Mitropoulos was in France for a one-week honeymoon while the campaign was relatively quiet. He had been bombarded with trans-Atlantic telephone calls at a small hotel next to Victor Hugo's house in Paris almost since his arrival. During the call, Dukakis was audibly very upset.

Mitropoulos told him that he didn't think Sasso needed to resign. He thought a leave of absence was adequate and that Sasso should be permitted to return at its conclusion, for the sake of Dukakis's candidacy.

Sasso was exposed to the same torrents of conflicting advice. Moreover, he had to reach a deeply personal decision before the evening news broadcasts, which were barely three hours away. As he explained much later, he could see only two choices for Dukakis, and they permitted no middle ground: he could go to the wall for Sasso, arguing that this was a badly handled mistake but essentially an in-house fiasco; or he could declare that Sasso's conduct had been wrong. In that case, he had to resign. Sasso did not believe going to the wall in a crisis like this was in Dukakis's constitution, and yet he sensed his anguished indecision. They spoke one more time on the telephone, and as Sasso told us later with lingering sadness but no evident bitterness, "We both agreed I had to go." In effect, Dukakis *let* him go.

To spare Dukakis embarrassment at making another public appearance to reverse that morning's decision, Sasso fell on his sword by going next door to a hastily arranged press conference at the Lafayette Hotel and announcing that he had resigned.

Sasso was a man whose heart was breaking. His dream of running a national campaign had shattered. He had let down and hurt his friend; occasionally bitter through his own hurt, Dukakis would later use the word "betrayal" when discussing the affair with some campaign aides. The state's aggressive political press corps, which had been simmering behind locked doors in the third-floor foyer at 105 Chauncy Street since the governor's press conference that morning, was noticeably subdued and shocked. "You know how I feel about this business and how I feel about Michael Dukakis," he began. "That makes this very difficult. I exercised a serious lack of judgment when I did this." He apologized to Dukakis, Biden, and Biden's family and supporters.

"As you know, I gave the governor my resignation today. I feel that is the best thing for this campaign," he said. "I thought it would be a story. The information was in the public domain. I did not try to distort that in any way. That is not an excuse for what I did. I know the kind of campaign that Mike Dukakis wants to run. That is not consistent with that. There are principles, values here that go beyond me and any individual and go to what he stands for."

"I knew it would hurt him," he said sadly. "I knew in my heart we would reach this day when I told him."

Back at the State House, the governor and his wife sat together with tears in their eyes. To friends and aides he described his loss in the most personal words, akin to losing a brother, an especially personal analogy for Dukakis, whose older brother Stelian struggled with mental illness and then died after lingering in a coma for months after being struck by a hit-and-run driver in 1973.

The day after Sasso's abrupt departure, Dukakis went to the campaign headquarters to tell his staff that he had made Brountas the active, rather than merely titled, chairman of the campaign. Corrigan quietly pulled him aside for a private meeting to tell him that he had sent the third videotape to NBC. That disclosure prompted a secret meeting among Dukakis, Brountas, and the top campaign staff about how to handle Corrigan's involvement. With Corrigan present for the discussion, his fate was discussed, at times as a political matter, at times in an earnest effort to figure out what was appropriate. Dukakis mostly listened, Brountas was noncommittal, and a few aides listed the pros and cons of keeping the skilled and devoted aide aboard. It was no idle or academic exercise: losing Corrigan following Sasso's and Tully's departure could easily have crippled the campaign at the top; he was its link to a rapidly spreading national organization, and at headquarters he was one of the few campaign officials with a personal link to Dukakis. In the end, it made sense to no one to continue a purge; Corrigan was Sasso's junior and subordinate and had done nothing more than make a delivery for him, and, unlike Tully (who resigned at once), he had not directly lied to the public on the campaign's behalf about what had happened. He was admonished for his secret messenger duty and subsequent silence, but retained.

Brountas began the search for a new campaign manager; he also decided that an internal investigation should flesh out details about the

John Sasso's eyes shine with his pain on the day he resigned from the Dukakis campaign in September 1987. (Photo by Keith Jenkins)

Biden tapes incident and put Boston attorney Dan Taylor, Dukakis's State House counsel during his first term, in charge of it.

The incident triggered a brief flurry of harmful attention in the national media, a media firestorm in Iowa, and (far more significant) a halt to Dukakis's political momentum both in Iowa and in the nation. In Iowa, the episode halted the campaign's quiet efforts to recruit key Biden supporters. Most of them flocked to the hot candidate of the moment in the state's constantly changing climate, Illinois Senator Paul Simon, whose roots were in Iowa-like rural, downstate Illinois, and whose folksy but ardent liberalism, mixed with a strain of fiscal conservatism, had helped him carve a constituency among the elderly as well as urban party activists.

On the other hand, within twenty-four hours it was apparent that the governor's basic political structure was holding firm. Some could not conceive of how Dukakis could run for president without Sasso. Others were furious with Sasso for not handling the episode better. Political insiders were more than a little stunned by the punishment. They felt all Sasso had done was "commit politics." That it was Sasso and Tully, not the governor himself, who had cast the first stone at Biden surreptitiously, that Dukakis had acted immediately when he learned the truth to take full responsibility and was on his way to the state for a more direct apology, gave his supporters something credible to say on his behalf. More objective observers thought Dukakis's handling of the affair had made him appear indecisive, which put a chink in his executive armor. The whole affair provoked less heat the farther one moved from the hothouse Boston atmosphere, where context and perspective can be foreign to the thumbs-up, thumbs-down political world.

The trip that became known as Dukakis's *mea culpa* Iowa tour began just two days later, early on October 2 in a high-school auditorium in Sioux City, the state's western metropolis. By chance, Sioux City was in the middle of Biden's strongest area in the state. Dukakis was nervous when he first appeared, trailed by a horde of blood-smelling reporters. But the atmosphere lost some of its electricity as the school's cheerleaders jumped and gesticulated their way through a spirited: "We know he is the B-E-S-T, Better than all of the R-E-S-T."

It would be difficult to maintain solemnity after an introduction like that, but with television cameras running, Dukakis did his best, declaring himself "saddened and apologetic about what happened to Senator Biden." He told 250 Sioux City Democrats that a presidential campaign is not a place "for people trying to hurt other people," and sliding past his indecision of two days before he added, "That unfortunately happened in my campaign without my knowledge and when it does happen you have to take action."

Dukakis plunged into a funk after losing his right hand man. Press secretary Patricia O'Brien holds the tape recorder. (Photo by Keith Jenkins)

Dukakis uttered some version of those words at nearly two dozen appearances from that Friday morning through Sunday afternoon, as he, a handful of aides, and a busload of reporters careened along the back roads in Western Iowa and on east toward Des Moines. By the time he was finished, he had said enough *mea culpa*s to absolve a chainsaw murderer, and abundant anecdotal evidence showed that the average Iowa Democrat either cared nothing about the incident or considered his forthright acceptance of responsibility more than sufficient (and for some, an attractive character trait, considering the still-fresh Iran-Contra scandal in Washington).

The tour also showed some limits on Sasso's banishment. One afternoon, Dukakis had impulsively told reporters who peppered him with questions that his now-former campaign manager would have "no role, formal or informal in this campaign," and in the evening a local attorney and Biden supporter wanted to know if Dukakis would rule out a position for Sasso in his administration should he be elected president thirteen months later; at last, Dukakis drew the line, refusing to commit himself, though several aides traveling with him and back in Boston, who harbored strong hopes that Sasso might still be able to return, thought he had needlessly foreclosed options he should have left for later.

Dukakis had no major endorsements pending that were called off because of the tapes incident, but some prominent politicians—notably New York Governor Mario Cuomo, Arkansas Governor Bill Clinton, Florida Senator and former Governor Bob Graham, and Atlanta Mayor Andrew Young—did pull back from relationships that had been warming. Most Democratic politicians were not particularly troubled by what Sasso had done, but they were bothered that Dukakis hadn't drawn the line and kept his campaign manager. Letting his best guy go suggested weakness and disloyalty. At least one, former South Carolina Governor Dick Reilly—a big Dukakis fan—was so turned off that very soon after Sasso's departure from the campaign he endorsed Dick Gephardt's candidacy.

Given Iowa's affinity for fellow Midwesterners, it cannot be assumed that but for the tapes affair Dukakis could have conquered the strong ties Senator Simon was already building in the state and which Congressman Gephardt would shortly cement with an unprecedented blitz of television commercials and powerful speeches. One cannot, however, ignore the fact that continued, uninterrupted progress by Dukakis both nationally and in Iowa might have produced a victory in the caucuses, which in turn would have put him in position to blow the rest of the field away by the time (March 8) of the twenty primaries and caucuses that comprised Super Tuesday.

How deeply the loss of Sasso hurt cannot be underestimated. Dukakis's sadness was palpable, but in real life as well as in public life a clear line divides grief from moping, and the governor crossed that line to his further and lasting harm. He all but suspended his intellectual, political, and stylistic growth as a presidential candidate, and he declined opportunity after opportunity for the better part of five months to engage his opponents in the give-and-take of normal debate in a nomination campaign.

Even in his deep funk, though, he could not ignore the imperative that he find a new campaign manager. He entrusted the task to Paul Brountas. The highly successful corporate attorney understandably felt thrust into a delicate political situation that was quite foreign to him; he had been a loyal and close Dukakis friend, chairing his gubernatorial campaigns and helping staff his state government, but a national campaign was completely different, and a national campaign under enormous stress was special. Brountas was not sure how widespread the knowledge that Sasso had leaked the Biden tapes had been within the campaign, or whether additional damaging disclosures might be imminent. Brountas's first thought, therefore, was to look outside for a new boss. With lawyerly diligence, he asked for help in compiling a list of 200 skilled and prominent Democrats, including members of Congress as well as state officials and Washington-based operatives; he made thirty telephone calls a day until he had reached everyone on the list, and he also took care to talk in person with each senior campaign staff member.

From the campaign itself, Brountas heard only one name, that of Susan Estrich. According to several of the senior staff, one reason they were unanimously united in favor of her appointment, along with a genuine desire to have her take over, was their hope that somehow Sasso would be able to return in several weeks or a few months and that having an internal replacement would make that more likely to happen.

Estrich had gone to Los Angeles to be with her husband for Yom Kippur. She wept on the long transcontinental flight for her friend's misfortune. By the last of the weekend she began to hear via her constantly ringing telephone that her name was in play back in Boston, but at the moment her professional life was in flux. Harvard Law School had been pressuring her to resume the full-time teaching her tenured position required, she was trying to handle a busy schedule as deputy campaign manager with general supervision over issues and speeches, and she was commuting coast-to-coast to see her husband. She also wondered whether she knew Dukakis well enough to deal with him as intimately as a campaign manager must, and to make the adjustment with no time for a gradual transition.

On the other hand, she would be the first female manager of a major presidential campaign, and though only thirty-four, her background in politics was as impressive as her intellectual achievements: senior aide in Edward Kennedy's 1980 campaign; handling platform negotiations at the New York City convention with the Jimmy Carter White House; top aide to Geraldine Ferraro while she wrote the Democratic platform in 1984 just before going on Walter Mondale's ticket; member of Mondale's senior traveling staff for the general election, along with future husband, then-speechwriter Marty Kaplan; and member of the Democratic National Committee with much experience in helping write the party's maddeningly complicated rules for the long primary and caucus season. Estrich can be charming, the only friend a person needs, penetrating with gaze and wit when provoked, a genuine intellectual and a back-alley political infighter who uses language that would make a sailor blush. She was more than qualified to be the pioneer. She decided to let fate decide.

Brountas brought four names to the governor. Estrich's was one. The others were Tom Kiley, the Boston pollster; Michael DelGuidice,

Mario Cuomo's former chief of staff; and Kirk O'Donnell, the former aide to House Speaker Tip O'Neill. Brountas and the governor say that each agreed on their first and only choice. Primed by Nick Mitropoulos and ready to say yes, Estrich had thirty minutes alone with Dukakis before the public announcement. The governor made a point of emphasizing his determination to campaign on his own merits and to stay on a lofty plane, post-Biden. In her own public remarks minutes later, she used the expression "positive campaigning" at least a dozen times.

After more than a week of unrelieved tension, the general applause, with muted murmurs of "out of her league" from the Democratic establishment, seemed to give the campaign a desperately needed emotional lift.

One of her very first moves had been to persuade Brountas to cancel a full-scale investigation of the campaign since Sasso's departure. If the truth were known, nearly all the staff either knew what had happened, had surmised what had happened, or had strong suspicions about what had happened (Estrich, from Paul Tully, had strong suspicions herself). But presidential campaigns are not like the Central Intelligence Agency, divided into airtight compartments; gossip and rumors are coins of the realm, and this campaign at the time was nearly all housed on two floors in a narrow old office building. Estrich saw no purpose to be served by lengthy interrogations of staff members to determine who knew what and when.

Her first move was to cancel Brountas's internal investigation into the tapes episode. The only people who had done something had come forward, she reasoned, and other than create an opening for the press to probe and produce still more stories about the affair, she failed to see the point. On reflection, no one disagreed, and the matter was quietly laid to rest.

Having dodged that bullet, Estrich's main priority was to maintain the appearance of a vibrant national campaign still making progress, even if a little subterfuge was required. She resolved that the campaign would take in $1 million for the month of October, surmising that the press would not downgrade a campaign that could take a body blow and still pull in that kind of monthly money. Ed Pliner, the campaign business manager, unilaterally held off recording for financial disclosure purposes the receipts from the September 30 fund-raiser, held the night before Sasso's resignation, until after the first of October; that helped produce the magic figure.

Legerdemain, however, could not disguise that Dukakis the candidate was flat as a pancake out on the hustings. He missed Sasso personally and politically, and worried about him. His sadness showed on his expressive face, which does not easily hide his moods with pasted-on campaign smiles. Dukakis's glum mood was also reflected in an almost petulant unwillingness to try new material in his speeches; his pen regularly crossed out new material and substituted familiar lines. For Paul Brountas, his friend went into a "two-month shell"; and Estrich, still trying to get to know the man well enough to advise him candidly, was bothered by his mopey moods.

As she said much later, he would return from the road convinced that no one liked him; and on the road, she felt he was campaigning without joy, performing his duties perfunctorily while his opponents, especially in the debates that were beginning to dominate the calendar, attracted much more attention. Dukakis told her he felt that the voters he was meeting, particularly in Iowa, saw him as a swarthy almost-foreigner who talked too fast and sounded funny. Dukakis had experienced adversity before in his public life, but although he was often called aloof and arrogant, he was also a dogged optimist as he went about his governmental and political rounds in Massachusetts; moodiness and brooding were unfamiliar in his persona. Indeed, Estrich said that she approved expenditures on polling and focus-group interviews in Iowa during this period, not so much because data were required for planning, but simply because she wanted to show him that the tapes affair had not hurt him and that in fact he was respected among Democrats in Iowa for his record, and was still very much in contention as the caucus campaign slowly began to heat up.

To remain in contention, however, and to move beyond contention toward victory, one must campaign vigorously and engage opponents when opportunity presents itself, not merely when attacked. Dukakis rarely did, and when he did it was almost never in the sustained way required to make a lasting impression in Iowa.

In November, Estrich made a critical hiring decision designed to beef up the campaign's high command, and in particular to fill Paul Tully's role for Sasso, that of overall strategist, developing a basic message for the campaign. Her choice, Tom Kiley of Boston, was one of the four who had made Paul Brountas' Final Four for campaign manager, but who had expressed reservations because he felt he didn't know Dukakis well enough. Kiley, a partner in a highly regarded consulting firm, had no previous connection with the campaign because his partner, John Martilla, had been Joe Biden's media adviser. A quiet, self-effacing, but intense analyst with a special background in polling, Kiley had got his start in his native Michigan nearly twenty years before, helping Richard Austin become mayor of Detroit, and had gone on to carve out a reputation as a mayoral campaign strategist. He was well known among party professionals nationally and came to Estrich highly recommended. He became her alter ego, accompanied her to meetings with Dukakis much of the time, and was the person she leaned on most for advice.

After watching and listening for a few weeks, Kiley wrote Estrich and Dukakis a long memorandum in December. He argued that the governor needed to broaden his message to voters in order to break out of the Iowa pack, that themes were needed that would soar beyond the mere specifics in his record or his ideas about the economy, which in this period carried little beyond an endlessly repeated belief in "good jobs at good wages," relieved occasionally by one-time speeches offering specific proposals. By elevating Dukakis thematically, Kiley argued, he would acquire a presidential voice. The idea, he added, was not to simply show emotion or compassion for people in need, but to embrace issues that themselves had emotional content.

Kiley and Estrich discussed these kinds of themes constantly. One that particularly appealed to her would have reached for "the larger, moral message" implicit in most Democratic Party ideals. That approach might have a chance of competing against the emphasis on peace and prosperity she expected from the Republicans in the general election. Estrich liked trying to define "the American character," what Americans are as a people, and how government could succeed by challenging the best instincts of its people and by representing their highest ideals.

As Estrich and Kiley recalled later, Dukakis never said no to any of their ideas, passed on either as memos or brief summaries delivered orally during fifteen- to thirty-minute meetings when he was back in Boston from the road, time jealously guarded for State House business. Instead, he would usually say nothing, taking their recommendations under advisement or putting memos in his briefcases, and then eventually communicating a curt, almost always unexplained rejection: I'm not going to do that, guys. That's not me. When speeches with new, soaring rhetoric were sent to him, the offending paragraphs were typically returned with large Xs through them. Instead he took refuge in rewritten versions of good jobs, good wages; $500-million local-development funds; criticism of the Iran-Contra scandal; and assertions about his own budget-balancing, problem-solving past. New to her job, and distracted by other headaches as she labored to establish herself, Estrich did not press the governor.

After several of these rejections in December, Estrich and Kiley realized that at least for the early voting states they had only one card to play: emphazing Dukakis's record, which they summarized with one word—competence. Particularly as Bruce Babbitt's campaign headed toward the rocks, Dukakis's record did set him apart from the others, but Kiley worried that the trouble with flying competence as a banner was that an opponent need only pick at a couple of mistakes among thousands of gubernatorial decisions to rip it down.

More out of exasperation than curiosity, Estrich asked Dukakis one day which issues actually touched him; the governor thought for a bit and replied, homelessness and the continuing conflict in Central America. That was enough to spark two visually powerful commercials, produced by a Boston-based consultant, Ken Swope, for the last few weeks of the campaign in Iowa. But nothing in the ads or in Dukakis's daily campaigning (beyond his record) set him apart from his rivals and staked a special claim to the presidential nomination. It was an especially unfortunate time not to be standing out, because the campaign in Iowa was in the midst of two major convulsions.

After nearly seven months of brooding in the Colorado mountains, Gary Hart decided early in December that if he was headed toward oblivion in politics, he wanted the voters to send him there, not the press. He announced his reentry into the race on December 16, just in time to make the filing deadline for the New Hampshire primary.

No event in the campaign since Hart's departure from it got the news coverage his second announcement received. An orgy of speculative media babble went on for more than a week. Then amid all this saturation coverage treating Hart's renewed candidacy as serious, polls were taken. They showed him to be a potential factor in the race, both in Iowa and nationally. A few voices suggested that there was less here than met the eye, that Hart had no money or campaign workers, and that most of the interest in him appeared to be far more celebrity curiosity than support, but this was *big news*, and it blotted out less sensational analyses right through Christmas.

From the first batch of Iowa polls, however, it was possible to see that the always-shifting sands in the state's landscape had shifted again in the Hart disruption, and that the big loser appeared to be Paul Simon. The Illinois senator's polling lead over his rivals had been substantial, but beginning in December a major crack formed in his campaign's foundation: an obvious contradiction between his endorsement of generous domestic policy initiatives and his vow to balance the hemorrhaging federal budget within three years of taking office. Gephardt had homed in on this economic contradiction, which he called "Simonomics," during a debate on NBC early in December. As the press picked up the point, Simon lost much of his earlier glow, scrambling to come up with a credible answer.

The many cross-currents in the volatile Iowa campaign met on January 15 before an overflow crowd of Democrats at the Des Moines Civic Auditorium for a debate sponsored by the *Des Moines Register*. Telecast statewide, it was the last opportunity for one of the candidates to make the major impressions, positive or negative, that might change the campaign's complexion in the final days. At that moment, the evening's drama was built around the mysterious personage, Gary Hart, who would either prove that he belonged after his eight-month absence or demonstrate that all the media hype about his reentry had been nothing more than that.

He wore a tweed sports jacket that set him apart from the somber blue-suited uniformity in the rest of the pack. But he was rusty from his months off the trail, it showed, and he was never again more than a campaign footnote.

Simon, put on the defensive by questions about his contradictory proposals, also fumbled badly. For the next week, he teetered over a major loss of support, and with Gephardt's appeal appearing concentrated among relatively conservative Democrats and residents of small towns and rural communities, the opportunity for Dukakis to make his move was clear. The opportunity, however, was not seized; Dukakis emphasized his opposition to any more aid to the Contras trying to overthrow the Nicaraguan government, he made a speech urging that the lessons learned by training and finding jobs for Massachusetts welfare recipients be applied nationally, but he did nothing that established himself in Iowans' minds with clarity and force. And then, with ten days to go until the caucuses, Simon's tottering candidacy was shored up when he received endorsement by the *Des Moines Register*, an influential recommendation considering the state's shifting political sands, which had been a fact of life for months.

For some reason, the publicity deluge surrounding Hart's reentry had hurt Simon more than anyone else. When Hart shuffled the Iowa deck of cards, the only part of Simon's support that appeared to hold was his liberal-leaning base, and even there he was getting competition from Reverend Jesse L. Jackson.

For the country as a whole, the big news in the first week of December was the visit to Washington by Soviet Communist Party general secretary Mikhail Gorbachev to sign the long-awaited treaty with President Reagan banning short- and intermediate-range nuclear missiles from Europe. Shrewdly, Dukakis arranged to be in Iowa while the summit was going on, speaking mostly about foreign policy in various appearances, and becoming in effect the summit's Iowa-based analyst. In Iowa newspapers and local television news broadcasts a Dukakis speech or press conference commentary on the meetings in Washington was often accorded more prominence than any story other than the summit itself. At least compared to the previous two months, Dukakis was slowly emerging from the two-month shell into which he had crawled after Sasso's resignation, and his improved performance came at a time when his Iowa campaign had been beefed up and was humming efficiently in its effort to contact Democrats individually in the endless search for supporters willing to, as the new buttons put it, caucus for Dukakis.

Dukakis also adopted a new basic campaign speech, designed if not to bring tears to voters' eyes, at least to package his ideas somewhat more effectively. All campaign long, Dukakis never stopped looking for a slogan. Although he was a program-centered chief executive, he searched endlessly for words that would work on a bumper sticker, which was how he viewed a "message." He failed in winter 1987, but for a spell he tried a somewhat lame, John Kennedy-suggesting phrase by attempting to summon America to "the next frontier."

As the Christmas holidays brought a welcome hiatus in the Iowa campaigning, the scrambled Dukakis—Simon—Gephardt—X-Factor race presented a situation that was ripe for a candidate who was willing to gamble, and on the day after Christmas it was Gephardt who went for broke.

From the depths of his summer and fall decline, Gephardt and his top aides began planning after Thanksgiving an unprecedented—for the Iowa caucuses—television blitz, as well as a major change in his campaign message. No longer would he simply be the candidate with several specific proposals with appeal for segments of the Iowa Democratic Party.

Now Gephardt wrapped his specific proposals in populist paper. He became the candidate of change against an elitist establishment. He offered himself as a fighter against the status quo with a battle cry, "It's Your Fight, Too."

And to drive it all home, his campaign produced hard-hitting television commercials. The most effective put his trade ideas in direct language: If a country like South Korea had restrictions on American exports that raised the price of a United States car to the equivalent of $48,000 (or so the ad claimed), then maybe the South Koreans would like to find out how many Hyundais they could sell over here for $48,000 apiece. With $250,000 behind it, the commercial designed by Gephardt media consultant and speechwriter Robert Shrum deluged the relatively inexpensive Iowa airwaves and filled a media vacuum. Gephardt soared, and his position improved even more after New Year's Day, when it was enhanced by news coverage of his new campaign themes.

The Gephardt campaign was built around a shrewd political judgment that if the universe of caucus participants on February 8 was roughly the same 90,000 who had turned out four years earlier, Gephardt would lose because he had little intrinsic appeal to the typical caucus-system Democratic regulars and activists. But he could not

credibly continue in the race unless he finished first. So it was decided
that his route to victory must involve a significant expansion of the
universe by attracting enough new participants to raise the turnout well
above 100,000.

Moreover, the need for a win was so great that his entire field
operation from the rest of the country, solely excepting New Hampshire, was stripped bare so that every available person was working
precincts in Iowa by mid-January. The advertising and organizational
blitz was backed up by a campaign message every bit as tough as the
commercials. A new Gephardt stump speech, unveiled January 6 at
Drake University in Des Moines, before a handful of students and the
first elements in the horde of journalists about to descend on the state,
identified an enemy—the establishment—the perfect foil for a populist
economic crusade.

The angry message connected with rank-and-file Iowa Democrats
at once, especially in the small towns and rural communities most hurt
by the decade-long agricultural recession then just bottoming out, as
well as in the manufacturing-based communities whose products were
hurt most by the overvalued dollar's damage to American exports,
which was just beginning to respond to the post-1985 devaluation.
Along with the intense media curiosity about Gary Hart II, and Paul
Simon's efforts to shore up his candidacy, the Gephardt populism drew
attention as the election year finally began.

By contrast, Dukakis opened the final round in the precaucus
campaigning far less dramatically, offering a message that continued to
touch several bases, but none memorably.

"Welcome to 1988," he said, beginning his final push in the United
Auto Worker—dominated city of Waterloo January 2. "The year we've
been waiting for. Because in November of this year, we're going to say
goodbye to the nuclear arms race and hello to an effort to build a peaceful
competition with the Soviet Union. We'll say goodbye to Star Wars and
hello to Star Schools. We'll say goodbye to a shooting war in Central
America and hello to a war against poverty and injustice and exploitation
throughout Latin America. We'll say goodbye to supply-side, trickle-
down, voodoo economics and hello to a strong and successful economic
partnership that will create genuine economic opportunity for every
citizen in this land."

Two-thirds of the way through this presentation—solid but stolid,
designed for applause but not cheers, sensible but not always sensitive—
came something that, though not exactly new, was different. After
citing the usual Democratic heroes from days past and reworking standard Democratic appeals to ordinary, average Americans, Dukakis
added, "I'm talking about Americans who speak for themselves, instead

of through the political action committees that are distorting and sub-verting the democratic process in our country."

After several more paragraphs denouncing PACs, Dukakis prom-ised that his first official act if elected president would be to resubmit legislation curtailing their spending clout in congressional elections. The bill had been stalled by a Republican filibuster in the Senate.

Not bad, but not nearly good enough for those at the highest echelons in the Dukakis campaign. Dukakis's remarks were all that was left of a strong proposal by Susan Estrich that Dukakis take on his two main opponents in Iowa, Gephardt and Simon, on this issue. Dukakis himself refused to accept contributions from political action commit-tees. For Dukakis the veteran political reformer this was a genuine issue of principle. (His personal fund-raising machine was so awesomely effective that PACs, always of marginal benefit at best in a presidential campaign, were never a temptation.)

Both Simon and especially Gephardt, however, were accepting PAC donations to their presidential campaigns. If widely publicized, this fact could cut into Simon's image of Trumanesque independence. But it could also deeply undermine Gephardt's populist war on the establishment. How in the world could Gephardt be the antiestablish-ment candidate if corporate America was financing his campaign?

Estrich tested the issue in focus groups and in broader public-opinion polls. The Dukakis campaign, like other campaigns, routinely used focus-group polling for in-depth assessments of public opinion. Focus groups are small groups of representative voters who discuss their feelings and reactions to candidates and issues under the direction of a trained discussion leader. Estrich concluded that making PACs the centerpiece in a final push toward the caucuses—with the contrast between Dukakis on the one hand and Gephardt and Simon on the other made explicit by the candidate himself—could turn the race around for the governor in a way no other issue could.

Estrich was not recommending an attack on character, or even an all-out assault on the opponents' positions. This, she felt, was the tactic presidential candidates used when handed a fortuitous match between their strengths and their opponents' weaknesses on issues of document-able importance to voters: You made the contrast explicit and pressed the advantage hard.

Estrich tried to persuade Dukakis that engaging Simon and Gephardt over their receipt of PAC contributions would pay large dividends. But she was turned down twice by a candidate who knew his own mind and was making it clear he was not going to budge. Dukakis worried about stirring memories of the Biden tapes by going on the offensive against another candidate. He was comfortable with the genteel tenor of the Democratic campaign, which contrasted sharply with the rapidly building, deeply personal enmity between Republicans Bob Dole and George Bush.

The one exception to this generally amicable atmosphere was Tennessee Senator Albert Gore, Jr., who was attacking all his Democratic opponents as captives of special-interest groups and liberal activists in Iowa, while he mobilized for war on his southern home turf after failing to organize an effective campaign in Iowa. It was still not clear whether the Gore strategy might have some merit, but the other six candidates were united in disliking his assaults, which they privately considered insincere coming from a senator with one of his chamber's most liberal voting records. If anything, Gore's behavior reinforced Dukakis's determination to avoid direct criticism of his rivals.

Word of the *Des Moines Register*'s endorsement of Simon began to spread late on January 17. That evening, Dukakis was scheduled to attend one of the staples in Iowa life, a girls' high-school basketball game. On the way out of Des Moines, his van was invaded by Susan Estrich and Iowa campaign director Teresa Vilmain, both determined to try one last time to light a fire under him. Estrich, who gave Dukakis his political intelligence cold, without embellishment, told the governor he was going to finish third in the caucuses unless he directly engaged Simon and Gephardt on their PAC contributions. As Estrich saw it, his appearance the next night at a party dinner in Dubuque on the Mississippi River was his last chance to make his rhetorical move, and combined with a press conference to call more attention to his comments, he could ignite a last-minute surge because Iowa Democrats were as anti-PAC as any constituency she had encountered. By now, Estrich was more than comfortable telling Dukakis precisely what was on her mind; in fact, a makeup person preparing Dukakis's face for a debate in western Sioux City several days before had been startled by the sharp words they exchanged while arguing the PAC issue just before the governor once again failed to raise it during a public forum. On this final occasion, Dukakis told Estrich and Vilmain forcefully that he had no intention of attacking candidates who weren't attacking him, and that was going to be that.

The next evening at the party dinner, Dukakis again denounced the influence of special-interest money in campaigns and declared, to loud applause, "My friends, under a Dukakis administration, 1989 is going to be the year we say goodbye to PAC money in American politics, and I mean it."

Not only did he say nothing about Simon and Gephardt, however, he would not even make it clear that his own campaign refused to accept PAC donations, which might have raised the issue at least by implication. Behind the scenes, though, the Dukakis campaign had begun to push the story to reporters, using the detailed reports of income and expenditure the candidates had to file with the Federal Elections Commission in Washington. It was a pretty good story, especially about Gephardt, who turned out to be beneficiary of more than two dozen corporate PACs, which were also giving to George Bush's campaign; but the information was flowing too late to greatly affect the Iowa campaign in its final days. The Simon camp, for which anything short of victory on their almost-home turf would be a severe disappointment, also weighed in too late with charges that Gephardt had made several major changes in his positions on major issues to accommodate the larger constituency in a presidential campaign.

Before leaving Iowa, Dukakis and several of his senior advisers wrestled with the question of how to treat Gephardt when they got to New Hampshire. At a meeting in the Hotel Des Moines late on caucus night, sentiment favored an immediate attack via television commercials, emphasizing both his receipt of PAC money and his many changes of opinion on major issues.

As before, however, Dukakis was unalterably opposed, and unlike his laconic replies to the previous two months of entreaties about a broader campaign message or raising PAC contributions as an issue, he elaborated this Monday night. He was determined, he said, to make running for president "fun," and if calculated assaults on his Democratic rivals were the only way to win, he was fully capable of folding his cards and heading back to Massachusetts with his head high.

On the other hand, Dukakis had every intention of campaigning aggressively in New Hampshire and of raising issues that brought him into conflict with Gephardt, such as his opposition to the specific retaliatory steps against American trading partners advocated by Gephardt; his opposition to Gephardt's advocating a tax on oil imports; and from the past, Gephardt's decision to vote in favor of passing President Reagan's income-tax cuts in 1981 after earlier efforts to change the controversial proposals failed. And Dukakis also fully intended to call in the chits his long opposition to licensing for a commercial nuclear power plant in Seabrook had given him, especially in the populous southern New Hampshire communities.

Sensing a third place in Dukakis's immediate future in Iowa, his staff began working overtime to lower expectations for his performance and to do all they could to raise expectations about the size of Gephardt's expected victory. As February 8 dawned the rough media consensus was that as an outsider Dukakis would get passing grades for reaching 20 percent of the first choices made in the caucus meetings, and that anything above 30 percent would earn Gephardt major plaudits.

As it turned out, the percentages in Iowa's complicated caucus system did not appear to crown a convincing victor: at 27 percent based on a never-completed count, Gephardt got the first place finish he needed, but his three-point margin over Simon was not spectacular, and the Illinois senator himself had no reason for chest pounding in his own numbers; Dukakis was at 21 percent in third place; and another 20 percent was split almost evenly by Jesse Jackson and Bruce Babbitt.

The raw numbers, however, provided only a portion of the information available that night to the journalists and politicians sifting through the results looking for meaning. According to a questionnaire filled out by more than 1,500 caucus participants for CBS News and the *New York Times*, the candidates' performances were far from uniform on February 8. Gephardt got fully 46 percent of the first choices by Democrats with high-school educations; his support was 42 percent among conservatives, and 38 percent among people more than sixty years of age. By contrast, support for Simon and Dukakis was more uniform in the low-to-mid twenties; the only exceptions were Dukakis's low, 12 percent showing among conservatives, and Simon's 15 percent result among Democrats with a high-school education.

According to another analysis of the caucus results done for NBC News, the Gephardt victory margin came overwhelmingly from rural Iowa; in the state's cities, the top three candidates ran essentially even, affecting judgments about how one could responsibly project the results beyond Iowa. In other words, the raw material did not add up to a convincing victory or a disappointing defeat for Gephardt on the one hand or Simon and Dukakis on the other. Also, special factors that Monday night heavily influenced most journalists' way of reporting the results. On the Democratic side, the Gephardt tidal wave had been a story for roughly a month by the time the caucuses were held; because he was expected to win but didn't win by a landslide, the temptation to be somewhat blasé about his performance was understandable. And much more important, the big story that night was on the Republican side. Bob Dole's victory was a foregone conclusion, but the second-place finish by television evangelist Pat Robertson over Vice President George Bush was a stunning upset and a deep embarrassment to the vice president, with the New Hampshire voting just eight days away. Against that dramatic development, the expected first-place finish by Gephardt could hardly compete.

Accordingly, when NBC's John Chancellor, concluding his on-air analysis of the result, said of Dukakis's performance, "Third place so far from home is no disgrace," the governor could be considered very fortunate. When Chancellor's words came over television, state director Charlie Baker's troops, watching from a restaurant in Manchester, New Hampshire cheered with pleasure and relief. Dukakis had been winnowed in. It was a liberated Dukakis who left Des Moines before dawn on February 9 and returned to New Hampshire and familiar turf.

4

The War of Attrition

Charlie Baker, Dukakis's New Hampshire state coordinator, called together his entire staff of eighty-five for a pep talk on the day of the Iowa caucuses. It was clear Dukakis would not come in first and could easily finish third. Baker wanted to make sure his people understood that their goal was victory the following week in the New Hampshire primary, regardless of what happened that night in the Midwest. When the staff presented him with an antique sword purchased from the second-hand shop next to the ramshackle headquarters in downtown Manchester, Baker brandished it in the air. The sword was a metaphor. The Massachusetts governor could not continue his candidacy without winning here. Iowa was different. Dukakis only needed to survive Iowa. New Hampshire, the quadrennial heartbreaker, was a must-win.

But New Hampshire was more than that; it was the gateway to a carefully planned route to the Democratic presidential nomination that had been mapped months before. The key for Dukakis's campaign was not the megaprimary a month later that was called Super Tuesday; the key spots were in the five minor events that would come before it: Maine, Vermont, Minnesota, South Dakota, and Wyoming. Domination in those small contests would create a perception of strength that would be critical to a good performance in the twenty primaries and caucuses on March 8.

After the Iowa caucuses, tactics becomes strategy in Democratic presidential politics. The nomination goes to the tactical master, the person who most skillfully navigates the treacherously complicated waters of Democratic campaign rules and events—as George McGovern, Jimmy Carter, and Walter Mondale have proved in modern times; however, an equally important corollary has just as frequently helped produce failure in general elections, namely, the tactics that win nominations are rarely relevant to the grand strategies that win elections. The great danger in a political war of attrition—which the Democratic primaries have become—is that it becomes an end in itself, leaving the winner unprepared for the far tougher struggle ahead. In the 1988 primaries, Dukakis mastered several skills that helped sink him in the fall: playing it safe, avoiding controversy, and emphasizing campaign field work over sending messages to the electorate.

Still lacking a rallying cry, a powerful theme, or a compelling message to voters summarizing what he wanted to do with the presidency, Dukakis relied on the image of a governmental chief executive against the remaining field of three legislators and one civil-rights movement figure: Richard Gephardt, Albert Gore, Paul Simon, and Jesse Jackson. He also relied on a Massachusetts-based fund-raising colossus, campaign leaders who knew how to pick the most inviting targets of opportunity, and a field organization of awesome size and skill that ran from New Hampshire to Texas, from Washington state to Florida.

Along the way, though, the governor was always vulnerable to the blow that took place in Iowa in 1988: an early win by a hot candidate with a message that connected. On February 9, that candidate was Richard Gephardt, who embraced the big-bang theory of presidential politics: Win an early victory and explode forward on media momentum.

Gephardt, his staff, and an accompanying press corps left the Des Moines Flying Service before dawn on the morning after the caucuses in a fleet of small jets. The scene resembled an evacuation more than a departure, with weary campaigners loaded down with luggage stumbling around in the dark waiting their turn to escape Iowa for the next contest in New Hampshire. Ed Reilly, his pollster, talked about the underlying factors that contributed to Gephardt's win the night before. "We're tapping into economic anxiety," he said above the hum of engines from his seat at the back of a tiny jet, recalling his man's powerful Hyundai commercial. "This is not about cars. It's about values."

"This is like fast-break basketball," he said. "We won Iowa. Now the important thing is to keep moving the ball."

The dynamic in New Hampshire would be Dukakis versus Can-

Charlie Baker kept the New Hampshire campaign staff focused on the upcoming primary despite the third place showing in Iowa. (Photo by Bill Brett)

didate X. Gephardt's job was to make Gephardt into Candidate X, *the* alternative.

Gephardt alighted from his plane at the Manchester airport with his wife Jane and his three children. "I am clearly the underdog," he said, immediately addressing his own heightened expectations. "Michael Dukakis is the clear favorite. The polls show that. He is a neighboring governor."

Then he went to a makeshift stage already crowded with nearly two dozen local supporters at a downtown shopping mall in Manchester. Bruce Springsteen's *Born in the USA* bawled from the sound system, and he made a pitch to be the antiestablishment alternative to the familiar governor. "Yesterday," he said, still high from his Iowa victory, "the Democrats of Iowa delivered an unmistakable message. This isn't just an election. It's a fight for America. And I've come to New Hampshire to tell you that it's your fight, too." He referred darkly to unspecified "forces of the other side" that would attempt to frustrate them.

The audience was a not-very-interested lunch-hour crowd that campaign advance staff had literally corralled in the mall. "We're going to take our America back from the vested interests, the entrenched interests, and yes, the establishment," he cried. "It's time to tell the forces of greed that enough is enough." He had the crowd hooked. By the time he finished his speech, voters in the audience were shrieking the refrain "Enough is enough" with him. This was a battle for control of our economic destiny, he said. If we lose this battle, "America won't be America any more."

It was powerful and potentially explosive stuff. But later that day at a motel in Portsmouth, the fire went out. Gephardt and his staff were numb with exhaustion. The campaign was broke. They mistakenly thought the momentum from his win in Iowa would carry them for a few days while they regrouped. Gephardt even left New Hampshire to raise money for television ads. Boston television time was costly. A thirty-second spot on a prime-time show like *Cheers* cost $14,000.

Meanwhile, Dukakis found his legs back on home turf. Much as he liked the good sturdy burghers in Iowa, he felt out of place there. He knew how to talk to the people in New Hampshire. The day after the caucuses, back in New England, he told Estrich, "It's good to be home."

The second day back, it showed. Although good television advertising can provide a major assist to a presidential candidate in a primary, it cannot supplant a strong campaign message delivered effectively each day. Unlike the general election, rarely is enough money available to fully saturate a state with advertising in a primary. As a result daily news coverage, the so-called free media, is a critical variable. For the 1988 New Hampshire primary campaign, effectively the eight days following

the Iowa caucuses, the news coverage was especially intense and vora-
ciously consumed by the relatively more informed and active people
who vote in the primary. Dukakis appealed to Democrats as the candidate of the future, the candidate dedicated to change, much as Gary
Hart had in 1984 when he won the Granite State primary. He cast
Gephardt and Simon as symbols of the political past, pushing protectionism and makework programs.

He was a happy, future-facing front-runner, but a critical ingredient in Dukakis's happiness was the barely functional candidacy of Paul
Simon. Enormous effort had gone into keeping the Illinois senator from
foundering in the final month of the campaign in Iowa, and so it was not
immediately clear how severely damaged he was. His second-place
finish had come close enough to Gephardt to diminish the Missouri
Congressman's first-place performance. Second place for Simon, however, had not been good enough to generate substantial campaign contributions, national political support, or cachet in New Hampshire.

For both Simon and Gephardt, New Hampshire was make or
break. Both candidates had to leave the state in the days following the
Iowa caucuses to raise money. Both candidates also resorted to borrowing tens of thousands of dollars within two days of the Iowa caucuses
while the well-financed Dukakis bought a healthy chunk of television
time well before the Iowa caucuses in all the markets serving New
Hampshire and dominated the airwaves on the Democratic side.

"The great irony is that Dukakis ended up better finishing third
than second," said Simon's pollster and top adviser, Washington-based
Paul Maslin, much later. "If Simon's race had ended in Iowa, New
Hampshire would have been a total focus on Gephardt and Dukakis. It
might have led to a closer result that [would have] kept Gephardt viable
through Super Tuesday. And Gephardt would have been much stronger in the industrial states than Al Gore. In a way, Iowa was very critical
in setting the stage."

Setting the stage has become Iowa's role. Within a day of the
caucuses, Simon knew he had no momentum in New Hampshire. He
also knew that his campaign could not survive a third-place finish there
and retain any credibility, much less raise any substantial money. From
Simon's perspective, *he* had to be the alternative to Dukakis, and so he
took direct aim at Gephardt, the only man standing between himself and
that goal. A tough television advertisement compared Gephardt's voting
record on Social Security, the MX missile, the B-1 bomber, nuclear
evacuation policy, and the minimum wage with his current, different
positions. It was particularly effective because Gephardt was not well
known in New Hampshire.

The Gephardt campaign was stunned, then angry. The campaign

legal counsel sent Mailgrams to New England television station managers demanding that they take the ads off the air, a strictly political ploy with no legal grounding. Simon's decision to mount an electronic offensive against Gephardt was a change in position that caused more than a little bad blood. For the three weeks before the Iowa caucuses, rumors swirled through the media hangout at the Savery Hotel bar in Des Moines that Simon would "go negative" before the final weekend. Gephardt's top aides had tracked the rumors like hunting dogs, but as the moment of truth arrived, Simon sent word that he would not make personal attacks on the airwaves.

With his back to the wall in New Hampshire, however, Simon welched on his word and his commercials hit the airwaves on the Thursday before the primary. For the nearly twenty pollsters tracking New Hampshire sentiment for various campaigns and the press, two elements were now in the mix: a forceful front-runner who was jabbing away at Gephardt, and a desperate trailing candidate who was clobbering Gephardt on television.

In most of the polls, public and private, Dukakis's support had inched down from 35 to 40 percent at the beginning of the week, and Gephardt had climbed above 20 percent. By the end of the week, however, Gephardt and Simon were in a death struggle for second place, which neither man could afford to lose, while Dukakis floated almost untouched above the battle as the candidates prepared for their one debate in Manchester on Saturday, a debate that put a grim Gephardt on the defensive.

Not until the final days, when it became apparent that Dukakis was getting away unscathed, did both Simon and Gephardt take aim at the Massachusetts governor. Gephardt played the tax card by raising the specter of the huge 1975 Massachusetts state tax increase in an ad first aired on the Friday night before the Tuesday primary. And Simon presented himself as a more caring candidate than Dukakis; New Hampshire voters knew he had had to cut social programs as well as raise taxes during his first term to eliminate an inherited budget deficit.

Gephardt's ad was not slick, but it emphasized the one heavy piece of baggage for even a Democrat to carry in the state—taxes. In America's Liechtenstein, a tiny tax haven with neither a sales nor a personal income tax, New Hampshire voters have a long history of rejecting even presidential candidates who can be tarred as taxers. Gephardt followed advice from Ed Reilly, who understood how effective using the tax card could be against Dukakis from working for Ed King in Massachusetts. Gephardt's ads sought to make a virtue out of his 1981 vote for the Reagan administration's tax cuts; he said he was proud of his vote, offered examples of how average citizens had benefited in the intervening seven years, and contrasted that with Dukakis's support for the biggest tax increase in Massachusetts history in 1975.

The attack came too late to establish a Gephardt-Dukakis race. New Hampshire voters, because of exposure to the Boston media market, which reaches 86 percent of the state's households, also knew Dukakis had cut taxes in his home state. But it was part of a vigorous windup to the New Hampshire campaign that enabled Gephardt to pass Simon at the finish, though not by much. During the long presidential primary season, the bright lights of scrutiny can shine on a candidate at any moment and test him to his limits. Sometimes the scrutiny comes after a major mistake, but often it comes right after an early triumph, when the candidate is expecting a wave of favorable, momentum-causing publicity instead. For Gephardt, his Iowa victory attracted scrutiny by both the press and his opponents, and he was slow to rise to its challenge. By contrast, Dukakis managed to get through Iowa, and then New Hampshire, without ever finding himself on the defensive over his long record as governor. He had been able to present himself as a sensible person with a record of accomplishment and a promise to face the tough decisions he saw ahead for the next president and to run the government with integrity and competence.

Gephardt's and Simon's last-minute shifts in tactics were too little too late. In his own advertising, Dukakis played on his popular positions against the Seabrook nuclear power plant, political action committees, and an oil import fee. Familiar and reassuring, he moved to Election Day with his lead intact, backed by an extensive field organization ready to shore him up should the situation change.

For Dukakis, the field organization was always critical. In Iowa, Steve Murphy, the savvy Gephardt campaign director, had muttered through clenched teeth: "They're emptying the bars in Boston" when veteran Massachusetts organizers, called from state, law, and academic offices—people like Robert "Skinner" Donahue, Tim Regan, and Ellie Moran—began to pop up in places like Davenport to tune the Dukakis organization for the final weeks in the Iowa campaign. The Boston operatives had enjoyed a collective reputation that bordered on legend since 1960, when Massachusetts Senator John F. Kennedy and a cadre of wise-guy Boston lawyers had snapped up the Democratic nomination. They showed up every four years.

The grunts in the field organization, however, were people who had worked on Dukakis campaigns for years, dating back to his first runs for the state legislature in the 1960s. They were just like the governor: suburban, liberal, good-government types. Longtime supporters would do anything to help him. It was not unusual for lawyers and doctors to do door-to-door canvassing. Margaret (MarDee) Xifaras, a Marion law-

Kitty Dukakis draped a replica of an Olympic gold medal around her husband's neck the night he finished first and "won the gold" in the New Hampshire primary. (Photo by Paul Benoit)

yer who had worked as a special assistant to Dukakis during his second term and held a masters degree in business administration in addition to her law degree, put on her storm boots and went slogging through the snow to bang on doors in Manchester for him on the final weekend before the primary; in politics, Dukakis style, she was not unusual.

Charlie Baker had carefully constructed an old-fashioned, grass-roots campaign organization in New Hampshire. The get-out-the-vote plan, prepared by the young Dukakis organizer John Geisser under the supervision of Baker and Corrigan, itemized the number of volunteers, telephones, and telephone calls to be made by date and by community. They assigned each region a specific number of rental cars, front-wheel-drive and four-wheel-drive vehicles, and vans. The definite and likely Dukakis voters who had been identified in the fall were contacted again by a campaign volunteer at least three times in the final week before the primary. Some were called a fourth time on Election Day to make sure they voted.

In the blue-collar city of Claremont, where he received 770 votes or 45 percent of the vote cast on primary day, a canvassing operation staffed by thirty volunteers visited 600 voters in person. Overall, the campaign contacted more than 210,000 households throughout the state and identified the presidential preference of almost 90 percent of the households where they could locate a family member. More than 2,000 volunteers from Massachusetts swarmed over the border to help for the final days. On Election Day, 123,512 people voted for president in the New Hampshire Democratic primary. Dukakis drew 44,112 votes or 36 percent of the vote, sixteen points more than his nearest competitor, Gephardt. He won every city but the largest, Manchester, where he was under regular attack by the *Union Leader* newspaper. Gephardt carried the city by 158 votes or 1 percent of the vote.

Expectations of the governor's performance in New Hampshire, however, were the real battleground. In 1968 and 1972 the winners in the New Hampshire Democratic primary had been perceived as losers because their rivals did better than expected. Dukakis consistently polled around 40 percent in public New Hampshire polls during much of the preseason skirmishing; however, his opponents tried to set his standard higher, arguing that 50 percent or less should be viewed as at least a moral defeat. But Dukakis campaign researchers discovered that no recent Democrat had ever won a contested New Hampshire primary by more than ten percentage points. They set that as an achievable benchmark, and Dukakis began to spout the statistic on the stump. Expectations were firmly shifted away from the 50 percent figure promoted by his rivals.

Once again, as in Iowa eight days before, the Republican results dominated the news coverage as George Bush came from behind to sweep past Bob Dole. On the Democratic side, the only mild suspense was in the Gephardt—Simon tussle for second, which damaged both men. Dukakis's victory margin was a solid, unspectacular 36.4 percent, over Gephardt's 20.2 percent and Simon's 17.4 percent. Setting the stage for their big chance down South, Jackson edged out Gore for fourth place, but both were well below 10 percent, and Bruce Babbitt's campaign ended with just 800 votes more than 1984's flash, Gary Hart, who was seventh.

According to a questionnaire-poll filled out by 2,200 Democratic primary voters for NBC News that day, Dukakis's support was relatively strong across the board: 39 percent among people who considered themselves strong Democrats, 35 percent among liberals, and 33 percent among moderates. For those looking for Dukakis's weak spots, Gephardt was once again strong among conservative Democrats, falling just short of Dukakis's by a 30 to 27 percent margin; and the governor was at his weakest in blue-collar precincts, especially in Manchester.

The sixteen-point margin was hailed as a significant win by the governor from next door, but the election night gaiety was tempered by awareness that much lay ahead.

The national media along with most of the presidential candidates essentially wrote off the next two contests—the Maine caucuses and Vermont's primary—to Dukakis because of his perceived regional advantage. Maine slipped in status from momentum-builder to a perfunctory pit stop on the way to Super Tuesday. Gephardt, Simon, and Gore packed up and headed South, but not Jesse L. Jackson.

Gerald Austin, Jackson's campaign manager, shrewdly spotted a competitive vacuum and, borrowing a page from the Dukakis strategy, moved swiftly to fill it. A liberal core in both states was waiting to be exploited by Jackson's candidacy. In Maine, Jackson had come out early in support of the striking workers at the International Paper Company mill in May 1987. It earned him undying gratitude in the state's labor movement. Austin spent $10,000 on Maine television ads for the final days before the caucuses on February 28, more than triple the previous Maine campaign budget. He dropped another $5,800 in Vermont, where a nonbinding beauty contest took place on town-meeting day, March 1. For very little money in northern states with minuscule minority populations, Jackson could boost his numbers and his own credibility as a candidate with an appeal that extended beyond black voters.

The Dukakis campaign slogan was Take Nothing for Granted. In Maine, the former state Democratic Party chairman, Barry Hobbins, a Gephardt supporter, puzzled about Dukakis's efforts in his state. "I don't know why he is spending so much money," he said one day over lunch in Portland. "He is shadow boxing, fighting a ghost that isn't going to appear."

It was, in fact, Jesse Jackson's specter that loomed. Both states foreshadowed the results and rivalry that would dominate the final weeks in the primary season. Dukakis won, but Jackson ran a solid second.

National media attention shifted to Minnesota and South Dakota, which voted one week after New Hampshire. Dukakis was strong from the start in both states, where he invested almost $750,000 to build campaigns from the bottom up. Minnesota had been a Dukakis target since the previous spring, when Celtics basketball star Kevin McHale, and two early Dukakis supporters from Minnesota, Pat Forceia, McHale's college roommate, and Gary Cerkvenik visited John Sasso at the temporary presidential campaign office in Boston's Park Square with a bullish memorandum saying that the economy was a big issue in Minnesota and Dukakis could win the state. Mondale, the 1984 Democratic presidential nominee and former senator from Minnesota, was fond of Dukakis. He never forgot the comfort the governor provided when he lost the New Hampshire primary to Hart in 1984. In Minnesota, Dukakis's chief competitor was Paul Simon. This old-fashioned liberal reminded some of another favorite son, the late senator and Vice President Hubert H. Humphrey. But Simon, limping badly by caucus day after his Iowa and New Hampshire disappointments, ended up running third to Jackson, who again was a surprising second to Dukakis. Simon then retreated to Illinois to wait out the southern tests. His campaign was essentially over, but Illinois politicians already slated as delegates persuaded him to stay in the race to enhance their chances of going to the national convention. The puckish senator also had the idea that he could be a power broker in a divided convention. That left the Super Tuesday contests to Dukakis, Gephardt, Gore, and Jackson.

After New Hampshire, Gephardt desperately needed a victory and zeroed in on South Dakota as the battleground. Dukakis held the lead until Gephardt unleashed a campaign advertisement over the final weekend ridiculing Dukakis as a tax-loving bumbler who knew nothing about agriculture but advised hard-pressed farmers to grow new crops of yuppie vegetables like Belgian endive. The Gephardt campaign sprang the ad on Friday night after the television stations had closed their sales offices for the weekend. It caught the Dukakis campaign by surprise. They watched helplessly as a fourteen-point lead dissolved and Gephardt surged into the lead to win the state by thirteen points. The loss was tempered by Dukakis's solid victory on the same day in neighboring Minnesota, his first victory outside New England.

The astonishing twenty-seven-point turnaround in South Dakota was a powerful message for Chauncy Street and Dukakis himself, who had resisted his staff's pleas that he go after his opposition with negative ads. Ken Swope, the Boston ad man, had warned that the campaign had two choices: take the guy out in one state, South Dakota, or in twenty, a reference to the states that would be voting on Super Tuesday.

The reverse, however, was supported by Dukakis himself, and most of his senior aides later agreed it was correct. By taking a media pounding in one state, Dukakis had in effect received dispensation to deliver a counter blow in twenty states, without being perceived as the heavy in the fight. Normally, attack advertising risks negative backlash, but after South Dakota the governor would have a chance to take a free shot in return, with a far larger potential payoff—the inside route to the nomination.

Dukakis, reluctantly but realistically, gave the high sign. As the race headed south, he agreed that the time had come to go nuclear on Gephardt.

Super Tuesday in 1988 was so big a political event on paper that it obscured its own meaning. As it began to take shape from coordinated votes in state legislatures around the South in 1985, it took on the character of *the* climactic event in the nominating season. How else was one to characterize a day on which twenty states—fourteen of them in or bordering on the South—would hold primaries or caucuses that would allocate roughly one-third (37 percent) of the delegate slots available at the Democratic National Convention? And if it was *the* climactic event in the nominating season, didn't that mean the South had finally risen as a national political entity in the Democratic Party, not just Jimmy Carter's base but the party's newly chosen battleground? Here in the South were buckets of national convention delegates and, later, Electoral College votes waiting for a candidate with enough sense to ditch liberalism and marry the millions of southerners who liked governmental activism if it produced growth and jobs but insisted on a strong foreign policy that kept the Soviet Union at a suspicious arm's length.

This interpretation was wrong. Fortunately for Michael Dukakis's presidential campaign, a thirty-two-year-old lawyer named Tad Devine had the presence of mind to look beyond Super Tuesday's obvious size to discern its true place in the system under which the Republican and Democratic parties select their presidential nominees. Devine had always been skeptical of the big-bang strategic theory that a candidate could bust out of the pack with a win in Iowa or New Hampshire and surge to the nomination unless that someone was Michael Dukakis. He saw the approach as a steady series of contests in which attrition would be the inexorable trend and it would always be critical to be ready for the next two contests.

On the surface, it is preposterous to speak of a thirty-two-year-old man as a veteran of presidential politics, and yet nothing else describes Tad Devine. At twenty-four, he had kept track of Jimmy Carter's delegate count in his holy war with Edward Kennedy; at twenty-eight he worked as number-two tactician for Walter Mondale's delegate operation; and now he was in charge of producing the delegate numbers for Dukakis.

The initial political inspiration for this tall, slender, intense lawyer had been Hunter S. Thompson. As a boy, sitting on a Rhode Island beach with two friends the summer after finishing high school in Providence, he had been enthralled by the zany writer's half-mad, half-brilliant account of the 1972 campaign, *Fear and Loathing on the Campaign Trail*. The three friends agreed that this was the life for them, not the anarchic, high-stakes thrills themselves, but working the gears in The Process. Four years later, the first of the three got his chance by being

Left: Leslie Dach, nicknamed Baby Doc, worked as communications director for the campaign. (Photo by Bill Brett) *Right: Susan Estrich, a tenured professor at Harvard Law School, was accustomed to being "a first" when she became the first woman to run a national presidential campaign after Sasso's resignation.* (Photo by Bill Brett)

Left: Susan Brophy, possessor of the most pronounced Boston accent in Washington, doggedly kept track of delegates during the nominating season and then became Estrich's assistant for the general election. (Photo by Bill Brett) *Right: Tad Devine, the onetime basketball star from Providence, Rhode Island, had uncanny insight into the mechanics of the Democratic nominating process.* (Photo by Bill Brett)

selected as an intern with Jimmy Carter's chief of staff, Hamilton Jordan, while still in college. In 1980, Tom Donilon found places for his two pals in the Carter operation—Devine, and another budding genius Anthony Corrado. Donilon continued to be the trailblazer, tapped very early to run Mondale's delegate operation, assisted once again by the rest of the Providence Three. Their work, which produced Mondale's nominating majority, showed an almost instinctive awareness of the critical link between process (the rules of the road) and strategy (the road itself).

But in 1988, Donilon had gone one way, as a top strategy adviser for Joe Biden, and Devine, after talking to Gephardt, chose Dukakis and moved to Boston. Carrado chose a different life, in academe, but would stay close enough to run Dukakis's national convention operation for Devine, and to assist on the logistical side when Donilon joined Dukakis in September to manage the campaign's preparations for the presidential and vice-presidential debates.

The Dukakis campaign strategists saw Super Tuesday as a test for discipline and targeting. Devine believed that caution was essential. Going overboard in an all-out effort to catch a huge majority among the roughly 1,300 national convention delegates on the line March 8, he felt, risked the worst kind of failure—not enough delegates to show for the effort, and not enough money left over for the next primaries.

Although fourteen of the contests were taking place in southern or border states, a handful of other primaries up north would give a careful strategist a tactical advantage. Months before, the Dukakis campaign had adopted a "four-corners" strategy for Super Tuesday. Anchoring the corners were Washington state in the Northwest; Massachusetts, Rhode Island, and Maryland in the Northeast; Florida in the Southeast, and Texas in the Southwest. The goal was to come out of Super Tuesday with the most delegates and enough money left over to fight in the major northern state primaries later on.

The Democratic and Republican nominating systems are a crazy quilt of individual state decisions and traditions and haphazard national party attempts to impose a modicum of order. They are quite different. Both Tad Devine in the Dukakis campaign and Lee Atwater in the Bush campaign understood that the rules and process dictate the strategy. Understanding this reality resulted in opposite views of Super Tuesday: to the Bush campaign it was everything, but for the Dukakis campaign it had to be balanced by greater attention to what came before and after. Their separate understanding is a major reason Bush and Dukakis faced each other in the general election.

Votes do not translate directly into the national-convention delegates, who determine the nominee. Most primary and caucus contests require a candidate to reach a threshold of the vote, usually 15 percent, in order to win one national convention delegate. That threshold eliminates fringe candidates, winnowing the field. For the same reason, the Federal Elections Commission withholds matching funds from campaigns that fail to win at least 20 percent of the vote in two consecutive primaries. Most Republican primaries are set up so that a candidate who wins a simple plurality of the vote in a congressional district will get *all* that district's delegates to the national convention. This preponderance of all-or-nothing situations in congressional districts makes a Republican nomination much easier to clinch early. Republicans like this arrangement because the earlier a party's nomination battle is decided the more likely that party is to win the presidency in the November general election, as demonstrated in five of the six elections between 1964 and 1988.

Surveying the landscape and the calendar for 1988, Atwater concluded that Bush need not win the earliest contests, such as the Iowa caucuses in February, or the New Hampshire primary, because of the immense harvest of delegates available to win almost outright on Super Tuesday. For the Republicans, Super Tuesday included sixteen primaries, including all the southern and border state contests the Democrats would also hold on March 8, but also including a primary in Atwater's native South Carolina three days earlier that could give its winner powerful media-driven momentum. It was therefore no accident that with the conservative South in mind, Bush never gave any of his opponents an inch of running room to his right, and was content to let Senator Bob Dole ride discontent with Ronald Reagan's economic and farm policies as much as he wanted in Iowa, while Bush emphasized his support for Reagan in staunchly conservative New Hampshire.

The Democratic system is different. It makes early knockouts very difficult, primarily because of changes adopted after the 1968 tumult, when Hubert Humphrey's nomination followed not one primary victory in a winter and spring of searing divisions over the war in Vietnam. Tad Devine summarized the changes well in a seminal memorandum on the looming primary season to Jack Corrigan and Susan Estrich in November 1987.

"The evolution of the delegate selection system in the last twenty years has dramatically affected the ways that a nominee can be chosen in the Democratic Party," Devine wrote. "In 1968, Hubert Humphrey did not enter a single primary, and only 1 percent of the delegates were allocated by mid-March. The reform movement of the seventies, away from closed process to a system which selected the vast majority of the delegates on the basis of primary/caucus results, has produced a process where delegates are more committed to candidates than to other sources of influence and authority."

Unlike his typical Republican counterpart, a Democratic National Convention delegate is most likely to have been chosen under a system known as proportional representation. In each congressional district, delegates are allocated according to size of the popular primary vote or caucus meeting preferences, once a threshold of 15 percent has been crossed by a candidate. The principal unit in a modern primary is the congressional district, not the state as a whole; the minority of delegates chosen statewide in a proportional system are also apportioned by the actual vote.

In the system as it stood in 1988, delegates were chosen in three other ways, and for the Dukakis campaign each was, Devine said, "a target of opportunity." Zeroing in on these targets would enable Dukakis to build the kind of lead from which a nominating majority was most likely to form. One selection system awarded a bonus national convention delegate to the winner of the vote in a congressional district. It was called "winner take more."

And the other system directly elected delegates as individuals, rather than as names on a slate pledged to a specific candidate; in this system a candidate could win all the delegates in a state's districts if the people running as his delegates won a simple plurality of the vote. Under pressure from Jesse Jackson and from liberals who still believed that fairness was the most important goal of a nomination system and that one-man—one-vote was thus the ideal, direct election of delegates was in disfavor, and after 1984, two of the largest states using it (California and Florida) switched to proportional representation and a "bonus" primary, respectively.

Finally, the Democrats also set aside a specific number of delegate slots for all members of their national committee, all Democratic governors, most Democratic congressmen and senators, plus five elder party statesmen. These Super Delegates were created in 1984 as a way to institutionalize the counsel of major party officials, and to woo many back to the presidential selection process. Many southern Democrats, in particular, had retreated to the sidelines because the post-1968 changes had diminished their role unless they ran for delegate as supporters of individual candidates. In 1988, 15 percent of the slots at the national convention were set aside for these Super Delegates, and because their selection was almost automatic, they could stay neutral as long as they wished.

To Devine, the challenge posed by the system was figuring a way for a candidate to break clear of his opponents under a system of proportional representation that was used by thirty-nine of the fifty-six contests in the season (The fifty-six contests would be held in fifty states and the District of Columbia, Puerto Rico, Guam, the Virgin Islands,

American Samoa, and among Americans living abroad.). Moreover, those thirty-nine events would govern selection of 2,017 delegates, nearly two-thirds of the convention delegates pledged to candidates, just under half the delegate population.

"Proportional representation methods severely limit delegate opportunities even in the largest states," he concluded in his memorandum, and then described precisely how they acted to make a breaking-out so difficult. "For example, in a four-delegate CD [congressional district] where two candidates break the threshold [15 percent at all levels of the process] Candidate A must beat Candidate B by approximately 20 percent in order to achieve a three-to-one split in delegates."

With three or more candidates, the one-for-you, one-for-me problem would only be worse. This was why, especially with front-runner Gary Hart gone from the race, the contest among six relatively unknown figures plus Jesse Jackson for the nomination was widely seen as unwinnable; this was why the concept of a brokered nomination or even a brokered national convention gained such currency even before the voting had started. And a main element in the brokered nomination scenarios was that of the 1,307 pledged delegates at stake on Super Tuesday in twenty contests, only one (Maryland) directly elected delegates, and five used the bonus rule (Florida, Massachusetts, North Carolina, Missouri, and Georgia).

"In summary," Devine wrote, "in the states with proportional primaries and caucuses in 1988, the delegate opportunities are severely limited by the nature of the system. . . . It is practically impossible in a two- or three-way race for a candidate to establish any significant margin of delegates in such contests. The opportunities for assembling large blocks of delegates will primarily exist in [direct-election] primary states, large-bonus primary states, and from the ranks of the unpledged delegates."

In specific numbers, eight direct-election primaries with 622 delegates were at stake, plus another nine bonus situations, with 948 delegates on the line.

On top of proportional-representation primaries, Devine specified another headache that 1988 would present—favorite sons, who included Dukakis (Massachusetts), Paul Simon (Illinois), Richard Gephardt (Missouri), Al Gore (Tennessee), and Jesse Jackson (the black community nationally, plus a special hold on huge chunks of Chicago and South Carolina). That was another reason significant pieces of the country would not truly be in play, which would further complicate assembling a nominating majority.

Finally, Devine's document was focused on the special significance that the calendar of events had for any campaign worthy of the presidency. Ever since a nobody named Jimmy Carter discovered the potential (for both national credibility and generating momentum) in the Iowa precinct caucuses, a new word had steadily crept into the nomination-season lexicon: front-loading, or movement by more states to the beginning of the process, lured by possible attention, influence, prominence, and even money from cash-endowed media and presidential campaign organizations.

Devine noted that more than 80 percent of the convention delegate slots would be allocated by the end of April in 1988, roughly ten weeks after the Iowa caucuses, including the 37 percent of pledged delegates who were at stake on Super Tuesday itself; but just as important, the time between Iowa and Super Tuesday had been condensed to twenty-eight days. Moreover, unlike 1980 and 1984, between Iowa and Super Tuesday would be events beyond the traditional New Hampshire primary.

"The southern promoters of Super Tuesday 1988 would have undoubtedly better attained the announced goals of promoting a moderate candidate by staggering the southern primaries throughout March," wrote Devine. "What they have probably produced is a system which will reflexively respond to the results of the pre-window period." The Democratic National Committee had established a "window," effectively a nominating season, within which states would hold caucuses and primary elections. Some states, eager to become the new Iowa or New Hampshire, broke the rules and set dates for contests before the opening date of the "window."

And that assumption produced Devine's first major recommendation: "Such a conclusion supports a strategy of total commitment to pre-window states, particularly in light of our real advantages in New England [three of seven pre-window events] and our ability to bring to bear additional significant resources."

For all practical purposes, that put an enormous premium on a strong showing in two midwestern states—Minnesota and South Dakota—that would select delegates on the same late-February day, one week after the New Hampshire primary. In one of the campaign's most important early decisions, Barbara Opacki, a veteran of field work in Dukakis's 1982 and 1986 campaigns, was dispatched by the fall of 1987 to assemble a non-Iowa midwestern structure.

With an eye cocked toward Al Gore—whose hopes rested on a national launch of his candidacy via the kind of clear-cut Super Tuesday triumph Devine considered highly improbable—he added an observation based on the likely preponderance of news coverage at the very beginning:

The fact that more than half of the network news minutes of coverage of the primary campaign traditionally will have aired by the day after the New Hampshire primary will effectively doom any candidacy which attempts to go into Super Tuesday without any established base vote. . . . The continued front-loading of the process in 1988 has undoubtedly accelerated this phenomenon, and the difficulty of emerging from the pack in 1988 will be heightened by the fact that there is a real contest on the Republican side which will compete for precious minutes / inches of coverage.

Even with Dukakis's rejection of advice to energize his Iowa campaign, however, and his decision to avoid assaults on his opponents with television commercials until one of them first used the tactic on him, the elements in Devine's assessing of the first seven contests as critical proved sound. Moreover, after Estrich, Corrigan, and Bob Farmer flew with Dukakis on a trip to Texas in mid-December to present the detailed budgetary recommendations, the governor accepted this fundamental Devine point: "This campaign must additionally take advantage of our resource advantage in states and attempt to dominate every event prior to Super Tuesday, even at the expense of having only minimal contact in states whose events occur within the window, including the Super Tuesday states themselves."

"Resource advantage" was a cryptic reference to a money-raising operation that far surpassed that of any other Democratic candidate in 1988.

In Massachusetts, Dukakis had always run field-intensive, low-budget campaigns. He was inclined to hoard resources rather than spend. For years he refused to own a credit card, and he had a hard and fast rule against campaigning on credit.

Enter Robert Farmer.

Dukakis later said that he could not have considered a national campaign without Sasso and Farmer. Sasso was a natural, but Farmer was an unlikely power behind the scenes. He is a bulky man with curly blond hair and blue eyes that blink myopically behind thick eyeglasses. He is aggressive but insecure, shy but eager for press coverage, brash but highly sensitive to slight. He can be volatile, argumentative, and thin-skinned but is able to laugh at himself. Once during a plane trip he began to argue vociferously over his schedule with his chief of staff, Tony West, a handsome young black man and recent graduate of Harvard College. West noticed another passenger reacting to Farmer's high-decibel ranting and quipped, "It's okay. He's my Dad." Farmer loved to tell that story on himself.

Farmer was born and raised in Cleveland and came East to attend

Dartmouth College in Hanover, New Hampshire. He graduated from Harvard Law School but never bothered to take the bar exam. He went into the educational publishing business instead. He made a small fortune and by 1980 was ready for a new challenge.

He had been raised Republican but as a liberal lost faith in the Republican Party much as conservative Democrats lost faith in their party of birth. In 1980, he volunteered to help John B. Anderson, Republican congressman from Illinois, raise money for his independent presidential bid. Farmer dreamed up an imaginative and effective strategy for persuading supporters to loan money to the candidate that would be repaid later.

He became hooked on politics during Anderson's 1980 campaign when he switched his party registration from Republican to Independent. After that campaign, he realized he was a Democrat at heart and switched again. As he cast about for a new project, he thought of Dukakis, then teaching at the Kennedy School at Harvard and readying for a comeback campaign in 1982. For progressives in Massachusetts, the rematch between King and Dukakis was nothing less than a holy war. They viewed King as the common lout who had slain the fair prince, Michael the Good.

Farmer arranged for a mutual friend to introduce him to Dukakis. Over lunch, he volunteered to be his finance chairman early in 1982. Dukakis was taken aback by the offer and demurred; he didn't even know this guy. Farmer then earned his title by raising money for Dukakis on his own. Three months later, Dukakis asked him to be campaign finance chairman for the 1982 campaign. Farmer helped raise $3.5 million for the campaign (compared to $600,000 without him in 1978).

Farmer ended up selling his publishing business for millions. He is a fit and energetic man with little to do and so he indulged his new love, politics, and became a full-time fund-raiser. He went from Anderson in 1980 to Dukakis in 1982 to treasurer of John Glenn's presidential campaign in 1984. He gradually evolved into one of the Democratic Party's most potent money-makers by the 1988 campaign, when he helped Dukakis and the Democratic Party break all fund-raising records and raise almost $100 million to underwrite the presidential campaign.

With Farmer firmly on Dukakis's side and the promise of sufficient funds to finance the campaign, the senior staff had the resources to establish field offices early in the key southern states of Florida and Texas; to spend the maximum allowed by law in Iowa and New Hampshire; to spend $2.2 million on the Super-Tuesday primaries, including $1.5 million in television and radio advertising; and to head north with $2 million left over when everyone else was broke.

It was a huge advantage. J. Joseph Grandmaison, the New Hampshire Democratic Party chairman, mused that it freed the Dukakis senior staff from making some hard choices. When the choice came between spending money on phones or television, they could do both. Bill Carrick, head of the fiscally strapped Gephardt effort, was impressed by the Dukakis campaign's resources. He could see the early organizational activity in places like Minnesota, Washington state, and Idaho. "They were not writing off any place," he said.

At 7:00 A.M. on March 16, 1987, the day Dukakis made public his decision to run for president, Sasso called Farmer at his Miami condominium. Kitty Dukakis called five minutes later. Farmer caught the first flight to Boston. He set up shop in a newly renamed "Presidential" suite at the elegant Meridien Hotel in Boston's financial district. He began by contacting each person on the 110-member Dukakis Finance Committee in Massachusetts. The committee was expanded to a 350-member presidential finance committee by recruiting the individuals who had given $1,000 to Dukakis's state campaign. The national finance committee eventually had 1,105 members, each of whom raised at least $10,000 for Dukakis. Kristen Demong, replicating a role she played in Dukakis's 1982 gubernatorial campaign, was the operational talent behind the fund-raising operation. With the diligence of a Repo man determined to repossess an automobile for failure to pay, she followed up on Farmer's contacts, closed the deals, and collected the checks.

Farmer was looking for established professionals, highly regarded in their own fields, who would be able to contact friends and relatives and raise money for Dukakis. It was Tupperware on a grand scale, with a political twist. Eventually, 900 people raised $10,000 for Dukakis from friends and acquaintances, 300 raised $20,000, 75 raised $50,000, and 23 raised $100,000.

To help him, Farmer recruited high-powered, persuasive, and dedicated individuals. He called them "ambassadors" and posted them to fertile constituencies. Alan Leventhal, a wealthy Boston real-estate mogul, signed on as second in command of the fund-raising operation. Nadine Hack, a wealthy, dedicated Democrat married to hotelier Jerry Dunfey, member of a well-known New England family, worked New York; George Danas, a Waltham businessman, and Peter Bassett, another Massachusetts businessman who owned a chain of Holiday Inns, worked the Greek community; Steve Grossman of the Massachusetts Envelope Company worked the Jewish community; John Battaglino, a Waltham businessman, went to California; Jon Rotenberg, a former state representative from Brookline who had worked on Soviet Jewry issues, went to Florida; Fred Alpert went to North Carolina, where he owned two furniture stores; Cathy Douglas Stone, widow of late Supreme Court Justice William O. Douglas, headed to her Washington-state home.

Battaglino had just sold his College Stores Associates bookstores chain to Barnes & Noble and, like Farmer, had the time and resources to devote himself to fund-raising. When Farmer called him, he was in Las Vegas with his son and three sons-in-law to attend the middleweight championship fight between Marvin Hagler and Sugar Ray Leonard. Farmer told him to forget the fight and join him in California, where he would have more fun helping him and Kitty set up a California fund-raising operation.

He left on the day of the fight and spent the next three days with Farmer and Kitty talking to people about raising money for Dukakis. On the third day, Farmer knocked on his hotel door and told him to stay a few days longer. Battaglino was incredulous, but he stayed fifteen months and raised $5 million for Dukakis in California, more than twice the $2.4 million raised by Mondale, a former vice president, in 1984.

One night over dinner at Grill 23, a fashionable Back Bay restaurant, early in the campaign, Senator John F. Kerry asked Farmer how much he expected to raise for Dukakis during the first federal reporting quarter. Farmer said he wanted to beat Joe Biden's $1.7 million first-quarter total and raise $1.8 million. You'll never do it, Kerry said. Farmer smiled smugly. Dukakis raised $4.5 million during the first quarter alone. At the beginning of the campaign, Farmer set modest goals that were routinely bested. He told Dukakis he could expect to raise $6.5 million by the time of the Iowa caucuses. In fact, the campaign had raised $17 million by that time.

Much of the money came from Massachusetts residents and Greek-Americans, the two financial mainstays in the Dukakis campaign. Although Greek-Americans make up only 1 percent of the United States population, they rank among the most generous in donating money to Greek-American politicians. It often seemed as though every Greek pizza-parlor owner in America was writing a check to Dukakis in 1987 and 1988.

Farmer raised the maximum allowed by law, $28.5 million for the primary campaign, well before the primary season ended. He labored under conditions stricter than those imposed by federal law. Dukakis refused all political action committee money, limited state employees' donations to $100, refused money from registered lobbyists, and forbade systematic solicitation of state contractors. He told Farmer that he should operate under the assumption that every person he approached for money would be interviewed by a news reporter. "Michael Dukakis taught me to be pristine," Farmer would often say.

Farmer traveled relentlessly, accompanied by two aides: the first handled logistics, the second sat in on each meeting and took notes. Farmer never once met alone with a potential contributor. With a watchful witness (usually Tony West, his chief of staff) always present there would never be a misunderstanding. The quid pro quo was not to be part of this campaign. Several times, wealthy men put in a request for an ambassadorship in return for a hefty donation. Once, a man asked for "an ambassadorship to an English-speaking country." Each time, Farmer abruptly ended the meeting and refused the money. The potential donor so eager for the English-speaking country later tried to give Farmer a $10,000 check to show he had no hard feelings. Farmer turned it away.

The presidential nominees receive $46 million from the federal Treasury for the general election. But Farmer helped raise $68 million for the Democratic Party's "Campaign '88" fund, which paid for get-out-the-vote work, generic party advertising, and party-building activity. In effect, it financed the field operation for the presidential campaign. Once again he labored under stringent conditions set by Dukakis: no corporate money, no PAC money, no union treasury money, no money from employees of government contractors, and no contributions greater than $100,000. The money was raised through direct mail, galas, and a major donor program. By the end, 148 individuals wrote personal checks for $100,000 each and 140 others raised $100,000 each. A committee of lawyers checked each contribution greater than $10,000. If they found a hint of impropriety, the contribution went back.

After the long campaign, Farmer was able to brag that Dukakis had not had to meet with more than five individuals or make more than five phone calls to raise money for a campaign that broke a Democratic fund-raising record.

With adequate financial backing, Dukakis could divide his time between his gubernatorial duties in Massachusetts and campaigning. The incremental nominating process and Devine's prescience conspired to build a head of momentum behind Dukakis's candidacy just as planned. Because the campaign had targeted the early contests, he acquired the image of the man to beat in the three weeks preceding March 8. The headlines were cumulative: victory in Maine; victory in Minnesota to match his loss to Gephardt's late television-commercial assault in South Dakota; victory in Vermont's primary; and a second place to Gore in Wyoming that was so close to a dead heat that some reported it in that way. Meanwhile, Babbitt had withdrawn, Gary Hart II existed only in media feature stories, Simon was out of the campaign except to help local Democrats win election as delegates from his home state, Illinois, and Gephardt was dangerously short of funds and exposed (because of his South Dakota gambit) to a full-scale Dukakis television assault in the Super Tuesday states.

As soon as Dukakis gave his permission, his media advisers went to work. Estrich had given ad man Ken Swope a list of Gephardt's political action committee contributions. Dukakis had refused to take any PAC money for his campaign, and Estrich thought the PAC list might provide fodder for an ad. Swope produced an ad showing the names of Gephardt's PAC contributors crawling across the screen like a televised Who's Who of corporate America.

They already had reason to believe this line of attack would work. Tubby Harrison had tested the PAC issue in a poll of Arkansas voters. When voters heard a description of a candidate like Gephardt, he drew 19 percent support. When they were told that this candidate accepted PAC contributions and had changed his positions on many major issues, the support thudded down to 4 percent.

Swope's PAC ad was aired in Texas and Florida a week before Super Tuesday. As the Dukakis high command hoped, Gephardt immediately dropped his populist message for a few critical days to respond to it. As soon as he did, Michael Shea and Daniel Payne, two other Boston-based ad men, weighed in with the coup de grace.

It was Shea's idea: find an acrobat, spray-paint his hair Gephardt strawberry blond, and show him flipping and flopping on the screen to represent Gephardt's shifts on issues. They auditioned gymnasts and chose a young man who looked a bit like Gephardt. They sprayed his hair, put him in a Robert Hall suit, white shirt, and red power tie. They rolled up his pant legs and then made him jump, flip, and flop for six hours. Payne came up with the idea of showing him diving head first through a circle. They used video tricks to make him go faster, slower, backward, forward. The ad was hilarious—and effective—because network newscasts magnified the effect by using both ads to illustrate stories on the shifting Gephardt positions.

The campaign bought time in areas where Gephardt was thought to be strong. Gore, meanwhile, borrowed heavily to do the same thing. Gephardt was being double-teamed and, being out of money, was unable to respond in kind. Gephardt's pollster, Ed Reilly, miserably watched the poll numbers tumble.

Despite having next to nothing to show from the February events, Albert Gore remained a force to be reckoned with in his native South, but as the campaign headed there the Tennessean's presence was discovered to be uneven; he was being pressed by Jesse Jackson everywhere in the Deep South, endangering his goal of being declared the clear winner of the day's southern and border-state contests, and Dukakis had the early advantage in the two largest states long ago understood by the

Dukakis campaign as just technically southern: Texas and Florida. Jesse Jackson also had a successful February. He demonstrated willingness to campaign hard everywhere but in South Dakota and Wyoming, and ability to press Dukakis in states where Simon's collapse made liberals willing to listen to somebody else, especially in Maine, Vermont, and Minnesota.

But even with the southern trends uncertain, his opponents' weaknesses had enabled Dukakis to close his fist over the rest of the Super-Tuesday landscape, with major delegate consequences. When Iowa gobbled up the Gephardt campaign treasury and organization, the congressman lost a golden opportunity to parlay support by House colleagues from Washington state into the kind of organization that could have done very well in its Super-Tuesday caucuses; the resulting vacuum was quickly filled by Dukakis. And above all, Maryland, the one primary directly electing delegates, with sixty-seven delegates at stake, was strongly contested only by Dukakis and Jackson.

The Dukakis campaign scared away the competition from Washington state and Maryland by pouring in major resources early. The other candidates bypassed the New England states of Massachusetts and Rhode Island, recognizing that they were firmly in Dukakis's corner.

From the earliest days in the campaign, Dukakis had targeted Texas and Florida for major efforts. Sasso had organizing rules which he pronounced regularly as a mantra and which were followed scrupulously. The first rule was to identify your base and lock it in, and the second was to reach out beyond your base. Dukakis targeted Mexican-Americans as his base in Texas, and Northeast retirees and Jews in Florida.

Texas posed special organizational problems because it was both a primary and a caucus state. Voters would vote in a primary to determine how 119 district-level delegates would be allocated and then, in a three-tiered caucus beginning with precinct caucuses that night, would determine who got the sixty-four statewide delegate slots. The initial goal was to get as many delegates as possible. No one in headquarters entertained the thought that Dukakis would carry Texas.

Early in 1987, while Dukakis was still exploring the possibility of running for president, top aide Nick Mitropoulos called Willie Velasquez, president of the Southwest Voter Registration Education Project, and told him that Dukakis was considering a run. Velasquez was a fiery, charismatic, and passionate leader whose work made him a heroic figure to Hispanics throughout the Southwest. He was universally viewed as the person most responsible for the rise of Hispanics to political power in the region.

Velasquez came to Boston for a meeting on January 19, 1987 with

Dukakis, Sasso, and Mitropoulos at the State House. Velasquez said that the governor drilled him for information on Mexican-American voters. Who are they? he asked. Where do they live? What motivates them? What do they care about? Whom do they respect? The Hispanic vote makes up as much as 25 percent of the Democratic primary vote in Texas. On Super Tuesday, Dukakis got 54 percent of the Hispanic vote in Texas, enough to give him the state. Velasquez stayed publicly neutral throughout the primaries, but after Dukakis won the nomination agreed to become a deputy campaign manager and work full time for the campaign even though he had just learned he was suffering from terminal cancer. But the cancer spread so rapidly that he died just three weeks later on June 15, 1988. Dukakis delivered the eulogy at his funeral mass in San Antonio.

The Texas terrain contained 19 media markets, 77 television stations, 254 counties, 6,800 precincts, and 31 senatorial districts. In October, Texas state director Tom Cosgrove hired six Texans. They built a centralized organization around a bank of personal computers.

Cosgrove, a professional operative who worked for Walter Mondale in 1984, set three goals for each Dukakis visit to Texas: build a big crowd to demonstrate excitement and popular appeal, deliver a message appropriate to Texas, and puncture expectations by going to a place where no one would expect a Massachusetts guy. In mid-October, Dukakis went to Longview, a community in conservative east Texas in the congressional district of the flamboyant Representative Charles Wilson. Wilson had let it be known he didn't think much of this guy from Massachusetts, whom he labeled a "pacifist Greek dwarf."

"No Greek dwarf can carry East Texas," he said.

On that October visit Dukakis delivered a national energy policy speech. The campaign taped the speech and flew the tape to Dallas. They bought satellite time and offered the tape to Texas television stations. Sixteen of the state's nineteen media markets picked up the speech. The message on energy was delivered statewide along with the subliminal message that Dukakis mustn't be a typical northern liberal because he was in East Texas, of all places. On Super Tuesday, the Greek dwarf carried Wilson's district and the state.

The campaign built its organization in the old-fashioned way, placing blocs of support one upon the other slowly, methodically, and relentlessly. They went after votes one at a time when they had to. Large states like Florida and Texas were conventionally viewed as states where voters would be more efficiently and effectively motivated by paid television advertising than phone banks, but the Democratic Party nominating system, based heavily upon a proportional-representation system, and the relatively crowded field conspired to reward this careful organizing.

Members of the Massachusetts political family and trusted friends went into the field. Jack Corrigan sent S. Stephen Rosenfeld, the governor's chief legal counsel and a lawyer with no political experience, and Paul Pezzella, an experienced political operative from central Massachusetts and one of the governor's legislative lobbyists, to Florida. Corrigan needled Rosenfeld by telling him that three things symbolized Florida—age, Jews, and crime—and Steve epitomized all three because of his prematurely gray hair, his Jewish heritage, and his criminal-justice expertise. Terry Bergman, a bright and dedicated thirty-five-year-old official from the state Office of Human Services and a Dukakis family friend, joined them.

Rosenfeld stuck closely to Sasso's golden rules for field organizing: identify your base and then reach out beyond your base. He identified the base as Broward County in south Florida, the most Democratic and fastest-growing county in the state. It had a large community of Jewish and northeastern retirees. The Tampa Bay area, with many New England retirees and a large community of Greek immigrants who worked in the sponge industry at Tarpon Springs, provided an additional opportunity.

Pezzella had a genius for spotting targets of opportunity. Ralph White, head of the Massachusetts Public Retirees Association, sent a letter to each of his members in Florida. The letter included a return card. The campaign received a stunning 80 percent response, and those former Massachusetts civil servants became the foundation of a Florida volunteer force.

Pezzella's field plan for the final thirty days was relentlessly detailed. Doubling shifts of phone-bank hours at fifteen locations, he also arranged for all the constituency-group leaders and elected officials who were supporting Dukakis to send letters to their associates. By election day the Dukakis campaign had identified 100,000 households favorable to Dukakis. During the final weekend in the Super-Tuesday campaign, the workers distributed 500,000 pieces of literature along the condo coast in south Florida.

Condos were the key in south Florida, and Terry Bergman set about organizing them. About 50,000 voters lived in the four Century Village condominium developments. The largest condo development in Deerfield Beach had 16,000 residents and 11,000 were registered Democrats. It enclosed eight precincts and two postal zip codes. The moderate-income condos were dominated by retired public employees, teachers, and transit workers with a history of political activism. In other words, they understood the relationship between the ballot box and a job and publicly financed benefits. They had thirty-nine Democratic clubs in Broward County and twenty-three in Palm Beach County. Bergman began to frequent the meetings until she became a familiar and welcome face.

Rosenfeld, taking advantage of his former title as chief legal counsel to the governor, acted as an ambassador to activists and key elected officials. He cultivated Bob Butterworth, the state Attorney General; Charlie Bryan, head of the machinists union; and LeRoy Collins, Democratic governor of Florida from 1955 to 1961 and chairman of the Democratic National Convention that nominated John F. Kennedy in 1960. The courtship paid off. Butterworth became chairman of the state campaign for Dukakis.

One week before the primary, Rosenfeld heard that Gephardt intended to hold a press conference in Tallahassee with twelve members of Congress who would then fan out across the state and campaign for him. Keeping with his "every day is its own campaign" philosophy, he went to bed worrying about how he would offset that good publicity for Gephardt. He woke suddenly at 4:00 A.M. with an idea and caught the 7:00 A.M. flight from Miami to Tallahassee. He went straight to the home of former Governor Collins and pleaded for a public endorsement. Collins agreed and wrote a letter dated March 3, 1988. "I am impressed with the strong qualifications of Michael Dukakis for the presidency," he wrote. "I will vote for him, and I hope that he is chosen by the people of Florida and the Nation, to be our next President. This is not a hasty or new decision. I have known Governor Dukakis for many years and have followed his career. . . . I believe he stands where the people of Florida want to stand."

Rosenfeld raced to a copy shop to duplicate the letter and then stuffed the copies himself into the mailboxes of the State House reporters at the state capital. The next day the Collins endorsement was the leading political story. In an unexpected stroke of luck, the Gephardt event never took place, and so Dukakis dominated the news.

By primary day the Dukakis campaign had spent five times more than any other presidential campaign on its field organization in Florida, $250,000. It had 200 telephones in use, 26 paid staff members, and more than 1,000 volunteers. The effort paid off. Dukakis won more than twice as many votes as his nearest competitor. He finished with 41 percent of the vote, followed by Jackson at 20 percent. Gephardt collapsed. He sagged 21 points in 12 days in Florida according to his own campaign polls and finished with 14 percent, followed by Gore at 13 percent.

On March 8, Pezzella, who was so exhausted that the dark circles around his eyes made him look like a raccoon, went to Sea Coast Towers, a condo complex in Miami Beach where Gephardt was speaking to the voters. Gephardt was endorsed by the district's legendary congressman, Claude Pepper, foremost champion of senior citizens in the U.S. House.

While Gephardt spoke, Pezzella nervously watched Dukakis volunteers hand palm cards to each person who alighted from a bank of elevators just yards away and directed each to a fleet of three dozen vehicles waiting to whisk them to the polls. He smiled to himself. He knew they would kill Gephardt and they did. Dukakis swept the 18th district, polling 15,188 votes to Gephardt's 4,325.

Even before February was over, three of the four corners spotted by John Sasso and Jack Corrigan a year before were secure: he held the front-runner's position in Florida, Maryland, and Washington state, and was able to concentrate resources in the final days on Texas. He was also able to treat the rest of the southern contests as a giant Chinese menu, carefully selecting the congressional districts most likely to produce delegates, rather than being forced like Gore and Gephardt to almost literally go for broke in trying to win states.

By the end, the senior staff, plotting from Tad Devine's original memo ranking each of the 171 Super-Tuesday congressional districts on a scale of one to five in importance for Dukakis, had targeted so carefully that Estrich coolly said no thanks to Bob Farmer's last-minute offer of an additional $2 million. Of the $2.2 million they spent on the twenty states, only $1.5 million went for media. Gephardt had only $687,000 to spend on the March 8 contests to $1.1 million for Gore. Gore's Tennessee address provided enough of a parochial appeal to make up for lack of cash. Jackson could count on his voters to get the message and get to the polls for him. He spent only $124,000.

"So far so good," Susan Estrich told us the night before the biggest primary day in American history. "We're looking for a super Tuesday."

She was almost right. Dukakis did not win Super Tuesday outright, but he did achieve his goals. His showing was equivalent to victory because the most important story on Super Tuesday was who lost (Gephardt), and who failed to win enough (Al Gore). Dukakis, Gore, and Jackson split the popular vote, but Dukakis edged the other two in delegates, winning 364 to Gore's 316 and Jackson's 354.

Communications Director Leslie Dach could anticipate from Tubby Harrison's uncannily accurate polling data how stunning Gephardt's defeat would be, as he and Gore exchanged places in state after state. Gephardt, he said, was going to finish a poor fourth in the overall balloting, but because of Jackson's strength in the Deep South, the prospect of a clear break-out by Gore seemed slight. Even more important, Dach pointed to the immense differences in the resources available to the three candidates once the dust cleared from the next day's ballot orgy: Dukakis would have $2 million in cash plus another $1 million in federal matching funds; Gore would be looking at a $1 million debt; and Gephardt would be at least temporarily broke.

To Tad Devine, author of the prescient targeting plan who had foreseen Super Tuesday better than anyone else months before, what counted was the way the race would look the next day. Gephardt and Gore, he told us, would be like football teams trailing late in a game—they would have to throw long, perfect passes: Gephardt bypassing Illinois for a last stand in Michigan's caucuses eighteen days later; Gore, probably forced to wait all the way until New York almost six weeks later unless he could establish himself somewhere else up North almost overnight.

"We've got the ground game," he said.

Devine also said Dukakis was beginning to score among the Super Delegates. The first breakthrough would be support by Colorado Governor Roy Roemer and state party chairman Buie Seawell, with that important western state's caucuses less than a month away.

As Super Tuesday night unfolded on television, the story was a big blob of numbers. Dukakis, however, was the early winner, when the prime-time audience was the largest, because of his easy-to-declare victories in the largest states; at home in Massachusetts, in Maryland, and in Texas and Florida. By contrast, Jackson and Gore were in tight contests in several southern states that weren't clearly resolved until quite late in the evening.

By the next day, however, the national story had become the Great Muddle. For the popular vote in the day's sixteen primaries, there was essentially a three-way tie: out of roughly ten million votes from more than 47,000 precincts, Jackson, Dukakis, and Gore in that order were within 65,000 votes of each other. Dukakis was first in the national delegate count with more than 450, and Jackson was just under 400 and Gore just under 350, a result that reflected Gephardt's inability to win any place but his home state, and his failure to even make the 15 percent threshold in states like Alabama, Arkansas, Georgia, Louisiana, Mississippi, North Carolina, and Virginia, where Jackson and Gore were able to divide much larger delegate pies.

"What's going on?" Jack Corrigan asked Devine's key associate, Susan Brophy, as the Jackson and Gore numbers kept swelling, aware that a simple claim of victory from the night's tabulating was not going to be so simple.

True, Dukakis had met his carefully framed goals with firsts in six of the twenty contests (Massachusetts, Rhode Island, Maryland, Texas, Florida, and Washington state); he had also come in second in Arkansas, Kentucky, and Nevada. After March 8, Dukakis's steadiness—a principal attribute for a marathoner—came to be appreciated as a huge advantage for him. Paul Maslin, the Simon strategist, described Dukakis as "Ol' Man River, he just kept moving along."

But Jackson had also finished strongly, and his strength was all the more noteworthy because he was decently positioned to do well in the two major coming events that month, in Illinois and Michigan. He won five southern states: Alabama, Georgia, Louisiana, Mississippi, and Virginia. And just as impressively, he finished second in nine others, including Texas (where he also battled Dukakis to a stand-off in evening caucuses that allocated half the state's pledged delegates), Florida, Massachusetts, Rhode Island, Maryland, Tennessee, North Carolina, Idaho, and Washington state.

Gore, meanwhile, was able to win only two Deep South states (Arkansas and North Carolina) to go with victories in Oklahoma, Nevada, his home state, Tennessee, and neighboring Kentucky. And he managed to finish second in five others: Alabama, Georgia, Louisiana, Mississippi, and Virginia. He had made his splash, but it was not the big one for which he had gone in debt.

And Gephardt, meanwhile, faded so badly that he could add only a distant second in Oklahoma to his victory in Missouri.

In some ways, the perfect metaphor for the Super-Tuesday numbers game were the caucuses on the tiny Pacific island, American Samoa. Only thirty-six people showed up, and they divided three delegate spots among Dukakis, Gephardt, and a lone Samoan, who remained uncommitted.

With less than a week to go before the megaprimary, the *Wall Street Journal* published a front-page article encapsulating the view, dominant at the time, of the Democratic race in the press and the political world that whatever might happen on Super Tuesday, the more important truth was that it was going to be almost impossible for any candidate to assemble a nominating majority; too many candidates were dividing up too many delegates, and after Super Tuesday there would not be enough delegates to be won in the remaining primaries to make a critical difference.

The day after the voting, this view was pounded home further in the overnight summary of the results by the Associated Press, as it had been on the network news specials the night before.

"The Democratic Presidential candidates on Wednesday found themselves stuck in a logjam of delegates in which nobody was likely to lock up the party's nomination when the primaries end in June," said the AP's opening paragraph. It concluded: "The odds are growing longer that any candidate can come up with the magic number needed to win on the first ballot at the Democratic convention in Atlanta."

In this and most other accounts, straightforward arithmetic was used to make the point. With Dukakis ahead in delegates on March 9, with 456.5, he would need to get another 1,625.5 to win the nomination, or 58 percent of the remaining pool, or roughly twice his support percentage thus far.

Tad Devine held a different view. His analysis was that between Super Tuesday and the end of April, several contests in large northern states would determine a first-ballot nominee, that during this period the Super Delegates' preferences would begin to be expressed, and that ultimately nearly all would move in the same direction. Accordingly, Devine felt that what counted most was not bragging rights about the Super-Tuesday results after a dozen proportional-representation primaries, but each campaign's condition as they all moved back up North. With Gephardt bleeding profusely and Gore unable to point to a northern state where he could do more than skirmish before New York's primary on April 19, Devine's conclusion was that the battle for the nomination was, as a practical matter, among Dukakis, Jackson, and a brokered nomination for somebody else (most likely to be Mario Cuomo). More simply, Devine believed Dukakis had the inside track to the nomination unless he blew it.

And he almost did.

5

The Last White Man

On March 9, 1988, the day after Super Tuesday, Jack Corrigan was sick
with the flu in Chicago. But even as he considered the terrain ahead
through bleary eyes, it looked smooth. He thought Albert Gore was a
short-timer now that the race had returned to the North; that Richard
Gephardt had been almost eliminated; that Paul Simon was an obstacle
only in Illinois. But he was worried about Jesse Jackson getting hot.
Jackson was the top story that night on the Chicago television stations;
he had momentum. Still, Corrigan felt Dukakis would win sooner or
later. "I could not figure out a strategy for the others to win the
nomination," he said. It was just a question of time.

Yet a strong sense of caution in the Dukakis high command tempered the elation at meeting their Super-Tuesday goals. "On March 9,"
said Tad Devine as he looked back at the post—Super-Tuesday landscape, "we thought the pressure on the other candidates to leave the race
would become enormous if we could sustain Dukakis through the
bumps on the road that were coming up ahead of us."

The bumps, however, would turn out to be large ones:first the
Illinois primary on March 15 and then the Michigan caucuses on March
26. The governor would face a genuine survival test in Wisconsin on
April 5, followed by presidential-sized temptations and challenges in the
wild New York political world before gliding for the remainder of the

primary season. Although he was the putative nominee after the New York primary on April 19, he had one more test to meet as the last white man standing against Jesse Louis Jackson, who insisted upon staying in the race to the end. An awkward racial reality kicked in as the minority candidate lost with monotonous regularity for six weeks.

The two men handled this sensitive situation professionally, but each put off the more important political challenge of making a deal that would enhance their party's chances of winning the White House. The result was an anticlimactic end to another tortuous Democratic primary season that set the stage for senseless competition for six more weeks until the Democratic National Convention.

Dukakis failed to use the precious time to deal with Jackson, to begin forging a relationship with the black voters he had neglected for too long, and to prepare for the assault on him from George Bush that every one of his senior advisers knew was coming. The urgings, the warnings were numerous, but Dukakis did not listen. The traditional mistake Democratic nominees have made in recent years has been their tendency to point too much toward managing the tumult in the national convention and too little toward the general-election campaign that begins the day after that convention.

For the nominee apparent, the path to victory had tested his stamina, his steadiness, and his political judgment; it had not, however, tested his ideas or subjected his long record as governor to scrutiny or subjected him to anything resembling the atmosphere of a general election. But for a while in March, it did expose many of his most damaging weaknesses.

After Super Tuesday, Devine's analysis assumed that the Illinois primary would be a problem. It was Paul Simon's home state and Jesse Jackson lived in Chicago. The Illinois system itself made a major Dukakis success unlikely. As one of the handful of "loophole" states still permitting direct election of delegates, the rules just about guaranteed Jackson a sweep in Chicago's overwhelmingly black congressional districts, and because Simon was both a southern Illinois-based politician and backed by Chicago's white Democratic power structure, it was very difficult to spot an opening in the state for an outsider in 1988.

On the other hand, Dukakis—no longer the regional candidate but a possible nominee—could not sit out any of the contests after Super Tuesday. Charlie Baker, dispatched to Illinois soon after his New Hampshire triumph, said, "You gotta be there." While Gephardt was making a desperate and valiant last stand in Michigan, Dukakis also had to make sure that his presence in Illinois kept Gore from making any unexpected northern breakthroughs on his way to New York.

The Illinois "loophole" primary system was a challenge for a campaign staff determined to steal at least a few delegates in the state. To make the best of the difficulty, Baker and his field director, Mike Whouley, another Massachusetts political operative, conceived a plan to sneak up on Simon and get on the statewide scoreboard through a handful of carefully chosen districts—those represented by Republicans, where the local Democratic organization was likely to be weak. They also aimed at the bottom of the Simon delegate slates in Chicago's congressional districts. The major slots had gone to local officeholders and politicians who would be impossible to defeat, but the rest of the Simon slots went to less well-known people, many of them fund-raisers. Because voters often stop marking ballots toward the bottom, the Dukakis campaign hoped that skillful organizing in the neighborhoods would produce some victories. It was a sensible plan. They intended to reevaluate it on the Friday before the primary and not make any heavy commitment to television advertising or raise Dukakis's in-person profile too high unless the governor's chances radically improved.

Initially his odds seemed to be on an upswing because Simon's national hopes had been destroyed in New Hampshire and Minnesota. Simon had remained in the race only at the behest of local Illinois politicians. Simon's image as a presidential candidate was weak and Dukakis's position as the possible nominee had piqued genuine voter interest. Big, boisterous crowds were showing up to hear the governor speak. At the same time, by the Friday before the primary, no clear evidence showed that Dukakis had a chance to get above third place and more than a handful of delegates. In Tubby Harrison's polling, Jackson had a solid base because of a lock on the black vote, which appeared to be about one-fourth of the likely primary electorate. Although Jackson's white support in a state where he is widely disliked was tiny, he seemed capable of getting 30 percent of the vote. Because of his wounded condition, Simon's position was harder to figure, but he was not an unpopular man. His polling lead slipped slightly going into the weekend, but it had not become a slide. Dukakis, meanwhile, had yet to crack 20 percent.

Everyone agreed with this view except Dukakis himself. The crowd response had convinced him he was hot and coming on strong. He insisted on an all-out push in the final days, including a $250,000-plus television investment that significantly raised not only his profile but also his stakes in the primary.

The commercial used for the final days made a purely political argument for Dukakis, the only time in the entire primary season when he asked people to vote for him for a reason that had nothing to do with his record or ideas. Over file footage of old political conventions, an announcer warned that "Some people would like to turn back the clock."

After a bow toward voters' power the announcer went back to the ominous and unnamed "they": "They say you must turn over that power to them at a brokered convention."

Arguing that Dukakis was the only person campaigning in every state, the commercial ended with the upbeat message that "On Tuesday, *you* can pick the next President."

It was vintage Dukakis and reflected his good-government, reformer roots. But in his campaigning Dukakis would not deliver the same message. He declined in press conferences that weekend to confirm that Simon was its target, even though the senator was saying five times a day that the convention would be brokered and that he wanted the Democrats in his home state to make him one of the big brokers. Just as important, the governor was not saying anything else that might generate enough attention to attract voters.

But Simon was still unsure about his lead over Jackson, and with Dukakis spending heavily on television, he decided on Sunday to play the ultimate trump card, always available in Chicago's polarizing political world—race. "The Dukakis game is to try and take votes away from me," said the usually progressive senator, "not so that Mike can be in first place, but so that Jesse can be first and knock me out of the ballgame."

Equating a vote for Dukakis with a vote for Jackson was the final push the Simon forces needed. The result in the popular vote was a decisive 42 to 32 percent margin for Simon over Jackson, while Dukakis slipped to 16 percent. Little consolation lay in Gore's being able to muster only 5 percent. Much worse, the Dukakis campaign was unable to elect even one delegate. From a national perspective, the real winner was the brokered convention that the governor campaigned and advertised against.

Contributing to the gnawing anxiety and frustration among Dukakis's top aides was the growing feeling that they were the target of a rotating band of snipers, not just the ever-present Jesse Jackson: Simon in Illinois, Gephardt in Michigan, Gore probably in Wisconsin. Senators, congressmen, governors, and state party chairmen were just waiting for some kind of clear-cut if not decisive post—Super-Tuesday Dukakis victory to start creating a bandwagon effect with endorsements and calls for unity, but the site for that clear-cut, decisive victory was proving maddeningly elusive.

"We're gonna win," Leslie Dach muttered the day after the Illinois voting, "but it could be a long spring."

Michigan had never been one of Tad Devine's carefully defined targets of opportunity, for two reasons. The first was its caucus system, which used proportional representation and sharply limited the extent to which a winning candidate could garner a significant plurality of the delegates (138). The second was Gephardt, whose tough stance on trade had endeared him to the state's powerful trade-union movement, especially the United Auto Workers, whose local leaders toiled hard for him. As of March 1, the Dukakis campaign had spent barely $25,000 of the more than $360,000 it would eventually invest in the caucuses.

But staying away was never an option for Dukakis. As the coming front-runner, he had to face the voters everywhere. He also had to take care in every post-Illinois contest that none of the also-rans, and especially not Gore, finished ahead of him. When the polls in Michigan showed Gephardt's support falling off markedly after his Super-Tuesday collapse, the state became winnable for Dukakis.

The Michigan caucuses, however, became a parody—a front-runner standing smugly on a platform of sand.

Dukakis began the week leading up to the caucuses on Saturday, March 26, by accepting endorsements by several local and state politicians, including Senator Donald Riegle. To secure Riegle's support, Dukakis agreed to publicly back the Senate version of the still-pending trade legislation which Riegle had co-sponsored, and which prescribed less drastic responses to documented cases of unfair trading practices than did Gephardt's House-passed amendment.

Though Dukakis had said the previous summer that he supported the Senate version of the trade bill, it was also true that he had said next to nothing about it since then, and in strongly criticizing Gephardt's amendment he had often said that the country needed an effective president, not new legislation. His embrace of Riegle's views just before the caucuses was therefore close enough to a flip-flop to earn the governor a steady diet of negative press stories. It was exactly the kind of political deal Dukakis had avoided throughout his campaign.

In a move that further enhanced his image as a smug front-runner, the governor left Michigan for two days before the caucuses to collect a major endorsement in the East (New Jersey Senator Bill Bradley), to confirm that he had begun talking seriously to Mario Cuomo, and to fly out to California to attend fund-raisers. Midway through this odyssey, a refueling stop in Detroit to accept more endorsements and outline his views on illegal drugs cast off the scent of condescension.

In contrast to Dukakis, Jackson took nothing for granted and never left the state. His Michigan campaign was managed by Joel Ferguson, a politically active developer from East Lansing, who played the caucus system like a violin for the Reverend. Ferguson spent his time and money organizing blacks all over the state, not just in the two overwhelmingly black congressional districts in Detroit. Because turnout for caucuses is much lower than for a formal primary, he reasoned that a high showing of black voters could produce victories nearly anywhere. To add to that base, he concentrated on communities with sizable populations of college students. The system itself facilitated his task because it was so easy for a voter to participate in a caucus. In practice, it resembled a primary. Instead of sitting through a two-hour meeting, a citizen simply had to show up at a polling place, mark a ballot, and leave. The Democratic Party's eligibility rules, moreover, were much less stringent than state voter-registration laws. But above all, Ferguson's candidate was a dervish of excitement in person, wisely scheduling events more outside Detroit than inside it, packing high-school gymnasiums, union halls, and churches, and campaigning night and day without significant competition from the underscheduled Dukakis.

Nonetheless, Dukakis appeared on the verge of victory as caucus day—a blustery, bleak, cold Saturday—dawned. He had editorial backing from the major Detroit newspapers and Gephardt was faltering. The public polls indicated a close race for the popular vote mostly because of Jackson's presumed dominance of Detroit despite Mayor Coleman Young's endorsement of Dukakis. But the polls showed Dukakis very narrowly ahead, and private samplings by the Gephardt and Dukakis camps actually showed the governor with a lead of 10 to 15 percentage points. The polls were all taken with a measure of skepticism, especially by the pollsters themselves, because of the vagaries in the caucus system, but it was almost universally assumed that with Jackson's support likely to be concentrated in Detroit, Dukakis's more even performance throughout the state would give him a plurality of the delegates at stake.

Almost from the beginning that Saturday, the ever-alert Dukakis field organization sensed trouble. Turnout in Detroit was massive. The Jackson campaign used buses and vans to bring thousands of people to the caucus sites. But reports that truly caused consternation told about the same kind of activity on a smaller scale in communities all over the sprawling state. As official results trickled into state Democratic headquarters in Lansing, it was apparent by mid-evening that Jackson was going to win big. Results came slowly because of the big vote and because some party officials sat on their results to keep clear signs of the Jackson victory off prime-time television. Ultimately, it was the Dukakis campaign, making a gracious gesture despite its gloom, which provided reporters with the information that made it possible to get the Jackson triumph into Sunday newspapers around the country.

For the front-runner, the numbers were awful: Jackson won the popular vote by 54 to 29 percent: 113,832 to 61,750. In his last hurrah, Gephardt got 13 percent. Using a conventional political strategy, Dukakis had aimed at matching the vote Walter Mondale had received to win the caucuses in 1984, and had exceeded it. This was the same strategic assumption that caused him to underestimate the Iowa caucus turnout earlier in the year. But even more astonishing was that Jackson beat Dukakis in delegates, 74 to 55, with nine for Gephardt. Ferguson's organization so dominated Dukakis's throughout the state that Jackson finished first in eleven of the state's eighteen congressional districts.

Back in Boston, Jack Corrigan tried to console his colleagues with an important point: Gephardt—once the most potentially dangerous foe up North—was now out of the race. Also, despite a targeted effort in Michigan's less populated communities in the northern part of the state, Gore had once again come up empty-handed. The raw numbers, moreover, did not tell the full story about Michigan. For example, 80 percent of Jackson's 52,000-vote margin came from Detroit's two majority-black congressional districts, and most of the rest came from black Democrats and university community members in smaller cities. In the heavily blue-collar communities surrounding Detroit, and in Macomb and St. Clair counties, where unemployment was relatively low, Jackson ran a distant third.

This was no time for consolation, however. As Dukakis's aide-de-camp Mitropoulos said with characteristic bluntness and accuracy, "Three strikes and you're out in this business." Dukakis had now whiffed in Illinois and Michigan, and the next stop was a state with a liberal Democratic Party membership, Wisconsin.

Jackson's victory unleashed a media storm of bottled-up, barely suppressed resentment against Dukakis: He's aloof; he's arrogant; he can't communicate with working people; he's all politics and no message. The brokered convention talk was revived, the Mario scenarios dusted off. Even allowing for the hype that infects all journalism, it was a richly deserved consequence of his March behavior. And to make matters worse, the Michigan results hit Washington on the Saturday night when the city's journalistic-political-governmental elite were having their annual Boys' Night Out at the Gridiron Club dinner.

Among those in attendance was John Sasso, who had wangled a late ticket earlier in the week. For more than five months, he had endured the tortures of exile in dignified total silence, and now, with Dukakis readying a final surge toward the nomination he had wanted to be visible for an evening, and it turned out to be the night the roof fell in on his candidate. When some columnists subsequently suggested he might return to rescue the campaign in its moment of trial, that only added insult to the self-inflicted injury. Far behind the scenes, however, Sasso's return was a question that had never really disappeared, and every so often an aide would urge Dukakis to think about it; he had always been dismissive, but within a few weeks he would begin to hear from campaign chairman Paul Brountas and Sasso himself.

Susan Brophy, Tad Devine's deputy, finally got back to her Boston apartment around midnight Saturday, long after the size of the Michigan debacle was clear. She had no sooner gotten in the door when the telephone rang. It was Anne Campbell calling from Washington, D.C. She is a Democratic National Committee member from the District of Columbia and a Super Delegate, one of the automatic 643 voting delegates to the national convention.

Already dispirited by Dukakis's defeat in the Michigan caucuses, Brophy was also feeling low because she knew that the operation she ran for the campaign, courting and counting delegate and other political support for Dukakis, would have to go on hold. The elaborate wooing of political endorsements was now a major symptom of all that was wrong with the Dukakis campaign, and at least through the New York primary on April 19 (assuming all went well and Dukakis started winning again) the governor would have to concentrate on reaching individual voters.

That Saturday night, Anne Campbell had called Brophy to get the latest Michigan numbers and to chat with a political friend.

"We talked about what a hit Dukakis had taken and how it was going to be worse in the press for the next several days, and I offered my own view that maybe he had one coming," Campbell later recalled. "But Susan was sounding so down, and while I hadn't really decided when I wanted to make my commitment I had been planning to be for Governor Dukakis for some time. So I told Susan to put me in her official delegate count the next day; she thought I was kidding at first, but she was so warm and grateful. I felt good, too."

Campbell was only one Super Delegate, but to Brophy's keen antennae, it was a signal that Dukakis's foundation of support remained strong. The next few days would prove Brophy and other senior campaign officials correct. Moreover, no sign of a Jackson surge was visible in the upcoming states: Connecticut, which voted on March 29; Colorado, on April 7, and above all Wisconsin, on April 5. Their interpretation of the Michigan results and the press criticism of Dukakis was that Dukakis needed to be a better candidate. He could not appear to be ignoring legitimate criticism that he was not connecting to working-class Democrats, that he was not identifying with the people who had not benefited from the unevenly distributed Republican prosperity and were worried about their economic future, that he was not spelling out anything that could give an undecided rank-and-filer a strong reason to vote for Michael Dukakis.

Pollster-strategists Tom Kiley and Tubby Harrison judged that Dukakis needed to think, not panic.

When Tom Kiley really needs to think, he often walks to his

downtown Boston office from his home in the Jamaica Plain neighborhood. It is a five-mile, seventy-five-minute respite from the telephone
and other office interruptions. On Sunday, March 27, Kiley's first
thoughts as he arose were that Dukakis was not facing a huge crisis, that
he needed some changes in style and emphasis. He doubted that polling
data he had received from Wisconsin the day before the Michigan
caucuses, showing roughly a twenty-percentage-point Dukakis lead
over Jackson, would change radically. By the time he had trudged
downtown he was fairly certain of his position, and Estrich (after five
months of constant, close association she called him "my new best
friend") agreed with him.

Their assessment was supported by the latest batch of polling
numbers from Tubby Harrison, and his interpretation of them. Unlike
Kiley, Harrison is a coiled spring of intensity, a night owl who broods
through his analyses. When he first moved to political candidates from
doing polls for the media, Harrison's reputation made him the kind of
guy you wanted numbers from without a lot of fancy analytical foot-
work. By 1988, his uncannily accurate record and his penetrating,
increasingly confident analyses had raised his profile considerably.
Campaign associates fondly claimed that with his bald dome and near-
sighted eyes magnified by thick eyeglasses, he looked strikingly like the
lovable extraterrestrial, ET. He also had help from two brilliant, up-
and-coming analysts from upstate New York, Clifford Brown of Union
College, and Lynda Powell from the University of Rochester.

The first test was Connecticut, where Jackson had impulsively
ventured following his Michigan triumph and was, Brophy aptly said,
in "a life-threatening situation." An exhausted Dukakis went to New
Haven that Sunday morning to address fellow Greek-Americans at a
church hall. "Yesterday we had a tough fight in Michigan," said the
visibly tired candidate. "I did not do quite as well as I hoped. As father
said to me over and over again," here he switched from English to Greek
to recite an ancient Greek proverb, "The sweetest honey is made only
slowly." According to Harrison, Dukakis's lead over Jackson had sagged
slightly on Sunday to roughly twenty percentage points after the news
about Michigan broke, but with Dukakis campaigning hard in Connecticut that very day, the lead was back up to nearly thirty points by
Monday. Causing more uneasiness were his first Wisconsin data following Michigan, which showed the governor ahead by the shaky
margin of eight points, which meant it was not yet clear how strong the
Jackson surge would be.

Tuesday morning was Dukakis's first full day back in Massachusetts since the Michigan defeat, and the first opportunity for a full-blown
meeting with his campaign staff. These meetings occurred informally,

after a more formal session to go over his recommended schedule for the next week or two. On this morning, however, Estrich went in to see him alone, and was then joined by Kiley, Corrigan, Dach, and Brountas. Dukakis was unusually relaxed as he joked with his advisers about their misplaced confidence the week before.

"Well," he clucked, "We were really geniuses until Saturday at five o'clock, weren't we?"

Estrich's early arrival to meet with Dukakis alone was as unusual as the two-page memorandum she brought with her, outlining a recommended strategy for the week ahead in Wisconsin. Among its principal recommendations: spend the rest of the week in Wisconsin, with no side trips; campaign hard and visibly in blue-collar cities and towns; raise the specter of four more years of Republican rule; produce a new television commercial with a strong message stressing the harm done working people by President Reagan's economic policies, and, using Dukakis's voice and image, identify more directly with working people's anger: promise to save jobs, not merely create them; continue avoiding attacks on Jackson but emphasize the choice to be made between them and invite voters to make it; and call a halt to endorsement prospecting.

Dukakis liked the ideas, making business-like nods as he read through the recommendations. He asked to see the advertisement copy when it was ready as well as the texts of three speeches, two major ones plus his basic remarks for routine appearances. Then he silently ripped the memorandum into shreds and threw them in a wastebasket, in keeping with his belief that campaign documents should be absorbed by the candidate and not preserved for journalists and other instant historians.

A Wisconsin victory would be up to Dukakis himself. Unlike many other places, the Dukakis campaign had little on the ground in Wisconsin. A few weeks before the Michigan caucuses, Corrigan, frustrated when he continually got no answer from the Wisconsin Dukakis office, flew out there and discovered that the campaign had only one rotary dial telephone. They hadn't allocated enough money to the state. He immediately moved twelve people in; after the Michigan caucuses, he again stepped up the pace.

Dukakis got to Milwaukee on Wednesday in time to make a tough speech at Marquette University, aimed at liberals and denouncing the Reagan administration's policies in Central America. At that time, he knew—courtesy of Tubby Harrison—that his lead in the state had opened up again into double digits. One reason appeared to have been the results in Connecticut's primary. Having raised the stakes by campaigning there, Jackson suffered a setback, albeit one on Dukakis's New England turf, losing to Dukakis by a thirty-point, 58 to 28 percent

margin. The result, however expected, was prominently displayed in
the Wisconsin press that night and the next day. With a deluge of
publicity still pouring into print and onto the air about Jackson, the large
lead Dukakis was building in Harrison's Wisconsin polls might have
been a powerful media counterforce. Dukakis's aides, however, privately reasoned that the bigger Jackson became in the press, the harder
he would fall, and Dukakis would rise if Harrison's data were accurate.
In its preprimary polls, the Wisconsin press was showing a much closer
race, a natural cause for internal alarm, but Harrison was riding as hot
a hot streak as a pollster ever had in the primaries, and the Dukakis high
command had not the slightest doubt that he was right on the money
again.

   For the national political press corps already encamped in Milwaukee, the alleged big moment for Dukakis was a speech his campaign had
scheduled in Serb Hall, the rebuilt temple of ethnic Democratic political
fable on the city's South Side. The speech was crafted mainly by his
campaign speechwriter, William Woodward, a quiet, bookish Capitol
Hill veteran who had been Massachusetts Congressman Gerry Studds's
administrative assistant, and who could write words to fit Dukakis's
difficult-to-follow, stop-and-go delivery style. Sasso thought Woodward was a genius and had recruited him to the campaign early. The
speech condemned the Reagan administration's overall economic record
and affirmed Dukakis's approach to government stressing balanced
economic growth steered toward regions left behind, guaranteed financial aid to all students eligible for college, called for a legal requirement
that employers provide basic health insurance for their workers, and
recommended emphasis on nonmilitary research and development over
Star Wars. These ideas were collected under the banner of "We've got
a future to build."

   From the national political reporters' vantage point, the speech was
at best a ho-hummer and more likely to be a flop. After all, with Jesse
Jackson supposedly on a national roll, and already drawing unheard-of
crowds in his first appearances around the state, the assumption was that
Dukakis would have to do something to match Jackson in the charisma
department or risk getting rolled over by this suddenly massive force.
Less heed was paid to a minority view in the press, based on hints from
Dukakis advisers, that his situation in Wisconsin was actually strong and
that the best strategy was not trying to match Jackson in either passion
(not possible) or liberal substance (impolitic), but instead to offer a
reassuring picture of someone who might make a good, confidence-
inspiring president and help working people.

   Dukakis also scored big in the all-important Wisconsin press with
his opening lines that night, referring to a local political development.

Wisconsin's primary, dating to the progressive movement at the turn of the century, is "open," meaning that any registered voters, of any party affiliation, may vote in whichever primary they choose. With the Republican nomination of George Bush now a foregone conclusion, the time was thus ripe for partisan mischief, such as tacit or overt encouragement of Republicans to vote for Jackson in the Democratic primary. The state's new Republican governor, Tommy Thompson, spoke glowingly of the excitement that had been generated by Jackson's campaign, remarks widely seen as a barely veiled invitation to Republican voters to cross over and vote for him. The danger in such maneuvers, though, is that they can be too cute, and this time they inspired a widespread backlash from Democrats able to accuse Thompson of meddling and encouraging people to use their vote for president in order to do mischief. As the Dukakis campaign saw it, the Thompson maneuver was also a backhanded way of acknowledging that the governor was the Democratic nominee whom Republicans feared most.

Accordingly, Dukakis opened his Scrb Hall speech by announcing that he was sending Governor Thompson a New England lobster with a note: "Dear Tommy, Many thanks for reminding the voters of Wisconsin that George Bush doesn't want to face me in November." That little opening, as intended, and not the presence or absence of passion in his prepared remarks, dominated the printed and broadcast reports on his appearance that night. No one knew at the time that the idea for that aside came from another fellow governor, Mario Cuomo, related to John Sasso in exile and passed on to Jack Corrigan and thence to Dukakis.

That night, Dukakis's television commercials began their heaviest bombardment of the electorate. In an ad produced by Ken Swope were photographs of working people who had suffered economic setback during the Reagan years: a farmer standing behind the auction sign for his dairy farm, factory gates carrying the sign "No Applications Accepted," an unemployment line, factory workers with folded arms glaring angrily at the camera, two little girls searching for food in a garbage can. As the pictures flashed on the screen, Dukakis said, "The human cost of seven years of Republican indifference is staggering. Who in this Republican administration could look right into the eyes of the laid-off factory worker or the homeless family . . . and say they had kept the promise of America?"

The commercials carried more weight than any Dukakis had so far aired in the primary season, not because their content was especially powerful or even different; they were special because this time the projected image of Dukakis was being reinforced all over the state by a dogged campaigner reaching for every hand and vote. The governor's schedule was as brutal as Jackson's, offering no evidence of confidence, much less smugness, as he rushed from audience to audience of mostly blue-collar workers and their families from Green Bay to Kenosha, from Racine to Oshkosh, from Waukesha to the state capital in Madison. In these appearances, Dukakis typically was all alone on a small stage after a brief introduction from a local Democrat, without a supporting cast of endorsement-offering pols. He would make relatively brief remarks and then take questions after inviting his audience to imagine he was already president and to ask questions they'd put to their president if they could.

Two days before the primary, the campaign had to face a scheduling dilemma over whether to make a quick dash to Colorado before the caucuses that would be held there on Monday. The initial Colorado results would be reported in Wisconsin while people were voting in the primary. That Jackson decided to go himself helped decide the issue for Dukakis, who made a quick trip out and back on Sunday after receiving reports that although Jackson could expect a strong showing in Denver and the university community in Boulder, the governor's campaign appeared in fairly strong shape despite a late start. On Monday evening, fairly quick reports came from caucuses in the Denver area, showing a modest Dukakis lead, but then the counting slowed to a crawl and Jackson began to complain that the results were being withheld by the Dukakis-supporting state party machinery to keep news of a presumed Jackson victory from reaching the voters in Wisconsin. The reports of Jackson's ire did not last more than a few hours before Estrich was on the telephone to Gerald Austin, Jackson's campaign manager. Dukakis's superabundance of campaign money made possible a world-class vote-canvassing operation that regularly provided it with vital information hours before official figures reached the press and other campaigns. Armed with a good cross-section of caucus results from all over Colorado, Estrich was able to tell Austin that Dukakis was going to win the caucuses by a clear margin, information that Austin used to stop the complaints from Jackson and thus to spare him embarrassment when the official figures were released.

As it turned out, though, events in Colorado had no effect on events in Wisconsin. The Wisconsin results came in a landslide almost precisely along the lines Tubby Harrison had foreseen. The overall numbers for the top three were impressive enough: 470,000 votes, or nearly 48 percent for Dukakis; 280,000 votes, or roughly 28 percent for Jackson; and 170,000 votes, or barely 17 percent for Al Gore, just enough to get him over the threshold to win delegates in seven of the state's nine congressional districts, though again a very weak showing because he had unloaded another sizable bundle of precious campaign dollars on television advertising.

The victory was a true triumph for Dukakis. Jackson carried one congressional district, the Milwaukee-dominated fifth, which had the largest black vote in the state, beating Dukakis by 48 percent to 36 percent. Outside that district, he was barely ahead of Gore, while Dukakis was beating him by roughly two to one. In Dane County, dominated by liberal Madison, where Dukakis had matched Jackson in a battle of the crowd counts at windup rallies the day before, Dukakis won by more than 8,000 votes.

Even more impressive were the majorities Dukakis piled up in the economically hurting blue-collar towns where Jackson had concentrated not just the previous week but in Wisconsin appearances dating back more than a year. The classic example was Kenosha, site of a Chrysler plant that company Chairman Lee Iacocca had announced he intended to close to a chorus of charges of sellout led by Jackson. After a well-attended meeting with local United Auto Workers Union members the preceding Saturday, which Dukakis followed up with a telegram to Iacocca asking him to reconsider his decision, the governor carried this symbolic bastion of blue-collar hurt by two to one. A two-week bath in the boiling cauldron of New York still lay ahead for Dukakis, but in the afterglow of his victory, even the most diehard Mario scenario writers in the political press did not hedge on what the Wisconsin primary's verdict meant: Michael Dukakis was a half-step away from clinching the Democratic nomination.

She was now only thirty-five, but Susan Estrich had twice already experienced the electric insanity in the modern New York Democratic presidential primary up close. Eight years before, she had helped Edward Kennedy parlay a Jimmy Carter goof (an abstention on an anti-Israel United Nations resolution) and a minirecession into a come-from-behind victory that kept Kennedy's nearly hopeless campaign alive; and in 1984, then preparing to help Congresswoman Geraldine Ferraro write the Democratic Party platform for that year's San Francisco national convention, she had watched with chagrin as Walter Mondale shouted to the skyscraper tops that he was more reliably committed than Gary Hart to moving the American embassy in Israel to Jerusalem. In her view, which she related to Dukakis crisply as they prepared to enter the most infested media snakepit in American politics, the New York primary would not be so much a contest for first place— which she thought Dukakis could nail down rather easily simply by keeping his cool while all around him were losing theirs—as it would be a test of his character and his political soul.

Nothing was more damaging to national Democrats in the Reagan era than the perception that they practiced special-interest group politics, that they would rent or sell little chunks of themselves to secure endorsement from this politician or that labor union at the expense of the broader public interest.

Dukakis had come through the primary season unscathed. He was vulnerable to the accusation that his national-policy ideas were vague in some key areas, but he had steered clear of extensive commitments, particularly the kinds that might cost taxpayers money or require an actual tax increase. And with a few exceptions as reminders of how painful the practice can be—notably his reendorsing the Senate version of the 1988 trade bill just before Michigan Senator Donald Riegle endorsed him—there had been almost no trading of promises or new positions for political support.

In the hothouse New York world, however, the past, willpower, and careful plans count for nothing. Dukakis was about to be tested by two powerful forces: Governor Mario Cuomo and the Middle East maelstrom-politics.

Some fourteen months before, Cuomo's decision not to be a candidate in the primaries cleared away the last obstacle to Dukakis's own candidacy. The mercurial governor, though, had never been able to completely let go of the possibility that he would become the nominee should none of the candidates come to the national convention with enough delegates to win. Whenever necessary, usually because of some statement by him that seemed to fan the embers of this possibility, the governor would make it clear that he would not run, that he did not expect a deadlock that would require brokering, and could not imagine how the nomination could go to someone who had not faced the voters. On the other hand, when pressed, Cuomo would answer hypothetical questions: in December 1987 he said that if his party's national leaders came to him as a group and implored him to be a candidate after a round of inconclusive primaries, he would not refuse. For most of 1987, these types of comments were very few because it was Cuomo's private judgment that Dukakis appeared to be the strongest candidate. After his *paisan* John Sasso (whom Cuomo thought was a world-class politician) resigned, however, the Dukakis candidacy no longer seemed so secure and Cuomo began to make more obvious noises.

After Dukakis came through the Super-Tuesday round of primaries with a small plurality of the delegates and headed north, where the most plausible route to victory lay in the coming industrial state contests, Cuomo again faced the issue of whether he would endorse him. While Cuomo raged at his inability to say anything about the presidential campaign without having the media read something into his remarks on his own possible candidacy, he commented with enough frequency to encourage those media interpretations. On a brief speaking trip of his own into southern Texas, however (Texas being one of those tea leaves no reporter could resist reading), Cuomo seemed to signal that an endorsement was not likely. By not endorsing he could avoid angering the other candidates' camps in New York, especially Jesse Jackson's. Cuomo also genuinely considered his endorsement presumptuous in the 1988 context. At the same time, he indicated he would keep his mind open in case political conditions changed. If Dukakis seemed home free by the end of March, he would probably hop aboard the bandwagon.

Shortly, before the March 26 Michigan caucuses, it appeared to Cuomo that conditions might in fact have changed, and in a telephone conversation with Dukakis the two men agreed they should talk in more depth through intermediaries. Cuomo designated his son, Andrew, a New York lawyer who frequently handled political matters for his father; Dukakis designated Estrich. Their first meeting in Manhattan on Thursday, March 24, went well. The next day, however, Andrew Cuomo called her in Boston and mentioned two troubling subjects. New York's black and Jewish communities, like so many others around the country, were at political odds and were preparing for a fresh round of conflict over Jesse Jackson, who advocated a Palestinian state and international administration for Jerusalem. Jackson had been suspiciously regarded by many New York Jews ever since he referred to New York City as Hymietown in 1984. Cuomo felt that New York City's polarizing Mayor Ed Koch might inject his egocentric personality into the conflict, and was eager to maintain his good relations with both sides. As a political leader with rare ability to broker difficult situations, Governor Cuomo's uneasiness was genuine.

On the telephone that Friday, Andrew Cuomo asked Estrich to consider recommending that Dukakis take two steps well before the April 19 primary. The first would be to publicly put Jackson on a "short list" of his potential running mates. The second was to make a shift away from Dukakis's previous qualified endorsement of a letter that thirty senators (many of them with unassailably strong pro-Israel records) had sent Israeli Prime Minister Yitzhak Shamir criticizing his unyielding position that Israel must retain the occupied West Bank and Gaza Strip, and criticizing his army's brutal handling of Palestinian demonstrations that had been attracting worldwide attention for months. To Estrich, it was clear that Governor Cuomo was to get credit for making Dukakis more supportive of two of his major constituencies (blacks and Jews together split roughly 50 percent of the vote in a typical statewide primary). Estrich informed Dukakis, and added her recommendation that this was precisely the kind of politics—the merits of the matters aside—that had so damaged Mondale's image in 1984. Dukakis agreed.

Twenty-four hours later, of course, the issue was moot. Right after

Dukakis lost the Michigan caucuses, Cuomo aides and then the governor himself made it clear that there would be no preprimary endorsement.

Dukakis, however, was far from free of the Middle East quicksand. As the primary neared, Al Gore, making his last stand, tried hard to cut into Dukakis's increasingly strong hold on a solid majority among Jewish Democrats in the state by moving closer to Shamir's positions. To his later regret, Gore undercut his thirty colleagues by criticizing the senators' letter, made it clear that as president he would never countenance formation of a Palestinean state on the West Bank, and beat Dukakis to the dubious distinction of capturing the endorsement of Koch, who declared (to *his* later regret) that Jewish voters would have to be "crazy" to support Jesse Jackson. Within New York's Jewish community and within the Dukakis campaign, Dukakis began getting strong advice to rule out countenancing a Palestinian state. Language making that clear was written into a major speech Dukakis was scheduled to give on April 11 to the prestigious Council of Presidents of Major American Jewish Organizations.

Dukakis considered the advice much more seriously than he had Cuomo's requests, but in the end he emphatically crossed out the paragraph at issue. As a potential president, he believed that the United States should not try to impose any peace settlement on an unwilling Israel; however, as a potential president, he also believed that chances for peace would be best advanced if the United States threw its great weight behind unconditional negotiations. In other words, he believed that the United States should not rule out anything that negotiation might even conceivably produce, and that included the possibility of a Palestinian state.

"I couldn't say that, I wouldn't say that," he told us a month later during a flight over the Midwest. "After twenty-five years in this business, you learn over time that you've got to be yourself."

As it was, Dukakis hardly ventured more than a millimeter from pro-Israel orthodoxy in his speech. He blamed Arab leaders' intransigence for the atmosphere that had produced the Palestinian uprising; he repeated a view he first expressed in 1977 that "Israel needs room to breathe" and thus should not be required to accept pre-1967 war borders; and he ruled the Palestine Liberation Organization out of peace negotiations until it explicitly renounced its own covenant equating peace with dissolution of Israel.

Millimeters count in New York on this issue, however, and Dukakis got no credit, and more than a little criticism, for his position, as well as for a flub during the question period corrected outside the auditorium, in which he seemed not to support Israeli sovereignty over Jerusalem. Critics included not only Gore, but another visitor to New

York that week, George Bush. At the same time, though, Dukakis retained the support he already had, long nurtured and bolstered by his wife's strenuous campaigning in public and in private; her Jewish heritage earned her nine mentions in her husband's speech to the Council of Presidents.

As the campaigns prepared for the final week, Dukakis at long last got something of a break from Mario Cuomo. To wipe out the last flicker of confusion about his hopes and intentions, Cuomo finally said categorically, ten days before the primary, that he would not accept the party's presidential nomination, not even if it were offered him on a silver platter at or before the national convention in Atlanta. The prize, Cuomo said, should go to a candidate who had earned it on the stump, and in his mind that candidate was going to be Dukakis; his Massachusetts colleague was, furthermore, apt to be a stronger nominee for *not* having needed Cuomo's endorsement.

The New York campaign's final week found Dukakis a clear frontrunner, but far from a shoo-in, and vulnerable to a mistake and to a strong message from his right by Senator Gore. The more reputable public polls showed Dukakis drawing low- to mid-forties support from the likely primary electorate, with Jackson about ten points back, and Gore fluctuating between 10 and 15 percent. From the polls, Jackson did not appear to have much of a shot at the 5 to 10 percent of the polling samples who remained undecided, which meant that the critical variables would be the size of the Gore vote and the black and Jewish voter turnouts. In Jackson's camp, the slender hope for a stupendous upset rested on Gore's receiving at least 20 percent of the vote, giving Jackson, at least on paper, a slight chance of edging Dukakis at somewhere between 35 and 40 percent.

From Gore's campaign, the chances of victory were seen as next to nil, but a Jackson upset over Dukakis could keep Gore's candidacy (as a credible alternative) alive. With New York media consultant David Garth (guru to both Mayor Koch and Governor Cuomo, but with not much of a record in national politics) calling most of the shots, the campaign planned to knock Dukakis and Jackson off stride with vigorous daily campaigning. The campaign's plans were significantly hindered, though, by lack of money. Moreover, any thoughts Garth might have had about using television commercials to bring down Dukakis's vote, as Representative Gephardt had at the last minute in South Dakota two months before, were discarded. There was Gore's future to think of, and he had already angered many leaders of the black community in Tennessee by criticizing Jackson, as well as several of his Senate colleagues, by criticizing of their letter to Israeli Prime Minister Shamir. As an attractive, intelligent, and experienced legislator with foreign-policy expertise and at least a toehold in the South, Gore was a possible option for Dukakis as a vice-presidential running mate.

For the final week in New York, Dukakis surely had more than enough money to bury Gore in an avalanche of counterattacking television commercials should the Senator put even one thirty-second negative advertisement on the air. Communications director Leslie Dach said, while the political world was waiting to see how Gore would play, "We're armed and ready; we have better missiles and more of them." Accordingly, while Gore jabbed at both his opponents, mostly on foreign policy, and above all on Israel, he campaigned in a positive vein, and although he never disowned Mayor Koch's divisive rantings (too much to ask, according to accepted political standards), Gore nonetheless endured them without supportive comment, and always with obvious discomfiture on his face.

The public polls on the Sunday before the Tuesday primary showed a confused picture. The *New York Daily News* poll showed Dukakis with a comfortable lead, but, using a statistically insignificant, one-day sample that showed a tight race, the paper misinterpreted its own data and published a Sunday front page screaming "Too Close to Call." By the weekend, daily samplings by ABC News were also showing a shaky, six-to-nine percentage point Dukakis lead over Jackson.

Dukakis, however, was back in stride and following his simple plan for New York, emphasizing jobs and economic justice in ethnic neighborhoods in the sprawling New York suburbs and upstate (the usually neglected half of the primary electorate) as well as ethnic neighborhoods in the city. And away from the crowds and the speeches, a hefty purchase of television time was pushing Dukakis's experience and (in a new twist spawned by Jackson's successful use of the issue) fighting a war on illegal drugs.

For public consumption, the Dukakis campaign's senior officials looked and acted worried as they had done in Wisconsin. On a frigid Saturday in Buffalo, while Dukakis was throwing out the first ball at a minor-league game in the city's new stadium (he bounced it in front of home plate), Corrigan solemnly intoned, "It's tight."

Not true. While Dukakis was inside the ball park enjoying his favorite sport, we stayed outside on two pay phones with the indefatigable reporter Maralee Schwartz of the *Washington Post*. From Tom Kiley and Tubby Harrison in Boston came word that Dukakis had begun to open up a solid lead again, meaning that without a last-two-days goof, the primary was now his to win. By late Monday, the public polls also began to suggest that it was time for Dukakis's big moment.

It was. The margin, like Wisconsin's, approached a landslide: 801,000 votes or 51 percent for Dukakis; 585,000 or 37 percent for Jackson; and 157,000 or 10 percent for Gore, who halted his campaign two days later with a graceful exit statement, saying Dukakis had shown that for the nomination race the voters had decided that in fact "competence is charisma."

Two days before the primary, Tad Devine sat down in his office and pieced together a memorandum to Estrich and Corrigan analyzing the race for the nomination, post-New York, from two vantage points: Gore stays in the race, or Gore stops running. Still at issue was whether Dukakis could assemble the 2,082 delegates needed for nomination before the convention convened in Atlanta, because roughly 60 percent of the delegate slots had been allocated as of the New York primary, and because Dukakis's lead over Jackson that Sunday was a slender 886 to 732.

"If only two candidates remain in the race after New York," Devine wrote, "MSD's ability to coalesce a nominating majority will be significantly enhanced. If large blocks of delegates elected as pledged to other, withdrawn candidates can be moved prior to 6/7/88 [the day of the last four primaries], MSD will be able to secure a clear majority immediately after the end of the nominating process."

In somewhat simpler English, Dukakis could win the nomination outright, without brokering. The nomination described in March 1987 as a "very, very long shot" in Dukakis's own words was now inevitable.

It hadn't started that way. As the workhorse in a race that had a few potential showhorses, Dukakis never stood out, partly because of a very early commitment to present a moderate image. The projection mostly reflected reality: the candidate had an unusual mixture of liberal and not-so-liberal ideas, strong durability, and steadiness. Dukakis had also resolved very early not to be a momentum candidate who could surge out front with a dramatic proposal or two. He had none in his head, or heart, and believed those who did, or relied on charismatic rhetoric or speaking styles, were either inviting critical scrutiny or likely to fade if primary voters focused on their broader and deeper presidential decisions. He had his large pile of money from his Massachusetts base and world-class fund-raisers. He was very lucky: several more prominent Democrats decided not to run, Gary Hart self-destructed, the Iowa results were good enough to keep him in the race, and his record never faced deep scrutiny in the heat of the campaign. But he also made a lot of his own good fortune: he correctly saw 1988 as a marathon and not a sprint; he ran without mortgaging pieces of himself to other politicians and interest groups; he persevered through a crisis that cost him his campaign manager; and with the nomination on the line, he won in Texas, Florida, Wisconsin, and finally New York because he made a stronger case and wiser political decisions.

Back in summer 1987, long before the race began in earnest, an editorial-page cartoon in the *San Francisco Chronicle* illustrated how the nomination would be won. The cartoon showed a pensive Snow White sitting alone on a two-seater porch swing, looking at seven hopeful dwarfs arrayed before her.

"Okay. . . . Heck. . . . The one with the eyebrows," she said.

The cartoon so appealed to Dukakis's wry wit that he made it part of his standard campaign speech back then, and his headquarters staff ordered tee-shirts with that line. Endorsements were then hard to come by, and any intimation of victory, however unenthusiastic, was eagerly embraced. But months later, with roughly ten million votes under his belt and the nomination within his grasp, that cartoon image was still appropriate. From out of almost nowhere and against hefty odds, he had won if not triumphed, survived more than dominated his opponents, and reached voters' heads if not their hearts, more because of who he was and what he had done in public life than what he had to offer as president. The man on the Omni Hotel stage that primary night in New York was a gray suit, but he wore well on a rack with several that wore out.

The day before the New York primary, a typical Democrat telephoned Susan Brophy in Boston. June Fischer, a Super Delegate by her membership on the Democratic National Committee, and a trench warrior from New Jersey, was eager to get recorded in the campaign's delegate count before New York voted.

"It was so important for me to stand up and be counted before the primary," she told us later. "I wasn't just getting on a bandwagon, I really wanted to do this."

June Fischer's 1988 campaign did not begin with Michael Dukakis, any more than it did for most of the more than twenty million people who participated in the long Democratic contest, in which Dukakis did not take his party by storm but slowly earned its highest prize.

"I was for Joe Biden," Fischer said. "I thought he had a little bit of the Kennedy mystique, the excitement, even some of the arrogance that makes the Kennedys so endearing. And I'd known him since 1974, when he came to help me in a pretty hopeless race for the House. I was absolutely devastated when he had to leave the race, and angry and bitter because of the Dukakis campaign's role in it."

And then, gradually, she changed her mind.

"I began to realize as the primaries were beginning that Michael Dukakis made me feel comfortable," she continued. "I don't want

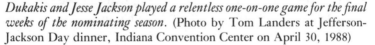

Dukakis and Jesse Jackson played a relentless one-on-one game for the final weeks of the nominating season. (Photo by Tom Landers at Jefferson-Jackson Day dinner, Indiana Convention Center on April 30, 1988)

another Ronald Reagan. I happen to think Jimmy Carter was a good president, and I know people want a more serious person."

Maine Attorney General James Tierney had observed, a few months earlier, "Michael Dukakis is a candidate you think your way to."

Thinking, however, requires information. As a new face on the national scene, Dukakis was known only to the distinct minority among the electorate who had participated in the Democratic primaries and caucuses, and even their knowledge was at best sketchy. After the New York primary, a hidden campaign began to see which side would introduce the governor first to the roughly ninety million people likely to vote in November: the Dukakis campaign with positive information, or the Bush campaign with negative information. Just as important, another race was on to fill in the different but almost equally large blanks about Bush: whether he had any identity other than as Ronald Reagan's vice president, whether he had a plan of his own about where he hoped to lead the country, whether his record constituted experience or whether Bob Dole's campaign commercial was correct, that he had left no footprints in a twenty-five-year trudge through public life. These hidden races were fascinating because each side was aware of the other's strengths, weaknesses, and likely moves; and each side processed its information and made its initial judgments at roughly the same time. The difference was that one candidate acted on the information he received and the other didn't.

Over Memorial Day weekend, George Bush made a critical decision to begin attacking Dukakis furiously as a far-out liberal, a decision his high command believed then and is convinced now was the key to his winning the presidency. The decision was much publicized at the time and has been since, but far less known is that at exactly the same time, Dukakis's senior strategists were reaching a similar conclusion about his potential vulnerabilities, which they considered extremely dangerous and which they thought should be addressed at once. But where Bush's advisers succeeded with their candidate, the Dukakis camp failed.

In the days before Bush and his top advisers gathered for the holiday weekend at his estate in Kennebunkport, Maine, Bush campaign pollster Robert Teeter had arranged for structured discussions with small groups of voters (called focus groups) in communities around the country where the election was likely to be closely contested. At one, in Paramus, New Jersey, the entire high command showed up to watch the participants through a one-way mirror, including Teeter, campaign manager Lee Atwater, and media wizard Roger Ailes. This gathering—which the Bush advisers attended because of its proximity to the coming summit with the candidate in Maine—consisted of two groups of conservative Democrats, Ronald Reagan supporters in 1984 but now leaning toward Dukakis.

In the discussion's key segment, the moderator asked leading, pointed questions: What if Dukakis opposed capital punishment for murderers? What if he had vetoed legislation requiring teachers to lead school children in reciting the Pledge of Allegiance? What if he had permitted murderers to have weekend passes from prison?

Quickly, the participants turned on Dukakis, majorities favoring him became majorities opposing him, he was fingered as a liberal, and previously identified positive attributes were forgotten.

The holiday weekend campaign summit microscopically examined these and other potential Dukakis vulnerablities. On Saturday evening Teeter gave Bush videotapes of the New Jersey focus-group meeting so that he could watch for himself. The very next morning, Bush told his advisers that voters appeared to know little about the governor and that they would respond if fed a steady diet of "information" about liberal positions and programs in his past. Just before the weekend conference ended, Bush was offered two alternatives that were really only one. Atwater's view, he said, was that Bush could hold off his attacks until after the mid-August Republican convention; Atwater felt that Dukakis's lead in the polls would be roughly fifteen percentage points going into the Democratic convention in mid-July, and that the love feast and Republican-bashing in Atlanta would quite probably bounce him ten points higher. On the other hand, Atwater said that Bush could launch his attacks at once, hoping to knock Dukakis's lead below ten percentage points by the end of the month, in which case the governor's lead would not be likely to surpass twenty percentage points after the Democratic convention, a dangerously but not irretrievably high margin, with the Republican convention still ahead.

Bush never hesitated at Kennebunkport: He chose the attack strategy, and the die was cast for the ensuing ugly spectacle. The attack had a lot of elements, but surprise was not one of them. The vulnerabilities Bush jabbed at were known in vivid detail by the Dukakis campaign's senior operatives. They had seen them in their own polls and focus groups; they had described them in detail; and they had struggled to develop strategies for dealing with them. Their ideas, however, unlike the plans of their counterparts in the Bush campaign, never made it past their candidate.

Dukakis's May 3 triumph over Jackson in the Ohio and Indiana primaries was the signal to shift planning for the general-election campaign into high gear. Tubby Harrison conducted polls to measure voters' sentiment in eight of the largest states. At least half those states would form the core in any Dukakis effort to reach 270 electoral votes and presidential victory. Beginning May 13, Harrison hit the phones, focusing on California, New York, Texas, Florida, Illinois, Ohio, New Jersey, and Michigan, states that represented 216 electoral votes.

Finishing just after the final round of primaries on June 7, he summarized his findings two days later in a memorandum to Estrich, Corrigan, and fellow pollster-strategist Tom Kiley (who had embarked on a similar exercise). He wrapped a veneer of good news around several ominous warnings.

At that very early stage, they found Dukakis ahead of Bush by double-digit margins in New York, Illinois, and Michigan; the governor was leading by much less convincing margins in California, Ohio and New Jersey; and he was behind in Texas and Florida. In short, despite his political honeymoon after his conquest in the primaries, it was clear even on the surface that after the bounces from the Democratic and Republican conventions canceled each other out, this was likely to be a close election.

But in analyzing his data, Harrison raised amazingly prescient red flags. Overall, he said, the results in the eight states pointed to some major weaknesses in Dukakis's position:

Left: Dukakis flattered a high school girl at her prom at Greenwood Community High School in Indiana on April 30, 1988. (Photo by Tom Landers) *Right: Nick Mitropoulos, Dukakis's "body man" for the campaign, accompanied Dukakis on the long, twisting campaign trail, even on the daily power walks like this one in Indianapolis.* (Photo by Tom Landers)

1. As a determinant of voter sentiment in the Bush-Dukakis matchup, opinions people had of Bush affected the trial-heat results more than opinions about Dukakis. Because Dukakis was so poorly known at this stage among the voters, it was primarily negative opinions about Bush that were affecting the race, much more than positive views of Dukakis.

   "This means," Harrison wrote, "that the race today is Bush's to lose, not ours to win, and fortunately he is losing it."

2. More than party registration or anything else, Harrison found that how voters perceived the candidates and themselves for their liberalism and conservatism was driving the horserace. Dukakis was benefiting because he was usually seen as moderately liberal and the vice president was seen as a relatively more extreme conservative.

   "Hence the vulnerability," he said on June 9. "If Bush is able convincingly to paint MSD as a liberal . . . he can reduce the distance between himself and the voters, and thereby turn the tables on us."

3. In trying to paint that liberal picture, moreover, Harrison discovered that any image of being "soft" on either crime in general or capital punishment for murderers "can hurt us quite a bit." "We are in part at the mercy of factors beyond our control," Harrison concluded. "We are ahead, but in many respects we don't have the initiative. These results argue strongly for taking steps very soon to go on the strategic offensive and move this campaign onto our own turf. . . ."

As early as May, moreover, the Dukakis high command had received enough signals from Bush and other Republicans and its own issues research and internal discussions to be sure that a negative assault was coming and that crime and patriotism-related subjects would be used to paint Dukakis as an extreme liberal. In fact, at a senior staff meeting at campaign headquarters in May, various campaign officials speculated about mock drafts of the Bush television commercials.

"Here's his first ad," Susan Estrich said one day. "There's this big black dude in his prison cell with street clothes on, whistling softly as he packs his toothbrush and a few incidentals before setting out on a weekend of pillaging."

Tom Kiley had another idea, imagining a Bush commercial that would begin with an aerial shot of Dukakis's home town.

"This is Brookline, Massachusetts," he had the announcer for the ad saying. "Here is where Michael Dukakis lives. But in this town, unlike the rest of the country, the town meeting has voted not to say the Pledge of Allegiance to begin its sessions. In this town, unlike the rest of the country, the official policy is to declare the place off limits to the strategic weapons that defend our country. In most American towns, people say the Pledge enthusiastically, and don't have their own foreign policy."

It was a diverting exercise, but as the primary season ended, the campaign had to settle on basic contours for a message in the general election. It then had three components and was well settled before Dukakis picked Lloyd Bentsen as his running mate and accepted his party's nomination in Atlanta.

The first component in the plan constantly emphasized the differences between Bush and Dukakis as public figures. It was designed to draw attention to Dukakis's record of accomplishment, his independence as a political figure, and his leadership ability as demonstrated by his accomplishments. It was also meant to keep attention on the squishy elements in Bush's political persona: his lack of personal accomplish-

Tubby Harrison, the oracular pollster, warned Dukakis about the fragile underpinnings of his campaign. (Photo by Bill Brett)

ments in public life, his privileged background, and his dependence on Reagan and others for the jobs he had held. All these factors had helped fuel some highly negative opinions of him among voters. Opinion polls were showing negative ratings for Bush of about 40 percent and above, a historically insuperable obstacle for a presidential candidate.

The message plan also envisaged an effort to link Dukakis in voters' minds to "people like me," to focus his domestic policy statements on proposals that would most affect those whom Estrich liked to call "average American families." At this time in the campaign, Dukakis's advocating federal assistance to locally operated and regulated child-care programs was a particularly important example, because of its appeal to women, but other such ideas included raising the minimum wage, requiring companies to give notice of intent to close plants and offices, making employers offer basic health insurance to their workers, and making a college education available to all qualified students.

And finally, the basic plan made a broad case for change in national direction and government policy, focusing on the noticeable, though not huge majorities of voters in polls who chose change over continuation of Reagan administration policies. From Estrich's perspective, Dukakis would call for a host of initiatives, from improved education to governmental efforts to help basic industries modernize, all designed to make the country second to none in the increasingly competitive international economy.

For that stage in the campaign it was an appropriate message. It was not, however, accompanied by a blueprint, a longer document setting forth the campaign's most important strategic principles as well as detailed steps for transforming the plan into a Dukakis victory.

Detailed blueprints can be overrated in presidential politics, but they can be critical in maintaining discipline for both the campaign and the candidate in the often chaotic campaign atmosphere. For Dukakis, though, the need was acute because ever since his comeback victory in the 1982 gubernatorial rematch with Ed King he had come to depend on John Sasso's quarterly memoranda.

"What's the plan?" and "What are my lines" were the two Dukakis queries most likely to be heard in meetings with his advisers. The initial three-part message he was given after the primaries ended had the advantage of hitting on three subjects—the middle class, Bush's negatives, and America's clout in the world—that touched a chord with voters. The message was also very broad, however, without detailed plans for driving it home every day and every week. The danger, seen at the time by senior campaign officials, was that without a genuine blueprint, the campaign was in danger of falling into the bad habit of living day to day, or worse, being suckered into almost daily responses to a sustained Bush attack.

While the message crafters labored, Estrich was able to delegate one task she knew would be accomplished with both skill and dispatch: arranging a campaign on the ground that was capable of winning the 270 electoral votes necessary to make Michael Dukakis president. The primary responsibility fell to Corrigan, assisted by Charlie Baker, architect of Dukakis's victory in New Hampshire who had gone on to perform critical field-organization tasks in several important primary states; and Charles Campion, a Dukakis supporter since childhood in the West Roxbury neighborhood of Boston who had national experience working for Walter Mondale, both when he was vice president and when he ran for president in 1984.

In the beginning, the Dukakis campaign approached its targeting decisions facing a daunting obstacle: the Republican Party's "lock" in modern times on the Electoral College. Twenty-three states with 202 votes had gone for the Republican nominee in each election from 1968 onward. Because of the aberrational victory by Jimmy Carter of Georgia in 1976, the task facing any Democratic nominee in 1988 was even more imposing than the lock implied, because the twenty-three states did not include several in the South which had gone for Carter in a brief burst of sectional enthusiasm, but which had voted for Ronald Reagan both times by hefty margins. In truth, if historical patterns were real, the Republican nominee could almost count on 250 electoral votes before he left his nominating convention.

"I started out by looking at this from the standpoint of the lock," Baker recalled after the election, "but maybe because this was all new to me, and I wasn't totally mesmerized by the recent past. I began to think that instead of concentrating on the lock, maybe the opportunity for us was the other way around. In other words, about half the Electoral College had consistently trended better than the national vote for Democratic nominees, in some cases a lot better. To us, this gradually seemed a better way to focus, if for no other reason than the fact that we had to lay a foundation for a Dukakis base."

For most of May and June, like their Bush counterparts, the field-operation chiefs sifted through a mountain of historical and current data, ranking the states by economic factors indicating some hardship as well as by political factors. Particularly useful was a deluge of voting statistics covering every precinct in the country that was made available to them by the National Committee for an Effective Congress, a liberal political-action committee. The precinct data were critical in developing a "persuasion index," a means for identifying all-important swing voters by comparing, say, the vote for a landslide loser like Walter Mondale to that for the most recently successful Democratic candidate for state auditor (usually a party-line vote).

By the last primaries on June 7, Corrigan was ready to make some basic decisions. The most vital was to keep more than 400 electoral votes "in play," or fully competitive, as long as possible. The Dukakis effort would have as much of a national aura as possible and keep the Bush campaign and its resources as spread out as possible.

Besides, he firmly believed that overall national sentiment as measured by the Bush-Dukakis trial heat in the polls would drive the Electoral College totals, not the other way around. This belief was a way of getting around the so-called lock: if Dukakis was supported by a majority of the people who voted in the country, at least 270 out of 538 electoral votes would simply be there to make him president. A corollary belief was that a majority was not to be found by a national assemblage of voting blocs, labor-union members, blacks, Hispanics, city residents, or poor people, the "quilt" that Jesse Jackson liked to use as an analogy. Instead, Corrigan decided the campaign must target voters much more broadly, and particularly that it must target the roughly ten million Democrats who had voted for Ronald Reagan in the 1980s, and the roughly one-third of the electorate not clearly wedded to either party.

The strength in his thinking was that its scale was grand enough to take Dukakis onto previously Republican turf in presidential campaigns in at least parts of the South, including Texas; in the suburbs; and in many agriculture-dominated states previously thought off-limits to a national Democratic figure.

Moreover, late in the spring after the primaries and for nearly two more months Dukakis was a candidate with very strong nonideological appeal. He was getting more than 20 percent of the Republican vote, he had a clear lead among independent voters, and was close enough to Bush among white males that his double-digit margin among females gave him a sizable overall advantage. Dukakis might be bland, even boring, and vague on major policy issues like the federal budget deficit, but a governor with an image of success in his governing past, who was optimistic about the country's potential and eager to face challenges stood in quite favorable contrast to the then-stumbling Bush.

But the weakness, as identified by Harrison's polls, was just as clear. This approach to the electorate depended dangerously on the Bush image of the moment, and did not impart a sense of urgency to protecting Dukakis's right flank while giving off the distinct signal to traditional Democratic groups (above all, to black people) that the governor was taking them for granted.

The fifty-state strategy—Dukakis's own idea and one he insisted on maintaining through the summer—would prove a costly mistake, needlessly diverting money and workers to places where the governor had no realistic chance at victory. As with so many other campaign matters, the Dukakis operation was warned about all this when Democratic election experts began trooping to Boston for consulting sessions as early as May. The situation described in voluminous detail by representatives from the National Committee for an Effective Congress was especially illuminating. In fact, the first time the committee's experts ran their data through a computer in a simulated election, they came up with a Dukakis defeat. Loosening their complex criteria a bit, they still calculated that the odds were just fifty-fifty that Dukakis could win 275 electoral votes, only five more than a winning majority, based on eighteen states and the District of Columbia.

The committee's people particularly warned the Dukakis campaign about New Jersey and Texas, both full-scale Dukakis targets. The experts' criteria showed that in New Jersey, Dukakis would have to win fully 75 percent of the persuadable voters in the state; they also said that it had a comparatively high ratio of white-collar to blue-collar voters, and that personal income in the state had jumped nearly 19 percent between 1984 and 1986. The chances for a Dukakis victory were estimated at a puny 34.5 percent. Dukakis, however, insisted that New Jersey was a clone of Massachusetts and that his chances were excellent.

In Texas, things looked even worse, despite the state's ailing oil and real-estate sectors. The committee's data indicated Dukakis would have to win nearly 80 percent of the persuadable voters and that his chances in the state were no better than 32 percent.

By September, the campaign narrowed its targets more carefully, but by then a great deal of money and a great many people had been wasted. The campaign's basic list of target states for the election was divided into three parts. The first consisted of the assumed Dukakis states, the places he had to win, including eight states with 86 electoral votes: the District of Columbia, Hawaii, Maryland, Massachusetts, Minnesota, New York, Rhode Island, and West Virginia.

The second, broader category included the sixteen "should-win" states with enough additional electoral votes at stake (217) to produce a Dukakis presidency: California, Connecticut, Illinois, Iowa, Michigan, Montana, New Jersey, New Mexico, North Dakota, Ohio, Oregon, Pennsylvania, South Dakota, Vermont, Washington, and Wisconsin.

And finally, ten states with 106 electoral votes were labeled "could-win" states, which would be worked just as hard as the others and kept in play as long as possible: Arkansas, Colorado, Delaware, Georgia, Kentucky, Maine, Missouri, North Carolina, Tennessee, and Texas.

The general Dukakis plan was levelheaded, not at all the product of adolescent political minds stuffed with the heady confidence that can come from winning a presidential nomination. In fact, it is remarkable for its tentative, not at all wild goals. The presumed base was conservatively estimated. Its relative lack of size, less than one-third the electoral votes needed for victory, was noteable. The should-wins were also conservatively chosen, and although in late spring Dukakis had leads in state polls in every one of them, the campaign's high command was well aware that New Jersey, California, and Ohio were likely to be very tough in the end, and that without them, indeed without New Jersey and Ohio (where Harrison's polls already showed the race to be close), Dukakis could win all his must- and could-win states and still be short of an Electoral College majority.

Also, Dukakis's base and the states he "should" win did not have a single electoral vote from the South. If the Republican lock reflected the country's conservative inclination in the Reagan age, then regional voting habits were likely to gradually reassert themselves as the campaign developed. To be sure, the opportunities in perhaps six southern states should be pressed to the hilt, but no prudent manager could count on any of them in his targeting, and the Dukakis campaign manager did not.

Indeed, Baker secretly began in May to work on a victory scenario that could apply even if Dukakis lost the popular vote to Bush. A minority president had been elected only three times in American history since the 12th Amendment to the Constitution, requiring that electors vote separately for president and vice president, was ratified in 1803.

"It always seemed to me that part of our job was to be ready for a worst-case strategy that would still elect Dukakis," Baker said much later, "and that I should never be so optimistic about his chances at any point to neglect it. Obviously, if the margin in the trial heats nationally in the late spring held up, there would be no problem. But it might not."

Baker could see how one candidate might win several states, including very large ones, by extremely narrow margins while the other candidate was winning a large number of comparatively small states by very wide margins; the scenario took into account the possibility that Bush could open up huge leads in much of the Deep South and some of the smaller states in the Rocky Mountains and the Southwest, but be vulnerable all over the Northeast, the West Coast, and the industrial Midwest. It was chilling to liberals imbued with notions of popular sovereignty to think like this, but they believed it was their job to cover all contingencies.

This thinking, of course, was just one more manifestation behind the scenes that several of his senior political aides were aware of how precarious Dukakis's position was. It was very clear that his election was considered anything but certain as he beat Jesse Jackson four final times on June 7 (in California, New Jersey, Montana, and New Mexico) and turned his attention to picking a running mate, dealing with Jackson, and preparing for the national convention that would present him to a mass audience nationally for the first time.

6

"America"

Senator Lloyd M. Bentsen was shaving at 6:30 A.M. in his Kalorama Square home in Washington on July 12, 1988 when the telephone rang. He almost didn't hear it because he had turned off the upstairs phones the night before so that he and his wife, B.A., could sleep without interruption from reporters checking to see if he had been asked to join Michael Dukakis on the Democratic national ticket as the vice presidential nominee.

The caller was Dukakis, who asked him right away, without pleasantries, to be his running mate. It took Bentsen no time to enthusiastically say yes. In keeping with protocol in such moments, Dukakis did not tell Bentsen that he had not made a final decision until barely twelve hours before the phone call, and that he had been genuinely torn between the tall Texan and a better-known American hero, Senator John Glenn of Ohio.

The joyous atmosphere—Dukakis immediately celebrated his choice as reestablishing the Boston-Austin axis that had improbably linked John Kennedy to Lyndon Johnson twenty-eight years before—was mostly superficial. For five miserable weeks, Dukakis had been wandering aimlessly. Throughout June, he had been so preoccupied with his search for a running mate that he neglected the equally important task of introducing himself to a country that was just beginning to get interested in him. And while Dukakis interviewed prospective running mates, Bush began to attack him with unprecedented venom as a far-out liberal who opened the prisons on weekends, opposed the Pledge of Allegiance, would strip the country's defenses, and wanted to raise taxes. Dukakis mistook the assault for desperation and rarely responded, but behind the scenes his high command took it as a definite challenge.

At almost the last moment, however, Dukakis himself caught his own slide. First, he made what may have been the most enthusiastically applauded choice of a running mate in modern times; then, less than two days before the Democratic national convention opened in Atlanta, he resolved to end his ceaseless dickering with Jesse Jackson and did so in a way that reinforced his image as an independent, forceful politician; and finally, he took a collection of quite ordinary words and turned them into a performance that for one shining hour made him look like a president.

The successes temporarily rescued him from a deterioration that became apparent in mid-June, when internal polls, analyses from his pollsters, and anecdotal information all pointed to a disturbing conclusion: Dukakis is vulnerable to a perception that he is more liberal than the average voter.

Just before final primaries on June 7, Susan Estrich asked her husband, Marty Kaplan, to draft a speech for Dukakis laying down a marker or two against the expected Bush onslaught, reminding both voters and (more important) Bush that they were watching him, and that Bush should expect an assault not only to fail but to add to his already considerable problems.

Focusing on the already significant amount of muck being hurled at them by Bush, Dukakis gave the speech late on the evening of June 7 at the Biltmore Hotel in Los Angeles, after a large crowd of supporters had enjoyed watching him place a telephone call on live television to his wife, who was in Boston recovering from spinal surgery for a ruptured disc.

"My friends, what a golden opportunity this is for us," he said. "What an opportunity for America to set our course for the next century. What an opportunity for Democrats to make our case with confidence. And what quicksand for our opponents if they waste this opportunity on mudslinging and name calling. Because the American people are not interested in what Mr. Bush thinks of me or what I think of him. They want to know which one of us has the strength and the ability and the values to lead our country."

Dukakis's private attitude toward the expected assault from Bush bordered on contempt. Shortly before the last primaries, we took a ride with him in a small private jet from Boston to Baltimore and back for a fund-raiser one evening. Asked about the increasing publicity and Republican attention being given to the escape a year earlier by convicted felon William Horton while on a furlough, Dukakis scoffed and said that would never become a real issue. The federal government had a far more permissive system, he said, and Ronald Reagan had operated a furlough program that had had worse problems than his when he was governor of California.

He also responded quickly and confidently when asked about another matter that the Bush campaign was discussing more and more: his veto in 1977 of legislation requiring teachers to lead pupils in daily recitations of the Pledge of Allegiance. Dukakis said that before the veto he had received an advisory opinion from the state supreme court that the legislation was unconstitutional, and he chuckled in mentioning that Republican Governor Thomas Kean of New Jersey, a Bush favorite who would keynote the Republican national convention, had vetoed an almost identical bill.

Dukakis made it clear too that he was the architect of the effort his aides constantly called the "fifty-state campaign" they were planning for the fall; he intended also to stick to his cherished plan for waging an intensive campaign in all fifty states, an idea many of his aides considered foolish; chatting with Nick Mitropoulos about a coming trip into the South, he mentioned that he was booked into Kentucky, complained that he had been there enough lately, and instead wanted the schedule changed to add stops in Mississippi and Alabama.

Four weeks later, his big lead had become at best a little lead. Dukakis's triumph in Atlanta has obscured that enormous slip. Bush campaign manager Lee Atwater had made clear, as they readied their attack strategy at the end of May, that its purpose was to knock Dukakis's polling lead well down into single digits. Had Dukakis run a vigorous, effective campaign in June, he could have maintained his large polling lead, and then jumped up toward the stratosphere with an uplifting performance at the convention. Jimmy Carter had thus built nearly a 30 percentage point lead over Gerald Ford in summer 1976, a lead that gave Carter enough of a cushion to sustain him through a long fall after Labor Day.

From double-digit margins in the published national polls shortly after the last of his spring primary victories over Jackson, the Dukakis campaign's first national polls showed him with only a fragile margin by the end of the ho-hum month. The first national poll for the campaign by Tubby Harrison and Tom Kiley (in June they had concentrated on surveys in the major battleground states), completed June 30, showed a Dukakis margin over Bush of six percentage points, 50 to 44 percent.

The good news from the poll was chiefly that Bush's improved standing was based primarily on the first stirrings of traditional Republican voting preferences in the Deep South and the Rocky Mountain states. Dukakis had not yet lost his strong leads in the eastern and central United States.

Kiley, whose initial memorandum on his poll was for Dukakis's eyes and done at Estrich's request in order to jar but not scare the candidate, made a similar point based on comparisons to the state polls he had been conducting as part of the running-mate selection. "An imprecise comparison with our previous state data shows that the narrowing of MSD's lead comes largely at the hands of certain constituencies—southern and western whites, Republicans, and self-described conservatives—who might have been expected to be somewhat more susceptible to attacks on MSD," he wrote the governor.

Harrison was chiefly troubled in his analysis by ideology, specifically the idea that would become known as the L word as the campaign progressed.

"These results," he wrote in his summary memorandum on July 2, "show that liberal / conservative ideology is becoming more important—to our detriment. Not only is Bush closer to the voters than MSD is in terms of perceived ideology, distance from MSD has more of an impact on the trial heats than distance from Bush does. This means that ideological differences are hurting MSD more than they are hurting Bush."

In his polling, Harrison regularly asked voters to rate themselves from very liberal to very conservative, on a scale of one to five. On the average, he found that the distance between where the typical voter viewed himself and where he viewed Dukakis was slightly greater than the distance from where he viewed Bush in considering ideology. That reading meant voters placed themselves closer to Bush than to the governor.

Kiley found a similar trend, and added in his July 1 memorandum that "this distance is sure to grow when Bush asks voters to consider furlough bans, taxes, capital punishment and similar issues, as he has in recent weeks."

"When we weigh in more aggressively with our middle-class economic issues we will broaden our advantage on this dimension once again," Kiley added, without noticing that the word "when" assumed a commitment that had not in fact been made.

Although a majority disagreed with the assertion that Dukakis was soft on crime, Harrison was worried that 37 percent of his interview subjects said they didn't know.

"These results," he wrote, "suggest that this issue is partly a blank slate on which to write an image: either we will fill that slate or Bush will."

Looking ahead, Harrison saw Bush's task as clear: emphasize good economic news and his foreign policy background, begin to moderate his conservatism, address his weak image by becoming more independent of Reagan, and hammer repeatedly at Dukakis as a liberal (especially on crime and taxes) to keep him on the defensive.

Harrison also considered Dukakis's tactical needs to be equally clear, including these:

1. "We must emphasize MSD's closeness to average people in understanding them, caring about their problems, talking their language and sharing aspirations."
2. "We must reinforce our advantages on the economy. What is indicated here is not a haggle over taxes and deficits, where we don't gain much over Bush, but some vision about rebuilding the basic sinews of the American economy."
3. "We must address our negatives," and here Harrison recommended tackling head-on the tax-spend image and concerns about crime.

Harrison also wrote, however, that the campaign had to move beyond merely tactical responses to the image-related danger signals he was reading in his polling data.

"What the campaign needs," he argued, "is a central, overriding call to arms to bring together the tactical points and give them a deeper dimension which people will understand and which people can relate to. And this should be built around what we are finding is the most basic concern and worry of the electorate: the failure of leadership to restore America's position in a changing world (especially America's economic position), and what that means to every American on an immediate, personal basis. This is the big picture. This constitutes the biggest failure of the Reagan / Bush administration—and the survey results show that people recognize it as such."

This kind of strategic message, Harrison concluded, would also block the Bush campaign's effort to tar Dukakis with the liberal label.

"It addresses the liberal / conservative outlook problem by asserting a deeper patriotism (which should allay fears of conservatives and especially our target conservative Democrats) and by providing a deeper justification for that patriotism than that provided by the rah-rah quality of Bush's patriotic appeals," he wrote. "Put differently, it turns the whole liberal / conservative dimension on its head, and gets it away from no-win spitting matches over abortion, the death penalty, and who raises or doesn't raise taxes the most."

Dukakis made no response to Harrison's oracular observations.

In Kiley's complementary opinion, Dukakis's comparative passivity in June had cost him an opportunity to continue to exploit a host of Bush weaknesses, both personal (too dependent on Reagan and having no accomplishments of his own) and class related (too much for the wealthy at the average Americans' expense).

> The serious doubts that American voters have about George Bush and his presidential capacity must be brought to the surface in the next few weeks. The reason Bush has closed the gap is he has successfully activated latent MSD vulnerabilities while we have not done the same in reverse.
>
> My concern for the next couple of weeks is that coverage of MSD will continue to be dominated by Jackson discussions, Veep speculation and convention planning, none of which do anything to build on favorable perceptions of MSD, to inform voters about MSD's record, or to effectively press the substantive case against Bush. . . . The simple fact underlying these poll results is that since the California primary Bush has been campaigning more aggressively and generating more helpful news coverage than MSD has.

This realistic assessment extended even to the most important component in Dukakis's lead in the national polls during this period—the storied gender gap. Unlike much of the press, the Dukakis campaign's analysts took very little comfort from the large leads the governor was enjoying among female voters. Harrison, especially, pointed out the much smaller Dukakis advantage among white women, Bush's higher standing up the income scale, and his much stronger position among married women. But much more important, he used differences between male and female attitudes about the economy to recommend the tactic that could have been what the Dukakis campaign never had until its final days: a thematic message.

Harrison wrote: "Those [issue] items which women felt were greater problems than men did were not associated with jobs and employment, but were associated with problems which would have monetary costs to families including the cost of college, the cost of medical / hospital care, the cost of long-term nursing care for the elderly or for those with elderly parents, affordable child care, and inflation and the cost of living."

Among men, by contrast, Harrison reported that attitudes toward the Bush—Dukakis horserace were affected more by their opinions about such questions as whether America's world power and influence were declining and whether unfair trade practices and other matters affecting the American economy's international competitiveness were serious problems.

"This should be tested further," Harrison wrote,

> but it seems that one way of reaching men is to make voting for MSD the equivalent of sending a message to Japan—and to the whole world—that we Americans are prepared to meet the challenges of the future which the world has hurled at us, and that MSD is a symbol of the desire for a reemergence of American power and influence in the world.
>
> On the level of the economy, to reach women, it is probably sufficient for MSD to emphasize costs, real wages, and real opportunities. In addition, believable plans to restore old industries, and build the high-paying, high-quality jobs of the future on which long-term economic prosperity and a growing standard of living depend will be telling arguments to women.
>
> But to reach men (who, after all, are now very optimistic about the condition of the economy) we may have to structure arguments about the economy in terms of becoming number one in the world economically again, so that voting for MSD is sending a powerful message for change.

Michael Dukakis wasn't interested. His initial reaction to recommendations for a theme of economic nationalism was dismissive: it's protectionism; it's the old Gephardt line; I want more trade, not less trade; I won't blame the rest of the world while our own financial house is a mess.

Even if Dukakis had been less negative, his thin campaign, stretched taut by planning for the convention and assisting in the search for a running mate, probably could not have accommodated a hard effort to prepare for the fall thematically; most attempts to expand the Dukakis ranks with senior officials, something the Republicans do with routine ease after their primaries, failed. After the New York primary, when it was clear Dukakis would be the Democratic nominee, many of the best and brightest operatives in the Democratic Party volunteered for the Dukakis bandwagon for the general election. The motives were surprisingly pure. Many had managed campaigns for rival candidates, but they wanted the Democratic Party to win in November. The dirty little secret among political operatives is that they are uniformly ideological. The Democratic handlers are as liberal as the Republican guns are conservative. Dukakis was not their first choice, but once he was the party's nominee, they would do everything they could to guarantee his success.

Robert Beckel, Mondale's campaign manager in 1984, argued that a transition group should be established to plan for the general election. In 1984, he had broken off in May and done the planning for the convention and general election for Mondale. It was essential. It was also a potential vehicle for bringing Sasso back into the campaign, and many others, including Nick Mitropoulos, were pushing at Dukakis to expand his primary team into a larger, more diverse group.

But the names went up and down a flagpole of rejection at the Chauncy Street headquarters, with few exceptions. For many, some grudgelike personal reason for rejection was enough. Dukakis expressed much distaste for "hired guns." (He inexplicably excluded his own cadre from this category of lesser beings.) There was also understandable reluctance to tamper with a team that was working well.

But some of the most outstanding Democratic operatives in America, many of them former Gephardt campaign officials, were rejected by the Dukakis campaign. Ed Reilly, a brilliant and articulate strategist, got thumbs down because he had been Eddie King's guy. Bob Shrum, one of the Democratic Party's best writers and thinkers, had once made a joke about phoning Jewish voters in Florida and urging them to back Dukakis because Kitty and Michael raised their children in both the Greek Orthodox and the Jewish faiths (Kitty Dukakis reportedly found the joke anti-Semitic, an observation that the many Jewish and Israeli leaders Shrum has worked closely with over the years would have found hilarious). Bill Carrick went down in flames because of lingering bad feelings over the Gephardt Belgian-endive attack. Some people in the Dukakis camp belived that Shrum and Carrick had spread the false rumor that Kitty Dukakis had seen the Biden videotape. Bob Squier had actually been fired by Dukakis in 1982. Not until many months later, when the campaign was in trouble, could these talented consultants, and others like two veteran Kennedy hands, Theodore Sorenson (John Kennedy's counsel) and Peter Edelman (a Robert Kennedy adviser), come aboard.

Some exceptions were striking. Dukakis hired Kirk O'Donnell, then running the Democratic idea factory, the Center for National Policy in Washington, to be a top aide. O'Donnell, a Bostonian, had gone to Washington to be Speaker Tip O'Neill's counsel and evolved into a widely respected blender of ideas and politics. Originally he was to have custody of Dukakis's message in both its paid television and live campaigning forms, but because he could not move to Boston until nearly convention time, he focused mostly on daily and weekly campaigning plans.

The Democrats once again did not do in 1988 that which the Republicans do routinely. In the Republican world, it's no sin to work for your guy in the primaries as if you were in World War III, but once the nomination is decided, you work for the nominee. The result is a talent pool of not just good but experienced people who are used to working together, and who reap the rewards in access and more clients than they can handle in the off season. In June 1988, however, Dukakis had no sense of his troubles; he was almost totally fixed on more immediate matters: Jesse Jackson, and his search for a running mate.

Few men in America were better prepared for the phone call answered that July morning in Washington than the veteran Texas senator. At the age of sixty-seven, Bentsen had the self-confidence and selflessness that comes with maturity. Although he was the very powerful chairman of the Senate Finance Committee and had won major legislative victories in 1988 in battles over catastrophic health insurance, welfare reform and international trade, he had reached the stage where he was ready and willing to take on the often frustrating job of vice president, assuming it would be a real job. What he had learned about Dukakis interested him, and he respected the Massachusetts governor's accomplishments and operating style. Senator John F. Kerry of Massachusetts, Dukakis's former lieutenant governor, had told Bentsen that he could expect to have a real and significant role in any Dukakis administration. Once it was clear he would be more than a symbolic figure or glorified official mourner, he was willing to help the Democratic Party win and govern as vice president.

Thirteen years before, he had tentatively explored running for the presidential nomination in 1976 during his first term in the U.S. Senate. He was able to raise money but drew little support and made little headway in a race that eventually went to another southerner, Jimmy Carter. In 1984, Mondale had considered him for the vice presidency, but he felt burned by Mondale's very public selection procedure, which he found demeaning when it exposed their sharp disagreements on issues and made it plain he had no chance of being picked. When the Dukakis brain trust put him on the short list in 1988, he said that he wanted no part of it if he was going to be embarrassed.

From the start, Dukakis was sensitive to criticism leveled at Mondale for his very public search in 1984, though he did understand that Mondale had operated that way partly to make it clear that he had won the nomination. "I don't think it's helpful . . . to do it with press conferences at the end of the driveway every time you talk to somebody," Dukakis told a State House news conference.

The careful work in selection was characteristic of Dukakis, who had always made significant decisions after extensive consultation and with tremendous care. The procedure followed by the Democratic ticket in 1988 contrasted starkly to Bush's casual manner of choosing

Senator Dan Quayle as his running mate. Selecting a running mate is the first truly presidential choice to be made by either candidate, and the methods reveal a great deal about these would-be presidents, which is why they are covered so closely by the press.

In late April between the Pennsylvania and Ohio primaries, when it was clear Dukakis was going to be the nominee, Michael Berman, a top Mondale aide, gave Corrigan a copy of the questionnaire Mondale used for vice-presidential hopefuls in 1984.

Corrigan passed it on to Daniel Taylor, a partner in the Boston law firm of Hill & Barlow and Dukakis's chief legal counsel during his first term as governor, and asked Taylor to update it. Corrigan assumed correctly that "one of the lawyers"—Taylor or perhaps Brountas— would run the vice-presidential selection for the campaign.

From the start, Dukakis's principal criterion was that the running mate be someone of stature who could serve as president if anything happened to him. Credibility was the watchword, more important than geography or foreign-policy experience. Top campaign staff assumed that the likely candidate would be a member of Congress with the Washington experience Dukakis lacked.

Selection did not start in earnest, however, until Dukakis designated Brountas as his quarterback on the vice presidency in May. That pronouncement was like putting a Sphinx in charge. Brountas, an essentially nonpolitical man, is the consummate legal counselor— discreet, thorough, and shrewd. Dukakis did not want the search to begin prematurely and so he discouraged his friend from even beginning work on his initial memo on the project. Finally, on a trip to Florence, Italy to visit his daughter, far from Dukakis's watchful presence, and just before the last primaries, Brountas began to outline the memo. Although he finished the memo several days before the June 7 end of the primary and caucus season, he held on to it. At midnight, as June 7 slid into June 8, he handed Dukakis the memo. They met for breakfast the next morning at the Century Plaza Hotel in Los Angeles to discuss its contents. The twenty-five-page memo and its attachments described a careful procedure for selecting a running mate. He covered the criteria that should be used to measure and judge a running mate, the history of other selections, and the lessons to be learned from them. From the start, Dukakis said it was not necessary that his second be someone who agreed with him on all issues, though he acknowledged that differences on major issues might be a problem.

The project was run by two teams of lawyers. The first team, headed by Daniel Taylor, conducted background checks on each potential candidate. Taylor put one lawyer in charge of each candidate. That lawyer, in turn, called upon other lawyers in Boston, Washington,

Dukakis campaign chairman Paul Brountas, the quintessential corporate attorney, had been one of Dukakis's best friends since Harvard Law School. (Photo by Joanne Rathe)

and the candidates' home states, and any other resources he or she needed to put together a complete personal profile on each candidate.

Another team of researchers, headed by Victoria Radd, a young lawyer on leave from the prestigious Washington firm of Williams and Connolly, began to assemble the public record on each candidate. They worked in Chauncy Street offices that were kept locked at all times and were off limits to anyone not working directly on the project. The secrecy led campaign jokers to dub it "the Manhattan project" after the supersecret federal project to develop the atomic bomb.

Taylor also retained a private investigative firm in northern Virginia, the Fairfax Group. He knew that some major media organizations retained private investigators to help check the presidential hopefuls' backgrounds, and hoped that by following the same procedure, the campaign would come up with the same sort of information first. Taylor also knew that a great deal of information, like credit records, was just a computer terminal away for a professional investigator.

He also asked each candidate to sign a waiver and allow one designated campaign lawyer to look at their raw FBI files. The lawyers who would review the records would keep that knowledge confidential. All the candidates agreed but one, Jesse Jackson, who was consistently balky at providing financial records and other documents requested by the lawyers.

While the lawyers began their work, Brountas headed to Washington a week after the final primary to meet with forty-five members of Congress. He not only checked potential candidates but systematically sought recommendations from leading Democratic officials. In private meetings without staff, he found these politicians remarkably candid and helpful. Everyone wanted to win in 1988. No one stinted in giving his most cogent advice to the counselor.

Eventually the two legal teams came together to produce a four-to five-page preliminary report on each potential candidate. Dukakis and Brountas saw these reports and cut the list of possible candidates further. As the list became narrower, the scrutiny became more intense. Taylor mailed a request for documents and more detailed personal information to each finalist. Brountas and the lawyer responsible for the candidate's background check sat down with each finalist alone and then met separately with each man's wife to ask if they knew of anything embarrassing or private that might become controversial if he became vice president. They purposely kept no written record of those meetings to avoid a paper trail that might subsequently prove embarrassing.

Some candidates seemed to rise to the top like cream, particularly after Senator Bill Bradley of New Jersey, a Dukakis favorite, and Senator Sam Nunn of Georgia, took themselves out of the competition late in June. Bradley told Brountas that it was not his time, it was Dukakis's time, and he wanted out before it got serious. Nunn, at Brountas's urging, agreed not to take himself out until he talked with Dukakis, but finally insisted he had no interest, a decision that disappointed several senior campaign officials.

The finalists were Glenn, Senator Albert Gore of Tennessee, Bentsen, and Representatives Lee Hamilton of Indiana and Richard Gephardt of Missouri. From a tactical standpoint, a congressman was less valuable to Dukakis than a senator. A senator could at least help carry his home state. But Dukakis was genuinely fond of Hamilton and deeply respected his primary rival, Gephardt, who scored many points with the Dukakis team for his articulate and sincere endorsement of the governor after the primaries. The governor was never enthusiastic about Gore. He felt he needed someone more seasoned who would better balance his lack of Washington experience.

The staff handed Dukakis a book with summaries of each candidate's background on Sunday night, July 10, after he returned from a campaign trip. It was time to decide.

On Monday morning, Brountas visited the governor at his home, and told us later that Dukakis said the choice was between Glenn and Bentsen, a choice about which Brountas said he felt neutral. He advised Dukakis to take his time and make more phone calls on his own. Estrich, however, said that her distinct impression was that although there were two finalists, she read Brountas's report on his meeting with Dukakis to mean the governor was leaning toward picking Glenn, who was closer to Dukakis on the issues, particularly aid to the Nicaraguan Contras, which Dukakis considered anathema and Bentsen had strongly supported. Jack Corrigan and Brountas are equally insistent that the governor was not then leaning either way.

The Ohio senator had a staunch Dukakis camp ally in Bob Farmer, who was his campaign treasurer in his unsuccessful 1984 presidential campaign. Kitty Dukakis too had thought Glenn would be a good idea. But Estrich, Corrigan, and O'Donnell wanted Bentsen, and they trooped up to the State House for a thirty-minute meeting with Dukakis late that afternoon to make their cases.

Politics never became a factor, mostly because Dukakis banned it as a consideration, but also because they had no conclusive evidence that selecting anyone would give the Democratic ticket a major state in November. Tom Kiley believed Glenn made a difference in his key state, Ohio, with twenty-three electoral votes, but Tubby Harrison disagreed and believed that only Sam Nunn could deliver a state to Dukakis. A minority opinion was that Gore's potential to deliver Kentucky as well as Tennessee (a twenty-electoral-vote parlay), as well as his having no clear liabilities and no major private business interests whereas Glenn and Bentsen did, should have made him attractive; several campaign sources later told us this was John Sasso's feeling, but he would not discuss the subject.

After talking with Dukakis, Brountas flew to Washington to meet with Jackson for the last time. The meeting had been scheduled for the previous Friday in Texas, but Brountas canceled it when Jackson again failed to provide the background information the campaign had requested. The campaign never received everything it requested—the major dispute was access to FBI files—but it had enough at the end to make an evaluation, and Brountas told us that no one was disqualified because of personal, financial, or other information the Dukakis campaign had about them.

At that private meeting, Jackson made it clear that he wanted to be the vice-presidential candidate, something he had not made clear until that moment despite more than a month of Jackson-driven publicity and speculation. He argued that he deserved it because he had won 6.6 million votes in the primary contests and came in second. He would balance the ticket, he said, because Dukakis was a conservative and he was a liberal. He also told Brountas that he wanted to be consulted on the ultimate choice—told ahead of time which way Dukakis was leaning and permitted to weigh in with his views before a final decision was made. On the spot, Brountas refused that request because none of the other candidates would be consulted in that way. But Brountas also promised Jackson, he told us later with a rueful smile, that he would not read about Dukakis's decision in the newspapers, and before he left Washington he wrote down Jackson's telephone numbers and scheduled locations for the next forty-eight hours. After a meeting that had its tense moments, both sides knew it was time for Brountas to return to Boston and for Dukakis to make his decision, and that it wouldn't be Jackson.

Later that afternoon in the State House, Estrich, Corrigan, and O'Donnell were making the case for Bentsen with Dukakis. Estrich, the law-school professor, prepared for the meeting as she would prepare for a major trial. She had her arguments ready and made them forcefully. She pointed out that Bentsen had been the legislative leader on issues that were going to be major themes in the fall campaign. He had real legislative achievements that addressed the dual economic issue of American competitiveness in the world and quality of life for working people. In the past year he had scored a congressional hat trick by leading the fight for legislation on plant-closing notification, trade, and catastrophic health-care insurance.

Although their polling suggested that Bentsen's presence on the ticket would not guarantee a Democratic victory in his home state,

Texas, whereas Glenn had a better chance of helping bring Ohio into the Democratic column, she argued that Glenn was a less reliable candidate than Bentsen.

Brountas had spent thirty minutes discussing Bentsen's personal finances with him in private. Bentsen left the U.S. House after three terms in 1955 for the private sector and the insurance business. By the time he returned to politics in 1970 (beating George Bush for the Senate seat), he was a millionaire many times over. His finances were potentially rife with problems from his many years as a successful business-man in wheeling-dealing Texas, and suggestions had been published that the senator might have had a dealing or two with the blind trust he had formed to manage his assets. But Bentsen handled every question thoroughly and with dispatch. This man was not likely to be tripped up by some investigative reporter; when the questions were all asked, he had obliterated, not merely answered them. In contrast, Glenn had been unable, some top Dukakis aides felt, to convincingly handle questions about his relationship with a contributor who had ties to the savings and loan industry. No one suggested that Senator Glenn had done anything illegal or even ethically questionable, but the hard time he had answer-ing questions forcefully was potentially troublesome. You cannot an-ticipate every question, Estrich argued, but you can measure a candidate by how well he answers questions now. The arguments persuaded Dukakis, above all the assertions that Bentsen was a choice who would make Dukakis look presidentially wise. When his advisers left, his choice was Bentsen.

After leaving Jackson, Brountas called Dukakis from Washington's National Airport before he boarded the shuttle to Boston. When he learned that Dukakis had settled upon Bentsen, Brountas became upset. "I don't want to do it this way. This is a once-in-a-lifetime decision," he said in a conversation overheard by an intrepid *Boston Globe* intern who had been dispatched to the airport to keep an eye out for him. Brountas worried that Glenn had not gotten due consideration and asked Dukakis to reserve judgment until they could meet again later that night.

That night at 10:15, Brountas, Estrich, Kitty Dukakis, and Cor-rigan sat with Dukakis at his kitchen table. They reviewed the case for Glenn and Bentsen, and by 11:30 P.M. Bentsen once again was the choice. Dukakis tried to call Bentsen on the spot, but the senator and B.A. had already switched off their bedroom phone and retired for the night and no one answered at their house in Washington.

Estrich was charged with calling the unselected, including Jackson, next morning and was on duty by 7:00 A.M. Brountas, however, had forgotten to give her the telephone numbers the night before. By the time she got the numbers and called Jackson, he had already left his hotel in Cincinnati and was on his way back to Washington. The Dukakis staff tried to reach him through his Secret Service detail in the air but could not establish contact. When Mitropoulos reached Ron Brown, the Jackson convention manager, that morning at about 10:00 A.M., Brown instantly knew that they were all in trouble.

When Jackson came striding through a terminal at Washington's National Airport, a reporter approached him and asked him for a reaction to Bentsen's selection. Jackson was surprised and angry but responded, "I am too controlled. I am too clear. I am too mature to be angry. I am focused on what we must do to keep hope alive."

But that night in an emotional speech before the NAACP, the spurned candidate bristled with pride and fury: "I will never surrender!" he cried, bringing the crowd to its feet. "One thing I know, I may not be on the ticket, but I'm qualified! That's what I know! Qualified!"

And now, because Paul Brountas hadn't given Susan Estrich a list of telephone numbers, the national impression of unity so vital for Dukakis at the national convention was in jeopardy. Or was something else involved? Despite the facts, was the real problem that Dukakis hadn't grasped the importance of forging a real political relationship with Jesse Jackson, just as this man from the suburbs had often had trouble in his career forging relationships with black people who weren't lawyers or doctors or college professors?

Jackson had not always wanted to be the vice-presidential choice. His desire for the job evolved. Jackson had a difficult time acknowledging he had lost his quest for the nomination. He seemed unable, as he had in 1984, to bring his campaign to a graceful end. The one difference in 1988 was his decision in May to bypass his campaign manager until then, Ohio political consultant Gerald Austin, and to hire a Washington lawyer and polished insider, Ron Brown, a veteran of Senator Kennedy's staff and presidential campaign, as well as of Democratic National Committee posts. Brown's selection was a clear signal that Jackson intended to make peace with Dukakis, and he was known to believe that because it was a certainty the governor wouldn't offer Jackson the vice-presidential nomination, Jackson shouldn't seek it. Many of Dukakis's senior aides were not only friends of Brown but were eager to have him join them after the convention; in fact, back in May he had tentatively agreed to join Kirk O'Donnell and Jack Corrigan in a political-affairs triumvirate. But as his response at a June meeting at the Boston headquarters with Estrich, Corrigan, and Democratic National Committee Chairman Paul Kirk showed, Brown played his Jackson role to the hilt. Although they all had known one another for years, they played clearly designated roles for this meeting. Kirk, as the head of the party, formally asked Brown if Jackson would withdraw from the race and endorse the nominee, Dukakis. When Brown, representing Jackson, said no, Kirk sagged with disappointment and Corrigan morosely shook his head from side to side. None of them liked Brown's suggestion that Jackson would end his candidacy on the eve of the convention.

The question that only Dukakis could answer was whether or not to put Jackson on the vice-presidential list. Dukakis decided he should be considered like the others. At first, right after the California primary on June 7, Jackson seemed unsure of his desires, but after a long weekend at a southern California luxury resort, Jackson had decided that he either wanted to be asked or wanted a very good reason why he wasn't being asked. Ron Brown thought his course was a mistake, but as Jackson began playing with the issue in public—saying he deserved consideration but refusing to say whether he'd accept a Dukakis offer—the vice presidency became an issue intensely interesting to many black Americans, who began to believe from Jackson's behavior that he had a chance, and knew what a gigantic moment it would be when the first black person was nominated for the national ticket of a major political party. Eventually, the emotions he helped create became a perceived source of pressure on Jackson, making it hard for him to simply turn off the whole subject.

On the other hand, Brountas told us later that not one recommendation in favor of Jackson came from anyone in a major position in the Dukakis campaign, and that he considered stopping consideration of him, in part for candor's sake, but also as a way of defusing emotions before the convention. Brountas said, however, he could not see how to single out and eliminate one vice-presidential hopeful and not any of the others, and so he didn't.

Fortunately for the governor, his campaign had been careful not to make antagonizing mistakes in its relationships with the Jackson forces as party platform and rules issues were worked on before the convention. Estrich knew better than almost anyone else the explosive potential in platform or rules issues at a Democratic National Convention. She had negotiated platform issues that gave Senator Edward M. Kennedy his symbolic victories in the 1980 convention that renominated President Jimmy Carter. She shared Dukakis's view that they should eliminate in advance any conceivable issue that the Jackson forces could use as a rallying point in Atlanta. When Jesse Jackson came to Atlanta, he would come only as a candidate fighting for his own candidacy, not as the spokesman for a popular cause, she resolved. And so Tad Devine went to work on rules and Corrigan plunged into the platform issues. In no time, nearly every specific issue separating them had been negotiated off the table except for a few platform points that Jackson insisted on trying to make in the form of convention-floor amendments. The Dukakis people, assured of a few symbolic fights that they already had the votes to win by a mile, then arranged for them to be debated outside of prime-time television hours.

At the end of June in the musty ballroom of a shabby downtown Denver hotel, the 152-member platform committee rejected Jackson proposals to raise taxes on corporations and wealthy taxpayers and to freeze defense spending, to recognize "self-determination" for Palestinians, and to ban first use of nuclear weapons in armed conflict.

They agreed to disagree on those items, with the knowledge that Dukakis clearly held overwhelming majorities to prevail on them, and so by the time the convention neared, they had nothing left to discuss. The Dukakis forces held a majority of votes at the convention and would not relent on any issue that might give ammunition to the Republicans. The most naive Dukakis convention delegate understood how Mondale hurt his candidacy with his proposal to raise taxes in 1984. They were not about to make the same mistake. In fact, that view was shared by many Jackson supporters, who had as much invested in a Democratic victory in November as the Dukakis supporters and were not inclined to take a suicidal plunge for symbolic reasons.

Tad Devine was responsible for working out some sort of compromise on party rules to similarly appease Jackson, who consistently complained that the rules discriminated against his candidacy by denying him delegates in direct proportion to his popular vote. In a session with Jackson representative Harold Ickes, a New York lawyer and veteran rules junkie, with Washington consultant Carl Wagner acting as broker, they agreed to reduce the number of Super Delegates, those unelected automatic delegates, to 10 percent of the total in 1992, and to eliminate the winner-take-all primaries that had given Dukakis so many targets of opportunity in 1988.

Thus, following the Bentsen selection, an angry Jackson's order to stop "negotiations" on convention issues after the missed telephone call was strictly for show. There was nothing left to discuss.

Brountas knew instantly when Jesse Jackson was irate by Jackson's way of addressing him. People joked about knowing Dukakis before he became Greek and described him as a Greek Yankee, but Brountas was truly a Greek Yankee, with his suspenders, bow ties (Dukakis ordered him to put the bow ties away for the duration of the campaign), horn-rimmed glasses, and button-down, sober, lawyerly demeanor. Jackson routinely called him "Lawyer Brountas." If he was angry he mangled his name and called him "Bronson." If he was pleased, he referred to him as "Paul."

For the six days after Bentsen's selection until the national convention opened, he was Bronson. At first, Dukakis could do nothing but apologize for his campaign's oversight, endure the near silence that greeted his own appearance at the NAACP convention, and prepare for his acceptance speech and some kind of dénouement with Jackson in Atlanta. Jackson himself faced a choice of either stimulating his followers' emotions or trying to cool things off; he chose to make things hotter, organizing a bus caravan to take him and an army of reporters to Atlanta all the way from Chicago. From Dukakis's standpoint, about the only good thing that came from the firestorm was that Jackson's angry response had taken the spotlight away from party liberals who might have raised a ruckus over Bentsen's selection because of his conservative positions in the Senate. Most awkward for Dukakis was his support for the multiple-warhead MX missile and the Contra rebels in Nicaragua, both positions directly contrary to Dukakis's strong views, and both having given him pause before naming Bentsen to the ticket.

Before Jackson's arrival on the Saturday before Monday's opening, staffs from the two camps began to meet in Atlanta, trying to figure out how—from the Dukakis perspective—the convention could help the governor get elected President, and how—from the Jackson perspective—their leader could exit on as "victorious" a scale as possible. The deliberations were complicated because no specific issue was left— slots on the national committee, party platform, party nomination rules, anything—that hadn't already been negotiated.

Accordingly, on his way to Atlanta, Jackson began to raise a new one, speaking vaguely about "partnership" with Dukakis, and about a "relationship" with him should he win the election. All along the bus route, the words appeared in Jackson's comments with increasing frequency. And they dominated a long speech he gave upon arrival in the steamy convention city to several thousand cheering supporters in Piedmont Park near the convention complex. To Dukakis and his advisers, that sounded like a call for commitments ahead of time to Jackson roles in a governmental transition or actual government that they felt would compromise Dukakis's independence if he were to become president, and would hurt him deeply in the campaign if he were to agree to anything like that.

The quickest way out for Jackson was clearly going to have to be a meeting with Dukakis. In staff meetings on Saturday, however, when the question of a time was raised, the Dukakis camp replied that the governor wanted to wait until after Jackson's scheduled speech to the convention on Tuesday night before making a commitment to a meeting. Jackson representatives and neutral brokers were flabbergasted. If Dukakis waited that long, they argued, he would not only be crudely suggesting that Jackson had to "behave" before he would see him, he

As a joke, a Jesse Jackson baseball cap was dumped on Dukakis's head after the two candidates made their peace in Atlanta. Dukakis's staff was not amused. (Photo by John Tlumacki)

would also risk two days of possibly disruptive behavior by more than 1,300 Jackson delegates on the convention floor and a possibly angry speech by Jackson instead of one promoting a united effort for the fall. Eventually, Dukakis got the point, and a meeting was arranged for early Monday morning. Only Jackson, Dukakis, Ron Brown, and Paul Brountas were in the Dukakis suite at the Hyatt, and according to all four accounts it was a monumental anticlimax. Jackson pleasantly tried to get Dukakis to understand that he wasn't demanding a piece of his transition or presidency, he was merely seeking his friendship. From his first words, it was apparent that the words partnership and relationship would no longer be used, and so the two sides spent the rest of their time talking about how they would talk about their meeting before nearly 1,000 reporters camped out in a ballroom below waiting for a press conference that would be telecast live. The ensuing love-in marked the beginning of Dukakis's convention, and just in time.

Now that television coverage has been sharply scaled back as conventions have become scripted coronations, party partisans dominate the audiences—in person and at home—at the beginning, for keynote speeches and routine convention business, even the actual nomination of the presidential candidate. For Dukakis—as well as for Bush a month later—the political challenge at the national convention is to present an image of order, with the nominee seen as comfortably in control; and to pull off a solidly spectacular performance in delivering his acceptance speech on the closing evening.

The early morning meeting with Jackson on Monday set the stage for a happy opening that presented Dukakis and his campaign as in control, without having made major concessions. As Thursday night loomed, the impression that things had gone successfully was nearly universal, but no one expected that Dukakis had anything spectacular up his sleeve for that evening, and in fact when an advance text of his acceptance speech was distributed, the impression was of a solid, unspectacular job that nonetheless would send his campaign into the general election on a positive note. Dukakis himself had joked that his wife had fallen asleep while reading the speech.

In short, no one had the slightest idea what was about to happen, including Michael Dukakis.

The evening had been carefully scripted to show Dukakis as a warm and loving family man, as a manifestation of the American dream, as someone with whom "average Americans" (Estrich's favorite phrase) could identify. Backstage in the small holding room, the air was thick with tension when Kitty Dukakis stopped by to wish her husband luck on his big night before taking her place in the family box out front. To lighten the mood, Dukakis approached his wife of more than two decades, held her shoulders, and looked at her intently. "You never told me you were Jewish," he said, cracking up everyone within earshot.

The night opened with music before more than 15,000 Democrats who were jammed into the Omni, a basketball stadium that convention manager Donald Fowler conceded would be "cosy" under the best of circumstances.

John Williams, the Boston Pops conductor, wrote a special "Fanfare for Michael Dukakis," and the governor's father-in-law, Harry Ellis Dickson, associate conductor laureate of the Pops, led the orchestra.

And then came Olympia Dukakis. At her moment of glory a few months earlier on accepting an Oscar for her performance in the movie *Moonstruck*, Dukakis's first cousin had brandished her gold statue in the air and cried, "Okay Michael, let's go!" With a few friends and aides in a Greenwich Village restaurant just before the New York primary, Dukakis had burst into tears in response.

On Thursday night, when cousin Michael would accept his prize, she made a return engagement to do the introductory honors. She was a Dukakis delegate at large from New Jersey.

When she walked onto the podium to the theme from *Moonstruck*, delegates gently waved standards that carried a silver moon crescent and star. She began her introduction by telling how her father Constantine and her Uncle Pan (Dukakis's father Panos) came to America in search of a dream. As she spoke, the first rumblings of an explosion of emotion began; 15,000 people shut up; backstage, her cousin ceased last-minute speech alterations and watched her intently on a television monitor.

"They had no money," she said of their fathers. "They didn't know the language. What they had were their dreams, a commitment to realize them and a willingness to make sacrifices for their children."

The lights then went off, and suddenly Olympia Dukakis was narrating a video taped just days before in Brookline, in which she talked about playing Ping Pong in the Dukakis cellar, arguing about politics and shooting baskets in the driveway with cousin Michael. She drove by the Huntington Avenue office building where Dr. Dukakis had his office for years and had once been robbed and badly beaten by a drug addict looking for drugs and money. "Crime is not political for Michael, it's personal," she said.

The video had been shot on the steamy Sunday before the convention opened by Dukakis media men Dan Payne and Michael Shea. The rush job had its mishaps but they were minimal and funny. Olympia, talking into the camera, was to drive a car into Dukakis's driveway. Performing her lines flawlessly, she drove into the wrong driveway. She also walked through the gymnasium at Brookline High School attended by Dukakis, his wife, and all their children; pointed out that the governor's famous tomato patch was in front of the Perry Street duplex where the sunlight was better; and then, with dramatic effect, pushed out from the garage an ancient, rusty snowblower that her cousin still insisted worked as well as the day he bought it twenty-five years earlier. "Mike gives the word frugal a new dimension," she said.

Backstage in a holding room, her cousin stood in front of a television monitor with his arms folded, fixed on his cousin's words, oblivious to the photographers and staff around him. "Michael and I have been fortunate but we are not unique," said this immigrant's daughter. "Millions of Americans have worked hard to realize their dreams. Extending these opportunities to everyone is what Mike is all about. Like our fathers before us, Mike believes in America anything is possible."

Suddenly, the silence in the holding room was broken by Bruce

Garamella, one of his top advance men, who was in charge of moving him to the podium for his speech.

"Governor," he said softly, "we have to go."

When the video faded and the spotlight returned to this accomplished actress standing on the podium at the Democratic National Convention, she said, "We all know that many Americans have come to this country with nothing—nothing but hope. Well, today one of their sons stands before you with the opportunity to be president of the United States."

Dukakis, with Nick Mitropoulos beside him as always, was now standing just behind the curtains at the entrance to the dark convention hall. He turned to his companion for a brief moment. "We've come a long way from the cafes in Iowa," he said softly.

"It's your night," Mitropoulos replied. "This room is packed. It's going to go like a tinderbox. Just go slowly. Knock 'em dead."

"Ladies and Gentlemen," Olympia Dukakis said, her professional voice cracking from emotion, "it is with honor and pride and with love that I give you Michael S. Dukakis."

"Okay, you're on," said Garamella.

"Here we go," said Dukakis, stepping forward.

The curtains parted, a spotlight turned on the opening, and music began to rise over the ovation. The song that became an anthem for the campaign, Neil Diamond's "America," roared from the sound system like an uncaged beast, drowning out the cheers of the capacity crowd and shaking the stadium rafters. The song celebrates the immigrant experience of those who leave behind the familiar to seek the promise of America. The driving, thumping bass beat of the music—you could actually feel it—heightened the emotions among thousands of delegates as the spotlight searched and then found Michael Dukakis as he walked onto the convention floor.

Mitropoulos had seen that song drive a crowd to a frenzy in a Chicago disco on the night of the Super-Tuesday voting, and had made a mental note to recommend it for the convention. The idea of walking Dukakis up to the podium from the floor was not only designed to dramatize the moment when the nominee came up from the people, it was also designed to show this self-contained, cerebral politician his new power to move and inspire, in almost desperate hope that he would use it.

"Far," sang Neil Diamond, "We've been traveling far / Without a home, but not without a star."

The governor was being mobbed by delegates. The Secret Service surrounded him in a protective wedge. Mitropoulos, carrying a copy of the speech in a vise grip, walked next to his boss step by step and had to shout to be heard above the din. Look up, he said, so the cameras will get your whole face. Take your time. Slow down. This is all for you. It's your night.

"Free, only want to be free / We huddle close and hang on to that dream."

Dukakis waved as he walked, occasionally gripping an outstretched hand and accepting a supporters' embrace. By the time he reached the podium, he was stunned by the surging waves of emotion pounding through the hall and washing over him.

"On the boats and on the planes / We're coming to America / Never looking back again, we're coming to America."

Long before his walk ended, supporters and friends from his home state, Massachusetts, were sobbing. They were so proud of him. Since they had arrived in Atlanta for the convention, it hadn't seemed real somehow. All those Dukakis signs seemed out of context. Atlanta, after all, is not exactly Springfield, Massachusetts. And all this fuss was over Michael, of all people. They were used to the Kennedys being bigger than life and somewhat legendary. But Michael? The guy who did his own grocery shopping with coupons and bought generic products to save a few pennies. Michael? For president?

"Home, it's a new and shining place / Make our bed and we'll say our grace / Freedom's light burning warm / Freedom's light burning warm."

Mitropoulos kept him from going to the stage for a second at the top of the stairs. For all his caution, the walk had gone a little bit too fast; the song was still playing. Now they could see James B. King, a veteran Massachusetts operative, granddaddy of advance men, who was running the podium, standing on the stage wired for sound, beaming with joy. Dukakis walked up the stairs to the platform with a bounce in his step and threw his arms in the air in a V for victory. After acknowledging the dignitaries at the back of the podium with a slight bow, he turned back to the crowd. He shook his head slightly, a gesture of incredulity as if he could not believe all this was intended for him.

"Got a dream to take them there / They're coming to America. Got a dream, they come to share / They're coming to America."

Dukakis shook his head again in amazement. He stood there soaking it in as "Stars and Stripes Forever" replaced "America" on the sound system. The introduction, the music, the wild emotion energized him as the staff had hoped. He then accepted the Democratic presidential nomination with the best speech performance of his life. The speech itself was vintage Dukakis and therefore devoid of soaring rhetoric or memorable lines. But the power of his performance invested the familiar, even prosaic words with new meaning.

When Estrich first raised the subject of his acceptance speech with

The Democratic Party nominees for president and vice president with their wives, B.A. and Kitty, stand before an enthralled crowd at the close of the Democratic National Convention. (Photo by John Tlumacki)

him, she recommended that the campaign's speechwriter, Bill Woodward, write it. A speechwriter has few great moments, and she felt Woodward had earned the opportunity to write the big one. But Dukakis countered that Ira Jackson, his former Revenue Commissioner and top adviser, now working as a bank executive in Boston, should take a whack at it. He had no strong thoughts of his own, and so Jackson did his own research into presidential speeches and came up with a draft that Estrich and Dukakis both rejected as too long and ponderous. With two weeks left before the convention, Woodward set to work with Dukakis. At the convention, Kennedy wordsmith Ted Sorenson changed one line and Jackson changed one paragraph, but it was essentially produced by Woodward and Dukakis.

During the practice sessions, Dukakis had been flat. In a practice room tucked out of sight beneath the podium, Mitropoulos, John Dukakis, and Kirk O'Donnell had acted as an audience, cheering and applauding, to determine the length of the speech as it would be delivered before the convention.

The speech was focused first on the dream that drew his parents to

America shortly after the turn of the century. He recalled the memory of his father, "who arrived at Ellis Island with only $25 in his pocket, but with a deep and abiding faith in the promise of America—and how I wish he were here tonight," his voice broke and tears glistened in his eyes, "He would be very proud of his son."

The American dream, he said, was what the Democratic Party was all about. He listed ethnic Democratic officeholders from across the nation, "Henry Cisneros of Texas, Bob Matsui of California, Barbara Mikulski of Maryland, Mario Cuomo of New York, Claude Pepper of Florida, and Jesse Louis Jackson."

The mention of Jackson's name drew a throaty roar from the Jackson delegates. Dukakis turned and waved to Jackson in the VIP booth. Jackson, beaming, responded with the thumbs-up gesture.

The tribute to Jackson was simple but eloquent, "A man who has lifted so many hearts with the dignity and the hope of his message throughout this campaign; a man whose very candidacy has said to every child—aim high; to every citizen—you count; to every voter—you can make a difference; to every American—you are a full shareholder in our dream.

"And my friends, if anyone tells you that the American dream belongs to the privileged few and not to all of us, you tell them that the Reagan era is over. You tell them that the Reagan era is over, and that a new era is about to begin.

"I don't think I have to tell any of you how much we Americans expect of ourselves," he said. "Or how much we have a right to expect from those we elect to public office. Because this election isn't about ideology. It's about competence."

As he recited that sentence, a piercing shriek came from campaign aide Victoria Rideout in the command trailer. She knew instantly that the Republicans would later use that line to charge that Dukakis didn't care about ideas. Woodward wrote the sentence into the earliest drafts of the speech after Estrich stressed to him aiming the speech at Middle Americans. If these voters base their vote upon ideology, we lose, she told him. This election needs to turn on the qualities and values of the individual, the area of Dukakis's greatest strength. As he wrote the speech, he thought that some of the most nagging problems left by the Reagan administration—the budget deficit, the decline in ethical standards, the trade issues—were not ideological questions so much as management issues. Issues of competence.

The speech was replete with familiar quotations and techniques that Dukakis had used in his annual state-of-the-state addresses in Massachusetts: he quoted John Winthrop, first governor of Massachusetts; he spoke by name of individuals whose accomplishments enriched and ennobled the nation; he recited the 2,000-year-old Athenian pledge always repeated at great ceremonial moments in ancient Greece.

He told them his special goal for the nation. It was the classic reformer view of government, the good-guy versus bad-guy view that had served him so well in Massachusetts where he rose to prominence because he offered clean government, unlike the scurrilous rascals who once gave the state a national reputation for corruption.

"My friends," he said, "four years from now, when our citizens walk along Pennsylvania Avenue in Washington, D.C., or when they see a picture of the White House on television, I want them to be proud of their government; I want them to be proud of a government that sets high standards not just for the American people, but high standards for itself."

"We're going to have a Justice Department that isn't the laughing stock of the nation—we're going to have a Justice Department that understands what the word 'justice' means."

"We're going to have a vice president who won't sit silently by when somebody at the National Security Council comes up with the cockamamie idea that we should trade arms to the Ayatollah for hostages. . . ." The crowd erupted with the chant, "Where was George? Where was George?"

". . . We're going to have a vice president named Lloyd Bentsen who will walk into the Oval Office and say,"Mr. President, this is outrageous and it's got to stop."

"My friends, in the Dukakis White House, as in the Dukakis State House, if you accept the privilege of public service, you had better understand the responsibilities of public service. If you violate that trust, you'll be fired; if you violate the law, you'll be prosecuted; and if you sell arms to the Ayatollah, don't expect a pardon from the president of the United States."

He spoke about the coming generation: convention keynoter Ann Richards's granddaughter Lily; Jesse Jackson's young daughter, Jackie; his own first grandchild, due to be born in January 1989.

"Yes, my friends, it's a time for wonderful new beginnings. A little baby. A new administration. A new era of greatness for America. And when we leave here tonight, we will leave to build that future together."

It was undeniably his finest hour. Seasoned pols from his home state shook their heads in amazement. The Duke had outdone himself, given the best speech performance of his life. The reaction was uniformly elated. The governor seemed overwhelmed. When Kitty came to the stage in her red silk dress, he grabbed her so hard, she was startled. For a moment, tears shone in his eyes.

His elation was shared by the party officials and also-rans who

After delivering the best speech performance of his career at the Democratic National Convention in July, the elated candidate grabbed his wife so hard that he startled her. (Photo by John Tlumacki)

joined him on the stage to House Speaker Jim Wright's booming introduction. Dick Gephardt gripped his hand and said, "We're going to win."

"The guy sounds like a president," said Bob Neill, a delegate from El Paso, Texas. Kathy Estep of Springfield, Ohio, another delegate, was sobbing. "He was presidential," she gasped. Norma Fenochietti, one of Dukakis's most hardworking and loyal political aides from Massachusetts, who began weeping at the moment he entered the hall and never stopped, said, "I can't believe it." Jeff Greenfield, the astute ABC commentator, said, "It was a speech that caused the Republicans to send out for an extra order of Maalox, Pepto-Bismol and Alka-Seltzer."

Michael Dukakis had indeed reached the high point in his marathon to the White House as he basked in the convention's adulation with glitter descending from the rafters and American flags rippling before him in a sea of red, white, and blue. At this heady time, he never suspected that he might never again experience a moment like this. The rest of the course would be a downhill run to defeat.

He had risen to a presidential moment, but as emotions gradually returned to normal—and it took several hours for Dukakis's closest aides and supporters—a few less than adoring thoughts remained. John Sasso couldn't help but notice that the text held not one memorable line or idea. And Tubby Harrison, his mind already focused on the coherent, cogent message required for the fall campaign, quickly noticed the same thing. But even they were totally swept up in Dukakis's willingess—finally—to *communicate* instead of speak. He had earned the right to soar in the polls, not by producing emotion, but by yielding to it, yielding to the Democrats' fierce, desperate desire to have a president again.

7

The Swoon

John Sasso was relaxing with his wife, Francine, and their two children on Martha's Vineyard, a bucolic island off the Cape Cod coast, when interrupted by a telephone call on Monday night, August 29. It was Paul Brountas, asking him to return to the campaign and to Boston immediately. Sasso had rented a vacation house for ten days, but he went to Boston the next morning, telling his wife he would be back the following day. He had been talking to Brountas and Dukakis about returning to the campaign since spring. He was ready to come back at any time in any capacity. But nothing had ever come of their discussions, despite tentative agreement from the governor as early as June that Sasso's return was desirable.

But this call was different. It was finally time, even past time. Michael Dukakis's presidential campaign was in deep trouble. Sasso never made it back to the Vineyard.

In the depths of the hottest August in a century, Dukakis allowed a post-Democratic convention lead of seventeen percentage points to vanish and become a nine-point Bush advantage in fourteen days. Neither polling margin reflected more than temporary post-convention glow, but that was all it took to reinforce what anyone could see: Dukakis was self-destructing, disappearing under a tidal wave of exquisitely framed and coordinated attacks designed to persuade the country, voting bloc by voting bloc, that he was a dangerous, incompetent liberal.

Again and again in recent years, Democratic presidential nominees have suffered the consequences of behaving as if the United States were France, where almost the entire official country shuts down for August. Modern presidential politics don't take August breaks, and neither do voters' minds, and there is no more a "traditional Labor Day start for the fall campaign"; every August since 1964, Democratic nominees have been severely hurt during this allegedly quiet month, and Dukakis (as a newcomer to the national scene) was warned explicitly in 1988 that he especially needed to be vigorous for the month following his nomination. His rejection of this advice made him a uniquely sitting target.

The attacks succeeded because the response from Dukakis was lame, ineffectual, and occasionally nonexistent. They also succeeded because Dukakis was not giving voters a reason to support his candidacy. Moreover, Bush was at long last offering thematic contrasts and standing on his own feet at his party's national convention in New Orleans. Dukakis had been advised long before his own convention that his best defense would be a powerful, positive offense in which he addressed average Americans' economic worries and their sense that the country was losing hold of its economic destiny. By the time the Republican convention opened on August 15, he had no real lead left. By the time the convention adjourned four days later, he was behind. Dukakis then made himself an even more inviting target by retreating to silence and to Massachusetts for much of the rest of August.

Within a week of the Democratic National Convention even Lee Atwater had taken to issuing statements attacking Dukakis for being a criminal-coddler. He charged that Dukakis had commuted the sentences of fifty-eight violent criminals during his nine years as governor—twenty-eight of them first-degree murderers. The Dukakis campaign came back with a lame explanation that governors routinely commuted sentences of prisoners.

Dukakis's own forays into *J'accuse*-land were less calculated, and rarely effective. On July 30, in Louisville, Kentucky, he accused the Reagan-Bush administration of lowering ethical standards, a familiar line, but when asked who he considered responsible for all the sleaze, his hubris got ahead of his political sense. "There's an old Greek saying that the fish rots from the head first. It starts at the top," Dukakis said. Although the facts of official malfeasance in the Reagan administration were well known, the Bush campaign immediately turned the tables by saying Dukakis was attacking Reagan personally. The governor knew he had goofed. Ever since Reagan's visit to Moscow in June he had been privately declared off limits for personal criticism by the Dukakis high

command. In one of their occasional telephone chats, John Sasso reminded him that he had goofed.

Reagan had his chance to get even four days later.

The Monday after the Democratic National Convention, senior
adviser Kirk O'Donnell got a phone call from "a federal civil servant,"
who, out of friendship, told him to expect George Bush's campaign to
spread a rumor that Dukakis had undergone treatment for depression in
the late 1970s.

It was an old rumor dating from the period following his defeat in
the Democratic primary at Edward King's hands in 1978, and it was
unfounded and totally false. It had circulated after Dukakis decided to
run for president, and now it was circulating again after his nomination.
It had also arisen during the Democratic convention when followers of
extremist eccentric Lyndon LaRouche distributed leaflets making wild
allegations about Dukakis's mental health. Now, the federal bureaucrat
was telling O'Donnell to expect rumor-mongering from the Bush forces.

Shortly after O'Donnell received this warning, the *Detroit News*
sent a questionnaire to both nominees, requesting their medical-history
records as well as statements from their physicians. The questionnaire
routinely went to the Dukakis press-relations office in Boston. Almost
at once it came to the attention of Mark Gearan, long a Dukakis aide,
who ran it.

As the week wore on, various campaign officials—including
O'Donnell, Gearan, and Press Secretary Dayton Duncan, Walter Mondale's deputy press secretary in 1984 who was hired by the campaign for
the general election—began to get inquiries from reporters checking a
rumor that the *News* was about to publish a story alleging that Dukakis
had sought psychiatric help ten years before. For some reason, rumors
in the 1988 campaign usually took this form: a report that a specific news
organization was about to go with a specific story. By Thursday, July
28, the rumors had become a major preoccupation for the senior staff,
and Dayton Duncan, who traveled with Dukakis, took one call in the
middle of the night from the *Los Angeles Times* requesting a comment;
Duncan declined, on the sensible grounds that there was no story on
which to comment.

With Dukakis touring several midwestern industrial states that
Friday, and with a regular press conference on his schedule, top campaign officials all agreed that if he was questioned on the subject, he
should reply that not only were the rumors false but that the newspaper
questionnaire would be answered.

No one asked a question about the rumors at the press conference
in Springfield, Illinois. But as the conference broke up, Dukakis was
approached by a small group of reporters, and Tom Squitieri of the

Boston Herald asked him if he was aware of rumors that he had sought psychiatric care after his older brother Stelian was killed by a hit-and-run driver in 1973, and again after he lost the election to Ed King in 1978. The governor shrugged and walked away.

The governor's nonresponse provoked some debate in the traveling press corps over how to interpret his shrug. Dayton Duncan weighed in with an emphatic on-the-record denial, though he had had to practically beg Dukakis to let him issue it. The governor, he said, "has never been treated for mental depression or mental illness of any kind, at any time."

But the governor's reaction to the question and Duncan's denial effectively kept the rumors alive through the weekend in press and political circles. The *Boston Globe* reported the Squitieri question, the shrug, and the Duncan response at the end of the daily Dukakis story in the Saturday morning paper. That weekend, reporters bombarded Dukakis headquarters with telephone calls, and Bush campaign officials and reporters discussed the subject with one another. The result was almost a frenzy behind the scenes by Monday, though not a molecule of hard information had materialized.

Dukakis was in Boston on Monday, and following a routine scheduling meeting with senior aides, the most senior ones—including O'Donnell, Estrich, and Corrigan—stayed behind. They had agreed in advance to make O'Donnell the point man. He would bring up the rumors and state the staff's unanimous view that the questionnaire should be filled out. Until that morning, O'Donnell had been most effective in dealing directly with Dukakis, and the governor enjoyed dealing directly with him. But on that morning, he decisively rejected the advice to answer the questions.

Dukakis had been through this difficulty before, after Gary Hart's debacle, when *New York Times* Washington editor Craig Whitney had authorized mailing an extremely long questionnaire to all the remaining candidates, demanding a wide range of information, including access to any raw files at the FBI, academic transcripts, birth certificates, and medical records. The request was absurdly intrusive and was withdrawn. This latest request, Dukakis said, was just like the earlier one, and he refused to respond to it.

O'Donnell tried to make the point that this was the general election, and with far more attention on everything each candidate did, no one could stand on the principle of privacy without appearing to give the rumors credibility as a political force. Dukakis rejected that argument out of hand, insisting that in fact the public would see the issue in the same way as he did. The governor, after all, had just finished almost two solid weeks of campaigning following his immensely successful convention. Unlike his senior aides, he had not had to field scores of phone calls from reporters, obviously hot on the trail of a hot rumor. Dukakis failed to see what his advisers were so anxious about.

It didn't take long for the tag team of Reverend Sun Myung Moon's *Washington Times* and Ronald Reagan to elevate the issue to real news. On Tuesday, the paper published a story that reported Dukakis's staff were calling newspapers denying unsubstantiated rumors about Dukakis's mental health. On Wednesday, both the *New York Times* and the *Boston Herald* mentioned mental-health "rumors" in news stories.

When a reporter for a Lyndon LaRouche publication, *Executive Intelligence Review*, asked Ronald Reagan about the rumors late Wednesday morning on August 3, Reagan said, "Look, I'm not going to pick on an invalid." His remark served as the legitimate news hook needed by the media to do a full-blown mental-health story on Dukakis. Although Reagan attempted to apologize for his tasteless remark later in the day by saying he had been joking, the unfounded rumor was nonetheless headed for the evening news.

At first it seemed as though the president's remark was a twofold gift to Dukakis: it woke him up and made him realize instantly that the only course available to him was full disclosure of his medical records; Reagan also put himself and Bush too close to the story, giving it the strong odor of campaign sleaze, and this taint was reflected in the evening's network-news treatment, as Bruce Morton of CBS reported that Bush campaign officials had been hyping the story behind the scenes.

As a result, not only did Reagan give Dukakis an opportunity to kill the rumors in one news cycle, the president also gave him a chance to look good, and he played the part with relish at a press conference across the street from his campaign headquarters shortly after Reagan retracted his comment.

No need to apologize, Dukakis said magnanimously, "We all occasionally misspeak." And a few hours later, his personal physician for many years, Dr. Gerald R. Plotkin, was produced to give a briefing, in mind-numbing detail, which included the governor's hemoglobin, white blood cell, and cholesterol counts.

But although the president looked stupid, the Bush campaign appeared at least partially complicit, and in the end Dukakis's response was skillful, still this burst of intense publicity raised questions about the governor that need never have come up. If he had been a surging candidate immediately after Atlanta (and he was), the mental-health story stopped his media momentum cold.

Late that evening, over supper at the St. Cloud restaurant in Boston's South End, pollster Tubby Harrison, though relieved that the mental-health story had appeared to end cleanly and without damage, talked of his much deeper worries about the campaign. Since Atlanta, he said, Dukakis had fallen from his presidential pedestal. Since the convention, the governor had said nothing, looked small, and acted as if he were in a city-council fight. What he needed most, Harrison said, was a strategic plan to guide his campaign thematically, so that each day's campaigning could be made part of a sharply defined whole. Without this kind of plan, Harrison said, the vital but day-to-day guidance being supplied by Kirk O'Donnell's aggressive work would be too helter-skelter, mostly defensive, too small-looking, or all three.

At that time, however, the governor was saying as little as possible. According to Kirk O'Donnell, he was fearful of getting tagged as another Democratic taxer and spender, and so he put off suggestions that he make specific proposals, worried that he would get caught in an endless barrage of questions about how he would pay for his initiatives. Examples of ideas that were either rejected or put on hold in this period are legion. Harvard Professor Lawrence Summers, who coordinated economic-policy issues for the campaign, researched a proposed commitment by Dukakis to preside over a 50 percent increase in the gross national product in the 1990s—in effect setting a goal for a return to 1960s growth rates. From Christopher Edley's issues shop came a fully developed proposal for national service by young people. And most of the initiatives that Dukakis eventually put forward in September and October, including higher education financing, health insurance, and drug law enforcement, were available to him in the summer.

On the other hand, while Dukakis was rejecting specific ideas or putting them off, he was also clamoring behind the scenes for a fully developed general-election battle plan, and he wasn't getting one.

The day after the mental-health rumors were put to rest, Dukakis looked good in the papers, but in person he was glum and distracted as he began a three-day swing from the South to the West Coast and back through Iowa. We spoke to him for several minutes in the front cabin of his airplane. He expressed amazement that news organizations would report rumors with no supporting information, and wondered aloud if this was a taste of what the general election would be like. He made his distaste plain.

His first stop that day was at the Neshoba County Fair in the steamy Mississippi town of Philadelphia, a stop scheduled as part of the fifty-state campaign fiction, even though Bush was already seven percentage points ahead of him there. Philadelphia is a famous site in the civil-rights movement lore, the place in 1964 where three young activists—one local black and two whites from the North—were murdered. In preparing his remarks for the appearance, speechwriters

Victoria Rideout and James Steinberg argued strongly for a reference to the anniversary, making the point that quite apart from the merits in observing such a major anniversary, failure to do so would almost certainly become a focus for press coverage. They were supported by one of the rising stars among black political operatives, Donna Brazile, who had joined Dukakis as a senior aide in late spring after service as Richard Gephardt's national field director. Rideout and Steinberg, however, despite their passionate entreaties, were told by Estrich and O'Donnell, late in the evening before the trip, that the subject was off limits.

On the plane the next morning, they got strong support from Paul Brountas, who also could not see how Dukakis could avoid the subject, in good conscience or as good political judgment. The result was nothing special, just a few lines linking the dark Mississippi past with the wrenching Boston struggle over school desegregation in the mid-1970s, and emphasizing each area's progress since then and that maintaining the progress was imperative. But on the way to the fair from a nearby airport, Dukakis sat next to Mississippi Secretary of State Dick Molpus, who advised him strongly to steer clear of civil rights; at the last minute—a frequent time for Dukakis speech decisions in the campaign—Dukakis decided to throw out all references to the past.

Instead, twenty-four years to the day since the three civil-rights workers' bodies were discovered, Dukakis told a nearly all-white audience of several thousand people fanning themselves in the fairgrounds grandstand that "It's time, in this Olympic year, to build a team for America that's not at half strength but at full strength. It's time, in this Olympic year, for America to settle not for the bronze, not for the silver; it's time to go for the gold."

The only national news he made was his failure to mention the anniversary.

That weekend, Dukakis drew large and enthusiastic crowds out West, but he left the general impression that he was a front-running candidate who was playing it safe. A regular exception was his unequivocal pledge to protect the California coast from oil exploration, but a rally in downtown Seattle on August 5, Dukakis sounded like the competence salesman in the Iowa caucuses:

> We're going to forge a new era of greatness for America. We're going to roll up our sleeves and go to work and build an economic future that will create good jobs at good wages for every citizen in every region of this land.

Dukakis got back to Boston Saturday evening, August 6, to welcome political news. In their latest national poll the *New York Times* and

CBS News had found that his lead over Bush was holding at a hefty seventeen percentage points. As word of the poll reached the Dukakis entourage late Saturday during a refueling stop-rally in Cedar Rapids, Iowa, the mood soared after more than a week of rough going. But even then, the high command had private indications that their margin was nowhere near that high, and that in fact they had already lost their post-convention "bounce."

The CBS-*New York Times* poll broke on the air on Sunday, August 7, and in print on August 8. By the following night, it was out of date, replaced on the public record by a Gallup survey that had Dukakis ahead by ten percentage points. Senior Dukakis aides attributed his dip in the second week of August to the sudden burst of national publicity over the mental-health rumors, but although the flap was certainly, Kirk O'Donnell said, a "momentum stopper" as a news event, little objective evidence says that it affected Dukakis's polling position; in fact, from hindsight it's apparent that the CBS-*New York Times* poll was an isolated survey that may well have reflected reality inaccurately.

The Dukakis campaign already had less rosy figures by the time the Gallup numbers were published. In fact, Tubby Harrison found Dukakis up by ten points, 52 to 42 percent, in a poll conducted between August 2 and August 4, a slip from the seventeen-point margin he had found immediately after the Democratic convention.

Harrison told us he had no evidence at all that the mental-health stories had any influence. He did find, he said, that nearly all the Dukakis slippage had occurred among the very voters who had given him his postconvention bounce: white men, especially those under age forty-five, who appeared to have flipped from strongly pro-Dukakis to overwhelmingly pro-Bush in less than two weeks. According to Harrison, the main cause was a sharp dip in the rating given his "presidential" qualities; he told us he had also spotted a surge in optimism about the direction of the economy and the country, and an increase in the importance of foreign policy to white men in determining their voting preference.

Six days later, after an update showed a still-stable ten-point margin, Harrison and his associate, Clifford Brown, analyzed the campaign in a memorandum to Estrich, Corrigan, O'Donnell, and Kiley. Harrison argues points with bulldog tenacity and the commitment of a true believer, which only increased as Dukakis continued to go it alone. His work in 1988 is remarkable for its consistency: the need for a grand campaign message based on restoring America's economic primacy in the world, emphasizing a strong defense and making tough proposals about crime, but also meeting the challenge of helping average Americans enjoy a decent, middle-class life.

"We came out of the convention looking big, strong, Presidential," the memo began. "The challenge was to maintain that image and take the fight to Bush during the weeks between the conventions."

"Instead, we seem to be bogged down in arguments with Bush on smaller issues and are largely reacting to his charges, instead of taking the fight to him and looking big. This lowers us to his level and means we are playing on his turf."

"Moreover, at a time when we should be strengthening MSD's image, we have been softening it with small visuals. Bush, in the meantime, by leveling strong attacks, has not only hurt us, but has addressed his wimp image as well. As a result, we are losing ground to Bush on 'Presidentiality' (especially among younger men), and the poll results show it. We have to take the play away from Bush again."

Harrison's analysis could be boiled down to a sentence: *something is wrong*. That view was shared across the highest level in the Dukakis campaign; the disquiet was uniform. It also was expressed in a companion observation: *something is missing*, and most of the senior staff identified that something as John Sasso.

During this period Sasso was, as always, supercautious in his observations to us, which he continued to offer only on condition that we make no attribution of any kind. He never dropped even a hint of the backstage machinations about him. He said, however, that without question Dukakis had fallen off his Atlanta pedestal, that he was "dickering" around in minutiae, and that he needed to go on the offensive about the country's economic future. Sasso told us that a strong offensive would make Bush's attacks seem petty by comparison, and get Dukakis beyond the need to engage in constantly defensive responses to the Bush attack.

No one at the top of the campaign opposed this general assessment. The difficulty came in translating it into a specific course of action. None of this discussion was meant to preclude a more comprehensive assault on Bush himself and his negative campaign tactics, as well as on the extremely conservative line the Republican Party seemed certain to follow in its national convention in New Orleans, which was to open on Monday, August 15. In fact, led by Estrich, O'Donnell, and Kiley, the campaign had begun around the first of the month to map detailed plans for bracketing the convention with a counteroffensive.

For months, senior Dukakis advisers had known that crime would be a problem for the governor, and that the Massachusetts furlough program—symbolized by one escaped criminal's grave crimes committed while on the run—would be the most likely vehicle for an all-out assault. By late May, everyone on Chauncy Street assumed that Bush would use the William Horton case. Indeed, by early June, Bush was citing it constantly, and by early August so-called independent organizations—Bush supporters who said they were acting on their own—were running anti-Dukakis television commercials in selected southern and western markets that used the Horton case as well as the menacing mug shot of the obviously black felon.

Estrich had already tried unsuccessfully to persuade Dukakis to tell two stories about his own family's direct experiences with crime: the mugging of his father at his office in 1977 and the hit-and-run murder of his brother four years earlier. The governor had used those stories in his comeback campaign in 1982 to counter King's strong position in favor of mandatory criminal sentences and capital punishment.

In early August, Estrich and the high command tried again, focusing on the Friday, August 12, before the Republican convention began. Their tentative schedule would put the governor that day in North Carolina, where one of the Horton television commercials was running, or in Jacksonville, Florida.

The plan called for a major campaign event, which New York ad man Ed McCabe would tape and use for a Dukakis commercial. As Estrich envisaged it, the event would touch all the bases she considered essential if Dukakis was to get in front of the furlough controversy: an explicit *mea culpa* about the Horton case by Dukakis acknowledging that it was a mistake but stressing that he had accepted responsibility and agreed to changes in the program; the two stories about his father and brother; information about the much more lax treatment of federal prisoners and the much looser furlough program in California when Ronald Reagan was its governor; and a strongly worded summary of Dukakis's law-enforcement record, focusing on the drop in the Massachusetts crime rate and the governor's widely praised efforts to coordinate the fight against illegal drugs.

The North Carolina event would also include endorsements of Dukakis by police organizations and unions around the country, and a strong denunciation of the pro-Bush television commercial by Dukakis himself (several Dukakis advisers believed that these early commercials were in part designed to see how strong a counterattack they provoked).

Dukakis rejected the entire plan brusquely, telling his top aides they were pushing him to go at Bush too hard, too early.

Estrich, O'Donnell, and their colleagues also strongly argued for an immediate response to the Republican convention, to be delivered on August 19, the day after it ended, when Dukakis would be riding a train through Illinois, Missouri and Arkansas. The focus in this counterattack was to be ideology, and it was timed to influence the national polls that would surely be conducted that weekend to measure Bush's bounce from the convention. For this plan, the focus was to be on a Republican

Party hopelessly stuck on the far right. The recommended speech lines included an assertion that the Republican Party was so far right it was wrong, and that it had completely left the mainstream of American political life.

Again, Dukakis brusquely rejected the advice. While his campaign train was rolling through the Midwest, Dukakis yelled at speechwriter——issues adviser Victoria Rideout to "take out the Bush stuff." But the governor's running mate did see the need to make a quick response. Lloyd Bentsen made speeches all day that Friday, calling the GOP convention "a Mardi Gras for the Moral Majority," and drawing contrasts between a right-wing party and the Democrats' feelings for middle-class families. In a general election, however, it is the candidate and not his running mate who gets the network news coverage, and Dukakis's silence meant the story belonged almost exclusively to the Republicans as they left New Orleans.

And what a story it was: Ronald Reagan's staged departure on the second day of the convention to leave the spotlight solely on Bush; his amazing choice of the junior senator from Indiana as his running mate; the firestorm of speculation and controversy about Dan Quayle's military service as a clerk-typist in the Indiana National Guard and his life of privilege; Bush's dogged defense of his decision; his ideological, new identity-supplying acceptance speech; Quayle's perfectly staged defense of himself among his Hoosier kinfolk in Huntington, Indiana, the day after the convention; and rampant speculation about all manner of possible skeletons in the Quayle closet that set scores of journalists on a wild chase.

In part, Dukakis's decision to say nothing as the Republican convention adjourned can be explained by a desire to let the Quayle controversy fester. His advisers had warned him, however, that the risk of silence was that if voters liked what Bush had shown them in his speech, Dukakis would be letting Bush bounce in the polls by default. On any given day, Dukakis's rejection of a speech, a strategy memo, or a line of attack could have a plausible explanation; however, Dukakis's behavior in August was so unusual because he was rejecting specific advice wholesale, running almost at odds with his entire campaign high command. In any event, he was without message, he was without lines of attack, he was staying too close to home, and he was unable to resolve the question of who should lead his campaign. And now, on the weekend after the Republican convention, a *Newsweek* poll had him trailing George Bush by nine points.

The staff had decreed that the week after the Republican National Convention was to be trade policy week. It took only one day, Monday, however, for Dukakis to step all over his own story by delivering a legalistic defense of his 1977 veto of the bill requiring school teachers to lead children in the Pledge of Allegiance.

"If the vice president of the United States is saying that if he was president and the United States Supreme Court said a law was unconstitutional and the attorney general said it was unconstitutional and he'd have signed it anyway, well, that raises very serious questions about what it means to take the oath of office," he said to a group of Massachusetts newspaper editors. "If the vice president is saying he'd sign an unconstitutional bill, then in my judgment he's not fit to hold the office" of president.

"I encourage children to say the Pledge of Allegiance," he said. "I say the Pledge of Allegiance. That's not the issue. The Republicans know it. . . . That law was unconstitutional."

As the pledge controversy droned on, the campaign had prepared precisely the kind of response Dukakis delivered that day, based on U.S. Supreme Court precedents dating from the attempts at persecuting Jehovah's Witnesses during World War II. The plan, however, had been to use it on a day when Bush was attacking Dukakis on the issue; on this Monday, he had only taken a question from his local audience, and the result was that the governor ruined the coverage of his comments on the trade deficit. Later, checking in by telephone with Estrich, Dukakis ruefully acknowledged his error, which had brought two more days of media attention on the issue, exactly what the governor didn't need.

Not only did Bush get in more licks, during this period he and other Republicans began to get personal and in a few cases truly dirty. The very same Monday, during the taping of a public-affairs program on a Blackfoot, Idaho radio station, Senator Steven Symms, a conservative Republican, claimed that Kitty Dukakis had burned an American flag during an antiwar demonstration in the 1960s. "I haven't seen this," he said, "but I've heard that there are pictures around that will surface before the election's over of Mrs. Dukakis burning the American flag when she was an antiwar demonstrator during the '60s." Kitty Dukakis emphatically denied the charge. She was living the quiet life of a young suburban matron and caring for her babies during the 1960s. No photographs even remotely resembling Symm's description have ever surfaced.

At the Republican National Convention, Bush made fun of Dukakis's height. The governor is five feet eight inches tall. "He said Dukakis was "short" on foreign policy experience, adding, "short, get it? short."

At a Bush rally in Los Angeles in the following week, comedian Bob Hope warmed up the crowd with more Dukakis "short" jokes. He said Dukakis loved to campaign "because he can kiss babies without lifting them up." He said that Bush was six feet two inches tall and Dukakis was the same height "standing on a horse."

Then he got into some ethnic "humor." "Remember when Nancy Reagan got into the White House, she bought all of that beautiful china? If the Greeks get in, they'll break it first thing."

The cumulative attacks were beginning to take a toll. Harrison polled Massachusetts voters in the week after the Republican National Convention and showed Dukakis with a negligible lead in his home state. When Dukakis saw the results, he was devastated. How could the people who knew him best be so alienated? His staff, sensing his shock, immediately reassured him. It's not you, it's the campaign. They still want you to be governor. It will be all right. He spent the end of the month touring his own state, again contrary to the advice of his campaign high command. In an annual ritual, he would bring state cabinet secretaries and officials to local communities for a day of intensive consultation.

Meanwhile, Estrich invited some of the Democratic Party's best political strategists to Boston for a meeting on Friday, August 26. The group included Thomas Donilon, Senator Joe Biden's senior adviser; William Carrick, Congressman Richard Gephardt's highly regarded campaign manager; and Robert Beckel, who had managed Walter Mondale's campaign and was then a rising star as a consultant and television commentator on his favorite craft. They met with Estrich, O'Donnell, Devine, and Harrison.

Beckel and Carrick did not attempt to hide their dismay. In a meeting filled with profanity, table thumping, and raised voices, they demanded to know why he was in Massachusetts. "Is he running for president of western Massachusetts?" someone asked, snidely. "End these press availabilities," roared Beckel. "If he keeps responding to the Bush attack of the day, he'll never get off the defensive." "Get ahead of this Willie Horton story. It's killing you." Of Bush, they screamed, "Cut his head off, garrote the SOB." Beckel emphasized and then wrote a memo on the middle-class squeeze. Carrick groaned that it sounded like someone he dated in high school. "Don't put that phrase in a speech," he advised. The consensus of the consultant's group was to attack Bush.

Estrich took the advice to heart. She understood far better than they did that something was very wrong. Dukakis was so determined to attend to state business that month, she had to wait days just to see him for a few minutes. She prepared a memo for the governor. "You have become the issue," she said bluntly, and then summarized his disastrous August: You have done two things in August, you have disappeared, and when you have appeared you have looked unhappy and miserable. Bush is defining the issues. We have to turn this thing, turn it hard, fast, and right away. In the three-page, single-spaced memorandum, she also warned Dukakis that the choice of Quayle was not hurting Bush any more, and that the consensus of the meeting had been that he should attack Bush on his own turf: middle-class problems. Bob Shrum, at her invitation, then drafted a speech for Labor Day, challenging the Republican notion of prosperity. There were two prosperities: one for the rich, the other for the rest of us. Dukakis found it too negative and rejected it.

But the attacks from the other side continued. On Tuesday, August 30, Bush tried a new tack, linking the Pledge of Allegiance and the furlough issues. During an appearance in Rocky Mount, North Carolina, with conservative Senator Jesse Helms, Bush said, "I can't understand the type of thinking that lets first-degree murderers who haven't even served enough time to be eligible for parole, out on parole [*sic*] so they can rape and plunder again, and then not be willing to let the teachers lead kids in the Pledge of Allegiance [*sic*]." Bush wasn't about to let the facts get in the way of good campaign rhetoric.

While Sasso worked out the details in his return to the campaign during that final week in August, the Bush high command took a tactical gamble that succeeded in turning the environmental issue into a plus for a candidate who had no business calling himself an environmentalist, a ploy that proved particularly cutting in New Jersey and California.

Environmental politics completely dominated New Jersey throughout summer and fall 1988. During one of the hottest summers in a century, swimming was prohibited along miles of sandy beach on the Jersey shore because of pollution. Medical and human waste and discarded syringes littered the beaches like seashells.

The New Jersey Democratic Party, commissioned a statewide poll from Paul Maslin to get baseline information on voters, and several focus-group discussions to probe Dukakis and Bush weaknesses in May. The focus groups, led by Stan Greenberg of New Haven, interviewed working women under forty-five, women over forty-five, and working-class men under forty-five. The results were as revealing as those conducted at about the same time in New Jersey by the Bush campaign.

The focus groups showed that people liked Mike Dukakis because he wasn't George Bush. They knew George Bush, and they didn't like him. They didn't know much about Dukakis but projected their expectations and hopes for an ideal president onto him. In one exercise, the group leader asked what would happen if there was a knock on the door and Bush walked into the room. He'd keep the motor running in the car, said one voter. He wouldn't come in here; this isn't the country club. If Dukakis came in? Well, that was different. He'd call me by my first name. He'd have a beer with us. They tested the furlough issue and found voters just didn't want to believe that Dukakis could be responsible for something so awful; they wanted to like him.

The results scared the staff in New Jersey. Dukakis was a sitting duck. They needed to erect a fortress of information around him so that by November at least an inch or two of protection would be left to which voters could cling.

The fears of the New Jersey troops were realized when Bush launched his "I am an environmentalist" campaign at the end of August. It proved to be an astonishingly successful exercise in saying black was white and getting away with it. He made claims that were directly contradicted by his record as vice president. In 1981, the Reagan administration attempted to eliminate the water-pollution program that would have financed cleanup of Boston Harbor. When Congress balked, the administration cut funding by half. Then Reagan twice vetoed the Clean Water Act. Bush himself was active in the Reagan administration's antienvironment record. When he was chairman of the administration's Task Force on Regulatory Relief, he protected big-business polluters by eliminating, weakening, or delaying environmental regulations. Former U.S. Senator Paul E. Tsongas said that Bush calling himself an environmentalist was like Bonnie and Clyde endorsing gun control.

But Bush literally sailed into Boston Harbor on a boat on Thursday, September 1. He laid blame for pollution of the harbor squarely on Dukakis, drowning out the Dukakis campaign officials' "fact sheets" that pointed to the Clean Water Act vetoes, the James Watts and Anne Gorsuchs whom Bush had loyally supported all through the decade. The governor tried to pretend that the political disaster wasn't happening by sticking to a California campaign schedule. The campaign had still made no effective response when Bush aired his deadly Boston-Harbor television ad at the beginning of September. The paid media were now reinforcing the message carried so powerfully for Bush in the press. Larry Rasky, spokesman for the Dukakis office covering New York, New Jersey, and Pennsylvania, began screaming, "This is aimed at New Jersey."

Rosa DeLauro, the Connecticut political operative who was running the tri-state campaign for Dukakis from New York, and Rasky, Joe Biden's former press secretary, sent a memo to Boston on August 26. They had become so frustrated at the lack of direction from the Boston headquarters that they put together their own message group, an impressive collection of twenty experienced pollsters, operatives, and politicians from the region. "The message group felt that, while Dukakis got a lift from the convention, the message did not prove as enduring as we might have hoped," they wrote. "With our message still unfolding, the Republicans can successfully raise doubts. A fully presented message here will not only provide an alternative picture of Dukakis, it will give a lift to this whole campaign structure, which is anxious to deliver the message on your behalf."

They recommended that the message for New Jersey, New York, and Pennsylvania have three components. The first was the economy. "You do not need to hear from us on this," they wrote. "Right now Bush has the edge on this thematic battle, though nearly all in the group thought the Democrats should be winning this battle by articulating, with some confidence, the public's anxiousness for their kids and the future."

The second message was "On your side," the tag that Dukakis finally seized upon two months later for the final days in his campaign. "New Jersey is a state with tough experience with corporate polluters, congestion, etc. They are ready, people believe, for a populist message that says Dukakis is on their side."

The final component in the message was the environment. "With the shore problems across the region, it is critical that Dukakis take the lead here. But right now, it was agreed, voters do not know whom to blame. The Reagan-Bush environmental record (anti-Clean Water Act, EPA, acid rain, etc.) is not yet an issue. The campaign needs to develop a formulation of the environmental issue that works, and New Jersey voters need to hear it."

There was essentially no response from Boston. Then early in September after Bush made an issue of Massachusetts's application to dump sewage sludge off the Jersey shore, Harold Hodes, one of the leaders in Dukakis's campaign in New Jersey and a former chief of staff with former Governor Brendan Byrne, became so frustrated that he flew to Boston to confront the candidate in person. This is crazy, he told him, we're getting hammered in New York and New Jersey. It's affecting Pennsylvania. He insisted the candidate return to the state as soon as possible to campaign. Dukakis readily agreed, and was back in New Jersey the following week.

But two weeks elapsed before Scott Miller received permission to cut a commercial responding to the Boston Harbor ad. Dukakis then vetoed it as too negative.

A response commercial did not make it onto the airwaves until October, and even then it was not a national advertisement but the initiative of a frustrated Tony Podesta, the California state director, who told Los Angeles media consultant Michael Kaye to cut his own spots on the environment, at least getting something on the air in California. The commercial featured pictures of the California coastline and contrasted Dukakis's endorsement by the nonpartisan League of Conservation Voters with Reagan's vetoing the Clean Water Act. "When you hear Bush talk about the environment, remember what he did to the environment," said the narrator.

With Labor Day just forty-eight hours away, Kiley, Harrison, and Harrison's assistant, Clifford Brown, tried to emphasize the extreme need to stick to a message in a memorandum to Dukakis, which was sent on Sasso's first full day back with the campaign. The campaign must focus on regaining the initiative on the economy and reestablish the notion that Dukakis stands on the side of average American families but Bush stands for the wealthy, they argued. The governor's major speech in Detroit on Labor Day had already been crafted and essentially approved; at issue now was whether Dukakis would understand how vital it was that he stick with his message. As his aides saw it: "Bear in mind that a majority continue to believe that 'George Bush stands for the privileged and the wealthy.' Therefore, when we talk about the economy this week, we have to remind people in the most forceful terms of the contrast between you and Bush."

"For example, you stand for every student getting a college education, Bush does not; you have a record on health care, and specific proposals for providing health security to every working family, while Bush voted against Medicare, recently supported raising Medicare premiums, etc."

"We mention these two issues because the latest polling results show Bush to be especially vulnerable on them. Once we have retaken the intiative on the foregoing, we can then expand our message to the larger theme of rebuilding the economy to meet the foreign economic threat."

Since spring, top officials in the campaign had tried without success to persuade Dukakis to make comprehensive, constant counterattacks against the Bush campaign's all-out effort to depict him as an extreme liberal who coddles criminals, is soft on defense, pollutes Boston Harbor, and scoffs at patriotism. Their failure had given Bush a month-long series of free shots that exacted a severe toll.

For all the agitation to respond to these attacks, however, advisers like Harrison were just as convinced that the most effective response was articulating—and then almost continuously repeating—of a positive message about the economy directed at the pressures on average families and the worry that the United States was losing its ability to control its destiny in an increasingly competitive international economy. With such a message, Dukakis would be on the high, substantive ground he had always sought, he would be speaking directly about the voters' troubles that were most likely to influence their votes, and above all he would be inoculating himself against negative campaign tactics that would appear silly and petty by comparison.

John Sasso stepped back into a tense, unfocused, beleaguered campaign after an eleven-month separation. He didn't come back to Michael Dukakis's campaign out of the blue at the end of August but after six months of behind-the-scenes discussions, machinations, and anguish that Dukakis was unable to resolve with a decisive act. The governor's lack of resoluteness in this matter, along with his inability to follow through with his original decision that Sasso should take a brief leave of absence for his transgressions around the Biden videotape are perhaps the two most harmful lapses in his entire campaign, and both occurred in the kind of situation most resembling a White House in crisis.

Dukakis's four-hour-long cave-in on the subject of Sasso's resignation on September 30, 1987, occurred in public. His much longer backing and filling over Sasso's return took place in secret.

John Sasso is the one thread that runs all the way through Michael Dukakis's presidential campaign. He was its progenitor, its guide, and the candidate's guide. When he made a big error in judgment and then resigned, his candidate was lost without his guidance. Up to the day the Biden tapes affair broke, Dukakis was slowly but surely growing toward true presidential status, and his campaign manager was about a stride ahead of him in preparing the governor to move beyond relying on his record in Massachusetts and his reputation for executive competence, and toward confrontation with the major questions of his time, and with the quantum difference between a president and a governor. It is a tribute to Sasso that this growth proceeded during his presence; it is an indictment of Dukakis that it stopped in his absence. If a major difference distinguishes the two men—apart from Sasso's fish-to-water affinity for politics—it is Sasso's acute awareness of his own limitations and his constant efforts to expand his knowledge and political vision, contrasting with Dukakis's tendency toward self-sufficiency, over-confidence, and denial when problems loom. In the campaign's early months, Sasso's unique ability to communicate with Dukakis, to nudge him beyond his relatively limited experience and sense of the country and the world, was beginning to pay discernible dividends.

When Sasso left, Dukakis was more than deeply wounded and unable to hide his sadness for the rest of 1987. His development as a national figure was arrested; competence, instead of a legitimate starting point, ended up being his mantra by default. And success in the primaries—a tribute to his steadiness, as well as to the skilled team Sasso left behind (including Susan Estrich and rounded out by Tom Kiley), but also the result of an ultimately weak field whose collapse left him alone against Jesse Jackson—rekindled the sense of self-sufficiency that made him think at times that *he* was capable of winning it all, and that he therefore didn't need John Sasso.

On the night of the Iowa precinct caucuses, adviser Francis O'Brien (a close Sasso friend) told Dukakis to his face that he should bring Sasso back at once, and the governor dismissed O'Brien's message on the spot. It was only February 8, scarcely four months since Dukakis had told reporters, impulsively, in answer to a question, that Sasso would play no role, formal or informal, in the rest of the campaign.

At first, Sasso and Dukakis spoke briefly and infrequently, though Sasso continued to talk to his many friends still high in the campaign and to offer advice when asked. He also passed on messages from other politicians who called him and assumed incorrectly that he still had a private pipeline to Dukakis. With Susan Estrich, Sasso conversed rarely. As the governor's fortunes prospered in the primaries, his success introduced an understandably human tension between these two who had long been associates and friends. Whenever gossip about them flared in the press, however, they always worked to defuse the tension, usually finding out that they had more to worry about from each other's "friends" than from each other.

According to Paul Brountas, he raised the subject of Sasso's return three or four times in private conversations beginning in April or May; he said he couldn't remember which. Mitropoulos began to work on both Brountas and Dukakis in April. After the Wisconsin primary, Mitropoulos urged the candidate to bring in a bigger team, arguing that plans for the general election should begin at once. After Sasso left the campaign, Mitropoulos talked to him by phone at least once a week. Eventually Brountas, who alone in the campaign's top echelon had urged Dukakis to let Sasso go, had a change of heart.

Brountas told us "He had been penalized," he thought, by spring 1988. "He had served his time, and at some point I thought we should have John come back."

Dukakis, however, said no, though never so firmly as to persuade Brountas to drop the matter. Dukakis was worried about how the issue would play in the press and how it would affect Estrich. According to Brountas, however, Dukakis had changed his mind by the time the primaries ended June 7. Indeed, the very next day, Dukakis had given an odd-sounding answer about Sasso in an early morning Los Angeles press conference.

He had been asked the same question scores of times, and always replied with the same dismissive answers, but on this morning he said, "I think we're going to continue with the team we have now," adding that he didn't "expect" to make any changes.

An hour later, in an interview in his car on the way to the airport and a flight east, we commented on his hedged language and asked if Estrich would be his campaign manager for the general election.

"Yes, indeed," he replied, "and Paul will of course continue as the chairman."

We didn't realize that Sasso's returning wasn't discussed with the idea that he would become "campaign manager" again. Brountas told us he had talked to Estrich in the spring about Sasso taking on responsibility in communications and advertising, possibly not full-time until fall.

Brountas said that by June, Dukakis no longer hesitated because of Sasso's role in the Biden tapes affair or even because of his statement that Sasso would have no role in the campaign. Instead, he told us Dukakis "had a considerable problem because Susan Estrich is the campaign manager, so that raised the question of where you would put John Sasso."

Sasso told us, as did Brountas, that he made it clear from his initial conversations, first with Brountas, and later with Dukakis, that he would do anything to help—full-time, part-time, communications, they could name it. As a practical matter, however, all involved knew that the instant Sasso came back, in any capacity, authority would immediately flow to his office.

Brountas thought Sasso would return after the Democratic convention. Nonetheless, it was remarkable that although Sasso went to Atlanta to do a live interview with CBS anchorman Dan Rather on the opening night, and stayed through Dukakis's formal nomination on Wednesday, the governor never talked to him in person, and didn't even make a telephone call to say thank you. So eager was Sasso not to present a problem that he hardly ever left his room in the Dukakis campaign's block of rooms in the executive tower of the Atlanta Hyatt Regency Hotel; indeed, after Dukakis was nominated, Mitropoulos and Corrigan were so insistent that Sasso come downstairs to the nightly campaign staff—press party in the hotel lobby that they went to Sasso's room and refused to leave until he got dressed and went downstairs with them.

Shortly after the convention, Brountas said he and Sasso talked again, and Brountas proposed that Sasso advise the campaign on general strategy, at first part-time, and then return to Chauncy Street full-time as of Labor Day. Brountas said this arrangement was agreeable to Dukakis as well as to Sasso. But nothing happened for another month.

Just hours before Sasso was called back to the campaign that Monday night in late August, the campaign had another horrid day that raised questions about who was in charge. The governor was touring

western Massachusetts on state business and the State House staff, eager
to make him available to local media to show he was hard at work despite
the campaign, scheduled a press conference. Estrich, aware of Bob
Beckel's warning that Dukakis was too accessible and that his press
availabilities were producing comments that stepped on the campaign's
daily message, abruptly ordered it canceled. After the cancellation
angered reporters, the campaign reversed itself and Dukakis held his
press conference, but the entire mess dominated the press coverage.
Mitropoulos got a call from an upset Dukakis that night; he left Cambridge next morning and headed down the Massachusetts Turnpike to
catch up with the governor in Amherst.

According to both Estrich and Brountas, the campaign chairman
told her early in August that Sasso might be back by Labor Day, as did
Jack Corrigan. Her response, she said, was that she would do nothing
to block Sasso's return, a less than ringing endorsement.

After being beckoned from the Vineyard, Sasso met with Brountas
and Mitropoulos late Tuesday at the Copley Plaza Hotel. Then he
headed to Brookline with Brountas to meet with Dukakis.

Estrich was still in the dark. "For me," she told us, "I would have
preferred that it happen the day after our convention, so it would look
like what it should have looked like, a move to greatly strengthen us for
the fall."

According to Brountas, Estrich's worry about the timing of any
move affected his own judgment, and he agreed that it was better to act
while the campaign was at its strongest in the polls, before the inevitable
tightening of the race occurred. Any perception of panic, no matter how
long the move had been in the works, would become reality in the
media-political world.

None of the participants anticipated, though, how disastrous August would be for Dukakis. After ten superficially successful days
following the Democratic convention, the governor first lost his media
momentum to the mental-health rumors, and then lost more than half
his post-convention polling lead by the time the Republican convention
opened on August 15, and then all of it after the convention adjourned
four days later with a "new" George Bush as standard bearer. Dukakis
was being pounded by Bush's attacks; he was rejecting advice and
proposals for counterattacks as well as for grander themes of his own;
he was also rejecting pleas from his advisers to campaign nearly full-time
on the road while he insisted on performing gubernatorial functions in
August; he had no basic plan for his general election campaign; and his
advertising conglomerate was not producing advertising to his or its
liking. In short, timing may have been a legitimate worry, particularly
out of respect for the woman whose leadership had held his campaign

together after its gravest crisis and led the surge to his nomination. But there was no longer time for such thoughts.

Estrich told us that she had resolved very early to stay away from the Sasso-Dukakis relationship. She had a feeling, however, that Dukakis had always assumed Sasso would return sometime. On the mature judgment that she shouldn't worry about what she couldn't control, she had simply concentrated on her demanding job; all she asked was that she be consulted if and when Sasso's return moved to the governor's front burner, though as it turned out he never did discuss the subject with her. As spring became summer, Estrich told us she never sensed any "Oh my God, we have to get Sasso back" urgency; instead it appeared to her that Dukakis, Sasso, and Brountas were slowly trying to work through the complicated emotions—hurt, anger, and guilt— that had been around ever since his resignation.

Although her relations with the governor had been smooth throughout the primaries, the two had never grown close. Several top officials in the campaign told us that Dukakis was almost always formal and distant in his dealings with her, and was frequently curt and cool; their meetings were mostly businesslike affairs that rarely lasted more than thirty minutes and usually consisted of little more than a decision-making run down a checklist. For all her brilliance and biting wit, Estrich is a sentient personality, easily wounded, and Dukakis's attitude hurt her. In August, his constant rejection of campaign-generated ideas drove her to despair, and to close friends she mostly blamed herself for not being able to figure out ways to reach Dukakis more effectively, and for accepting too easily decisions she should have fought more persuasively. In fact, she hardly saw Dukakis at all in August, even though he was in Boston much more than he had been previously; often, it took a day or two for her to arrange brief meetings and to bring in new campaign officials, especially the advertising team.

For help in dealing with Dukakis, she had turned initially in winter 1987 to Tom Kiley, who had been her key strategist for the rapid succession of primaries and caucuses that had made Dukakis the apparent nominee by the Wisconsin primary in early April and the inevitable nominee after New York on April 19. In June, however, friends of each noticed a strain in their relationship and attributed it to Kiley's repeated efforts to bring top executives from the Hill Holliday agency— where John Sasso worked—over to manage the campaign's television advertising, an idea Dukakis rejected.

Estrich told us that she and Dukakis had a clear disagreement over her advocating early and harsh attacks on Bush. Both for specific speeches—a constant bone of contention between campaign staff and candidate in August—and general strategy, Estrich was constantly leading the charge for a steady fire at Bush in speeches and advertising, and Dukakis was constantly turning her down. Dukakis was also quick to take a blue pencil to his speeches, crossing out new material or flights of rhetoric and replacing them with dry but primary-vintage Dukakis themes.

As she saw it in August, the campaign's Boston high command had no influence on the campaign on the road. With Labor Day approaching, she discussed this subject with Kirk O'Donnell and Jack Corrigan. O'Donnell was already up to his ears in planning the campaign's daily and weekly messages, and so Corrigan volunteered to join the road show. Of the three, he had the closest relationship with Dukakis from his period as Sasso's State House alter ego, and he had already overseen establishment of the campaign's national field organization, which was the campaign's most smoothly functioning component and could probably be run by his deputies.

Behind the scenes, the agitation for Sasso's return began to spread among the high command, involving not just Brountas and Dukakis but also Corrigan, Harrison, Kiley, and O'Donnell.

"Okay, we just didn't do it," Brountas told us. "It just kind of dragged on."

Indeed, on Saturday, August 27, Sasso rented a house on Martha's Vineyard for a ten-day vacation with his family, a definite sign he expected nothing to happen, despite nearly three months of top-level vacillation that had left the disciplined politician, accustomed to decisive if unpleasant decisions, just short of disgusted.

Brountas said no specific event precipitated the call to Sasso on the evening of Monday, August 29. Other senior campaign officials, however, told us the prevailing view was that the point of Sasso's return was reached one week earlier, when Harrison finished the Massachusetts poll showing the state to be a statistical dead heat. Events on that Monday also drove home to all the chaotic state of affairs in the deeply troubled campaign, with Labor Day just one week away.

According to Estrich, she was summoned to a State House meeting with Dukakis Wednesday morning by Brountas, who told her what would happen. He said she continued to express "concern" about the timing, reminding him of her view that the public perception would be one of panic, as well as that she was being replaced. Her session with the governor lasted fifteen minutes.

Estrich and Brountas each told us that in addition to retaining the campaign manager post, the campaign's division heads would continue to report to her, and she would be a full participant in all top-level activities. As for Sasso, Brountas said he would take over the advertising operation, develop general strategy, and draft the general-election plan that Dukakis still craved. But most important was the unspoken fact that Sasso would deal with Dukakis; with that in prospect, Estrich felt truly relieved.

The next three days were a blur of secret meetings to prepare for a Friday announcement. The day before it, a gloating George Bush toured dirty Boston Harbor, grinning proudly as he held a *Boston Herald* aloft with its front-page headline on the newspaper's own poll showing the race was even in Massachusetts. The perception was indeed one of panic.

Estrich put on a brave face at the press conference announcing Sasso's return on the Friday morning before the long Labor Day weekend. She likened Sasso's return to the return of a long-lost family member. She kept a fixed smile on her face throughout the public event at the Lafayette Hotel, making a point of embracing Sasso in public, praising him lavishly, and applauding his return; but the strain was apparent. The smile was gone as soon as she returned to her office.

Much as she needed someone who could get through to her balky candidate, she resisted Sasso's return, particularly late in August when the campaign was ailing, because it was an almost explicit indictment of her.

When Sasso, accompanied by Estrich and Brountas, walked into a meeting room at the Hotel Lafayette for the announcement of his return, the room exploded in sustained applause and cheers. Word of his return had sped like a rifle shot through the Boston political community that morning. Dozens of overjoyed friends had rushed from their offices all over downtown Boston to cheer him. Sasso basked in the warmth of the audience. He expressed his joy at the events that had allowed him to "rejoin the campaign and do very much what I love." The palpable relief among the Dukakis partisans had to be disheartening for Estrich; she could not help feeling pained.

Estrich had won tenure on the Harvard Law School faculty by age thirty-two. Defeat and setback were as alien to her as to the high-achieving Dukakis. Her pride was deeply wounded, as were her feelings, and each was an avoidable pain, had Dukakis acted decisively in June or July. Although Sasso had been a friend since the 1980 Kennedy campaign and was the one who made her deputy campaign manager at the beginning of the effort, their friendship had suffered during his absence. When the campaign succeeded, political wiseguys, ever skeptical about a young woman's ability to perform in the male-dominated political world, were inclined to credit Sasso's unseen hand (a hand that did not exist) behind the scenes. When things went wrong, she caught the blame, as a surrogate for Dukakis.

In public, Dukakis kept his former aide at arm's length during his time of political isolation, stoically unwilling to compromise his public promise that Sasso would have no role in his campaign. From Estrich's viewpoint, Sasso was definitely in Elba. She called him only twice looking for advice during his eleven-month exile.

Dukakis never delineated lines of responsibility between Sasso and Estrich. You guys work something out, he said. This omission made for a difficult and touchy transition, with Estrich retaining her title but the real power gradually drifting to Sasso, who had the governor's ear and became a rallying point for a beleaguered campaign moving into its final eight weeks.

8

Willie and the Duke

For America's most famous felon, Christmas day 1988 was distinguished only by a day off from cooking in the kitchen at the Maryland Penitentiary. As he sat alone in his cell with a cup of coffee, he suddenly caught himself rocking back and forth to a silent rhythm, a common sight in institutions that house the mentally ill. He stopped, startled by this inadvertent motion of his body. Another inmate called out, "Hey man, whatcha doin'?"

William Robert Horton, Jr., talked about that moment two days later with an embarrassed laugh. It showed, he said, that years of prison life had taken a toll on him. He was getting "institutionalized," he said. It was a rare revelation from this guarded and wary career criminal, whose escape from a Massachusetts furlough and violent escapades hurt Michael Dukakis's presidential candidacy more than any other issue.

Michael Dukakis's candidacy was premised upon his record and his character. For much of the campaign, the basic message seemed to be: Vote for me because I'm better than the other guy. When he accepted his party's nomination, he declared that the election was about competence, not ideology. As soon as it became apparent that Dukakis would be the Democratic presidential nominee, the Bush strategists decided to destroy the candidacy by destroying Dukakis and his public record. The Bush campaign fixed upon hairline cracks in the Dukakis record and pounded them until the cracks opened into crevasses. They convinced millions of Americans that Dukakis was not only a flaming liberal but dangerous and risky. They used his veto of a bill that would force school teachers to lead children in the Pledge of Allegiance to paint him as unpatriotic. They used the prison furlough program to show he was a criminal coddler. They blamed him for the pollution in Boston Harbor and turned "competence" into incompetence. They capitalized upon the economic downturn that led to a state revenue shortfall turning the Massachusetts "miracle" into the Massachusetts "mirage."

Nobody runs for any office without some kind of record, and it is axiomatic that no campaign subjects a record to scrutiny like one for the presidency, as well as that governors and legislators—because they have made thousands of individual decisions and votes, each vulnerable to skillful misrepresentation or justifiable condemnation—are especially at risk. In the age of computerized libraries and Xerox machines, the possibilities for microscopic examination are all but limitless. Accordingly, all serious politicians, but above all those contending for the presidency, are elaborately prepared for the inevitable assaults— defensively as well as for counterattack; all, that is, except for Michael Dukakis in 1988.

The Bush campaign had a most compliant victim. Dukakis's campaign advisers warned him explicitly that an assault of this kind was a certainty, and advised numerous, vigorous defensive and counteroffensive measures as early as spring 1988. Dukakis, however, did not take either his potential vulnerability or Bush's commitment to exploiting it seriously; he believed the attacks were preposterous and would be seen as such. Dukakis also rejected urgings that he counterattack as early as June, insisting on his own that this kind of campaign would interfere with the specific proposals on issues he wanted to make, and that he was not yet well enough known as a national figure to mount an all-out assault on Bush.

His advisers, though, all believed strongly that a campaign attack or charge that isn't vigorously answered is certain to stick. They insisted that the record of a long-term governor who had made thousands of decisions was inherently exploitable, like that of a legislator who has cast thousands of votes on issues that can easily be warped to fit the needs of a thirty-second television commercial.

Hanging over researcher Terry Bergman's desk at campaign headquarters was a copy of a letter from Charles D. Ravenel, a Democrat from South Carolina who had run for the U.S. Senate against Strom Thurmond in 1978 and been defeated by a reelection campaign managed by Lee Atwater. The letter had passed through several hands before S. Stephen Rosenfeld handed it to Bergman late in May, telling her, "This is the reason your job is important." The message contained in that letter was eerily prescient.

"My very strong belief," wrote Ravenel on May 18, 1988, "is that Atwater is the premier negative strategist in American politics. I have the deep suspicion that Atwater will begin hitting at Dukakis very early, perhaps even before the convention, in order to put in place a higher and pervasive negative attitude about Dukakis. If Mike does not respond right away he could risk having the negatives well set in the minds of the Americans before he could begin to change them.

"The Bush campaign has all the money in the world and can afford to do this on a massive scale and do it early," he wrote. "If you are weeks or even a month behind in terms of preparing countering ads and buying time, it may be too late. It would be fighting an uphill battle for the rest of the campaign. I strongly urge that a full-scale defensive effort be made ready right away."

That full-scale effort never took place and the Bush campaign proceeded to destroy the foundation under the Dukakis candidacy. The most effective weapon turned out to be a thirty-seven-year-old con named William Horton.

Horton looks nothing like the glowering, ferocious figure in his mug shot. Nothing is remarkable about his ordinary features except the latticework of scars on his nose. He has a boyish, slender physique and neat, close-cropped hair and beard. His appearance is deceiving. He is a textbook felon, a classic product of deprivation and violence who has spent almost his entire adult life behind steel bars. He is unschooled in the ways of civilized society. He has nothing approximating middle-class values. He is uneducated in the traditional sense as well. He never got past the eighth grade. Judge Vincent J. Femia, the Maryland jurist who sentenced him to two consecutive life terms in prison plus eighty-five years for terrorizing, assaulting, and robbing a young Maryland couple in their suburban home, said he had no conscience. Nothing in Horton's demeanor, history or behavior contradicts the judge's opinion.

Horton was born August 12, 1951 in Chesterfield, South Carolina to William and Sara Horton. He was the fifth of six children in his father's first marriage and his mother's second. One of his siblings died as a child. His father, a city trash collector and a heavy drinker, shot and injured Horton's mother when Horton was age four or five. His father was convicted and imprisoned for the shooting. His mother recovered from her wounds but abandoned her children to the care of relatives and left South Carolina for New York. An aunt assumed responsibility for young William. But the background of family violence and effective loss of both parents took its toll. According to his prison file in Massachusetts, he did "average to poor" work in school until grade seven when he went truant. He left school for good after grade eight. While in prison much later in Massachusetts, he prepared for but failed the high-school equivalency examination. He was first arrested when he was thirteen for breaking and entering and sentenced to a juvenile correctional institute. After six months, he was released but arrested six months later on another breaking-and-entering charge. He was sent back to reform school and a lifelong pattern of lawbreaking and incarceration was established.

His adult criminal record began in South Carolina in 1968. While other teenagers were getting ready for the high-school prom and graduation, the sixteen-year-old Horton was charged with assault with intent to kill and carrying a concealed weapon (a knife). He allegedly attacked a man during a barroom fight. He served three years in prison and when released moved to Lawrence, Massachusetts to be near relatives. He lived with a woman and fathered a daughter. He was known to police. Between 1971 and 1974, he was arrested every year and charged with eleven separate offenses, including public drunkenness and disorderly conduct, assault and battery, distribution of a controlled substance, and nine separate motor-vehicle violations. Like other career criminals, his offenses grew more serious with his age. At age twenty-three, he was charged with the ultimate offense, murder. Joseph Fournier, a seventeen-year-old gas station attendant in Lawrence, was stabbed nineteen times and his body dumped into an oil drum during a robbery of $276 on Saturday night, October 26, 1974. (The story, often reported and repeated during the campaign, that Fournier had been sexually mutilated was false.) Three young men including Horton who had left a party to rob the gas station were arrested on November 8, 1974 and charged with murder and armed robbery. They were found guilty after a trial on May 22, 1975 and received the mandatory sentence of life without parole for the murder and twenty- to forty-year concurrent sentences for armed robbery. The other two men are still incarcerated in medium-security prisons in Massachusetts.

The police never determined who actually stabbed the teenager. According to one law-enforcement source, one of Horton's codefendants allegedly confessed to the murder, but his testimony could not be used in court because police had neglected to read him his rights. Some believe that Horton was in the car with a needle in his arm during the murder. He was a drug user. Still others believe he was the one who stabbed the teenager. For a trial under the state's felony murder rule, it was not necessary for the prosecution to prove who did what, only that all were involved in the crime.

Horton was sent to Walpole State Prison, the only maximum-security prison in the state, which is now known as Cedar Junction, a concession to the Walpole townspeople, who were offended by association with the most violent and dangerous criminals in the state. He made license plates in the metal shop. His prison record described him as a loner with "many associations during his lifetime but very few friends."

The Massachusetts prison system, like others, operates on an incentive system. Good behavior and time served warrant moves to lower security. The system, like all others in the United States, is based upon the community-reintegration model of corrections. Corrections officials throughout the nation have concluded that locking up prisoners in secure facilities for their entire sentence was an enormous failure in the late 1960s. Prisoners actually became worse in prison, and once released, committed crimes that put them behind bars again. The community reintegration model gradually reintroduces a prisoner to society by gradually reducing the security and increasing personal responsibility, freedom, and exposure to the outside world.

Over the years Horton incurred eleven disciplinary infractions, including possessing stubs of marijuana cigarettes and a syringe, fighting with another inmate, and refusing to follow the guards' orders. Horton was known by other inmates to have a drug problem while in prison. His behavior followed the pattern typical of long-term offenders: denial, adjustment, testing the limits. He eventually appeared to adjust and to have figured out the system. To get into a less secure environment, he had to follow the rules, and so he did. After eighteen months at Walpole, he was moved down the hill to Norfolk, a medium-security or walled facility that is less strict than Cedar Junction. He was held there for thirty-five months before being moved back to Walpole after authorities found him in possession of the syringe and betting slips. After two more years at Walpole, he was able to get a move back to Norfolk, where he stayed for three more years. He finally went to the Northeast Correctional Center in Concord, also known as the Concord farm, a minimum-security prison, in September 1984, where he learned to cook, acquiring his first marketable skill at the age of thirty-three.

Like other inmates in minimum-security facilities, he was on an honor system. If he followed the rules, he could stay in a relatively free environment. At any time, anyone could walk away from a minimum-security prison, which is nothing more than a dormitory. Just before he secured his first furlough in August 1985, he was approved by an independent screening board to work with the mentally retarded at a state mental-health facility in Boston. This highly successful program used inmates to provide direct patient care. For a while, a professional familiar with his work with the retarded thought he actually might be turning a corner and acquiring the social skills and values he would need to qualify for a commutation and a return to society. This is an isolated memory of Horton. After his escape, officials had trouble finding anyone who even remembered him. He was an almost invisible prisoner. There was nothing special about him.

His good behavior was eventually rewarded by qualification for the furlough program. To qualify for a furlough, he had to have served more than ten years of his sentence, be in minimum security more than sixty days, and not incur any major disciplinary infraction within thirty days of applying for a furlough. He was clearly on the commutation track. "I tried my best to be normal," he said during an interview at the Maryland Penitentiary after the election, "to stay out of serious trouble for ten years. Then I tried to get the paperwork in motion. No one owed me no favor. I did no favors. I get along because I conduct myself in a mature manner."

"I behaved myself," he said. "My greatest hope was to get a commutation. I did not feel that I deserved to be in prison in the first place." In retrospect, Dukakis administration officials call Horton's release a huge mistake. But an intensive internal investigation into his case found that he qualified for a furlough under current guidelines, his furlough sponsors were suitable, and the formal review process was followed in his case.

The review suggested that the system may have been faulty by failing to adequately instruct furlough sponsors on procedures and by failing to treat each furlough for lifers as a special privilege rather than a routine practice. The most experienced officials, however, say that nothing was inherently wrong with the system. They say it's impossible to bat 1.000.

After he successfully completed his first twelve-hour furlough in August 1985, the system assumed he was trustworthy. Because he had been a disciplinary problem early in his incarceration, prison officials could credit themselves for having "rehabilitated" him. The extraordinary success of the furlough program may also have lulled prison officials. The escape rate for lifers was .02 percent. During the entire life of the program only eleven convicted murderers escaped while on furlough, and most of the escapes took place in the early years of the program before Dukakis was governor and tightened eligibility. None of the escapees is at large today. The Lifers Group at Norfolk told state Representative Larry Giordano of Methuen that Horton curried favor by acting as an informant. The lifers had been led to believe that Giordano might drop his opposition to the furlough program if they could convince him Horton was an exception, just a bad guy. Other lifers pegged Horton as a hard-core criminal. They referred to him as someone with "larceny in his heart," the inside term for a chronic offender, someone with a criminal mind. Horton denies he was an informant and the investigation into his case found no evidence that he curried favor in any special way.

His furlough sponsors were a woman whom he met while in prison and then a sister-in-law. Between August 4, 1975 and May 3 and 4, 1986, he successfully completed nine furloughs. On those furloughs he went to the movies, visited his daughter, went shopping, and took his daughter to church. Everything seemed to be fine, but later investigation showed that the brief tastes of freedom had whetted an apppetite for more in Horton. His first sponsor, a pen pal who wrote to him when he was incarcerated at Walpole and then visited him almost weekly for six years, was never aware of the specifics about his crime until after he escaped. She told investigators that she had to persuade him to follow his approved itineraries on his last few furloughs with her because he wanted to go to parties with friends and take late-night trips to the beach. She told him she was postponing any more furloughs until she was convinced he had "calmed down." Instead, he switched sponsors. His sister-in-law was unaware that he was supposed to remain with her at all times and had no idea that he was supposed to follow an itinerary. She was his sponsor during his tenth furlough, when he made the move he concedes was "the stupidest mistake of my life."

At dawn on a weekend morning on June 7, 1986 while on furlough in Lawrence, he broke the rules. He left his sister-in-law's home in a car to visit a woman. The detailed hour-by-hour itinerary for his furlough, approved weeks earlier, listed no such visit. He had no driver's license, and accompanied by his female friend, he drove through a blinking red light without stopping in Methuen at 5:22 A.M. He mistakenly thought a blinking red light meant proceed with caution. He did not learn that motorists are supposed to come to a full stop for a blinking red light until told during this interview. ("Not in Boston," he insisted, doubtless remembering how Boston's notorious drivers flout traffic laws.) A police officer flagged him over to the side of the road. Not realizing he had broken a minor traffic law, he incorrectly assumed the officer recognized him, although he gave him a false name, William Crawford. While the police officer checked to be sure the car was not stolen (it belonged to his sister-in-law's neighbor, and Horton had no registration with him), Horton waited uneasily in the car. He knew that if he was reported he would be sent back "behind the wall," back to a higher-security prison, probably Walpole, because of his original offense and sentence. He watched the officer through his rear-view mirror, and when the police officer alighted from the cruiser again and began walking back to Horton, Horton thought he was pulling out his service revolver. He gunned the car and took off.

"What would you have done?" he asked in a way suggesting he saw no other course. "I went out of bounds. It was the stupidest mistake I ever made in my life."

"I blame myself because I escaped. That was my mistake. I blame myself. I figured I would have to go back to Walpole. It takes five, six, seven years to get out of there. I thought I would never get out again. I did not want to go through that. It was not easy for me to get up" through the system."

He had also won $5,000 in the Massachusetts Lottery that weekend. He headed south and worked in construction in Florida, where he met a man from Maryland who was involved in drug dealing. He went back to Maryland with him, worked for a few weeks as a mechanic, but quit when the boss ran his fake Social Security number through a computer and discovered it was false. He was then using the alias Tony Franklin and living with his friend in the same neighborhood as Cliff Barnes and Angela Miller. Although he felt relatively safe when he was working as a carpenter or mechanic, he had moments of unease. "People look at you strange and you never know if someone is like an off-duty cop. I knew I could not go to my family. I did not even call my family," he said. His family did not learn his whereabouts until he was arrested in Maryland ten months after he escaped.

Horton will not discuss the Maryland case in any detail. He claims he is innocent and makes vague allusions to involvement by others, whom he will not identify. He wants to overturn his conviction. "People say this guy has no hope. I don't feel that way," he said. "I don't feel I will be here for the rest of my life and become a vegetable. I don't believe that. I know for a fact that won't happen." He has seized upon some technicalities as a defense: police failed to conduct a blood test to show he was the rapist of Angela Miller (now Barnes); the government failed to recover the knife that was used to cut off her clothing and torment Clifford Barnes; he was too stupefied by pain-killing drugs to hear his rights read to him in the hospital after his capture. "I was in the wrong place at the wrong time. When I came to this state [Maryland], I was associating with some people who knew the Barneses. One thing led to another," he said.

The evidence that he was responsible and acted alone, however, is overwhelming. Only minutes after the couple escaped from their home, the police chased and caught Horton, who was driving the red Camaro Z28 that had been taken from the victims' driveway. The Camaro was filled with their property. Horton's pockets contained the heart-shaped locket and engagement ring and other jewelry that had been taken from Angela Miller, who was raped twice by a masked intruder. She saw her assailant once without his mask and identified him in the courtroom as Horton.

According to his court testimony, Clifford Barnes, a twenty-eight-year-old manager of an auto-repair facility in Washington, D.C., drove home from work in a red Z28 Camaro on April 3, 1987. He stopped by the white house with the blue trim at about 7:15 P.M., planning to meet friends later at the Ramada Inn. His live-in girlfriend, Angie Miller, was out with the girls. He took off his shirt and tie and went into the bathroom. When he heard floorboards creak he called out, "Angie, is that you?" In response, the bathroom door burst open and a man with a gun entered, throwing him to the floor.

". . . He started pushing me off the toilet hollering 'lay . . . down, you don't know who you're messing with' and he pulled the hammer back when it was on the side of my head," he said.

"He—I kept trying to turn my head and he kept telling me 'If you look, I'll kill you," he testified. "He was telling me that he was doing this to protect himself, that he was paid to deliver me to someone, that he was not going to hurt me. . . . I told him I didn't have much money. He said, 'You think I'm a . . . thief. I'm not here to rob you. You don't know who you're . . . with. Somebody paid me to do this. You've been . . . with the wrong people.' "

He testified that his assailant used a sweater to blindfold him and then tied him up in the basement. During the evening, Barnes said that Horton lacerated his chest and stomach with a knife as he demanded the location and Private Identification Numbers of his bank money cards. Horton was wearing a stocking mask. He identified him later in court by his voice.

Angie Miller, a project analyst for a defense company, returned home after an evening out with her girlfriends just after 2:00 A.M. She testified that a masked man with a handgun accosted her in the hallway and threw her to the ground. He then tied her up in the bedroom and demanded her bank cards.

"I was extremely frightened," she testified. "I was thinking that Cliff was already killed and in the basement and I just, I knew I was next." She said he cut her clothes off with a knife and raped her while he held a knife to her throat and a gun at her head.

The assailant then tied her up in the bathroom and returned to the basement where Barnes was tied. Meanwhile, she got free of her blindfold and saw his face briefly when he returned. "He said he had to mess me up for what I had done, for getting loose, and for seeing him, and I convinced him that I didn't see him," she said. "He started to rub the gun up against my neck and my face and making threats about messing me up for what I had done. He said, 'You hate me. If you had the gun, you'd shoot me.' I said, 'No, no. Please just leave us alone and we'll forget about it,' and he would start getting upset because he said I was lying and he said, 'You think I do this because I have to?' He said, 'I don't have to do this sort of thing.' He said, 'I choose to do this sort of thing,' and just making references like that." She said he raped her a second time.

Meanwhile, her desperate boyfriend worked himself free in the basement at about 6:00 A.M. and ran to a neighbor's house to get help. As soon as he realized Barnes was out of the house, the man believed to be Horton fled in the red Camaro. Miller also got free during this time and joined her boyfriend at the neighbor's house.

A police officer spotted the car about two and a half miles away from the Barnes residence near the Livingston Square Shopping Center. It was stopped at a red light on Old Fort Road near the intersection with Indian Head Highway. When told to pull over, Horton gunned the car and headed north in the southbound lane straight toward another police cruiser. The two cars played chicken on the highway and when the cruiser swerved, Horton passed by in the Camaro, but collided head-on with a second police cruiser. Horton kept going north in the southbound lane for two miles until the car broke down. The officers testified that he alighted from the car, pointed the gun at them and ran across the grassy median of the highway. Shots were flying. Horton was shot four times in the arm and stomach. Prince Georges County police fired thirty-six rounds of handgun ammunition and four shotgun rounds at him. Barnes's .22 automatic pistol, which was taken from the house, had two safety devices on it. Horton never got the second safety off the gun and did not return the fire. He fell on Indian Hill Highway when shot the first time and dropped the handgun. He got up and kept running toward a housing development. He fell a second time in a wooded area, but again got to his feet and kept running. He was finally captured in the backyard of a house on Murray Hill Drive.

"During the car chase, I realized that prison had affected me," said Horton later. "I thought I wanted to die rather than go back to jail. My thought was I wanted to die. That is why I ran. Because I knew I did not have a running chance. I did not want to go back to jail. People don't have the slightest clue about what goes on in jail. You could be in the tier at any moment when someone would lose his mind and you could be dead. People died like fireflies [in Walpole in the early days of his incarceration]. I think a lot of people in prison should not be there because they are not mentally right." Because of his injuries and because he never fired a shot, Horton was particularly offended when charged with attempted murder of the police officers. He was found innocent of those charges.

Some people familiar with the case have speculated that Horton may have falsely thought Clifford Barnes was wealthy. His job as manager of an auto-repair shop called for him to test drive the repaired cars. He often drove home the most expensive and sporty cars. Because he was living in the neighborhood with the man he had met in Florida, Horton could have noticed this succession of fancy cars in the driveway at Barnes's Proxmire Drive home and concluded Barnes had money. Only five months earlier, a married couple from the same community, Oxon Hill, had been arrested in connection with the murder of Dennis White, described by police as the biggest cocaine dealer in the region, and his fifteen-year-old daughter, Donna. When police found the decomposing bodies of the father and daughter at their Camp Springs home in spring 1986, they also discovered more than $1 million in cash hidden in the attic, the largest cash recovery ever made by county police. During the interview Horton confirmed that he knew about this case.

The fantasy about "the big score" is common among those incarcerated for long periods of time. The masked assailant of Clifford Barnes and Angela Miller told them that someone had sent him and was insistent that they give him their automated money cards and PIN numbers. This theory would explain why Horton stayed in the house after finding little of value, waited for the couple to return home, and then stayed with them until dawn. According to police, he got into the house by breaking a basement door early on the morning of April 3, 1987.

His declaration of innocence is also consistent with the textbook profile of a sociopath and career criminal whose life has taught him that anything goes and nothing is out of bounds if it profits him. He is egocentric and projects a heroic image of himself as a tough-minded loner against the world.

"I raised myself," he said with a defiant tone when asked about his childhood. "I don't make excuses. I have not had an easy life but I had a life which I still do have. It turned out negative but it could have turned out positive. As long as you have life you have a chance. At a certain age, you have to learn by yourself. You can't blame your family, your mother, father, sisters, brothers. To me that is a crutch. I like to think I am mentally strong."

"I'm not a follower. I'm not the type of individual who feels you have to be with any crowd to survive. I don't have time to worry about what others think," he said.

"I think I can achieve anything. I feel I can achieve anything. I don't think I'm dumb, stupid or naive. I feel good about William Horton. I can be arrogant. It keeps people away that I don't want to associate with.

I socialize but not to the point where I would regret any affiliation. You can only be what you want to be."

Although he appears to have adjusted quickly to the prison in Maryland just a few blocks from downtown Baltimore, he complained that he did not fit in. His notoriety had set him apart. "I'm not the average prisoner," he said. Prison guards keep a closer eye on him than others, he said.

He still seems genuinely puzzled about how his case became such a major issue in a presidential campaign. "More was made of this issue than should have been," he said. "More important people have escaped from furlough than William Horton. Dukakis did not do anything. He did not originate the furlough program. He simply chose not to abolish it."

He professed to hold no bitterness toward Bush.

"I don't dislike the man," he said. "I don't know him. I feel bad about what he did to me. He made things worse for me. What good is bitterness going to do me? All I can do is take what they give me and fight back. Laying around and weeping for something is wasted time, wasted motion. I don't allow myself to be miserable."

"I think the issue [Bush] was trying to raise was a racist issue because I was black. Bush sent the message that blacks are more apt to create serious crimes. It bothers me that they don't know who I am. I was not given an opportunity [to tell my side]. I'm not into self-pity. I think I am that way because I taught myself how to be strong. I teach myself every day."

"When I first got sentenced to Walpole, I could not believe I was in jail for a first-degree murder charge. People think I'm some kind of Jesse James. I know who I am. I'm not going to be bothered by what people think. That is not to say I would not like to make changes in my life. I'm a very realistic person in the way I feel and think."

The notoriety his case attracted during the campaign made it impossible for him to be returned to Massachusetts custody as he wished. He gets few visits in Maryland because his family and friends cannot afford to travel to the prison. Before his trial, his public defender plea bargained with the county prosecutor's office. If Horton had agreed to plead guilty to at least one count of rape, he could have received life sentences that would run concurrent with his life sentence in Massachusetts and would have been allowed to serve the sentence in Massachusetts. He refused to accept the deal. By the time the trial took place in October 1987, the presidential campaign was well under way and the Horton case had sparked an outcry in Massachusetts.

When he sentenced him for the Maryland crimes after a trial that attracted heavy press coverage, Judge Femia refused to sentence Horton in a way that would allow him to serve his time in Massachusetts. "With all due respect to the citizens of our sister state Commonwealth of Massachusetts," he said, "I'm afraid William Horton is their Arthur Goode and I'm not prepared to take the chance that Mr. Horton might again be furloughed or otherwise released. . . . I would strongly urge the people of Massachusetts to not wait up for Mr. Horton. In fact, I would ask them not to bother to put a light out for him because he won't be coming home. He now belongs to the state of Maryland." (After walking away from a Maryland mental hospital in 1976, Arthur F. Goode III raped and killed a boy in Florida and another in Virginia. He was put to death in Florida in 1984 for murdering the nine-year-old Florida boy.)

Horton has little interest or knowledge of politics, but expressed regret that his case hurt Dukakis. "Dukakis would have been the best president for black people, for poor people," he said. "Dukakis cares. That is the difference. I knew that. I'm not a dummy. Most good presidents come out of the Democratic Party. I think we're coming to a very selfish society. Bush's presidency means we'll have a society built on what can you do for me. When you take and elect George Bush over Michael Dukakis, that's sad."

Horton exhibited little emotion until he talked about the fate of the other lifers back in Massachusetts. After he escaped, there was public uproar over the furlough program in Massachusetts. A citizens' group began a petition drive to abolish all furlough programs. Dukakis resisted until it became clear that the entire program could be repealed by referendum. He relented and agreed to eliminate the program for those serving life without parole in order to keep furloughs for other prisoners. As the bill wound its way through the legislature, the Corrections Department feared that other lifers might attempt to escape if they knew they would no longer be able to experience those brief hours of freedom. And so all the lifers were roused without notice in the middle of the night during a system-wide roundup and taken back behind the wall to medium-security facilities.

"That is the thing that hurts me the most," said Horton. "I'm not the first individual who left on a furlough in Massachusetts and across the country. All of a sudden they make an issue of William Horton."

"I did not want [the lifers] to be punished by what I did. I did not feel people should be punished twice. I wasn't the first guy to escape. I won't be the last. Obviously there should be a furlough system."

"Prison is just a warehouse. They are not here for rehabilitation or anything else. It's just a warehouse. The programs are there to take advantage of, to get a move," to lower security.

Furloughs, he said, are "a valuable tool for inmates and the administration because it makes the administration look good. It's good for the inmate and taxpayer because it helps people reunite with their family and friends. It gives people hope. It gives you a chance to see how society has changed. After a long stretch in jail, you don't know how to walk down the street any more. It's like being a baby all over again. I think it's needed. You can't take a person and put them in jail for ten, fifteen, twenty years without ever seeing daylight and expect them to be rehabilitated."

He is most worried about the rape charges brought against him. In prison society, those convicted of sexual crimes are shunned. "The most important thing to me is proving I did not rape anybody. I don't want that on my record," he said. "It hurts me to be charged with rape."

Vice President Bush incorrectly claimed that Massachusetts had a unique and unusually lenient furlough program. In fact, corrections professionals with national experience describe the Massachusetts program as in the mainstream. Furlough programs were established throughout the nation during the wave of prison reform following the riots and deaths at the state prison in Attica, New York in 1971. They are widely viewed in corrections circles as a practical tool to reintroduce prisoners to the community. While on furlough, an inmate can go to school, interview for a job, and reestablish family relationships. In Massachusetts, the program was introduced in 1972 by Francis W. Sargent, a Republican governor who preceded Dukakis in office. Republican Governors Nelson Rockefeller of New York and Ronald W. Reagan of California introduced their own furlough programs. By 1988, every state had some form of temporary release program, and inmates convicted of murder were eligible to participate in those programs in the federal system and in thirty-six states, including Massachusetts where the state Supreme Judicial Court ruled in 1973 that murderers had the right to furloughs.

The mandatory penalty for first-degree murder in Massachusetts is a life sentence without parole. The penalty is stiffer than many other states impose. The sentencing structure in most states allows murderers to be paroled, except in special cases such as murder of a police officer, a double murder, or a case in which the victim was tortured. "Massachusetts is actually tough on murder," explained Professor James Alan Fox of Northeastern University, who has studied the issue in depth. The average length of prison time served for first degree murder in the United States is eleven years. In many states, William Horton would have been paroled and out on the street before he even qualified for his first furlough in Massachusetts.

Critics of the furlough program suggested that this sentence meant that the prisoner was never to be released from prison. But modern corrections policy assumes that most prison inmates (95 percent, in actuality) will leave prison some day, and that includes lifers, who are considered a particularly good risk because they have the lowest recidivism rate of any category of offender. The first-degree lifers in Massachusetts who eventually win release from prison do so because their sentences are commuted from first- to second-degree murder by the parole board and the governor. This commutation makes them eligible for parole after fifteen years. Obtaining such a commutation is not easy. Only about one in every ten convicted murderers ever has his sentence commuted. During the fifteen-year period between 1972 and 1987 (spanning four governors' terms) only thirty-six lifers won commutations to second-degree murder in Massachusetts. They served an average 19.4 years before being released. Almost half of those commutations were first-degree lifers serving felony murder sentences. For an extremely high percentage of convicted murderers, the murder is their first felony conviction. Although friends and families of the victim never forgive or forget the crime, corrections professionals have found that many of these inmates can safely be returned to society. Some learn a lesson and mature behind bars. For others, authorities judge that they have paid as much as can reasonably be expected for a mistake that may have been isolated, if grievous.

Not all first-degree murders are cold-blooded, premeditated killings, despite the charge. The murder one category in Massachusetts includes felony murder. A teenager driving a getaway car during a holdup in which a cashier is killed by someone else could be convicted of murder one even though he did not pull the trigger. This conviction, in fact, happened in the original Horton case, when three men were convicted of first-degree murder although only one may have actually committed the crime. Most of the women who are convicted of murder one in Massachusetts are guilty of felony murder—they became peripherally involved in a killing because of a boyfriend or husband who was the actual killer. In many cases, the trigger man might cop a plea and plead guilty to second-degree murder but the wheel man might claim innocence but be convicted of felony or first-degree murder. Under the sentence structure, the actual murderer will be eligible for parole after fifteen years, but the accomplice, who may not even have witnessed the killing, will serve life without parole.

Furloughs were considered vital in commutation proceedings in showing that the prisoner could handle freedom. A total of 69 percent of the first-degree lifers commuted in Massachusetts between 1972 and 1987 had received furloughs prior to commutation. In any case, only about one in every six lifers ever qualified for the furlough program in Massachusetts, and only after passing through a five-tiered review.

Corrections professionals said that furloughs made the difference between an angry man and an adjusted man returning to society. Numerous studies have shown that the recidivism rate is double for inmates
released without furloughs. Furloughs also relieve prison tensions. The
Massachusetts correctional system, like those of other industrial states,
is 150 percent over capacity. The state-prison population has more than
doubled since 1980.

The Dukakis campaign was aware of the political danger in the
crime issue and furlough program long before the Bush campaign.
Within weeks of Horton's arrest in Maryland, corrections officials had
given the campaign a list of experts who would publicly defend the
program. In a June 21, 1987 memo, Steve Rosenfeld, then working as
Dukakis's Florida state director, recapped the highlights in a Dukakis
trip to Florida on June 16 and 17 and stressed getting out in front of the
crime issue. "The issue of crime is just as important as we have believed," he wrote. "The death penalty will come up—it did during our
visit, several times—and we must get our anticrime message out first so
it does not sound like a defensive attempt to explain away our opposition
to the death penalty, but rather a positive, successful message, giving us
a framework to deal with the death penalty when it does come at us."

Jim Carpenito, a Salem, New Hampshire lawyer who was
Dukakis's coordinator in that southern New Hampshire community,
was troubled by the shrill coverage of the furlough issue by the Lawrence (Mass.) *Eagle Tribune*. A poll conducted for the Dukakis campaign
showed that the *Tribune* was the primary source of daily news for 11
percent of the Democratic primary voters in New Hampshire. Carpenito called state campaign director Charlie Baker. We're getting killed, he
said. What are you going to do about it? Baker began reading the *Tribune*
every day. The newspaper's fixation on the furlough issue was so
complete that it bumped the U.S.—U.S.S.R. summit off the front
page. In response, Baker scheduled "police weekends," led by Essex
County District Attorney Kevin Burke. Law-enforcement officials from
Massachusetts held press conferences and campaigned door to door in
New Hampshire during the final months in 1987. Eventually, Dukakis
swept southern New Hampshire because those voters were getting the
furlough news in a broader context with Dukakis's record as governor.

But if the Dukakis campaign was sensitive to the issue long before
the public was aware of the controversy, the Bush campaign was not far
behind. While the Democrats were still playing out the primary string,
the Bush high command essentially declared Michael Dukakis the Democratic presidential nominee at the end of March 1988 by naming
Andrew H. Card, a former Republican state representative from Hol-
brook, Massachusetts, director of opposition research.

Card, a youthful forty-one, had been a fairly progressive Republican legislator on Beacon Hill. He gravitated naturally toward the types of suburban reform issues that Dukakis embraced in Massachusetts. Like Dukakis, he was also an ambitious man. In 1982, when Dukakis went up against King in the rematch campaign in the Democratic primary, Card launched a long-shot campaign to win the Republican gubernatorial nomination. The race left Card with good will and unquenched ambition. He soon moved to Washington to work in Reagan's White House. He and his brother-in-law, Ronald Kaufman, a native of Quincy, Massachusetts and experienced Republican operative, were the first to set up shop in New Hampshire for Bush's 1988 campaign.

Card had ample first-hand knowledge of Dukakis. His legislative career overlapped Dukakis's first term in office. The Republican National Committee had been compiling background information on Dukakis and other prominent Democrats for a long time. The files were turned over to the Bush campaign, which had also been saving news clips on Dukakis and the other Democratic hopefuls throughout the campaign season.

When Card moved back to the White House payroll later in spring 1988 to take over the job of special assistant for intergovernmental relations for Reagan, the search-and-destroy mission on Dukakis fell to Jim Pinkerton, director of the campaign research shop. It was immediately apparent to Pinkerton that the campaign would have to puncture the Massachusetts miracle and undermine Dukakis' record in his home state.

A week before the New York primary, Senator Al Gore, in the *New York Daily News* debate at Madison Square Garden, attacked Dukakis for giving weekend passes to criminals. His campaign had learned of the state furlough program from an article in the pro-Republican *Washington Times*. Pinkerton was puzzled by the remark. He knew nothing about state or federal prison furlough programs and it sounded strange to him.

Pinkerton tracked down Card, who was still working on the campaign, to find out more about these "weekend passes" for criminals. Card remembered a brief flap over the furlough program from 1976 during Dukakis's first term. The legislature had wanted to prohibit murderers from participating in the program. Dukakis disagreed. The Supreme Judicial Court had already issued an opinion upholding murderers' rights to participate in the program. He pocket vetoed the bill that would have outlawed participation and instead tightened eligibility for the program by requiring that inmates serve at least five years of their sentence to participate. That was the first of several steps taken to stiffen eligibility and administration of the program. During Edward J. King's term, a lifer escaped and King responded by increasing the eligibility

criterion to ten years. In response to the Horton case, Dukakis tough-
ened the program for lifers twice before finally agreeing to eliminate it.
In June 1987, he announced new rules including requirements that the
superintendent of each correctional institution personally interview and
assess each furlough candidate, that psychiatric exams be made of each
first-degree lifer before approval of a furlough, and that furlough sponsors be investigated and interviewed quarterly. In August 1987, he
announced more rules, including the requirement that the inmate serve
12½ years to be eligible for furlough, creating a three-person advisory
board of parole board members to advise the corrections commissioner
on suitability of furloughs for first-degree lifers, and notifying the
victim's family about the pending furlough application. The tougher
rules failed to blunt the demand for revoking the program. Dukakis
agreed in March 1988 not to oppose the ban. As a result, the penalty for
first-degree murder in Massachusetts is now effectively stiffer than the
penalties in most other states.

Unless explained in context, furlough programs may sound irra-
tional to those who assume prisoners are locked up for the duration of
their sentences. Card explained the issue to Pinkerton and added, "If
you think that is crazy wait until I tell you about the Pledge of Allegiance."

In May 1977, during his first term as governor, Dukakis had vetoed
a bill that would have required school teachers to lead students in the
Pledge of Allegiance. He felt the legislation was unconstitutional and a
state Supreme Judicial Court advisory opinion agreed with him. The
state court suggested the law would violate school teachers' First
Amendment rights. The state advisory opinion was based upon a 1943
U.S. Supreme Court opinion that upheld the rights of children of
Jehovah's Witnesses not to recite the pledge because of their religious
prohibition against swearing allegiance to material objects. The state
legislature, feuding with Dukakis at the time, passed the bill over his
objections, and the House broke into a chorus of "God Bless America"
after the vote.

Pinkerton and a team of researchers whom Atwater referred to as
the "thirty-five excellent nerds" were looking for examples of Dukakis's
liberalism. They knew that Republicans win national elections if the
opponent can be identified as a liberal. Atwater, frazzled by campaign
responsibilities, asked Pinkerton to summarize the "best"—that is, most
damaging—issues on one 3 by 5 inch index card in mid-April. Pinkerton
complied with a card jammed with issues, including state tax increases
from 1975, state spending statistics, the pledge, furloughs, and defense-
related issues like Dukakis's support of a nuclear freeze.

Just weeks later in May, Terry Bergman was asked to perform the same service for the Dukakis campaign. Bergman had worked in state government and on campaigns for Dukakis since 1975. She joined S. Stephen Rosenfeld in a defensive research operation in that month. Under their direction, former aides were asked to prepare detailed reports on specific areas of political vulnerability from Dukakis's long public record. They were told to write the attack as the Republicans would and present the issue in the worst possible light, compile all facts and figures on the vulnerability, develop defensive talking points, find something similar in Bush's record at which to counterpunch, list credible third parties who could be called upon to offer a defense, and provide original documents and news clips.

Rosenfeld asked Bergman to prepare a memo summarizing the ten areas in which Dukakis was most vulnerable to criticism and attack. Her May memo was uncanny. She listed every issue that the Republicans would use over the summer and fall to define Dukakis as a dangerous, risky liberal. She listed: (1) the rate of state-government spending and first-term tax hikes; (2) the increase in the size of state government; (3) "excessive regulation"—business regulatory practices from the first term; (4) criminal-justice issues, including prison furloughs and commutations; (5) inexperience on foreign policy; (6) the Dukakis "sleaze" factor, including corruption of his former education adviser and Sasso's involvement in the Biden tape episode; (7) manager versus mismanagement, including deaths of children in state foster care, the current budget shortfall, the continued high welfare caseload, the polluted condition of Boston Harbor, controversy over locating a new prison, prison overcrowding, and conditions in the state mental hospital at Bridgewater; (8) social liberalism, including veto on the Pledge of Allegiance bill; (9) taking credit for the Massachusetts miracle; and (10) the Massachusetts miracle versus the decline in manufacturing jobs in the Commonwealth.

The furlough issue proved to be the most damaging for Dukakis when coupled with his opposition to capital punishment. The Bush campaign was able to use the issue to create the perception that Dukakis was a fuzzy-headed liberal and sympathetic toward criminals despite a record in Massachusetts that showed violent crime had dropped 13 percent, drug convictions were up fivefold, police employment was up, and the homicide rate was the lowest among the major industrial states. After Atwater passed on the information provided by Pinkerton, Bush made public references to the furlough program in late spring. The program was prominently featured in his first pointed attack on Dukakis on June 9 in Houston before the Texas Republican Convention.

"His values are too often, in my judgment, out of the mainstream," he said in an address criticizing Dukakis for being soft on crime, in favor of high taxes, and more skeptical of America than some of its enemies.

The speech established a Bush pattern of using isolated "facts" out of context to create a negative view of Massachusetts and its governor. Although Bush had been an incumbent vice president for eight years, he cast Dukakis in the role of incumbent with a record to defend, a tactic that put Dukakis on the defensive. The response, if made, rarely caught up to the original charge.

The Dukakis campaign issue staff mistakenly thought that data showing the Massachusetts furlough program to be a mainstream correctional tool would kill the stories. Tom Herman, an issues adviser to the candidate, headed to the back of the campaign plane to explain the issue to the traveling press corps after Bush on June 18 leveled another furlough attack. The press jokingly referred to the briefing as "Herman's Furlough 101."

"We thought, obviously erroneously, that facts were facts and the program was mainstream and we were showing it was mainstream and the story would go away. We didn't think it would stick," he said. In May, Tom Cosgrove, then running Dukakis's primary campaign in New Jersey, warned Dukakis that the furlough issue was going to be a problem there. Dukakis responded, "But the federal government has a furlough program." Because the Massachusetts program was just like dozens of others, including the federal program, he thought there was no issue.

But other senior campaign aides were agitating for a counteroffensive. Estrich, herself a rape victim, had written a book called *Real Rape*, published a year before. She instantly understood the power in the image of a black man raping a white woman. She wanted the governor to address the issue frontally, to admit it had been a mistake and tell people he had ended the program for lifers; to tell of his own experiences with crime, an elderly father bound and robbed by a drug addict, a brother killed by a hit-and-run driver; to point out the similarities with the federal furlough program; and to recount his own record on fighting crime and drug abuse.

Still other senior campaign officials believed the less said about furloughs the better because it was a no-win issue. No matter how many facts and figures they provided, the public would never buy weekend passes for criminals. On occasion, the campaign was able to mount effective counterattacks. The day Pennsylvania Senator Arlen Specter came to Boston to criticize Dukakis on crime, the Dukakis campaign arranged for him to be literally surrounded by a pack of Massachusetts law-enforcement officials, who effectively shot down his message. Specter couldn't even get the first word at his own press conference. Massachusetts Attorney General James M. Shannon, in a mock serious tone, welcomed the senator to the state and explained that the district attorneys, sheriffs, police chiefs, and others surrounding him all worked together on the governor's anticrime council. "We're glad you're here today, Senator," he said. "So why don't you take in a game at Fenway or something; just please don't gum up the working relationship all of us have in Massachusetts."

That counterblast was rare, however. Bush added furloughs to his stump speech. A week after the June 9 critique during a speech to the Illinois Republican Convention in Springfield, he said that voters should ask Dukakis why he let "murderers out on vacations." Four days later in Louisville, he first mentioned the name "Willie" Horton in a speech to the National Sheriffs Association and told how Horton escaped while on furlough and attacked a couple in Maryland. Bush's attacks became increasingly shrill. Clint Eastwood's answer to crime was "Go ahead. Make my day," he said. "My opponent's answer is slightly different: 'Go ahead: Have a nice weekend.' " On Labor Day in California, in a voice that rose to a shout, he cried, "No more furloughs for people to rape, pillage and plunder in the United States." On October 7 in Medina, Ohio, Bush attacked Dukakis as the "furlough king."

The Bush campaign actively fanned the flames. Mark Goodin, the chief campaign spokesman in Washington, kept a mug shot of Horton taped above his desk at campaign headquarters to remind him to mention the case to reporters. One Bush aide was quoted as saying that the only question was whether their television ads would show "Willie" Horton with or without the knife in his hand. In late October when Horton, in a phone conversation with a Gannett News Service reporter, complained that Bush had lied about his case and said, "Obviously, I am for Dukakis," the Bush campaign gleefully billed his comment as "an endorsement."

"Did you hear about Willie's endorsement?" Atwater asked reporters traveling with the vice president in Michigan. "I assume the reason he endorsed him is that he thinks he'll have a better chance of getting out of jail if Dukakis is elected. I don't know if Dukakis would let him out, but I think there'd be a better chance." Atwater made this remark after being forced to apologize for another wisecrack about "Willie" being Dukakis's running mate. Early in July, Atwater told a Republican gathering about a *Reader's Digest* article on the Horton case. "There is a story about a fellow named Willie Horton who, for all I know, may end up being Dukakis's running mate," he said. He mentioned that he saw Jesse Jackson standing in Dukakis's driveway on the news, "So anyway, maybe [Dukakis] will put this Willie Horton on the ticket after all is said and done." He and others in the Bush campaign denied the attacks were aimed at stirring racial hatred and fears. Atwater, particularly, said he was sensitive to that sort of thing because a white southern boy like him would be suspected of such tactics. But this white southern boy, born in the same year and state as Horton, always used the diminutive in referring to Horton. He called him "Willie," just as white men traditionally addressed black men in the South. A white criminal would be more likely to have been called "Horton."

Dukakis's record was, above all, wrecked with skill by the Bush campaign's television advertising team, one of whose main members had direct experience with furloughs. The two most effective ads in the Bush campaign were produced by Dennis Frankenberry, a partner with the Milwaukee-based firm of Frankenberry, Laughlin & Constable. The first showed scenes of sewage and pollution in Boston Harbor and charged Dukakis did "nothing" to clean it up. The other Frankenberry spot showed a prison with a revolving door and attacked Dukakis's "revolving door" prison furlough policy. The ad, filmed in grainy black and white at Utah State Prison where Gary Gilmore was executed in 1976, was considered the most powerful in the 1988 campaign.

Frankenberry had had his own brush with the law and first-hand knowledge of corrections programs. In 1985, his red sportscar struck and injured two teenagers on a bicycle, and he fled the scene. His blood alcohol level tested at twice the legal limit. He pleaded guilty and was sentenced to ninety days in the House of Correction. For the sixty-eight days he actually served, he was released from prison for twelve hours each day in a work-release program.

The Bush campaign also had help in publicizing the Horton case from the *Readers Digest*, which commissioned a graphic seven-page story on the case called "Getting Away with Murder" for its July issue. Reprints of the article were distributed in many states. Two so-called independent political action committees also made and broadcast television commercials on the tragedy. The American Security Political Action Committee broadcast an ad called "Weekend Passes" throughout the South during the summer, displaying a mug shot of a threatening Horton. In October, a group called Committee for the Presidency, Bush supporters in Los Angeles, made ads with Donna Fournier Cuomo, the bitter sister of Horton's original victim, and Cliff Barnes. The camera zoomed in for intense closeups of these victims telling their stories and blaming Dukakis.

The committee that featured Bush's picture on its letterhead with the subtitle "George Bush Victory Fund" sent Barnes and Fournier on the road to hold press conferences in seven cities in California and Texas in October. Barnes appeared on the Oprah Winfrey, Geraldo Rivera, and Morton Downey, Jr. television shows. The Bush campaign helped news reporters contact and interview these victims. Ugly leaflets that invariably included Horton's ferocious mug shot were mailed to Reagan Democrats in a massive direct-mail campaign run by state Republican parties and right-wing sympathizers. William Horton became a familiar face to Reagan Democrats in rural Texas, suburban Detroit, and ethnic neighborhoods in Chicago. An anti-Dukakis videotape showed George Hanna, Sr., father of a Massachusetts state-police trooper who was killed in the line of duty, standing at his son's grave. He hated Dukakis because of Dukakis's opposition to the death penalty. A picture of a knife dripping blood was on the videotape cover.

One reason the charges were so damaging is that in each a grain of truth glistened through the murk of distortion and gave each charge some credibility. Dukakis *was* a liberal. He *had* strongly endorsed the furlough program as an effective rehabilitative tool. He *was* skeptical of the military. He *did* think that private ownership of handguns was dangerous and a mistake. He *was* a card-carrying member of the American Civil Liberties Union and *proud* of it. He *did* think it wrong to force school teachers to lead the Pledge of Allegiance. And Boston Harbor *was* polluted. For ten long years he had been governor of Massachusetts, a progressive state with a long and liberal tradition of activist government and high government spending and taxation. The Massachusetts legislature was at the forefront in protesting the war in Vietnam. Massachusetts was a laboratory for exploration and change fostered by dozens of fine universities.

Little in government is black or white. Always mitigating factors can be found. And so dozens of issues could be exploited. Massachusetts was one of three states that regulated BB guns. It led the way in imposing a mandatory year in prison on anyone caught carrying a handgun without a permit. Issues plucked out of the context of their times could also take on different connotations in 1988. At the height of the Vietnam war, most citizens thought that if eighteen- and nineteen-year-old soldiers were old enough to fight and die for their country, they were old enough to have a beer. But by 1988, with teenaged drunk-driving accidents epidemic and the military draft a historical footnote, public opinion had swung the other way, in favor of an age twenty-one drinking limit. Prison reforms adopted in the early 1970s as a reaction to prison riots and high recidivism rates were seen as unduly "soft" in later, hard-line times.

Still other issues bubbled like a poisonous subterranean stream through the ranks of ideological conservatives and fundamentalist Christians. Dukakis was described as a supporter of satanism because he awarded a Paul Revere Patriot Citation to self-declared "witch" Laurie Cabot of Salem, Massachusetts. The citation was a tourist gimmick awarded to children visiting the State House and gave the honoree the right to graze his cattle on the Boston Common. He was also accused of supporting bestiality, an issue that generated much merriment in the upper reaches of the Bush campaign, although they never went public with it. They never needed to because their surrogates were spreading the stories through the religious right. A comic book published by Anthony Kane & Associates in Garrisonville, Virginia purported to tell "The real story of Mike Dukakis." The title page billed him as "The World's greatest quick-change and slight [sic]-of-hand artist!" It featured a cartoon sketch of a man in an open raincoat chasing a panicked pack of chickens, elephants, giraffes, dogs, and cats. Protesters dressed in bunny suits greeted Dukakis and his wife at public appearances. At one event Kitty Dukakis was greeted by a protester dressed as Little Bo Peep. She carried a sign that said Keep Dukakis Away from My Sheep.

The comic book turned innocuous events that had occurred twenty years earlier into major issues. In Massachusetts, citizens have the right of free petition, which means that any citizen can drop a bill into the legislative hopper by asking his state legislator to file it for him or her. In 1970, state Representative Michael S. Dukakis of Brookline was asked to file five bills to update the state's archaic blue laws by his constituent Bill Baird, the well-known reproductive-rights advocate. The bills called for repeal of the laws against fornication or sex outside of marriage, against blasphemy, against unnatural and lascivious acts with another person, and the crime against nature (bestiality). Under the blue laws, which remained in effect through Catholic church influence, it was still a criminal offense in Massachusetts for two unmarried adults to engage in sexual relations. Birth control was illegal in the state until the early 1970s.

In one of the truly remarkable campaign moves, Bush succeeded in putting Dukakis on the defensive with the environmental issue. The weapon was Boston's historic harbor, which had been a repository for garbage and other detritus since the American Colonists pitched tea into it two hundred years ago. Harbor clean-up did not become a government or widespread public issue until well after a more environmentally sensitive era dawned. When Dukakis first took office as governor in 1975, the Executive Office of Environmental Affairs had just been created. Evelyn F. Murphy, later Dukakis's lieutenant governor, then a bright Duke University-educated Ph.D., was the first state Secretary of Environmental Affairs.

Murphy had to pick her best shots during the first Dukakis administration as she tried to get the new cabinet office off the ground. The office pasted together the old Department of Natural Resources and some agencies from the Department of Public Health. Despite his reform-minded bent and suburban background, Dukakis was never

Bush literally sailed into Boston's harbor at the end of the summer and used the murky ocean water to deliver a scathing indictment of Dukakis's record as governor. (Photo by Wendy Maeda)

much of a nature fancier and displayed little fervor for environmental issues. Murphy decided to make protection of the environmentally sensitive Georges Bank, richest fishing grounds in the world, her environmental priority. She convinced Dukakis of the issue's importance. He backed her, thinking about Massachusetts fishermens' jobs, and Massachusetts led the way in litigation to block oil drilling on Georges Bank in the late 1970s.

There were other problems with harbor cleanup. Because the Environmental Affairs office was brand new when he came into office, no comprehensive plan was on hand for a clean-up project. The primary treatment plant had long ago proved inadequate in treating Greater Boston sewage. A proposal to build a massive primary and secondary treatment plant on nearby Deer Island had Winthrop citizens up in arms. They correctly raised environmental objections about the plant.

Harbor clean-up would have cost $1 billion in the 1970s and federal money was available for 90 percent of it. (By 1988 the cost had grown to a stunning $6 billion.) But Dukakis had also inherited a $500 million budget deficit in 1975 and he could not come up with the 10 percent or $100 million for the state's share. The Metropolitan District Commission (MDC), an agency in the Office of Environmental Affairs, studied the issue from 1975 to 1978 and concluded that the state should put all its money into primary treatment and ask the federal government for a waiver on secondary treatment. Primary treatment separates liquid from solid wastes and removes about 70 percent of the contaminants. Secondary treatment removes an additional 10 percent of the contaminants at double the cost. In other words, primary treatment would cost $1 billion and secondary treatment, $2 billion. Dukakis's successor, Edward J. King, agreed with the strategy and filed the request for a waiver with the federal Environmental Protection Agency in September 1979. (Bush's vacation hometown, Kennebunkport, Maine applied for and received a waiver for secondary waste treatment under the same program.) The EPA was supposed to act on the waiver within one year. But it did nothing until 1982, when the request was rejected. Dukakis defeated King in 1982, and in that same year the city of Quincy, which borders Boston on the south, filed a lawsuit against both the state and federal governments demanding clean-up of the harbor. Dukakis came back into office in 1983 and requested a second waiver to buy time while he empaneled a blue-ribbon commission headed by former Governor Frank Sargent to make recommendations for a harbor clean-up plan. It recommended establishing an independent commission with a mandate to conduct the massive project. Dukakis filed the legislation creating the Massachusetts Water Resources Authority in 1984. It passed the state legislature in 1985, and the state is now implementing a $6.6 billion clean-up project.

Boston Harbor, however, is still filthy; it was a fissure in Dukakis's record, and the Bush campaign turned it into a political San Andreas Fault; and, most important, Dukakis let it happen.

Finally, the Bush campaign turned its guns on gun control, particularly in states like Texas (where huge billboards looming over the highways said: "I don't believe in people owning guns." Michael S. Dukakis); the Rocky Mountain states, Colorado and Montana, where Dukakis had an opportunity to do well, rural sections of Pennsylvania and other eastern states like Maryland, where a gun referendum was on the ballot. The National Rifle Association, which has 2.8 million members, acted as the principal Bush surrogate. The October issue of its monthly magazine *The American Rifleman* featured a black background with the words: "I do not believe in people owning guns, only the police and military. I am going to do everything I can to disarm this state." The quote is attributed to Dukakis on June 16, 1986. He denied ever saying such a thing. The source of the quote was Michael Yacino, long a Dukakis hater and the leading gun lobbyist in Massachusetts, who claimed Dukakis made the statement during an impromptu four-or five-minute meeting in his office. "He's lying," said Yacino when asked about the denial."I don't care what he is saying. That is what he feels." Although it is true that Yacino was the sort of person who heard what he wanted to hear, it is also true that Dukakis was no gun freak.

Dukakis, as a lifelong resident in a congested urban area and as governor of a densely populated state, had long considered gun control a public-safety issue. He had favored strict controls on firearms throughout his career as the wisest course to discourage private citizens from having weapons lying around their homes where they might cause an accidental death, be used in committing crimes of passion, or be stolen by criminals.

The hardliners in the NRA consider any regulation a direct threat to their "constitutional right" to bear arms. In his annual Handgun Control Week proclamation, Dukakis said he did not agree with that reading of the Constitution. He did not think people had the right to bear arms. For all that, however, Dukakis was not, as one of his criminal-justice advisers said, "a disarmament freak." Even during the unsuccessful referendum to ban sale and possession of handguns by private citizens in 1976 (which he supported), he expressed reservations about finding the money to reimburse citizens for their handguns and the gun owners' constitutional rights of privacy. Nothing in his record suggests he opposed ownership of guns by hunters and sportsmen.

The gun-control issue epitomized the cultural gulf between Massachusetts and the South. The threat of street crime is a real one for residents of urban neighborhoods in the North. They see the gun as the primary weapon of destruction. In states like Montana and Texas, the gun rack is standard equipment on pickup trucks. A man's gun is familiar, like a household appliance. The gun is an inherent part of the ethic in the West. Gun ownership, a rite of passage to manhood, is considered essential for protection.

The National Rifle Association went after Dukakis with a vengeance. They taped radio ads featuring actor Charlton Heston, who played Moses in a 1950s epic on Biblical times, and bought air time on radio stations in twenty states. In the ad Heston said, "The right to own a gun, especially for self-defense, is under serious threat." He criticized Dukakis for being against the death penalty and mandatory sentences for drug dealers and for supporting furloughs for prisoners. "He also did everything he could to take guns away from honest citizens. That was in Massachusetts. Now he wants to do it all over America," he said. The ad prompted John Sharp, a Texas Railroad commissioner and chairman of Dukakis's Texas campaign, to mournfully comment, "I never thought I'd see the day that Moses lied."

But he did, and the tactic met the only standard set by George Bush in 1988—it worked.

9

Made with Worms

The image flickering on the television screen is a grim Michael Dukakis in shirtsleeves. His arm rests upon a television set that broadcasts a Bush campaign commercial. The commercial features news footage of a ridiculous-looking Dukakis riding in an M1 tank. As the camera zooms in to show Dukakis smiling giddily from beneath an Army helmet, the narrator charges that Dukakis has opposed "virtually every defense system we developed. . . . And now he wants to be our Commander-in-Chief. America can't afford that risk."

Dukakis snaps off the television set in this commercial within a commercial and barks: "I'm fed up with it. Haven't seen anything like it in twenty-five years of public life, George Bush's negative TV ads: distorting my record, full of lies, and he knows it."

Late in October, the Dukakis campaign produced this commercial, called "Counterpunch," and television advertising in Campaign '88 came full circle: a television ad about another candidate's television ad. Counterpunch was a metaphor for the Dukakis campaign's advertising, a belated exercise in damage control that mirrored the campaign's shortage of decisiveness, experience, and leadership at the top.

The Dukakis advertising was a genuine source of wonder in the political world throughout fall 1988. For all the problems moving from the primaries to the biggest of all political stages, it seemed unthinkable

Dukakis climbed into an M-1 tank at a manufacturing plant in Sterling Heights, Michigan, for a campaign "visual" on September 13 that ended up in a Bush campaign commercial. (Photo courtesy of Associated Press and Wide World Photo)

that any advertising program could be this bad. How, people wondered, could the campaign be almost completely without advertising during the critical weeks in September, as full-scale assaults by Bush hit the national airwaves? How could Dukakis put $3 million plus behind a performance that appeared to be a morality play (with actors) about Bush's commercials and then yank it off the air within ten days? How could the candidate himself check scripts on trade policy line by line, searching for anything that might smack of jingoistic rhetoric aimed at the Japanese, and then allow onto the air in Ohio an almost openly racist commercial using the Japanese flag that was put together by Jesse Jackson's former campaign manager? How could one presidential campaign generate 1,200 scripts for television advertisements in one month?

The advertising failure was colossal, stupendous, dramatic, intricate, but also at times side-splitting, thigh-slapping, head-scratching. It was a failure that needed long and complex roots because it was far too gigantic a goof to have been produced by one lone bumbler. To produce a failure this sweeping took scores of people, meetings, committees, plans, proposals, outlines. It was a failure that could at almost any moment in summer and mid-fall 1988 have been corrected, even transformed into triumph, but internal rivalry, a balky candidate, and some fatally flawed judgments kept it tearing at the increasingly tattered fabric that was Michael Dukakis's presidential candidacy.

Advertising could not have elected Dukakis; it didn't elect George Bush. As politicians have invested more and more millions in television commercials in recent years, its influence has sometimes been exaggerated. The United States is more than a nation of video-addicted, semiliterate zombies whose every opinion about themselves, their country, their world, and their leaders can be manipulated with relative ease by thirty-second bursts of artfully and scientifically constructed stimuli. It isn't quite that simple; advertising matters, but it cannot be isolated from other parts of a political campaign. What matters is how well the advertising fits, or indeed whether it fits at all, with the basic message and themes a candidate is sending to voters, and whether his communications strategy is skillfully and effectively enough executed that the themes and the message regularly penetrate the increasingly thick cloud of information that surrounds the modern citizen in an age of mass-produced data.

Within three weeks of his nomination, it was apparent that Dukakis himself had real trouble communicating, and that he was vulnerable to an all-out assault from a Republican campaign that was limited by no standards other than effectiveness. At the core of his vulnerability was the almost blank slate he was in most potential voters' minds as the general election began. Of all the tired lines in politics, few have retained validity like this one: if your slate is blank, you either write on it at once or you can be certain your opponent will do the job for you. Advertising could have helped Dukakis considerably as he left his Atlanta experience, precisely because so many of the gaps involved basic questions about his personality, character, and record.

But instead of helping Dukakis to define himself and his message and draw contrasts with his opponent, his advertising program hurt him. In the general election, the Dukakis campaign, after production expenses, bought about $25 million worth of advertising time on national and local television stations. By dramatic contrast, the Bush campaign bought more than $45 million worth of advertising air time. In other words, voters were almost twice as likely to see a Bush commercial as a Dukakis commercial in the fall.

As near as those involved can figure it out, the Dukakis campaign ad men spent roughly $6 million producing their material, which amounts to 20 percent of the campaign's purchase of television time. The Republicans spent less than 10 percent on production. And finally, the campaign's sputtering, ever-changing, and therefore ineffective commercial message reached the public as forty-seven individual advertisements. The Bush campaign produced thirty-seven commercials, but 40 percent of the available cash was put behind fewer than six, reflecting the clarity in their message.

The reasons for the disaster were complicated:

1. All early efforts to plan an advertising campaign were derailed by the constant, top-level preoccupation with the missing meister, John Sasso, who was working as an executive at the largest advertising agency in New England as he waited from spring to late summer for the call to return to the campaign. Advertising proposals were advanced and rejected, often depending on whether or not they had a component involving his return to the campaign.

2. In Sasso's absence, top-level campaign advisers under orders from campaign manager Susan Estrich put together a plan that even they doubted would work. They had advocated, without success, a counterplan in May that would have used leadership from the executives in the advertising firm Sasso had joined. Versions of the plan were still being floated around Chauncy Street in August.

3. Dukakis and Susan Estrich differed early and often on whether Dukakis should attack Bush, and if so, how. The hotly controversial advertising Sasso approved after his return—the so-called "packaging" ads—was at least partly designed to slide around the governor's objection to negative advertising.

None of this was apparent, except to a small circle of Dukakis aides, as the campaign emerged from its victories over Jesse Jackson in Ohio and Indiana on May 2 with a mandate to get serious about the general election.

While riding in a car with Dukakis during the New York primary campaign in April, Estrich told him that it was time to expand the media team. Her initial thought was to go to the two most prominent Democratic media men, Robert Shrum and Robert Squier, but Dukakis had a rocky history with both and brushed off those suggestions. He blamed Shrum for the Gephardt campaign's Belgian-endive attack in South Dakota and had fired Squier during his 1982 gubernatorial campaign.

It was June before Tom Kiley, under instructions from Estrich, began to recruit political and commercial advertising firms to make up the Future Group. The idea was to draw the best in the business into an ad hoc advertising group to create "cutting-edge" advertising for the

Dukakis campaign, much as the Republicans had been doing with commercial firm talent for years with the November Group and the Tuesday Team, the advertisers who worked for Richard M. Nixon and Ronald Reagan.

Kiley had opposed the idea and had particular reservations about the wisdom in putting together a group of "strangers" to develop campaign advertising. He endorsed the concept of combining political and commercial talent but thought it too much to expect "strangers" to work well together. Behind the scenes, he argued long, hard, and unsuccessfully that John M. "Jack" Connors, Jr., president and chief operating officer of Hill Holliday Connors Cosmopulos Inc., the largest advertising agency in New England and a growing national powerhouse, be brought in to manage the advertising effort. His agency would not be directly involved because some of its larger advertising contracts prohibited the firm from doing political advertising. But in a May 26 meeting with Kiley, Connors told him he was willing to take a leave from his agency. He was Boston-based, politically savvy, familiar with Dukakis and his record, and his firm ranked among the best in the nation. He had the experience and contacts to handle a three-month, $46-million ad campaign with ease. Connors had been former Boston Mayor Kevin H. White's advertising man during the early part of White's political career, and he and Kiley knew each other from their joint involvement in the particularly divisive 1975 mayoral campaign, still part of Boston political lore.

Hill Holliday also held an added bonus for the Dukakis campaign: John Sasso was working there.

Ironically, Kiley's idea didn't involve Sasso, though by summer, Kiley was among those top Dukakis aides who believed Sasso should be back for the fall and the general election campaign. Realizing his diplomatic error, Kiley actually apologized to Sasso for not telling him what he was trying to do. The Kiley plan called for Connors to come to the campaign with a handful of his most talented people, some with political backgrounds, and oversee both hiring other creative talent and producing Dukakis's campaign advertising. Very quickly, Connors worked up a detailed plan. A vital element in that plan called for spending up to $6 million almost immediately after the Democratic convention for early advertising to establish favorable images and introduce Dukakis to the broader general-election audience. This idea, also supported by most of the advertising people later assembled by the campaign, was based on the theory that the governor was not well known and had a very short time in which to become well known before the general-election campaign accelerated after Labor Day.

According to Estrich, she presented the proposal to Paul Brountas, who in turn gave it to Dukakis, and she heard back from Brountas very quickly that the answer was no; she did not press Brountas to have Dukakis reconsider and did not herself raise the matter with the governor. According to several other senior officials of the campaign who were present for discussions of the Hill Holliday idea, Estrich was not a proponent of it, and they speculated among themselves that the reason was that this plan would provide a route back into the campaign for Sasso; to this day, Estrich says otherwise. When Kiley kept pressing for the idea, after the rejection, she rebuked her closest adviser from the primaries with sharp words, which she quickly regretted.

Later in that summer, Dukakis told Jack Corrigan, another supporter of the idea because he felt commercial advertising talent should be managed by people with political knowhow as well as knowledge of Dukakis, that he had been bothered that Connors's firm had a small account with a state agency and feared a public perception of favoritism.

Dukakis, ever sensitive about public ethics, also had reservations about using Connors because of a much larger piece of indirectly related business. Hill Holliday had held the lucrative state lottery advertising contract for years, and although that contract is let by state Treasurer Robert Q. Crane, a separately elected official, not the governor, Dukakis worried about the appearance. The *Boston Herald*, the tabloid that is part of Rupert Murdoch's publishing empire, had already printed speculative stories, which were false, even suggesting a causal link between the lottery contract and Sasso's employment at Hill Holliday.

That was not the primary reason for his hesitation, however. When Brountas broached the subject to the governor, Dukakis puzzled over why they would want to bring in Connors. Nothing against Jack, but isn't John Sasso doing the same thing? he asked. Couldn't John do this? If we're going to go to Hill Holliday, we ought to bring John back. Brountas had already told Dukakis he felt that Sasso had served his sentence, done his time, been penalized enough for the Biden tapes affair. And Sasso knew Dukakis far better than the advertising people being mentioned. Their view that Sasso's return and the Hill Holliday proposal were interchangeable revealed a fundamental misunderstanding of Sasso's role in the campaign, his job at the ad agency, and the advertising needs of a national campaign. Even more remarkable is that the governor, in isolation, made a critical decision about a critical element in his general-election campaign without fully airing the issue with his top political advisers.

Francis O'Brien, a veteran of the Mondale and Ferraro campaigns with additional experience in the entertainment, advertising, and public-relations worlds, then agreed to help Kiley locate commercial talent. O'Brien had also supported the Hill Holliday proposal, but no time was left to continue the argument; the campaign needed advertising people, and it needed advertising. He and Kiley spent a month together in New York before the Democratic National Convention interviewing and recruiting advertising executives. By mid-July they had assembled a team including Gary Susnjara, president of American operations of the British advertising and public-relations giant, Saatchi & Saatchi, as day-to-day manager; Edward A. McCabe, the advertising man who created the Frank Perdue chicken commercials; Scott Miller, an experienced political advertising man from Sawyer/Miller; Mal MacDougall, the man responsible for anti-Democratic commercials run in 1980 by the Republican National Committee, who nonetheless had been a big Dukakis fan from the time he lived in Massachusetts; Hank Bernhardt of Rhode Island; Michael Kaye of Los Angeles; Frank Mingo of New York, who specialized in advertising aimed at the black community; and Daniel Payne and Ken Swope of Boston, who produced Dukakis's primary campaign ads.

The plan was to have Susnjara run the business end of the operation and have Miller work with the Madison-Avenue creative talent. But it never quite worked as planned. The team lacked one powerful manager with both political and advertising experience and the mandate to make decisions. Ultimately, Miller, who was supposed to be a manager and not a producer of ads, became the principal ad man for the campaign, producing about thirty ads.

Late in July, Scott Miller and Michael Kaye visited Dukakis at his State House office.

"Both Kaye and I said, you've got to define yourself before they do. You are standing on a platform two miles high made of toothpicks. People are positively curious. They want to know you. Therefore, go up early and often. Talk about your record and platform," said Miller. They anticipated an ad that never surfaced. They assumed that Roger Ailes, the advertising Prince of Darkness behind Bush, would go on the air with testimonials from Massachusetts residents debunking the Massachusetts miracle.

Kaye immediately sensed a problem. None of them had a close relationship with the candidate. They had no history, no trust. He expressed to Miller his worry that no one had the long relationship with Dukakis needed to build an effective advertising campaign for him in the short time allowed.

A number of advertising professionals recommended that Dukakis go on the air early. Despite his success in winning the nomination, people knew little about him. He needed to get on television to fill in the blanks and make a preemptive strike in some vulnerable areas. But when it came to preemptive advertising, Dukakis's own innate caution came into play. Kiley was inclined to husband campaign resources until after Labor Day. Dukakis agreed. No ads were aired although Kaye prepared a flight of positive ads cut from the convention highlights to broadcast before the Republican National Convention.

By August, an in-house team of ad writers was writing scripts for advertisements on an economic populism theme. The theme was carried out in two ways: as the middle-class squeeze, which eventually evolved into Dukakis's rallying cry, "We're on your side"; and as America losing its preeminent place in the world because of Republican policies. The campaign discovered by polling that men and women reacted very differently to the economic message. Women responded to the middle-class squeeze issues, but men were more moved by the big-picture competitiveness issues.

Delivering the message was another matter. Estrich could not order an ad into production unless Dukakis approved the script. But Estrich, totally new to this part of general-election campaign work, sent Dukakis very few scripts and he approved even fewer. His reluctance to go negative was still a problem, and she continued to press for a strongly negative thrust both in advertising and on the stump.

In one major attempt, the campaign staff had planned to take the battle to Bush immediately after the Republican National Convention late in August. The theme in the ads was a blatant steal from Reagan's anti-Mondale attack in 1984, when he said Mondale was so far left he had left the country. These ads would say the Republicans, a bunch of rich right-wingers, had left Main Street and the mainstream behind. Dukakis considered that approach too negative. The ads were never produced.

The top campaign staff also made a strong effort to respond to Bush's criticism of the Massachusetts prison furlough program, just before the Republican convention, using an Ed McCabe crew to tape a proposed denunciation by Dukakis in North Carolina of commercials already being run in battleground states by Bush campaign supporters. That idea too was rejected by the candidate.

Dukakis was only one obstacle, however. Throughout August the ad men produced advertisements that were not quite right. McCabe produced a biographical spot that Kiley and others loved, but it tested badly in focus groups. The bio spot was a sixty-second ad featuring old still photographs of immigrants on Ellis Island, Dukakis's parents and Dukakis at different times in his life: as a student, as a soldier, as a young politician, as governor. With lyrical music in the background, a narrator said: "The American dream is two immigrants coming to America, meeting, and building a good and happy life together."

"The American dream is working hard and being rewarded for it.

It's living in a decent home and giving your children quality education."

"The American dream is the hope and the belief that a boy or girl can go as far as their abilities can take them, no matter how humble their beginnings."

"The American dream is raising a son who grows into a man who could actually become the president of the United States. A man who has lived that dream and will fight to protect it for every American."

The spot winds down with a clip from Dukakis's acceptance speech. He says: "If anyone tells you that the American dream belongs to the privileged few and not to all of us you tell them that the Reagan era is over and a new era is about to begin."

The narrator returns with the close: "This November vote for Michael Dukakis. Vote for the American dream."

The campaign staff said the reference to the Reagan era had to go. Polling data showed that Reagan's popularity was moving toward an all-time high for him. Any crack at Reagan would boomerang. But McCabe resisted changing it for two weeks.

Despite the eventual change, voters failed to respond to the ad as the staff did. "It was a beautiful spot," sighed Kiley, who had it repeatedly tested, not wanting to believe it didn't work with voters. "But for too many people the spot celebrated Mike Dukakis's dream and not the American dream." It never aired.

The advertising team, moreover, rarely functioned as one. Both McCabe and Kaye proved difficult and balky (though in their defense, neither was getting adequate direction from the campaign). Both resisted making any changes in their product. Kaye cut spots that needed fine tuning, which he flatly refused to do. Miller was supposed to be directing but ended up remaking the commercials. When it became clear that Kaye would not revise his ads and it would take two weeks to get McCabe to remove a sentence from one of his, the campaign staff decided that it would be quicker and easier to have Miller produce new spots.

Dukakis's well-known repugnance for negative ads aside, there was clearly a management problem. Many of the ads were only slightly off, by a matter of degrees. Without a clean line of authority to one boss with political skill, nothing could break through the campaign bureaucracy.

Miller produced an environmental spot to counter the Boston Harbor attacks but did not receive permission to produce it until mid-September, two weeks after the Bush ad on Boston Harbor began airing. Dukakis thought Miller's response was too negative and it was never used. A remarkably similar ad ordered up by the California state director ended up on the air in October.

"There was a sort of consensus strategy," said Miller. "There were

David D'Alessandro, a hard driving corporate executive, devised a last ditch advertising strategy that amounted to little more than damage control. (Photo courtesy of John Hancock Co.)

many, many people with veto power and tack-on power. On a given day any one of ten or eleven people could stop something by having reservations; at the same time anyone could tack something on."

"McCabe was brilliant but he was missing a piece. All the commercial people were," said a senior campaign adviser afterward. "They needed to be educated. Their ads were off by five degrees. There was nothing wrong with the team but we needed a strong sense of people who had been in this before to manage this creative process. We needed a strong link to the message in the campaign. Ads don't drive messages, it's the other way around. We had a tough time in this campaign settling on a theme and the ads show that."

McCabe had dreamed up the "it takes a tough man to make a tender chicken" commercials for Frank Perdue. But like most commercial advertising men, he had avoided political work. It was time-consuming, unprofitable, and fairly thankless. But by 1988 he headed his own agency, McCabe Communications, and was ready for a new challenge. When O'Brien called him at the end of June, he was ready to lend his talents to the cause. He was considered brilliant and at forty-nine it could be assumed he was at the top of his game, though his performance never came close to his imposing reputation.

A week after Sasso returned to the campaign in September, he spoke to Kiley about the campaign's advertising. It soon became clear to Kiley that Sasso had in mind completely revamping the operation, yanking all spots then being broadcast, halting any production of new ones, and new leadership.

Sasso discovered the advertising team was bogged in bureaucratic inertia. Some campaign observers, lapsing into black humor, suggested the Future Group should be renamed the December Group because nothing was likely to get done until a month after election day. Sasso felt the advertising team needed a very tough, very aggressive manager.

During his eleven-month exile from the campaign, Sasso worked as a vice president at Hill Holliday, which held the advertising contract for John Hancock Mutual Life Insurance Company. While there, he met David F. D'Alessandro, the thirty-seven-year-old president of the corporate sector in John Hancock who was known as a very aggressive wunderkind. His rise from public-relations man to corporate president had taken four years. D'Alessandro's responsibilities included nurturing the corporate image of the $44-billion John Hancock companies. He had overseen production of the award-winning John Hancock Financial Services ad campaign "Real Life, Real Answers," which broke new ground in commercial advertising with cinéma vérité, slice-of-life vignettes purporting to show the financial dilemmas of potential John

Hancock customers. The ads won kudos from the advertising industry and the style was later copied by AT&T and Apple Computer.

D'Alessandro had been passed over for the top-management job on the advertising team in July when a well-regarded advertising executive warned Estrich and Kiley that he had a reputation for arrogance and not listening to others' opinions, and was politically inexperienced. D'Alessandro had some definite ideas about advertising, however. He wrote Kiley a letter on July 5 in which he recommended the campaign pursue three major themes. The first was titled "Dukakis Can Make It Better" and would play on the quality of voters' economic lives. The second would define Dukakis and show how he differed from Bush. The third was anti-Bush advertising that would concentrate on Bush's lack of decisiveness and failure to lead.

"Many people in America appear to be voting against Bush rather than for Dukakis," he wrote. "As Bush closes the difference in the polls and promotes his own image as well as attacks Dukakis, you must fill the image gap with Dukakis's leadership abilities and decisiveness messages.

"This will serve to negate Bush's ability to render Dukakis as inexperienced and simply not 'ready for the job' and counterpoint his specific attacks (Massachusetts miracle, crime, etc.).

"One does not have to be a rocket scientist to invent these three themes," he wrote. "One does, however, have to be highly disciplined to stick to these three themes. I cannot emphasize enough how important it is, as stated earlier, to consistently drive the advertising against these themes and their clear message.

"Proactive creative [material] will be vital," he wrote. "Rather than wait for Bush to attack with what you believe are Dukakis's 'underbelly' sensitivities, make some commercials which proactively demonstrate the positive points dealing with the 'attack issues.' Aggressiveness here will help the candidate to not appear to be 'back-pedaling' or being defensive in editorial exposure."

Sasso felt D'Alessandro was capable of providing the aggressive leadership needed for the advertising effort. As of Labor Day, when he prevailed upon D'Alessandro to join the campaign, five ads were on the air: New Era, a spot cut by Scott Miller from Dukakis's Democratic National Convention speech; Tough and Responsibility, two spots on Dukakis's record, also done by Miller; a generic anti-Republican spot made by Republican-turned-Democratic ad man Mal MacDougall focusing on the federal budget deficit, and an ad for Texas featuring Bentsen's role in the recently adopted plant-closing legislation.

At the core of the current advertising were the commercials about Dukakis's record, which Kiley (and Roger Ailes in Bush's campaign) felt were doing an effective job of presenting facts and images about lower crime rates and a strong economy that would provide some protection for Dukakis against Bush's attacks. He then had planned to move on to commercials using Dukakis in person to present snapshots of his ideas to improve average American families' economic lot. Also, negative advertising would be built around a theme that Bush was a weak figure who had failed in his Reagan-administration assignments, especially the war against illegal drugs.

D'Alessandro's job was initially described as liaison between the advertising staff and the campaign senior staff. When Kiley went to see him September 12, he thought it was to discuss content and plans, but D'Alessandro quickly made it clear he was preparing to completely redo the campaign in his way. Given his clear mandate from Sasso to fix the management problem, D'Alessandro moved forward and displaced Susnjara within days.

D'Alessandro found an astonishing collection of 1,200 scripts for ads that were never approved and never produced. The tenth-floor office was literally knee deep in unapproved scripts. Scripts were in the drawers, scripts on the desks, scripts in the planters. D'Alessandro likened the atmosphere to a French prison from the Papillon era. He would open a door, only to find six people feverishly working on scripts that never won approval.

It became apparent to him that the advertising effort was being driven by the written word rather than pictures. The three people whose approval was most essential, he thought, were all linear, logical thinkers. They were: Dukakis, the Harvard-trained lawyer; Estrich, another Harvard-trained lawyer, and Tom Kiley, a pollster. On September 12, D'Alessandro had told Kiley that it was going to be tough to be polite as he made his changes because of time constraints; Kiley came to see that as a huge understatement.

D'Alessandro first conducted an inventory of scripts and personnel and fired some of the local advertising writers who were producing the reams of scripts. He felt Democratic Party operatives had a faulty mind set. They were always looking for the silver bullet, the one ad that would tip the race. By contrast, the Republicans saw advertising as a marketing strategy and a series of ads that implemented it. He saw nothing sophisticated about the Republicans' 1988 ad campaign. He pegged it as vintage 1972 marketing, something an ad agency would have done back then to introduce a new car to the public. Michael Dukakis needed the same type of marketing strategy to sell his candidacy to the American people, he thought. At this late date, however, little could be concocted beyond a belated exercise in damage control.

Making a highly unusual move, he scheduled a gathering that later became derisively known as the Shoot-Out for September 19 in a room at the luxurious Ritz Carlton hotel in the fashionable Back Bay next to the Boston Public Garden. D'Alessandro, a miserably unhappy Susnjara, and two people from the W. B. Doner agency of Baltimore sat at a table. D'Alessandro had worked with Doner before he joined John Hancock four years earlier. A week before the Shoot-Out he gave twenty-one assignments based upon seven concepts drawn from the general election plan that John Sasso had just written. He insisted upon storyboards (frame-by-frame facsimiles of images to be used in the ads) because the campaign seemed to be devoid of visuals. He knew that four days later he would be presenting a marketing strategy—the first and only comprehensive marketing strategy in the campaign—to Dukakis for his approval.

Advertising veterans were insulted by the audition. They felt well known and established enough to bypass something like an audition. But D'Alessandro decided an audition was the most efficient way to find the right creative talent. He was looking for two types of agencies: a political agency to turn out the negative or comparative ads and react swiftly to campaign developments, and a traditional ad agency to do the more cosmic visionary commercials to sell the candidate.

Sawyer/Miller impressed him as the best political agency with the most firepower in research and ability to turn out commercials rapidly. The agency displayed fifteen storyboards in their ninety-minute presentation. In addition to Scott Miller, Mandy Grunwald, a talented advertising professional with the firm, would work on the account. The Doner agency was picked to do the more visionary commercials that would emphasize Dukakis's aspirations for the country.

Among those who did not make the cut were Daniel Payne and Ken Swope, two Boston-based advertising men who had made all Dukakis's primary-campaign commercials. Payne had done the advertising for Dukakis's 1982 and 1986 gubernatorial campaigns, and his commercial presenting Dukakis and his record to Democratic voters throughout the long primary season was the view of the governor that the people who voted for him saw more than any other.

D'Alessandro was not impressed by their presentations, and more important, Dukakis was dissatisfied with their work. He thought the impulsive but highly creative Ken Swope was intemperate. And the only Payne ad he had liked was the anti-Gephardt flip-flop ad used in March. He wanted to fire him. Estrich gave Payne a chance to work his way back into Dukakis's good graces by arranging for him to make the Dukakis biographical film featuring his movie-star cousin Olympia for the Democratic National Convention, a widely praised political documentary that preceded Dukakis' walk to the convention stage to make his acceptance speech.

Dukakis's treatment of Payne struck several campaign colleagues as both misguided and callous, but he was adamant.

On September 23 at the Hotel Lafayette, D'Alessandro presented the candidate with a comprehensive marketing plan complete with storyboards and a detailed time line. Sasso, Estrich, Corrigan, and Bob Farmer were also there, along with Washington political consultant Robert Squier; New York investment counselor Michael Delguidice (an intimate of Governor Mario Cuomo), and Senator Bill Bradley of New Jersey, who had come to Boston to help Dukakis prepare for his first debate with Bush two days later.

D'Alessandro opened the presentation by showing three of McCabe's worst ads. One featured actors playing heavily accented foreigners who lavished praise on policies that allowed them to buy up chunks of American industry and real estate cheap. "In the last eight years, we and other overseas investors have bought $1.2 trillion worth of the United States," says the first foreign businessman.

A British businesswoman then trills, "Now we own a lot of your country and we want to own even more!"

An Arab businessman ends the spot with his fingers crossed, saying, "So our fingers are crossed that you keep things exactly as they are and vote for ... George Bush." Although the idea was fair, the execution veered right into jingoism.

Another ad attempting to criticize Bush's poor performance on fighting drug trafficking showed mountains of powder labeled "cocaine" in shaky letters and ended with a sneeze. It was unintelligible.

We won't have "pedestrian political ads"; this is what we won't do, he said, pointing to the McCabe spots, which he knew Dukakis would hate. Bob Squier, a producer of "pedestrian political ads," squirmed with frustration. Estrich injected that they needed some "pedestrian *negative* political ads."

The original plan included five phases. The first two were indirectly anti-Bush. D'Alessandro's major proposal—to which Sasso had alluded in his first conversation with Kiley two weeks before—were the famous packaging ads, which in concept resembled his "Real Life, Real Answers" campaign for John Hancock. The ads would show cynical Bush-handlers played by actors wisecracking and plotting ways of packaging Bush and his positions in the face of Dukakis initiatives on major issues. The ads were designed both to fan voters' suspicions that Bush was a pawn of his keepers and to introduce Dukakis's positions on issues.

The second anti-Bush ads were to be done with celebrity endorsements featuring movie stars like Robert Redford, Woody Allen, and Meryl Streep. Dukakis wondered aloud if Woody Allen was exactly the right person to be going after the Republicans for cutting Social Security benefits. The presentation continued.

The next phase would feature "Dukakis the man" speaking directly into the camera and making a pitch for the programs and policies he favored for the nation. The ad campaign would end with two series of positive ads. The first were the "Imagine" series, whose concept was designed to get voters to sense the positive results that could flow from Dukakis's election and implementation of his ideas, particularly for middle-class families. These positive ads, produced by Jim Dale of W. B. Doner of Baltimore, offered a vision of a better country. One spot showed children in a playground: "Imagine a place where children come out to play without fear or drugs or drug dealers. Is that too much to expect? As president, Michael Dukakis will be on your side. He'll declare a real war on drugs. Double the number of drug agents and slash aid to countries that allow drug traffic."

Another featured a supermarket checkout counter and a troubled young couple exchanging a worried look over a checkbook. "Imagine a place where families don't have to stretch two paychecks for the life one paycheck used to bring. Is that too much to expect? As president, Michael Dukakis will be on your side. He's committed to giving earning power back to the American worker."

The final "Imagine" ad replayed images from all the earlier "Imagine" ads and featured an original song called "Anthem" that concluded thus:

"Someday soon, Here in America / A brighter future is what we're going to see / The Best America / The Best America / The Best America is yet to come."

The original strategic plan had called for the close to be McCabe's "I Believe" ads. According to McCabe's petulant, self-promotional account of his experience with the Dukakis campaign in *New York* magazine in December 1988, D'Alessandro was initially impressed by the concept. McCabe introduced it to D'Alessandro by singing a chorus of Frankie Laine's hit song, "I Believe," over the telephone. His idea was to fit pictures to the lyrics and have the song sung by someone like Whitney Houston.

This is how he described it in his *New York* article.

"I believe for every drop of rain that falls . . . "

[footage of burned-out South Bronx tenements]

"a flower grows"

[the camera finds a small garden in bloom]

"I believe that somewhere in the darkest night . . . "

[dejected workers filing out of a shut-down plant at the end of a day]

"a candle glows."

[dissolve to a late-night labor-management bargaining session ending with agreement]

"I believe for every one who goes astray . . . "

[a littered, polluted beach]

"Someone will come to show the way."

[a group of citizens moves in and starts to clean up.]

Although McCabe's work clearly had not passed muster among the senior campaign staff, Scott Miller persuaded D'Alessandro to give McCabe a second chance because they had already paid him so much money. He hasn't gotten a hit yet, maybe with time he will, Miller said. "I Believe" never ran because when it was tested in focus groups, voters found it confusing. "Is this a bank commercial?" asked one puzzled guinea pig. Privately, the senior political and advertising people thought the commercial sophomoric and technically far too busy, and it set off much scorn and laughter.

Late in September, the campaign and the reconfigured ad team were faced with a choice: mount a defensive action against the Bush offensive or introduce a new dynamic into the race that, if successful, would stabilize the race and give them time to regroup. They went for the latter. That was the point of the packaging ads.

Sasso's fear at the time was that the race would break wide open and Bush would move into an insurmountable lead. Dukakis's own credibility was in shreds. Sasso had nightmares about the 1988 race turning into a replay of 1984, when Walter F. Mondale was routed by Ronald Reagan. It made no sense to put their man on the air to set the record straight. They were being bombarded with so many negatives that they had to flip the race somehow. Their polling data showed that voters were more likely to believe that Bush was susceptible to his handlers' whims.

While the Dukakis campaign dealt with the internal challenge from Jackson in June and July, Bush went on the offensive immediately after the primary season closed in June. He stepped up the battle after the Republican National Convention with harsh attacks on Dukakis. So-called independent groups, financed by the same people contributing to the Bush campaign, did the same with tough television ads highlighting the William Horton case.

As Bush was slashing Dukakis on the stump and in the press, a contrary view was being carried in his advertising. The Bush campaign began its advertising with positive spots showing George Bush's red-haired granddaughter rushing into his arms in slow motion. "I want a kinder and gentler nation," the vice president says as he lifts his granddaughter into the air and plants a kiss on her cheek. "The President," a narrator intones, "The heart, the soul, the conscience of the nation."

That changed on Labor Day when the Bush campaign attack ads began to reinforce the negative message being carried in the press.

The Bush attack ads moved in concert with the message being delivered by Vice President Bush on the stump, where he had been lambasting Dukakis since early June for being a "card-carrying member of the ACLU," for being against the Pledge of Allegiance, for coddling criminals, and for lacking mainstream values.

The damage was already deep and the Dukakis campaign had already spent hundreds of thousands of dollars producing scripts and ads that never aired. The Bush campaign essentially established a negative first impression of the Massachusetts governor for many voters with Bushs' rat-ta-tat-tat attacks on the stump, which were brought home with deadly force through the post-Labor Day paid advertising. "The damage was done by September 10," said pollster Edward J. Reilly, who joined the campaign for the last month to conduct focus-group polling on the ads. To make matters worse, D'Alessandro pulled most Dukakis campaign commercials off the air during the mid-September week while he was considering the new material, authorizing only about $500,000 for New Era and ads from the primaries, including a spot that featured a teenager working in a pizza shop because he couldn't afford to go to college; this was precisely when Bush's negative material was first pouring onto the airwaves. Sasso felt a bit helpless at the paucity of suitable ads on hand. But he hoped that, as history showed, voter opinions tended to freeze in the four or five days before a major debate, and that might limit the damage.

At the September 23 session, Dukakis approved the ad campaign immediately. His only reaction was to ask whether he should be called Mike or Michael. For some reason he associated this debate over his name with advertising. Earlier in his political career, he had always been called Mike in advertising, although intimates always called him Michael, Sasso being a rare exception. Dukakis brought the same topic up when introduced to McCabe in July at the State House. With polls showing Dukakis shrinking in public esteem, the staff quickly agreed that Michael was the way to go. He needed to be made bigger, not more familiar and smaller.

By the time of the September 23 presentation, Dukakis understood the need for negative advertising, but he told D'Alessandro to make sure to get him into the ads in a positive way when possible. He said he understood that would not always be possible, but he wanted some balance.

With Dukakis's approval secured, D'Alessandro went to work. Sawyer/Miller produced the first packaging ads in one day. They went on the air one week later, on September 30. With a one-week heavy buy, about 6 percent of the advertising budget, the ads would tell voters to reserve judgment: "They're trying to sell you a package; wouldn't you rather elect a President?"

"We never expected people were going to take away specific issue information from the ads," said D'Alessandro. "We were looking to exploit one message: Bush is politically expedient. He will do what his handlers want."

"We knew that if we went the traditional route, people would turn off. We wanted to make sure we were not zapped," he said.

The packaging ads created a stir in media circles. Other consultants criticized them as too vague and subtle. Some senior campaign staffers, including Estrich, believe they were awful, and failed. Others, including pollsters Tubby Harrison and Ed Reilly and Corrigan remain convinced they were working. The packaging theme clearly was being picked up. "Packaging" became an operative word in the campaign. The news media reinforced the message. Indiana Senator Dan Quayle came across as so thoroughly packaged during the vice-presidential candidate debate on October 5 that he was forced to publicly "break free" from his handlers on October 10 to show he was his own man. The *New York Times* ran a major article on Bush as a packaged candidate.

"Bush began to look even more political in our polling," said D'Alessandro. According to Reilly, the pollster working with him, voters in focus groups reacted strongly to the packaging ads: they either loved them or became angry with Bush—consistently. Reilly was convinced that the ads hit a responsive chord.

Sasso had been back at the campaign a month when he called Ed Reilly, his rival strategist during Dukakis's bitter comeback campaign against Ed King in 1982, and Gephardt's pollster and senior adviser in 1988. Reilly had been passed over in spring when the Dukakis team for fall was being assembled; Sasso asked that he join him now.

I have nobody around to make decisions, he told his former foe: this will scare you when you see it. When Reilly arrived, Sasso sent him next door to D'Alessandro and his first assignment: test the packaging spots among voters in selected swing-voter neighborhoods in a New Jersey suburb, in Des Moines, and in Detroit.

From the focus-group polling, Reilly learned that voters needed to see the spots a couple of times to understand them. But it occurred to him that these ads could turn into a serial soap opera, in which viewers would become familiar with the characters and look forward to the next installment. He also learned that the ads gave these critical swing voters a psychological vehicle for changing their minds about Dukakis. The Bush campaign by then had totally ruptured the governor's relationship with swing voters, who make up between 15 and 25 percent of the electorate. The message in the packaging ads—they are manipulating you—gave voters a way to return to their formerly high opinion of Dukakis. These were voters who did not want to vote for George Bush because he was a Republican and certainly not Ronald Reagan. The ads were not aimed at 51 percent of the electorate but at the critical swing voters who would make the difference on election day.

In a companion national survey, Reilly learned that voters thought the Bush campaign was being less than honest with them and believed that Bush was being run by his handlers. The robotic performance by Republican vice-presidential candidate Dan Quayle in his debate with Senator Bentsen put "afterburners" on that perception. If voters needed additional proof, that debate provided it.

During a late fall strategy meeting, an exhausted Sasso gazed across the table at Ed Reilly, who was equally exhausted from working twenty-hour days for Dukakis. "You know," he mused, struck suddenly by the incongruity of their collaboration, "I spent six years thinking up ways to fuck you."

Reilly met the gaze head on. "Same," he responded.

Just prior to the second debate between Dukakis and Bush, Tubby Harrison sent the top campaign staff two memos, along with his latest national poll results. On October 10, just after Lloyd Bentsen's dramatic trouncing of Dan Quayle, he was showing a narrow five-point Bush lead, 50 to 45 percent, a four-point margin shift from the previous week, which he said had come "primarily from the debate, with some additional help from the packaging spots."

Harrison's analysis was an attempt to concentrate on states and regions where the ads had been most heavily aired (the East and far West), and he was convinced that in those places they worked, and that they were likely to increase in effectiveness the more they were aired.

Kiley, however, believed the evidence was soft. And Estrich hated the commercials and voiced her opinion vehemently. At times the tension between Sasso and Estrich became so bad that D'Alessandro in one meeting suggested, "Can't we just close our eyes and act like Republicans?" The decision-making style of the campaign was based on reaching consensus. If any one among ten senior staffers had reservations, that would be enough to block a change in rotation or approval of an ad. Despite Sasso's position, Estrich's views still carried immense weight.

Her adamance and the strongly negative press reaction persuaded Sasso (who at times felt rusty and unsure in his job after so long an absence) to pull the packaging ads off the air after nine days; after placing the advertising in D'Alessandro's hands, his key initiative was now history.

The overall communications plan had three objectives: to stabilize the race, to set the record straight in battleground states, and to air positive ads that showed more of Dukakis the man. The next phase called for running hard-hitting anti-Bush ads in key markets. It was little more than damage control.

The issues in the negative ads paralleled some of those in the negative spots first distributed by the Bush campaign in August. While ads criticizing Bush's environmental record appeared in California, others criticizing Bush's record in fighting drug trafficking were released in Texas, and another spot, showing a Social Security card being cut to bits, aired in the Midwest.

The plan called for taking advantage of developments in the campaign and exploiting unforeseen opportunities. Dukakis's performance in the first presidential debate resulted in two ads from his closing statement, which were more effective than his showing in the debate itself, and they were broadcast the next night. Quayle's shaky performance in his vice-presidential debate prompted them to move to exploit the public's unease about his qualifications, a minor issue with swing voters, in Harrison's dissenting opinion. The day after the Omaha debate, two ads went up. The first was a packaging spot showing Bush strategists worrying about Quayle and suggesting he be replaced. The second presented a dramatic tableau of *New York Times* headlines showing vice presidents taking the oath of office after the president's death or abrupt resignation, and a vacant Oval Office. An ominous thumping heartbeat provided the background noise. Miller produced the heartbeat spot on his own without first securing script approval from the campaign in order to protect its integrity. He sent it to the campaign fully produced.

After the second presidential debate on October 13, the plan called for the Dukakis ads to go positive. Their effectiveness, however, was marred by Dukakis's disastrous showing in the debate. Each showed Dukakis sitting in the Brookline living room of Jack Connors (the would-be advertising chief) talking about difficulties in raising a family in modern times and the need for the country to become number one in the world again.

With the governor's chances reduced to less than minimal, the most interesting drama in the Dukakis advertising became an almost comical wait to see if McCabe could produce a usable commercial before the election, and how high his final expenses would be. Undaunted by rejection, he kept proposing spots. D'Alessandro strung him along, fearing a public outburst from the volatile ad man. And, left essentially to his own devices, McCabe kept producing ads that never won approval. Not one of his ads ever made the air. On occasion, his ideas veered into the whacky. He suggested that one anti-Quayle spot actually feature a quail. The ad would show a confused and frightened quail against the pounding of a human heart. The heart stops and a narrator says, "Just remember . . . he'd only be a heartbeat away."

When this idea was presented to D'Alessandro in September, he told the ad man that most Americans had no idea what a quail looked like. McCabe expressed surprise because he often ate quail for lunch in chic Manhattan restaurants. Another anti-Quayle spot featured two armed thugs in a cabin who were holding a man captive. The man, dressed only in his undershorts, would be bound by ropes. When he turned his face, the viewer would see it was actor Robert Redford, to whom Quayle fancies he bears a resemblance. The message would be "They've taken Dan Quayle away."

Sasso exploded with anger when he heard about that concept. The campaign had poured half a million dollars into this guy, and now he wanted to produce a commercial likely to generate sympathy for Bush's running mate. Sasso then laughed. It was absurd.

Another spot, called "Hawk v. Dove," would show a hawk and a dove fornicating in a tree. They turn into an eagle, which speaks with Michael Dukakis's voice, and then soars into the sky.

Amidst all this chaos, the state campaign directors were screaming for air cover as they tried to keep Dukakis afloat in battleground after battleground. The lack of advertising response to the most effective of the anti-Dukakis Bush spots drove them to desperation, and then to the unheard-of response of unilateral action. Reilly referred to the strong, almost autonomous state directors as "nation states." Anthony Podesta in California contacted Michael Kaye in Los Angeles and worked with him on a response to the Boston Harbor spot that attacked Bush's environmental and crime positions and presented a clip from Dukakis's effective "On Your Side" speech. Ray Strother, once Gary Hart's media man and briefly Albert Gore's before Super Tuesday, who was in Texas to do ads for Bentsen's Senate campaign, cut some spots for the presidential campaign being run there by Tom Cosgrove. Gerry Austin, Jesse Jackson's campaign manager, worked up some trade spots for Ohio. One, featuring a Japanese flag, was sloppily produced but delivered a clear, if borderline racist message.

The ads became more combative and raw at the very end of the campaign. In one spot called "Rich," the campaign made a blatant populist appeal. It accused Bush of favoring tax breaks for the rich and opposing Dukakis's program of tax enforcement. In the ad, a candy sampler with the stitched words "The Rich Get Richer" appears on the screen. "Remember the old saying: The rich get richer?" asks the narrator. "Now George Bush wants to make it the law. That's right. Tax avoidance and tax breaks for the rich and nothing for the rest of us."

Podesta worked on an ad called "Furlough from the Truth" attempting to paint Bush as a hypocrite by highlighting a worse tragedy in the federal prison system. Angel Medrano ran way from a federal halfway house in Arizona and raped and murdered a young pregnant woman. The ad—which also ran nationally—showed the murder victim being carried from a house in a body bag and a mug shot of Medrano, though it never mentioned his name to avoid criticism—which came anyway—that the spot was anti-Hispanic. Podesta wanted to show the woman's gravestone, etched with a woman and the words: "Please don't forget me." The ad ran but that scene was vetoed by the campaign. "They put lies on and we're talking about good taste," groused an angry field operative.

"Their strategy, if there was one, was to create something from his Massachusetts record. When that record was totally destroyed by the competition, there was nothing left," said Mal MacDougall late in October. "I guess they were caught off guard. A lot of people in the Dukakis campaign thought the Republicans would run a more positive campaign and make Bush into a statesman. Once you start reacting to someone else's strategy, your strategy falls apart."

The disarray in advertising was a manifestation of a greater problem, however. In the two weeks following the Republican National Convention, Bush had seized effective control of the campaign by attacks carried by the print press and on network television. He had also been transformed by his effective acceptance speech and by his handlers into a man with a new image, that of a strong, independent leader. Against all that, Dukakis showed nothing, and the image disparity became worse after Labor Day when Bush's negative advertising began running.

It was at the end of October that the Dukakis campaign began attacking the attacks, the ultimate confession of weakness.

In one of these, he tried to hit back at perhaps the most photogenically embarrassing moment of the fall campaign, his famous tank ride. Dukakis had taken a ride in an M1 tank at a manufacturing plant in Sterling Heights, Michigan during a week when he was focusing on his embattled national-defense positions. Jack Weeks, his campaign trip director, thought it was a great visual. Bush had been photographed in similar settings. The first time around the course Dukakis, his head poking from the top of the tank, looked fine. But then he put on an Army helmet in order to talk to the company president through the two-way radio built into the helmet. He looked ridiculous, and was photographed spinning around the course looking like a plastic toy with a sickly grin on his face. The visual turned into a disaster. The network news shows broadcast it that night, and the footage was often repeated.

Roger Ailes, Bush's media man, was inspired by the network news footage of Dukakis in the tank to use it in a Bush campaign ad. That ad raised doubts about Dukakis's ability to serve as commander-in-chief and warned that a Dukakis presidency would be dangerous.

Within days, the Dukakis campaign broadcast a response, the Counterpunch ad, which was cut in eight minutes during a New York City taping session. On October 21, the campaign went public, condemning Bush for his negative attacks.

The election would be held in two weeks. Behind by roughly double-digit margins in the polls, it was too late for advertising to make a difference. But only then did Dukakis's campaign seem to hit a passable stride. Ads produced for use in swing states were almost uniformly hard-hitting by the end of the campaign. Ads contrasted Bush's inaction or failures on the environment and drug fighting with Dukakis "results." An ad called "Fourteen thousand" accused Bush of sitting by while "his" administration furloughed 14,000 drug dealers from the federal system while Dukakis took action and changed his own furlough program in Massachusetts. Too little, too late.

Nothing more strongly symbolized Dukakis's inability to perform on the grander stage in a general election than his majestically botched advertising. In the early days, when it counted, he did not lack for plans, proposals, ideas for useful advertising; even in September ways could be found of salvaging the campaign. In many ways, the overall failure was driven by the more important failure to present voters with a coherent, consistent theme and message in any forum.

Toward the end, D'Alessandro came upon Sasso sitting in his office with his head in his hands and offered this analysis. He told him that the Bush-Dukakis campaign was like a soft-drink rivalry between two major manufacturers of cola. Company A decides to launch a new product ahead of Company B. It runs advertising in the South saying that "Our product is great cold but the product made by Company B is made with impure water." Then they go to the Midwest and say "Our product is great with lemon but the drink made by Company B is made with worms." When Company B begins its own ad campaign and says "Our product tastes great," Southerners say "Yeah, but it's made with dirty water." And in the Midwest they say, "Oh no, I know it's made with worms."

10

The Ice Man

Some of the wealthiest, most powerful, and best-connected Democrats in the nation gathered to celebrate Robert Farmer's fiftieth birthday on September 18 at the Meridien Hotel in Boston's financial district. Farmer, a political Midas, was the person most responsible for raising almost $100 million for the Dukakis presidential campaign. The governor could not miss this social engagement. To the rustle of silk and click of wine glasses, Dukakis moved through the elegant crowd that night, shaking hands and greeting acquaintances.

His oldest friends, however, noticed that he was upset, just going through the social motions. He apologized to several of them about the state of his campaign. He acted as though he had let them down. Over and over he promised it would get better. To J. Joseph Grandmaison, campaign manager from his 1974 gubernatorial campaign and now New Hampshire Democratic Party chairman, he almost wailed like a confused child: "Where did the seventeen points go? How do you lose seventeen points?"

In the heat of a general-election campaign, no task is more nearly impossible than recovery. Nominees with clear advantages and momentum going into September usually win eight weeks later; turning the tide requires an extraordinary act of resolve and discipline because the margin for further error is nonexistent. As a rule, a newly energized

The Boston Police Patrolman's Union endorsed Bush at a press conference in East Boston. Bush is surrounded by Bob Guiney, union president, to his left, and Don Murray, the union vice president, to his right. (Photo by Wendy Maeda)

campaign message with simplicity and punch is essential—at best one powerful negative theme and an equally powerful positive one emphasized again and again, and synthesized with special planning and care for the nationally televised debates that have been a fixture in the season since 1976. In other words, recovery requires exactly the opposite of the face Dukakis presented to the country after Labor Day.

September was a daily struggle to turn the surging tides of negativism. It is an axiom in presidential politics and a sad commentary on journalistic whimsy that polling, by and large, drives press coverage. This axiom never proved to be truer than in fall 1988: George Bush was ahead, and Michael Dukakis was behind. Positions had been reversed in June and July, but September was when the momentum-plasma of press coverage really counted and flowed into George Bush's veins, a daily life force. The polling numbers were interpreted to mean that the Bush campaign was working, effective, and tough and that the Dukakis campaign was chaotic, ineffectual, and weak.

By its very nature journalism tends toward excess, and the torrential press focus on Dukakis's problems obscured the truth—the race was in fact quite close. The bounce Bush got from his nominating convention was never larger than the nine-point, 50 to 41 percent lead a Gallup Poll for *Newsweek* gave him the weekend after it adjourned; by Labor Day, the prevailing Bush margin was in lower single digits.

Because the holiday weekend had begun with the announcement of John Sasso's return in an atmosphere of crisis, however, the *story* of Sasso's return was inevitably a large negative for the Dukakis campaign, and magnified the Labor Day focus on Dukakis to see if the situation improved.

At first it did not: Dukakis disliked and quickly discarded a new economic message in a Labor Day speech; a Federal Aviation Administration official grounded Dukakis's plane temporarily in Chicago; antiabortion demonstrators infiltrated his rallies with two days of heckling and nearly began fistfights, and, in an inexplicable crack at a press conference, Dukakis hinted he might deploy Strategic Defense Initiative hardware some day (if it worked) after a year of calling Star Wars a fantasy and a fraud.

At first, Bush seemed his crisp, scripted self, banging away at liberalism, "Willie" Horton, and the Massachusetts "mirage," with only an occasional retreat into silliness like his declaration that September 7 was Pearl Harbor Day.

Handed both the crisis atmosphere and seeing no clear, major change in the candidates' styles or messages, the Chauncy Street high command hunkered down for bad polling news. It came fast. In a survey completed September 8 that sent shudders through the building, Tubby Harrison found Bush ahead by twelve points, 53 to 41 percent, with Dukakis now clearly painted into a liberal corner and Bush well ahead on strength-related imagery and other presidential qualities. Now worry was genuine that the margin might swell toward a landslide and effectively doom the campaign before it could mount a true counterattack.

Though their relationship was almost irretrievably awkward, Sasso and Estrich did not preside over separate and hostile fiefdoms. Sasso quickly brought in a number of people to help him with his strategic responsibilities, but for the first two weeks his own focus was mostly on advertising and on formulating a general campaign plan for Dukakis. This concentration left vast areas of major importance and responsibility to Estrich. They did not usually work as a team, but they were on the same team.

Sasso moved very quickly to use his influence with Dukakis to get him to stop returning to Boston for State House duties at midweek; henceforth, his returns would be mostly on Saturdays and his departures mostly on Sunday afternoons. He also decided after the twelve-point-deficit poll to take 5 percent of the campaign's advertising budget out of the final days in the campaign and put it to work immediately, behind commercials that sold Dukakis as a leader and listed favorable details from his record (he cut taxes five times, increased workers' income, pioneered the first universal-health-program in the country, reduced crime by 13 percent, and so on)—spots Bush advertising man Roger Ailes later said he considered highly effective.

On the other hand, Dukakis's substantive campaigning unfolded according to plans made in August under Estrich. In September, Dukakis began to focus on what the campaign and press called the middle-class squeeze. The political idea behind this message was that it appealed to elements of the more traditional Democratic vote including women, blue-collar workers, and minorities who might be expected to return to the Dukakis cause most easily.

The second half of the economic message was to be a focus on meeting the economic challenge from abroad, aiming the political appeal mostly at white men. Dukakis, however, was still arguing with his advisers, Sasso included, on this topic, wary as always about appearing protectionist and jingoist. As of Labor Day, he agreed to use rhetoric promising to "bring prosperity home" and cited statistics about the increase in foreign ownership of American real estate and business assets; however, he used even this material infrequently, reflecting his misgivings.

A useful illustration of Dukakis's unwillingness to deliver the full weight of a message Harrison had convinced the rest of his colleagues would be successful can be seen in some sentences from a draft of his Labor Day speech to a rally in Detroit. He did say: "The time has come to bring prosperity home to America, to every home in America, to stop ignoring foreign competition and start beating it. . . . To stop hiding our heads in the sand and realize that we've got a fight on our hands, that we're in a battle for the economic future of this country."

But he did not say: "The Republicans haven't done a thing to open new markets for American products overseas; we'll insist that the price of free trade in America be an end to protectionism in Europe and Asia."

And, still skittish about being negative, he also did not say of Bush and Dan Quayle: "After months on the campaign trail, he's offered America nothing but a fading echo of the past and a running mate who is simply not qualified to be president or vice president of the United States."

Nonetheless, Dukakis was beginning to be less ineffective, and his campaigning took on a serious, if not telegenic tone that slowly began to stand at least as an earnest, responsible contrast to the ceaseless rat-a-tat-tat of Bush's attacks and flag waving. In August, part of Dukakis's rejection of specific ideas and strategies had flowed from his insistence that Labor Day was when the battle should be truly joined and his feeling that he had let his gubernatorial responsibilities slide too much and wanted to spend more time in the state before that became impossible. That insistence may have been wrong and naive, taking a lesson from history—Republican aggressiveness and Democratic disorder and lassitude had produced hideous Augusts in 1972, 1976, and 1984—but it was real.

In the background, however, the campaign worked hard throughout the month to produce several initiatives that were unveiled in the first three weeks of September: a proposal to provide post-secondary education to all who qualify for it via loans paid back through payroll deductions; proposed nationalization of his Massachusetts initiative requiring most employers to provide basic health insurance for their workers and a companion proposal offering universal care to uninsured pregnant women; three major speeches that put more flesh on the long-neglected bones of his national-defense positions; and complete proposals to step up the war on illegal drug trafficking, beginning by doubling the number of Drug Enforcement Administration agents.

He also finally decided to hit back at Bush's attacks, using a speech at East Texas State College on September 9 as his forum. He raised the specter of modern McCarthyism, adding that "The American people can smell the garbage." The speech, drafted by Washington consultant Robert Shrum (now helping regularly) was a success in the press, though it was delivered on a Friday (a tough news day because Saturday newspapers are small). It also played well because on the same day Bush committed one of his many excesses on the William Horton case, bellowing in Illinois that "Willie Horton got out and raped and murdered again, and I oppose that kind of program." Horton, of course, did not murder while on escape. The Dukakis speech also delighted his running mate. Lloyd Bentsen had tried to persuade Dukakis that unanswered charges stick, but had finally retreated into frustrated silence on the topic. On this day, however, he tried positive reinforcement and telephoned a strongly upbeat analysis to Dukakis. As so often happened, however, Dukakis mistook one speech for a response and didn't return to the theme for eleven days.

When he finally did, it clicked again as a powerful contrast to Bush's style and tactics. Dukakis had begun September 20 in Houston, where his health-insurance proposal was outlined, but its initial press reception was frosty because traveling campaign staff members were poorly prepared for specific questions. On a flight to Kentucky early in the afternoon, Steve Engelberg (a Washington lawyer and veteran of Walter

Mondale's wars who traveled with Dukakis in the fall), sensed negative media accounts and recommended that the governor draw a sharp contrast in his Kentucky remarks between his own efforts to raise issues important to millions of Americans and Bush's appearance that day in a flag-making factory in New Jersey. The results were unusually harsh stories about Bush's campaigning and favorable attention to Dukakis on network news shows that night.

Two days later, Bush went for symbolism again by returning to Boston to accept endorsement by the anti-Dukakis Boston Police Patrolmen's Association. On September 1, Dukakis had given the vice president almost a free shot when he came to view the foul waters in Boston Harbor by keeping to a California schedule. But on the same day as the Patrolmen's endorsement, September 22, the Dukakis campaign answered with a rally of its own in Boston, pulling in speakers like Mario Cuomo and leaders of police groups from around the country, and blunted Bush's raid in the national media coverage.

In this critical period, when the bottom could have fallen out, the slowly developing contrast between a candidate offering substance and a candidate limited to symbols, helped Dukakis first to stabilize his perilous situation and then to make steady improvement. Fourteen days after his report of a twelve percentage point deficit, Tubby Harrison checked in on September 22 with a summary of Dukakis's steady climb back. He was in the fight again, trailing by six points, 50 to 44 percent, with voters about to suspend further judgment, anticipating the first debate.

"Bush's onslaught on liberal / conservative seems to have run out of steam," Harrison wrote to the high command "We have found that people are moved by our messages about the so-called middle-class squeeze and about making America number one again economically. People also seem to be moved by the argument that MSD has specific policy intiatives and a record, especially in the area of 'squeeze' concerns and drugs."

The debate, in short, presented a genuine opportunity to transform the campaign.

Since the 1960 debates between John F. Kennedy and Richard M. Nixon, televised joint appearances had again become a fixture in presidential politics after 1976. Back in August, chairman James A. Baker III and his top associates in George Bush's campaign gave the Dukakis campaign a take-it-or-leave-it offer: two presidential debates timed with roughly three weeks between the last one and Election Day, or no debates at all. The offer reflected the Bush high command's lack of confidence that Bush could handle the spontaneous, uncontrollable, high-stakes, high-pressure event, and in private they prepared themselves to abandon the idea of debates entirely should Dukakis not take their offer.

But he did. According to his negotiator, Paul Brountas, he saw his job as getting Dukakis at least two chances, though he wanted three and would have jumped at four, to turn around a campaign that then seemed likely to be difficult. Brountas's position also reflected his supreme confidence that the quick-thinking governor could "win" any confrontation. Ever since Dukakis moderated the public-television show *The Advocates* in the early 1970s, the governor had handled himself well on the cool medium of television.

Within the campaign, only a few, primarily represented by Tubby Harrison, took the position that Dukakis should hold out, citing a 1987 agreement between the two national party chairmen. Before the election year began they had arranged to hold three debates watched over by a bipartisan commission they created. Moreover, if that meant no debates, Dukakis should say, fine, and then attack Bush as a quitter and welcher, but more important, base the rest of his campaign on tough, middle-class themes and hope to prevail without a dramatic debating breakthrough.

With the number of nationally televised encounters limited to two, the debates mattered even more to Dukakis. For him, more than for Bush, it was critical that he use the two ninety-minute slots of prime television time to deliver his message with power and clarity and do what he could to shift the tone and tide of the campaign. Ever since Nixon "lost" his 1960 encounter with Kennedy by appearing dark and sweaty on television, style mattered more than substance, though an inadvertent gaffe on substance could be extremely damaging. In getting Dukakis ready for the debates, his preparation team stressed this fact of modern political life.

But Dukakis muffed it.

On Sunday, September 18, a small group of Dukakis's most important advisers gathered at his home in Brookline to talk about one of the few events left in the general-election campaign that could change its complexion, change its very substance: the governor's first debate with George Bush, all set for the following Sunday in Winston-Salem, North Carolina. The group included Sasso, Estrich, Brountas, O'Donnell, Mitropoulos, and Victoria Rideout, a domestic-issues specialist on the campaign who also helped write speeches.

One additional participant was a portly, cherubic-faced young Washington lawyer out of Providence, Rhode Island named Thomas Donilon, who had assumed barely two weeks earlier the herculean task of coordinating the candidate's preparation for the debate. They had little time and much stress, but Donilon had prepared a ten-page memorandum setting forth a general theory about the event, built around three main strategic points that he used to frame the discussion.

The first was that Dukakis had to be the "appropriate aggressor" for all ninety minutes in the debate, not like some whiny, contrary kid or a savage prosecuting attorney, but the governor had to crowd the vice president throughout their joint appearance with a panel of reporters and keep the entire discussion on his terms. The second point was that while walking that careful line between aggressiveness and meanness, Dukakis had to rough Bush up, to beat him clearly, so that his negative ratings in follow-up national polls would rise. To accomplish this control, he should persistently emphasize the weak links in Bush's record that showed lapses in judgment and failures to perform—from the Watergate period, when he was Republican national chairman, right through the Iran-Contra scandal—and Bush's inability to coordinate the nation's war against illegal drugs with anything more than publicity stunts.

Finally, and most important, Donilon's theory of the debate emphasized that every answer Dukakis would give in the ninety-minute event had to fit into a larger theme. Unfortunately, no larger theme had the candidate's backing at that critical juncture. The weak reed of competence had already been severely bent by the Bush campaign's skillful attacks, and the postprimary concepts of character and leadership ability (meant to create a personal contrast) had been just as deeply eroded by Bush's New Orleans transformation combined with Dukakis's poor campaign performance. Now two specific ideas were in front of Dukakis; they were not contradictory, but for a ninety-minute program he had to pick one of them. The first was the squeeze on middle-income Americans that he had been emphasizing with occasional consistency since Labor Day; the second was the idea that it was time for the American government to change direction and not stand pat so that the nation would flourish in the 1990s. Dukakis was not yet ready to embrace Tubby Harrison's passionate recommendations to stress a commitment to putting and keeping America at the top of the world's economic heap.

Initially, Dukakis found himself uncomfortable with both ideas. They were too vague, he said, they had not been thought through completely, and in that standard Dukakis phrase about things he doesn't especially like, "They're not me." Around the table that day, and for the next five days, his advisers would debate fiercely, often in his presence, whether his thematic focus should be on the middle-class squeeze or the need for change; a political consultants' shouting match that seemed to Dukakis to have all the intellectual vitality of "Tastes Great" vs. "Less Filling."

From Estrich's perspective, Dukakis appeared to be looking for a perfect mirror that reflected him and reflected Bush, an exercise that would have helped three months earlier. One theme Dukakis seemed to like was supplied that week by Theodore Sorensen, who wrote so many of John Kennedy's best speeches and who advised Dukakis off and on during the fall: George Bush is not a stand-up guy, he said one day, and Dukakis is; Dukakis has grappled with tough questions in public life, he has ideas that will help average Americans, but Bush does not. Another strong advocate of this approach was Victoria Rideout, a talented idea person who had written speeches for Geraldine Ferraro in 1984 and helped run the issues section of Dukakis's reelection campaign in 1986. In a conversation she had with Dukakis, he all but approved the stand-up-guy approach.

In many ways, that Donilon had been able to stage-manage the preparation to this juncture was miraculous. He had come to Boston August 26, at Susan Estrich's request, to discuss the campaign privately with Bill Carrick and Bob Beckel. Following the meeting, Estrich asked Donilon (they had traveled together on Mondale's plane in fall 1984) to stay behind; time was very late, she confessed, but she needed help and wanted him to come to Boston to handle the debates.

Donilon, who agreed without hesitation, is proof that the Democrats do not lack the talent to run and win presidential elections. He was only thirty-two but had been Joe Biden's senior adviser in 1987, handled delegate-wooing for Mondale in 1984, and been the wunderkind for Jimmy Carter's renomination in 1980. He was, moreover, both a conceptual thinker and adroit at the nuts and bolts of campaigning. Within days, he obtained a leave from his law firm, severed his consulting links to CBS News, and arrived in Boston to pick up videotapes on Great Dukakis Debates of the Past.

Donilon landed squarely in the middle of the chaotic Estrich-to-Sasso transition, was unable to see either of them, and was told by Jack Corrigan to slow down because he wasn't sure his deal to work on the debates was still on. The day Sasso's return was announced, Sasso talked to Donilon, now camped in Rhode Island to wait out the headquarters crisis, and told him his debate job would have to be reevaluated. Sasso finally phoned him back on Labor Day and told him that he and Dukakis (whom Donilon had shaken hands with twice before in his life) wanted him very much.

As of Labor Day, the so-called book with material on domestic issues for use in the debate read like it had been prepared by college interns, and had to be put together from scratch. Rideout took on this huge task and turned issues into shape for actual use as two-minute answers and one-minute rebuttals in the debate. The book on foreign policy was four inches thick when he first picked it up, Donilon said, and it had to be distilled, with Georgetown University Professor Madeline Albright, Dukakis's principal foreign-policy adviser, directing, and a new crew of experts brought together for the debate preparations.

The books could not be ready for Dukakis's study until that Sunday, September 18, with one week to go, but that was no special problem for a man who had been through forty joint appearances with his opponents during the marathon primary season. Two things were a special problem: (1) getting the supremely confident Dukakis in shape to make a good personal impression on voters, and (2) deciding which theme to emphasize to lift his answers and rebuttals above the press-conference format.

Preparing form and content for his answers on important issues within the two-minute rule proved to be excruciatingly slow work. Donilon and his foreign-policy helpers had to work overtime to convince the governor that his constantly referring to the Reagan administration's efforts to aid the Contra guerrillas in Nicaragua as "illegal" might be accurate, but was also impolitic and formalistic. On the Wednesday before the debate, it took the preparations team—swollen by far more staff members than necessary, Donilon felt—three hours to refine answers and rebuttals for three questions on economic policy.

Nonetheless, the atmosphere was bright and Dukakis was cocky and confident as he breezed into the Lafayette Hotel Presidential suite across the street from campaign headquarters for his dress rehearsal early Friday evening. As a gag, because Bush had used the suite earlier in the year, a squash racket's handle was left sticking out from under the bed as Dukakis entered and took his place behind one of two podiums set up for the ninety-minute drill.

The governor then proceeded to get slaughtered.

In real life, Robert Barnett is a top-flight Washington lawyer who represents several network news correspondents and authors (including, these days, Kitty Dukakis). But in his Walter Mitty life, he is George Bush; Barnett played Bush to help Geraldine Ferraro prepare for her debate in 1984 and he was back again by popular demand in 1988. With a massive Bush clipping file, a prodigious memory, an instinct for political debate, and a useful combination of Bush's breezily cheery personality and his own tiger's skill at rhetorical combat, Barnett is the perfect person to practice with because the actual debate could never be as bad as a session with him. He peppered Dukakis mercilessly with barbed assaults emphasizing liberal sins and weaknesses. Dukakis tried to fight back, but was gradually reduced to mumbling stock campaign phrases, sometimes barely audible. When his torture was halted, a severely shaken Dukakis sat down, acknowledged that he was terrible, and said he had a lot of work to do.

The dress rehearsal had been videotaped by one of the Democratic Party's top political consultants, Robert Squier of Washington, D.C., who had worked with Dukakis in 1982 until fired in a tiff over advertising. He came back to help that fall as a spot assignment. With so little time left before the debate, Squier boiled down his advice: he told Dukakis that when he took a question he should begin his answer by addressing his questioner, but within seconds switch so that for the bulk of it he was addressing that symbol of the American people in late-1980s politics—the television camera. He told Dukakis that he must not do anything while Bush was speaking, so that the occasional camera shots showing both men would not display disdain, contempt, or some other unbecoming expression on his face.

Later that evening, Sasso rode with Dukakis to Brookline to continue the discussion about a theme for the encounter. According to Donilon, Sasso pitched for the theme of change. Before the decision was made, however, a lurch exposed the political and intellectual chaos in the exercise to sharpen focus. Before Sasso and Dukakis left that evening, the governor had been quite explicit about his strong interest in the proposal put forward by, among others, Vickie Rideout and Ted Sorenson, that he concentrate on portraying himself as the candidate who was standing up for the average American's interests and who had stood up to challenges all his life, whereas Bush had spent his career, and his vice presidency, ducking every tough one that came his way.

The next day, however, the word came back to the preparation team from the governor himself that Dukakis would emphasize the case for change and in effect try to wrap economic worries like the pressures on middle America and the country's ebbing primacy into an even larger bundle that would form a clear departure from Ronald Reagan's era. In some ways, though disagreement remained, the entire high command was at least relieved to know that a strategic message had been agreed on, however tardy the decision was. Nonetheless, although many saw the general attractiveness in a message that emphasized moving national policy in different directions after Reagan, several Dukakis advisers, notably Tubby Harrison, worried about it. By being the candidate for change, Dukakis might needlessly expose himself to a Bush barrage designed to associate that change with needless risk, which was precisely the Bush campaign strategy. For that reason they urged the governor to make his message twinspecifics: relief for America's middle class and restoring the country's position in the world economy. But Dukakis had made his decision, or at least he appeared to have.

Still, for the candidate, the exercise had been confusing. He needed to walk an extremely fine line between aggressiveness and meanness. He came much too late after too much infighting to a theme he should have embraced at least two months before and still wasn't sure about. And he had spent only part of an evening with a top-notch television adviser; George Bush had been under guru Roger Ailes's thumb for nearly a year.

The next morning, on the flight to North Carolina, Dukakis stared out the window for much of the ride from his customary perch in the Sky Pig front cabin. Vickie Rideout came over, sat down next to him, put her arm around him, and made small talk.

I don't know about this case for change, Dukakis said to her, I don't know if I feel comfortable with it—one more example of his inability at key moments in the general election to act decisively and to stick to his decisions.

Dukakis was in a Winston-Salem hotel suite by Sunday afternoon, and worked on his material until an hour before the debate started at 9:00 that evening, the most important session being a ninety-minute drill on questions that Donilon called "off-the-wall," dealing with personality, reading habits, family influences, and the like. After a long public life buying suits off the rack in the famous Filene's Bargain Basement in Boston, he had repeatedly refused to buy a new one at full price. This time, Nick Mitropoulos had acted unilaterally and got him one. Dukakis's acceptance of it mirrored his entire attitude toward preparing for the debate. Donilon had heard all the stories about his rejecting advice throughout the campaign, and especially in August, but he had found the candidate eager to learn, actively seeking direction, and willing to change, as might befit someone whose campaign was in deep trouble.

In the final few hours, Dukakis seemed to his advisers wound tight as a top, and jumpy when his wife interrupted the last session to insist he pose with her and his children for the long-delayed family Christmas-card picture, which took eight shots before the photographer was satisfied.

Ready or not, it was time to go. Standing in the wings at Wake Forest, Dukakis and Mitropoulos spotted Bush and Ailes standing directly across from them. "Go get him," urged Mitropoulos as Dukakis began to walk on stage.

He got him on substance, but in their first encounter Bush succeeded in projecting a warmer, more approachable persona than the tightly wound governor. Far more important, however, Dukakis left his game plan in the locker room.

Bush turned his slightly goofy manner into an endearing quality and savagely turned Dukakis's coolness into a negative. When Bush got tangled up on weapons systems, confusing Midgetman with Minuteman and MX, he immediately turned the goof to his advantage by blurting, "It's Christmas. It's Christmas." The reference was to his gaffe earlier in the month when he confused September 7 with December 7, Pearl Harbor Day. While everyone was laughing *with* him, Bush stuck in the knife, "Wouldn't it be nice to be perfect? Wouldn't it be nice to be the Ice Man so you never make a mistake?"

Although most Americans ideally might want a president who was smarter than they, they had also been conditioned during the eight-year Reagan presidency to want a president they could *like*. Dukakis was more serious than Bush, more articulate, more overtly aggressive, scored many more debating points, and, ultimately, was less likable. Bush telegraphed nearly every one of his one-liners with a toothy grin that said, Look at me. Look at what I am saying. He was a doofus but a nice doofus. Dukakis made substantive points while Bush scored with emotional and folksy ones.

Bush was well prepared by his handlers. He pushed every hot-button social issue at every conceivable opportunity and effectively painted Dukakis as an out-of-the-mainstream liberal. In his first answer, to a question about drugs posed by Jim Lehrer of the McNeil-Lehrer News Hour, he mentioned the word "values" six times. He never defined those values, allowing the viewers to fill in the blanks with their own values, but he delivered an unmistakable message: My values are your values, not like those of this other guy. Dukakis found himself defending essentially liberal positions throughout the debate, reinforcing the value question for swing voters who tend to be less liberal than he.

Bush spoke in folksy idiom. He denounced a cocaine scene that was treated with humor in the popular movie *Crocodile Dundee*; Dukakis talked about a "drug-running Panamanian dictator."

Bush swirled the cloak of incumbency around himself. In defending the Reagan-Bush administration's dealings with Manuel Antonio Noriega, he said, "The other day my opponent was given a briefing by the CIA. I asked for, and received, the same briefing. I am very careful in public life about dealing with classified information, and what I'm about to say is unclassified." There was an implicit suggestion that maybe the other guy had not been so careful. "Seven administrations were dealing with Mr. Noriega," he said. "It was the Reagan-Bush administration that brought this man to justice."

He wound up the answer by accusing Dukakis and "those pickets out there" of trying to "tear down seven different administrations." He made protest and criticism sound un-American. He turned his refusal to tell the advice he had given President Reagan on the Iran-Contra matter into a test of loyalty to his president.

And then, in the exchange that captured the debate's essence, ABC Anchorman Peter Jennings asked Dukakis about his passionless style.

"Passionless?" asked Dukakis.

"Passionless, technocratic—the smartest clerk in the world," responded Jennings.

The governor's response did little to dispel the rap. "Peter," he said, "I care deeply about people, all people, working people, working families, people all over this country who in some cases are living from paycheck to paycheck, in other cases they're having a hard time opening up the door of college opportunity to their children, in other cases don't have basic health insurance which for most of us we accept as a matter of course, assuming we're going to have and we're going to pay the bills we incur when we get sick, and somebody who believes deeply in genuine opportunity for every single citizen in this country. And that's the kind of passion that I brought to my state."

Bush, as ever missing no chance to take an antiliberal line, denounced Dukakis's "misguided passion," mentioning Dukakis's support for the Shea bill, an expression of anti-war sentiment, which would have exempted young Massachusetts draftees from fighting in the undeclared war in Vietnam. He made Dukakis sound unpatriotic for backing the bill. He also quoted Dukakis as saying, "I am a card-carrying member of the ACLU," the American Civil Liberties Union.

When Jennings asked him if using the phrase "card carrying" in speaking of the ACLU was intended to suggest Dukakis was "less than patriotic," Bush responded by referring to the ACLUs First Amendment cases and declared righteously, "I don't want my ten-year-old grandchild to go into an X-rated movie."

In contrast, Dukakis's counterattack sounded rote. "Of course, the vice president is questioning my patriotism," he said, his face and voice expressionless. "I don't think there is any question about that. And I resent it, I resent it."

Dukakis was at his best in calling for presidential leadership to end the problem of homelessness: "You know, back after World War II, when we had hundreds of thousands of GIs who came back from the war, we didn't sit around, we went out and built housing. The government was very much involved, so was the housing industry, so was the banking industry, so were housing advocates, so were nonprofit agencies, so were governors and mayors, and people all over this country who believed deeply in home ownership and affordable housing. Now that's the kind of leadership that I want to provide as president of the

United States. This isn't a question of a little charity to the homeless; this is a question of organizing the housing community."

But Bush scored in his rebuttal. The interest rate was half what it was during Jimmy Carter's presidency, he said. He disdained the "old Democratic liberal way of trying to build more bricks and mortar . . . if we spend, and spend, and spend that is going to wrap up the housing market and we'll go right back to the days of the misery index and malaise that President Reagan and I have overcome, thank God for the United States on that one."

Nor did the Bush partisans in the audience help Dukakis. When he said, "I'm opposed to the death penalty. I think everybody knows that. I'm also very tough on violent crime," he was interrupted by a gale of laughter.

Bush's worst moment came when he said he hadn't "sorted out" the appropriate penalty for women who have abortions, but denounced abortion with outrage in his voice. The next morning, his campaign chairman, James Baker, called a press conference to personally set the record straight and state that Bush did not intend to penalize women for undergoing the medical procedure.

Dukakis, in contrast, was coolly logical. "I think what the vice president is saying is that he's prepared to brand a woman a criminal for making this decision."

One of the most telling exchanges came over Bush's endorsement of "a thousand points of light," volunteer efforts to meet human needs.

"Being haunted—'a thousand points of light'—I don't know what that means," said Dukakis. "I know what has happened over the course of the past eight years. These programs have been cut and slashed and butchered, and they've hurt kids all over this country."

Bush rebutted, "What troubles me is that when I talk of the voluntary sector and a 'thousand points of light' and a thousand different ways to help on these problems, the man has just said he doesn't understand what I'm talking about. And this is the problem I have with the big-spending liberals. They think the only way to do it is for the federal government to do it all."

It was an hour into the broadcast before Dukakis got around to mentioning the word "change" in response to a question about Bush's charge that his defense policies amounted to unilateral disarmament for the United States and only then in referring to the "forces of change" sweeping the rest of the world. It was Bush who used the "change" word to his advantage. In his closing statement, he declared, "Yes, we want change, but we are the change, I am the change. I don't want to go back to malaise and misery index."

Sasso led a charge of happy Dukakis warriors into the governor's holding room after the post-debate pleasantries on the stage had ended. He was elated. "You won, don't you know you won?" he bellowed at his somewhat unsure candidate. Possibly the mood around Dukakis reflected that after more than six weeks of pure Hell, they had sensed their man's superior command of facts, subjects, and rhetoric; and the first verdicts from press analysts and quickie polls reported the same conclusion.

It was only later, after a boisterous rally, and among a few other senior campaign officials back at Dukakis's hotel, that Sasso began to think through the debate again and to reach a different conclusion about its result. On reflection, it seemed to him that Dukakis had not achieved any of his broader goals, and that nearly all the debate had covered subjects that left Dukakis holding a liberal bag, no matter how effectively he argued his points. Sasso decided against sharing his thoughts with Dukakis that night, preferring to let him keep his upbeat mood; but he did talk with him in depth next day, as additional information and opinion began to surface that Bush had projected himself as a more likable person, even though he had presented his political case poorly—a distinction that matters to people who focus their voting decisions on The Man, and who get their notions primarily from television.

Margaret Garrard Warner of *Newsweek* said it perfectly in a question to Dukakis in the second debate: "Governor, you won the first debate on intellect and yet you lost it on heart. . . . The American people admired your performance but didn't seem to like you very much."

By the third day after the debate, the polls began to show how accurate this judgment was. In the Dukakis camp's surveys, Bush's lead moved back to eight percentage points, and it reached nine points, 51 to 42 percent, on the eve of the critical October 5 meeting between Lloyd Bentsen and Dan Quayle in Omaha.

Unlike the disorder at the top of the ticket, the Bentsen campaign ran like an autonomous satellite smoothly spinning in its own orbit. Although the younger Boston staffers promptly adopted the nickname coined by *Boston Globe* columnist Mike Barnicle, "Oil Can Lloyd," a play on his Texas constituency and nickname of a Boston Red Sox pitcher, everyone (including, on occasion, his wife for forty years, B.A.) addressed him as "Senator," with all the deference the title implied. The Dukakis senior staffers were impressed by Bentsen. He exuded a leadership presence that could not be denied. He was elegant, patrician, dignified. He looked like someone central casting would send over to play the part of a southern senator. They respected him and, like Dukakis, were not only pleased but proud of the choice. They were also so overwhelmed by the challenges in the fall campaign that little time was left to tinker with the Bentsen campaign.

Bentsen initially acted as Dukakis's ambassador to the South and to the disaffected Reagan Democrats who needed to be brought back into the Democratic family if the ticket was to be victorious. The Republican tactics immediately became apparent to him in his forays into Texas and other southern states. He conveyed his worry to Dukakis in telephone conversations and at breakfast meetings. Bentsen was not reluctant to provide counsel to Dukakis, but it was not his style to be extremely forceful. I've been down there, he would tell him. We're being nicked by this stuff—on the Pledge of Allegiance, gun control, defense, the furlough program. We have to deal with it. It was frustrating to him and his campaign staff as the Dukakis campaign made no effective response. They could sense that Bubba in Lake Charles, Louisiana was turning away from the Democratic ticket.

The vice-presidential candidates' debate was a special challenge for Bentsen, who shared his staff's nervousness about Quayle. It had nothing to do with his qualifications, intelligence, or experience. It had everything to do with Quayle's movie-star good looks, the rigidity in the debate format, television's limitations, and the easily exceedable low expectations set for Quayle's performance.

They all believed that Quayle was selected mainly because he was telegenic. By contrast, Bentsen looked even older on television than his sixty-seven years. The camera mercilessly magnified each wrinkle on his sun-weathered face. Bentsen also, like many other veteran legislators, spoke Senatese. Asked about some social ill, he was more likely to talk of a piece of legislation than to give a crisp ideological or emotional response. Senators Edward M. Kennedy and Robert Dole had the same difficulty in communications when they ran for president.

Researchers had dug through the files and come up with a mini-debate between Bentsen and Quayle on plant-closing legislation broadcast earlier on the MacNeil-Lehrer News Hour on public television. They had heard that Roger Ailes, Bush's media adviser, had watched the tape for hours on end. Bentsen, as chairman of the Senate Finance Committee, had favored the legislation that required companies to notify workers before shutting down. Quayle led the Republican opposition to the bill. The staff watched the tape with sinking hearts. Quayle clearly bested Bentsen in that televised encounter even though Bentsen was in command of the more politically popular side. Former Indiana Senator Birch Bayh, ousted by Quayle in 1980, talked to Tad Devine at length on the phone. He warned him not to underestimate the kid, as he had.

The staff held the first mock debate at the Ritz Carlton hotel in Washington. Standing in for Senator Dan Quayle was Representative Dennis E. Eckart, a thirty-eight-year-old Democrat from northeast

Ohio. Eckart prepared rigorously for the sessions. He felt that Quayle was picked because he was the quintessential media politician. To that end, he obtained more than seventy videotapes of Quayle performing. One night, Eckart's nine-year-old son came upon his father watching the tapes. "Dad," he asked. "Why are we watching Republicans?" Eckart interviewed Bayh at length, talked to reporters who had covered Quayle in Congress, and subscribed to a media service to obtain videotapes of Quayle's performance on the stump.

An adept mimic, he mastered Quayle's mannerisms, including his hand brush to the hair gesture, and buried himself in Quayle's public record so that he could parrot the Indiana Senator's rhetoric as well as his positions on any issue. He cracked up the briefing team when he arrived at the hotel suite in Washington with a golf tee jauntily tucked behind one ear and a putter in his hand. He leaned the putter by the podium and took his place.

He knocked the first question right out of the ballpark. He was aggressive and forceful and lambasted Dukakis as a left-leaning softie, out of the mainstream. Bentsen seemed to be ignoring Eckart's rhetoric and instead tried to respond directly to the questions being posed by Robert Barnett and staffer Mike McCurry, who played reporters. He acted as though the debate were a press conference.

When the session ended, the briefing team sat in dead silence. "Holy Jesus," thought one senior Bentsen aide. "This is awful." The debate format demanded one-liners, not reasoned argument, and those were not Bentsen's forte. The staffer regretfully recalled the story about the crusty old senator who was told to respond in two minutes and replied, "Son, it takes two minutes for a U.S. Senator to clear his throat." Bentsen himself seemed frustrated by his own performance. When he left the room, Tom Donilon tried to bolster spirits. Dukakis was just as bad in his first session, he said: these guys just need a little practice to get into the swing of things.

Unlike Dukakis, Bentsen had no qualms about being scripted. In his first rehearsals, he literally read the answers from his debate book. Later, having learned his material, he would answer the questions by making exactly the same points in his own words.

On the Tuesday after the Bush-Dukakis debate, Tom Donilon flew to Kansas City for his first meeting with Bentsen. It lasted more than four hours, starting with an exhaustive review of Dukakis's record and positions, point by point. The preparation team's biggest aim was to keep Bentsen from being left mute about some obscure fact in Dukakis's Massachusetts record. They compiled a huge briefing book summarizing every conceivable issue.

The Kansas City group was an amalgam of Democratic Party and

Bentsen veterans as well as Dukakis aides, including a brilliant young Washington attorney, Victoria Radd; the spokesman for the Democratic National Committee and Bruce Babbitt's former campaign manager, Michael McCurry; former Bentsen aide and speechwriter Steve Ward; and former chief Senate aide, Joe O'Neill, on leave from running the National Retailers Association. These regulars on the Bentsen traveling staff were joined by Susan Estrich; Jim Johnson, Mondale's 1984 campaign chairman; and Bob Shrum, the one-time Kennedy speechwriter who had worked for Representative Richard A. Gephardt earlier in the year. That Saturday, the full team, including Dukakis foreign-policy adviser Madeline Albright, met with Bentsen in his Washington office. They established goals for his debate: he should emphasize Tubby Harrison's theme of economic nationalism, and stress major contrasts with Quayle, including his experience, that he was a combat veteran, Quayle's published comments at odds with Reagan-administration policy on arms control, and Quayle's vote against child nutrition programs. And finally, Bentsen must vigorously defend Dukakis, particularly on crime and national defense. They agreed Bentsen should force Quayle to debate Bentsen by needling him on things he could not ignore that would prove how significant the choice was.

That night, Shrum rescripted Bentsen's debate material into short answers and rebuttals to possible questions. One of Donilon's theories was that although debate questions from a panel could take infinite shapes, a candidate needed to be ready to give only about ten answers to the basic political topics in the campaign, and that even though he should begin by dealing with the specific aim of a question he should always round out his answer by making his larger points. To get the debate material into shape, Shrum was up all night, with his usual fortification: a rare steak, two martinis, and three cigars.

On his way to Austin for the final preparation session before going to Omaha, the senator sat at the front of his airplane hunched over the huge book, studying each page. Once in Austin at the Four Seasons Hotel, Eckert and McCurry took turns playing Quayle. To help Bentsen rest while videotape of his rehearsals was being played back for review, Donilon got him a bar stool on which to sit behind his podium. Bentsen insisted that Donilon and O'Neill critique each performance.

Michael Sheehan, a Democratic media consultant, reminded the candidate that the first two sentences in his answer were the most important. Whatever it is you want to say, say it right away, he instructed. He harped on listening to Quayle. He'll say something that will strike you as wrong. You have to be ready to react immediately and take advantage of what he said. He also reminded Bentsen that he had an opportunity to make silent comments on Quayle's remarks because of the camera angles that would show Bentsen in the background during Quayle's responses. You can convey a great deal with a shake of the head, Sheehan said. Bentsen absorbed the lesson, the opposite of Dukakis's no-reaction instruction.

But it became clear during the preparatory sessions that Bentsen was still stiff. He could not memorize answers verbatim. He also had little patience with role playing. He knew it was necesary and even useful, but it wasn't real for him. His attitude showed in his tepid performances. When they left for Omaha, the staff was still queasy. The expectations for Bentsen's performance had gotten out of control. They feared that all Quayle had to do was show up and not drool on camera to neutralize the encounter.

McCurry suggested they do one more practice session on the morning of the debate in Omaha. Bentsen was a different person. He delivered crisp answers and did his closing statement better than he ever had before. The staff applauded.

During the light and camera checks later that day, Quayle was tense and tight and Bentsen was relaxed. Quayle said little during his walk-through, responding in monosyllables to Roger Ailes's barked orders. His wife, Marilyn, conferred intensely with the staff.

By contrast, a relaxed Bentsen swept in with an entourage. A member of Bentsen's staff suggested that his wife practice coming to the stage to congratulate him, as she would after the debate, in order to check the camera angles. Dissatisfied with the first embrace, they had her rush the stage a second time. This time Bentsen swept B.A. off her feet in Clark Gable style. Everyone laughed.

The bipartisan Commission on Presidential Debates, established by the two political parties, had hoped to hold the vice-presidential candidates' debate in a posh old theater in downtown Omaha, Nebraska, but the road show of the Broadway musical *Cats* was scheduled for the theater that week. The debate was shifted to the Omaha Civic Auditorium, where Randy "Macho Man" Savage and André the Giant had squared off days before for the World Wrestling Federation title. (Both were disqualified because they spent too much time outside the ring.) Although the auditorium was draped with curtains to cut it down to more intimate size, producers of the event thought that the sports-arena atmosphere made the audience less inhibited than it might have been in a proper theater. The negotiators had insisted that supporters be seated on the same side of the auditorium as their candidate. They failed to realize that the candidates would be speaking into cameras on the opposite side of the stage, and so at all three forums the candidates found themselves staring into the opposition's hostile faces.

As the live television debate began, moderator Judy Woodruff of the MacNeil-Lehrer News Hour told how significant this debate was: "based on history since World War II, there is almost a 50—50 chance that one of the two men here tonight will become president of the United States."

Woodruff asked the first question of Quayle, a version of the question on everyone's mind. "Why do you think that you have not made a more substantial impression on some of these people who have been able to observe you up close?" she asked.

Quayle responded as he had been coached: "The question goes to whether I am qualified to be vice president, and in the case of a tragedy, whether I'm qualified to be president. Qualifications for the office of vice president or president are not age alone. We must look at accomplishments, and we must look at experience. I have more experience than others that have sought the office of vice president. Now let's look at the qualifications and let's look at the three biggest issues that are going to be confronting America in the next presidency. Those three issues are national security and arms control, jobs and education, and the federal budget deficit. On each one of those issues I have more experience than does the governor of Massachusetts."

So far so good. Quayle tossed off technical arms-control terms like telemetry and encryption, throw weight and megatonnage.

In his one-minute response, Bentsen raised the stakes. He said the debate was about the presidency, not the vice presidency, because "if tragedy should occur, we have to step in there without any margin for error, without time for preparation, to take over the responsibility for the biggest job in the world, that of running this great country of ours. To take over the awesome resonsibility for commanding the nuclear weaponry that this country has."

For the first part of the debate, Quayle spouted the more cutting lines, as expected. He hammered Dukakis as "one of the most liberal governors in the United States of America." He referred to Dukakis as "Tax Hike Mike" and said Dukakis told farmers to grow Belgian endive. "That is what he and his Harvard buddies think," he sneered.

Quayle defended his votes to delay cost-of-living adjustments to people on Social Security by accusing Bentsen and Dukakis of favoring the same. He attacked Dukakis for doing "virtually nothing" to clean up the polluted Boston Harbor.

In the hall, Quayle seemed to have the edge. But as the debate wore on, he began to seem increasingly programmed. The panel of journalists had met earlier in the day and agreed to flout the rules negotiated by the campaigns, which called for no follow up questions. They decided to follow-up one another's questions if the responses seemed unsatisfactory. Brit Hume of ABC News asked Quayle a second time what he would do if he suddenly became president. Quayle delivered the same answer he had given to Judy Woodruff's opening question. At first he had sounded like a robot, reciting the same reply over and over; now he began to get incoherent.

His inadequate reply caused NBC anchorman Tom Brokaw to go back to the same question. "Senator Quayle," he said. 'I don't mean to beat this drum until it has no more sound left in it, but to follow up on Brit Hume's question, when you said that it was a hypothetical situation, it is sir, after all, the reason that we're here tonight because you are running not just for vice president."

Quayle, sounding agitated, began to talk again about his experience. "It is not just age, it's accomplishments, it's experience. I have far more experience than many others that sought the office of vice president of this country. I have as much experience in the Congress as Jack Kennedy did when he sought the presidency."

The camera shot captured Bentsen widening his eyes in surprise. Then came his rebuttal. He shook his head almost sadly. "Senator," he began. "I served with Jack Kennedy," he paused for effect. "I knew Jack Kennedy. Jack Kennedy was a friend of mine. Senator, you're no Jack Kennedy." The crowd exploded and Quayle recoiled like a child who had had his face slapped. Backstage with the technicians, Edward M. Fouhy, a veteran network television executive and executive producer of the debates, exclaimed, "That's the sound bite." Joe O'Neill and the briefing team shrieked with delight in the holding room. Deadly silence reigned beyond the curtain that separated them from the Republican holding room.

Quayle managed to come back with a "that was really uncalled for, Senator," but looked and sounded like a pouting child. Bentsen turned back to him with an elegant and cutting retort, "You're the one that was making the comparison, Senator, and I'm the one who knew him well. And frankly, I think you're so far apart in the objectives you choose for your country that I did not think the comparison was well taken, Senator." The rebuke in that final biting "Senator" was brutal.

Congressman Dennis Eckart, the Quayle practice stand-in, had been convinced that Quayle would try to compare himself to the late President John F. Kennedy, but some members of the briefing team expressed disbelief that Quayle would have the nerve to compare himself to the last great Democratic hero. Eckart, however, had seen Quayle do it repeatedly on videotape in places like Bismarck, North Dakota and other small Republican backwater towns to which Republican handlers had sentenced the vice-presidential hopeful.

When Eckart, playing Quayle, suggested for the first time in a practice session that he, like Kennedy, was prepared to lead a new generation to greatness (he called it his "soaring like an eagle" answer and it was one of forty-six hypothetical questions that he had guessed might be asked), Bentsen reacted viscerally. The Texan dropped out of the rehearsal mode and said, "Senator, you can't say that."

The "You're no JFK" line had been kicking around in the Dukakis campaign for about ten days. When Andy Savitz's quick-response team was asked to prepare some lines for Bentsen's debate from Boston, issues staffer Sam Buell offered it as an example of the sort of one-liner they needed. During debate preparations, the briefing team had suggested that Bentsen say George Bush was no Ronald Reagan. But Bentsen never delivered the line in practice.

The debate was essentially over. Bentsen tired toward the end and was confused by the flashing lights that indicated speaking turn. He thought they were broken when, in fact, they were working properly. But that made no difference. He had served up the line that would be broadcast for days and make the headlines.

Quayle began to deteriorate noticeably. He seemed distracted and rattled. Bentsen may have been weary but he seemed even more confident. McCurry turned to Tad Devine—the Dukakis staff's liaison for the campaign—in the holding room and excitedly said, "He is just popping him at will."

The next day Bentsen called Eckart from Texas, where the vice-presidential candidate was campaigning. "You're a hell of a lot tougher than he was," Bentsen said.

Later that fall Bentsen delivered a speech in the U.S. House chamber to stir up the Democratic congressmen for the election. Eckart went to the Republican podium in the well after Bentsen's speech, put his right foot on the leg of the podium, gripped the front of the podium and stared aimlessly into space, an uncanny copy of Quayle's debate demeanor. He began to ape Quayle's clipped speaking style and asked Bentsen if he'd like to take the opportunity to answer serious questions about his qualifications.

Bentsen, never missing a beat, went back to the microphone and said, in an exact replica of his October 5 timing, "Congressman, I know Dan Quayle. I've worked with Dan Quayle. I served with Dan Quayle and Congressman Eckart; you're no Dan Quayle." He brought down the House.

The day after the debate, a jubilant Dukakis campaigned with his running mate in Texas. His campaign rushed to release two new anti-Quayle commercials. One showed Bush handlers talking about what a disaster Quayle had been and discussing the possibility of replacing him. The other was even more direct. It showed front-page *New York Times* stories of vice presidents taking the oath of office after the president's

death or resignation. Then as a heartbeat thumped ominously in the
background and the camera zoomed in on a still photograph of the Oval
Office, the narrator explained that after months of consideration Bush
had made his personal choice for vice president, J. Danforth Quayle.
"Hopefully," he said, "we'll never know how great a lapse of judgment
that was."

It sounded powerful; it even looked powerful; however, very little
evidence shows that this kind of advertising or message-sending was
politically powerful. As poll after poll showed in the fall, once you got
past recognizing that Dan Quayle was a very controversial person about
whom most people had substantial doubts, these feelings affected the
preference between Bush and Dukakis almost not at all. Most Quayle
haters were partisan Democrats, but Bush's selection of him did not
appear to alter preferences among the moderately conservative citizens
whose votes were still up for grabs; no one would deny, however, that
the debate gave the Democrats an enormous emotional boost, and it
showed on the stump for the next day or two.

Unlike Dukakis, George Bush was nowhere near his junior partner
the day after the Omaha debate. Rich Bond, a senior Bush staffer
traveling with Quayle went into a full damage-control mode and even
tried to minimize the importance of the vice presidency. "Dan Quayle's
role in this campaign is to run for *vice* president," he said. "Dan Quayle
is not running for president. Dan Quayle is running for *vice* president."

With some finality he announced that "George Bush will be the
major focus going into the weekend. He will make news today." Sure
enough, Bush raised his public profile to divert attention from his
beleaguered second by announcing a crime-fighting proposal that included doubling spending for prison construction and prosecuting as
adults juveniles as young as fifteen for some felonies.

Within ten days of the vice-presidential debate, Bentsen had risen
to celebrity status on the campaign trail. He was being mobbed like a
rock star on college campuses. Jack Corrigan described him as a "folk
hero." Of the four candidates on the two tickets, he came across as the
most presidential. Many Democrats were quietly muttering that the
ticket order was reversed.

On October 18, the day after an NBC-*Wall Street Journal* poll
showed Bush ahead by seventeen points following Dukakis's second
debate debacle, Bentsen delivered a blistering speech to the Democratic
Leadership Conference at the University of California at Los Angeles.
The courtly senator had seen enough. He had come to have real affection
for Dukakis, and on this day, he went ballistic. "We have witnessed—
through the combined efforts of the Republican Party and their nominees for president and vice president—one of the most outrageous

displays of negative campaigning ever seen in the history of national politics," he said.

He denounced the "utterly vicious onslaught of distortion and character assassination from the Republicans directed at the patriotism and honor of my running mate, Michael Dukakis."

"They've said things about him that we wouldn't say in Texas about a rattlesnake on the lawn at a church picnic. They don't seem to mind if what they say is untrue. They don't seem to worry if it's misleading. They don't seem to care that what they do is downright mean."

"It's just like the half-baked proposals they dish up in the name of debate. If it sounds good, say it. If it sells, package it. It if looks good, nominate it."

"We've been a little too flabbergasted sometimes to make a proper response," he said. "Mike Dukakis and I deeply believe in the value of honorable, spirited debate. But I don't think we ever imagined that George Bush and the Republicans would be so willing to debase that precious currency of our democracy by conducting a campaign that resembles a demagogic race for county sheriff instead of president of the United States."

Rating Bentsen's performance in the context set by the other nominees in 1988 is unfair because he surpassed a much higher standard.

11

The Final Debate

John Sasso's telephone rang and woke him out of a sound sleep at 6:00
A.M. on October 13 in Los Angeles, not quite dawn. It was the morning
of the final debate, Dukakis's last big chance to make a major move and
change perception of the race from that of nearly inevitable defeat to a
horserace. A very worried Nick Mitropoulos was calling from his own
room in the Bonaventure Hotel's collection of cold cylindrical glassed
towers. "I have to see you. Come to my room. He's sick," said Mitropoulos. The governor had an inflamed throat and could hardly speak
above a whisper. Mitropoulos, alarmed, sent someone to find a ther-
mometer and called a doctor.

"Who'd you call?" asked Sasso, jolted wide-awake by the prospect
of one of 500 journalists gathered in Los Angeles for this final debate
finding out about a sudden visit from a medical doctor. He showered and
went to see Dukakis himself at 7:00 A.M. In eleven hours, Dukakis was
scheduled to walk onto the stage.

Paul Brountas later said Dukakis had had a definite touch of something viral: a sore, almost raw throat and a low fever, and he had hardly
slept during the night; he looked sick. Mitropoulos watched him take
lozenges for his throat, maybe a couple of aspirin, but wasn't aware of
any antihistamine remedy or other medicine that might have made him
drowsy.

Dukakis canceled his 10:00 A.M. debate practice session, agreeing instead to see a few people—media consultant Bob Squier, Tom Donilon, and Sasso—in his room for an hour.

Estrich stopped by the suite briefly and talked to him about the trade-deficit figures released that day in Washington. She left Dukakis's debate book with him, along with the short game plan of positive and negative debating points that had been prepared for him. After he passed around the closing statement he had written out himself, she left. She would not see him again until after the debate.

At no time did any senior member of Dukakis's staff give a thought to trying to delay the debate, although they worried about whether he was sharp and capable of absorbing a great deal of debate advice that seemed contradictory on the surface: be tough but likable, press Bush constantly on his vunerabilities but concentrate on delivering a clear message about restoring America's economic primacy. Even at this late hour it was not clear to the senior staff how rough Dukakis was prepared to be, and now he was lumbering around his suite popping lozenges so that he could speak above a whisper. The atmosphere was starting to have the unmistakable scent of defeat, a far cry from the gritty determination that marked preparations for the occasion.

A debate between presidential nominees is a fascinating anomaly. On the one hand it entails elaborate preparations by the candidate and his advisers, with reams of polling data, lengthy bull sessions, tense rehearsals, and even tenser meetings between the candidate and his most intimate confidants. But it is also a show featuring the candidate alone— rehearsed but live, ultimately on his own. To be successful, a candidate himself has to construct the bridge between the equal imperatives of being elaborately prepared and having the faith in himself and his advice to take a deep breath and execute his plan, of deciding what to say and planning how to say it. With all the chips on the table, Dukakis walked into his two debates with Bush possessing the raw material for an effective performance, and on each occasion completely discarded his plans. That kind of failure is entirely personal, which is why debates can be so dramatically revealing no matter how closely scripted they are.

Five days earlier, Dukakis had shown up at Boston's Park Plaza Hotel to place himself in Tom Donilon's hands again. When he walked into the rented suite that Sunday, October 9, a slick preparation book was waiting for him with a smaller group of advisers who were no longer arguing in front of him about tactics or grand strategy. The night before, Dukakis had watched a videotape of the first debate. That exposure brought home to him the impression he privately called his warm-and-fuzzy problem. He told his team he wanted to work on his technique and he wanted to show more of himself. Bob Squier was unavailable that day, so for some practice questions and answers he was advised by consultant Michael Sheehan, who had helped Lloyd Bentsen the week before. The advice was simple: smile, slow down, gesture more expansively, stop playing the accordion with your hands, and tell a few stories to illustrate points.

The preparation team agreed, with no apparent resistance from the candidate, that he must be very aggressive cn the issues that came up. Donilon said, "to push Bush hard and rap him." As the preparation went forward, the two primary areas of concentration were: foreign policy (more foreign policy than before Winston-Salem); and crime and other "liberal" issues, on which it was considered essential that Dukakis mount a strong counterattack.

This time, all had reached consensus about an all-inclusive theme to hit at every opportunity. That theme, Donilon said, was Tubby Harrison's concept of making and keeping America the number-one economy in the world. By now this theme had strong support from the entire high command. Watching Lloyd Bentsen push this point again and again in his debate with Quayle had impressed Dukakis, who finally agreed with this recommendation as well.

The governor and his entourage flew out to Los Angeles on Tuesday, had a debate workout with Bob Barnett, and scheduled a full day of meetings for the next day, the day before the debate.

But according to Estrich, Dukakis was in a bad mood, flat, and argumentative with his staff on Wednesday. He talked about a just-released Louis Harris poll showing him just two percentage points behind Bush. In a rambling assessment of the race, Dukakis said he was making real progress, that it was now very close, he felt, and that his favorite analogy—the marathon—still seemed appropriate.

Several of the senior campaign officials around the room exchanged alarmed glances. To Donilon, the ominous implication in Dukakis's attitude was that he might be having second thoughts about being aggressive in the debate, might be thinking that a cautious presentation seeking to avoid major mistakes would preserve what he appeared to believe was his momentum. Eventually, Dukakis retired to his suite, with Sasso close behind.

The senior staffers immediately erupted with profanity. "Do you know something I don't know?" Bob Squier inquired of Estrich, half wondering if the campaign might have received some late poll indicating a surge (in fact, the latest survey had the Bush lead widening slightly to eight percentage points). Donilon quickly piped up that, on the contrary, "All the white men in America that are for Dukakis are probably sitting right here at this table."

More seriously, he reviewed the campaign's evidence of a move to within five percentage points following Quayle's debating debacle, and then a slide back. Squier added that as of that day in the once-winnable state of New Jersey, Dukakis was essentially out of the race.

Sasso heard from the group while he was on Dukakis's floor, and after checking with the governor, he reported firmly that Dukakis was under no illusions about his precarious position. Estrich said, however, that when Sasso rejoined the staff group, which included herself, Squier, Donilon, and Kirk O'Donnell, he told them that Dukakis had a real concern about presenting a positive image, and wanted them to "re-package" attack material to make it shorter.

From this time on, the preparation exercise lost its focus. The staff had been working on a one-page summary like a football game plan, with positive and negative messages that Dukakis should concentrate on transmitting during the debate. Now, however, a genuine question in Donilon's mind was whether they had "closure" (meaning Dukakis's assent) for their game plan, and he saw that as essentially a staff failure to make a convincing case to him.

Dukakis was still being hurt by Bush's exploitation of the Horton case, and so the staff recommended that regardless of the content in a crime question, he be aware that it might be the only crime question. Therefore, he must deal with the specifics quickly and then describe how his father and brother were victimized, summarize his own crime-fighting record and the subsequent drop in the state crime rate, tell about the federal prison and Governor Ronald Reagan's California prisoner furlough programs, and accuse Bush of cynically and irresponsibly exploiting an issue he didn't know anything about.

Then, twenty-four-hours before the most important ninety minutes in his campaign, the Dukakis debate preparations were jolted by ABC's "World News Tonight." For the entire first half of the thirty-minute broadcast, anchorman Peter Jennings effectively declared the campaign over. This conclusion was based upon a "poll" of more than 11,500 registered voters that had been taken over the extraordinarily long period of twenty days, from September 20 through October 10, in all fifty-one of the country's voting jurisdictions. The horserace results from the survey showed a small Bush lead, 51 to 45 percent; however, the network used the results from the fifty states plus the District of Columbia to declare that fully 400 electoral votes were either "firm" or "leaning" to Bush. Jennings occasionally hedged, but his report was declarative and definitive in tone as well as content. On the night before the second and climactic debate, and with twenty-six days left in the campaign, a television network called the election over except for the voting. The network devoted another hour to the subject on its "Night-line" program that night. The *Washington Post*, ABC's polling partner, rejected that approach for a far more cautious presentation of the same data in the next day's newspaper; according to the *Post*, Bush was more clearly ahead in the contest for 271 Electoral College votes in some ways than he was in the popular vote, but the big debate was that night, the race was extremely close in most of the largest states, and Bush's overall six-point margin left Dukakis alive, if clearly trailing.

High atop the Bonaventure Hotel, the "news" slugged Dukakis and his senior advisers. Back in Boston, however, the fury against ABC was confined to its arrogance, its methodology, and its timing. For the race itself, Tubby Harrison was convinced that the popular vote was in fact slightly worse than ABCs six percentage-point margin, and that Bush's lead was increasing. Harrison considered the ABC Electoral College predictions silly so close to the debate, but he also had no illusions about Dukakis's situation.

No, he said, Bush's lead in the national horserace had not narrowed beyond a slight change after Dan Quayle's Omaha debacle. In fact, he said, he was not sure that Quayle would matter significantly in the end unless the election was already too close to call.

From the tone and content in the press coverage, a visitor from Mars might have thought Bush was ahead by twenty percentage points and had locked up 400 or even more electoral votes. Nothing could have been further from the truth. In fact, Bush was drifting, and although Dukakis wasn't clearly gaining on him, at least not in a way that could be called a surge, the governor's position was slowly strengthening during the first week in October. Dukakis's progress, however, appeared to halt just prior to the debate, only sharpening the internal debate over whether his packaging advertisements were mistakenly pulled just when they were helping him.

Never one to gild a lily, Harrison nevertheless felt obliged to write on October 7 that "things may, therefore, be turning around."

In two national polls, on October 2 and 3 and on October 4 and 5, the day of the Bentsen-Quayle debate, Harrison recorded a nine-point Bush lead. On the surface, that was no clear change from the eight-point Bush lead he found at the end of September after the first debate. The regional distribution of Harrison's numbers, however, *was* different. In the more recent survey, Bush's lead had jumped in the mostly abandoned South, but his margin had dipped in the East, fallen in the central states to a statistical dead heat, and the race remained deadlocked in the West.

Among more likely voters, moreover, Bush's margin over Dukakis dipped from nine to seven percentage points; but much more intriguing, Harrison saw a marked change among his "opinion leaders," a group of respondents who were seen as certain voters, who always vote, and who were following the campaign closely. Among them, after trailing the week before, Dukakis had moved into a slight lead.

On October 6 and 7, Dukakis's standing improved more noticeably, to a 50 to 45 percent deficit. Because most of his improvement stemmed, though, from Bentsen's annihilation of Quayle in their debate, it was difficult to know whether it was simply an opinion "bounce" or whether it might prove more lasting.

"This improvement *did not come* from any significant improvement in MSDs personal-quality or job-capability comparisons with Bush," Harrison cautioned the campaign high command in a memorandum accompanying his numbers, "nor did it come from any gains on the liberal-conservative outlook front."

Instead, the gain was mostly from undecided voters. The debate was an unmistakable factor, but Harrison also mentioned "some additional help from the packaging spots."

By this time, the spots had been aired far less often in the South and the Midwest than in the rest of the country, and so Harrison focused on a search for their influence in the Northeast and the Rocky Mountain and West Coast states.

"In those three regions, the spots did have an impact on the trial-heat results," he wrote. "After controlling for party, outlook, and the other demographic variables, MSD's trial-heat total was about six points higher among those who had seen the spots than among those who had not—and Bush's was six points lower, for a twelve-point margin difference."

The effect, Harrison stressed, was not on opinion of Bush or of Dukakis; rather, the spots simply appeared to affect voting preferences among people who said they had seen them.

On the eve of the debate, though, Harrison's latest poll showed Bush ahead by 51 to 43 percent, a three-point increase in his margin. Because the Bush campaign's high command had also detected Dukakis's comeback, it had increased its barrage of negative television commercials; these ads, and the Dukakis campaign's "packaging" commercials' being off the air may have driven the governor down a bit.

Above all, Harrison's predebate poll showed how tarred Dukakis had become with the liberal label's pejorative connotations. Fully 30 percent of the poll sample called Dukakis very liberal, and among white men the number was 36 percent, compared to just 6 percent of the sample who thus described their own ideology; the overall very liberal description of Dukakis had now risen more than 50 percent since the Democratic convention.

With exquisite irony, Debate Day opened with bad polling news, a strategy that was less than crystal clear, and a sick candidate. As all during the general election, glimmers of hope would flicker for them, only to be regularly doused by fresh disappointments. The triumph of his running mate, Lloyd Bentsen, over Dan Quayle eight days before had become history very fast. Dukakis had used the issue of Bush's judgment in choosing the Indiana senator for a day out on the road, and his advertising people had quickly tried to milk the debate more by rushing out new commercials; however, the campaign's internal polls had made it clear almost since Bush picked Quayle out of the blue in New Orleans that for all the doubts about whether he could chew gum and be vice president at the same time, the controversy about him excited partisan Democrats, not moderate-to-conservative voters who were now soft in their presidential voting allegiance. In other words, the people who would decide the election didn't care about Dan Quayle.

Moreover, for the week after Omaha, Dukakis was unable to make or sustain good impressions in his daily campaigning, the kinds of impressions that can move polling numbers. After trying to milk Bentsen's victory for a day, for example, the governor went to suburban St. Louis, where he deplored the sharp increase in foreign ownership of American business and real-estate assets, only to learn as he was leaving an automotive parts plant that it had been owned by an Italian concern for the past decade. And the next day he finally told the stories about his father and brother as crime victims, in a speech at Bates College in Maine, only to be upstaged by the college's notable alumna, his mother, Euterpe. In her strong, clipped, almost-Yankee accent, the eighty-five-year-old Mrs. Dukakis accused Bush of "mangling the truth" about her son and implying that, "presumably because he is a first generation American he doesn't love the flag quite so much."

She was speaking out in disgust, she said, adding, "I am telling the truth because my son refuses to do so, but since I am a surrogate I can."

As he rose to speak, Dukakis almost solemnly intoned, "That, my friends, is a very, very tough act to follow."

Dukakis's only truly good day before the final debate had come on Columbus Day when he unveiled an innovative housing initiative on Long Island and then walked with Mario Cuomo and John F. Kennedy, Jr. down Fifth Avenue in the city's annual parade.

Bush and Dukakis met on the UCLA campus in Westwood. Although Secret Service agents and police-escorted motorcades make driving in the Los Angeles area tolerable only for presidential candidates and other huge-shots, Dukakis's aides had planned to move him from downtown at noon for a quick tour of the debating stage, and then to hold him in a suite at a nearby hotel until show time.

After the routine walk-through at the debate site, Dukakis went with Sasso, Mitropoulos, Squier, and Donilon to the luxurious Westwood Marquis for more discussions and practice. Dukakis was still feeling poorly, and his aides agreed to wait while he rested.

He fell asleep at 1:00 P.M. For Dukakis a nap usually takes fifteen or twenty minutes. As he slept his aides chatted among themselves in the suite's living room. At 2:00 P.M., still no sounds came from his bedroom, but Sasso and the others decided to let him rest a while longer. At 3:00 P.M. Sasso could stand the wait no longer, and Mitropoulos was sent in to wake Dukakis. Dukakis got up, but after a few more minutes, his aides no longer heard noise from the bedroom, and realized he had fallen asleep again. Despite their uneasiness, they did not firmly rouse him until 5:00 P.M., an hour before the debate began. Fifteen minutes later they went downstairs to ride over to the auditorium. As they walked through the hotel lobby, Mitropoulos noticed a well-dressed, familiar-looking man seated on a couch writing furiously; it was Bernard Shaw, the Cable News Network anchorman who would be the debate's moderator and would ask the first question of Dukakis that night. Mitropoulos wondered briefly what it would be.

In a column after the August 1987 debate in Iowa between Dukakis and Richard Gephardt, Hunter Thompson, father of gonzo, flood of consciousness, journalism, had written that Gephardt's error had been in not realizing that Dukakis is a mongoose, a rodent famed for its skill at killing poisonous snakes. Mitropoulos would afterward remind Dukakis to be the mongoose at every debate. Just before the governor walked onto the UCLA stage, Mitropoulos said it one last time, "You've got to be the mongoose. Be tough. Be aggressive. Be yourself."

According to Donilon, Sasso also did his best to rouse Dukakis mentally as they left the holding room to proceed toward the stage. All the way down the walkway, he kept repeating to the governor, "Be aggressive, be aggressive, keep at him." As they got to the edge of the stage, Sasso pointed at Bush, waiting in the opposite wing, "That guy can't be president," he said emphatically as he gave his boss a gentle push.

"I think he was [still] sick," Donilon said.

By that moment, expectations for Dukakis's performance in the second and final presidential debate were out of control. The consensus was that he had to hit a grand-slam home run to get back into the fight for the final twenty-six days in the campaign.

And within moments after the first question the expectations thudded to the ground like a weakly hit foul ball.

Hours before the public debate a private, spirited discussion had occupied the panel members, including Ann Compton of ABC, Andrea Mitchell of NBC, and Margaret Garrard Warner of *Newsweek*, over the first question Shaw intended to ask Dukakis.

Shaw told us later that he had observed throughout the campaign that none of the presidential candidates ever answered a question. Rather, they used questions as opportunities to spout campaign rhetoric. He had also noticed that voters had a hard time getting a "feeling fix" on Dukakis. He seemed cold, robotic. Because Bush was criticizing Dukakis for being soft on crime, Shaw thought that a pointed personal question on the subject might not only elicit a real answer but would also show any emotion in Dukakis's thinking on a major issue in the campaign. He decided to ask Dukakis if he would favor the death penalty for the criminal who raped and killed his beloved Kitty. Earlier that day, the other three panelists argued with him about that question. They insisted it was much too personal. He should never use Kitty Dukakis's name.

According to Warner, the panelists discussed Shaw's planned question after a rehearsal at UCLA that morning, and shared with him their doubt about his wording: it was likely to make the audience recoil and to shock Dukakis, but not necessarily to produce the answer or the emotion he was seeking to elicit.

Shaw felt that the personal angle was just the point. He knew the governor treasured his wife Kitty above all others. His only fear going into the debate was that Dukakis might knock the question right out of the ballpark and Shaw would be criticized for having tossed the Democratic candidate a softball of a question. He walked onto the stage holding his breath but convinced it was the hardest question he could ask him; later, his panelists agreed.

Dukakis never flinched, never blinked when Shaw posed the raw hypothetical brutalization and murder of the woman he so loved, and whether he would favor the death penalty for her killer. In fact, the answer came out with the methodical logic one might expect in response to a question about rural electrification.

"No, I don't, Bernard," replied the governor, "and I think you know that I've opposed the death penalty all of my life. I don't see any evidence that it's a deterrent, and I think there are better and more effective ways to deal with violent crime."

That was it on the topic; no mention of his wife, no stories, as agreed, about his father and brother. And then Dukakis suddenly lurched homeward:

"We've done so in my own state, and it's one of the reasons why we have had the biggest drop in crime of any industrial state in America, why we have the lowest murder rate of any industrial state in America." And then Dukakis lurched again, this time toward drugs, as if he'd pressed the wrong button on an information-retrieval system:

"But we have work to do in this nation; we have work to do to fight a real war, and not a phony war against drugs."

And on he rambled, suggesting that he would call a hemispheric summit to organize an international battle against drugs, and reach young people in the schools, and help the police, and double the number of narcs, and then maybe there wouldn't be so much drugs and people would be safe in their neighborhoods.

As Dukakis delivered his leaden response, Shaw thought, "Governor, that is not the right political answer."

It was a loose, direct, but not brutal Bush who then made the values contrast and the style contrast with his rebuttal.

"Well, a lot of what this campaign is about, it seems to me, Bernie, is to a question of values. And here, I do have, on this particular question, a big difference with my opponent," he began.

"You see I do believe that some crimes are so heinous, so brutal, so outrageous—and I'd say particularly those that result in the death of a police officer—those real brutal crimes, I do believe in the death penalty. And I think it is a deterrent. And I believe we need it, and I'm glad that the Congress moved on this drug bill, and it finally called for that, related to these narcotics drug kingpins. And so, we just have an honest difference of opinion. I support it, and he doesn't."

It was then Bush's turn to face Shaw.

"Now to you, Vice President Bush. I quote to you this from Article III of the 20th Amendment of the Constitution: Quote 'I, at the time fixed for the beginning of the term of the President, the President-elect shall have died, the Vice-President-elect shall become President,' meaning if you are elected and die before Inauguration Day . . ."

"BERnie!" Bush cut in with his best Poppy Bush affectation of mock shock and dismay, and the audience dissolved into laughter.

Shaw pretended not to notice and continued with his now utterly fractured question: "*Automatically, automatically*, Dan Quayle would become the forty-first president of the United States. What have you to say about that possibility?"

Naturally, Bush supported his man Quayle, and Dukakis's rebuttal had not one direct criticism of the senator's qualifications to be president.

To Susan Estrich's trained eyes and ears in one of two holding rooms near the stage where she sat with her husband, Marty Kaplan, and fund-raiser Bob Farmer, the debate's disastrous trend was crystal clear five minutes after it began. John Sasso was so upset that he resolved not to attend the postdebate mob scene in the press room, where campaign higher-ups are dispatched to feed quotes to the ravenous, reaction-crazed journalists. But Donilon, convinced that Dukakis had been thrown off balance by Shaw's first question and immediately struck by the silence in the senior staff room during the debate, compared to the jubilant cheering in the holding room during the first one, still thought the opening was not an irremediable disaster, and told us he wasn't particularly bothered. One reason the Dukakis campaign had wanted a panel of journalists instead of just one moderator-referee, he said, was that it meant a constant stream of questions and therefore opportunities to come back dramatically from a bad answer and deliver the kind of statement (like Lloyd Bentsen's on John Kennedy) that could turn the debate around.

But that night, though the opportunities kept coming, the one answer never did.

Even as Dukakis dully uttered those first nonresponsive words, a syndicated cartoonist in the crammed pressroom at the debate site brutally caricatured the governor's inept response, so brutal, that he never considered shipping his drawing for publication. It showed a sprawled, lifeless Kitty Dukakis with a huge knife sticking out of her back, with Dukakis standing over the body, announcing: "I have implemented a five-point program to deal with the rape and murder of my wife, and as soon as she's in the ground I'll be convening a multilateral conference involving the NATO nations and OAS. . . ."

The first question set the standard for a perfunctory performance by Dukakis. He was never really bad, but in the high-stakes climate, he failed to project warmth, emotion or even ease. At first he seemed wound up and tight, but Bush came across as much more relaxed. Bush made more expansive hand gestures, used opportunities to make parenthetical jokes and asides, and continued to slap at Dukakis, almost at will, for being "liberal," a word he pronounced with distaste.

Bush once again showed ability to connect with television viewers. His sincerity quotient soared. He was friendly. He called Bernard Shaw "Bernie" and Dukakis addressed him as "Bernard," pronounced in the French way. Bush occasionally fractured his syntax and seemed to be talking about things out of context, as when he defended Quayle's comparing his experience to that of John F. Kennedys' at the time Kennedy sought the presidency. But Bush forgot to mention Kennedy's name and so when he said, "You know, Lloyd Bentsen jumped on Dan Quayle when Dan Quayle said he's had roughly the same amount of experience," some viewers may have wondered what he was talking about; but it didn't matter.

What counted on television was that Bush was a stand-up guy as he portrayed Quayle as a young and helpless victim of "such a pounding, an unfair pounding" and himself as his champion.

"Three times since World War II," responded Dukakis, "the vice president has had to suddenly become the president and commander-in-chief. I picked Lloyd Bentsen because I thought he was the best-qualified person for the job. Mr. Bush picked Dan Quayle and, before he did it, he said, 'Watch my choice for vice president. It will tell all.' And it sure did. It sure did."

That was better, but Dukakis was soon thrown into the position of governmental scold, the bearer of bad news, the political Cassandra. He warned that the national debt would get worse without effective leadership and tough decisions. The next president would need to make "tough and difficult decisions" on defense spending. The federal government faced "limits" on what it could spend.

"We cannot continue to tell the American people that we're going to build all of these systems, and at the same time invest in important things here at home, and be serious about building a strong and good America. And that's the kind of America I want to build," he said. It may have been thoughtful, but it wasn't what he needed to convey to the public at this critical juncture.

Meanwhile, Bush kept pushing his values buttons, punching out words like "strength," "values," "naive," and "liberal," and using buzz words like "unilateral disarmament" and "freeze" to characterize Dukakis's defense positions. He promised not to appoint judges who would "legislate from the bench." He accused Dukakis of raiding his state pension fund and mocked Dukakis's proposal to beef up tax enforcement and collect unpaid taxes as "this idea of unleashing a whole bunch, an army, a conventional-force army of IRS agents into everybody's kitchen."

When Margaret Warner asked Dukakis if he believed that a president had to be likable to be an effective leader, the governor explained that he was a serious person. He used the word *serious* or *seriously* seven times. "I'm also a serious guy. I think the presidency of the United States is a very serious office. And I think we have to address these issues in a very serious way. . . . And I'm going to be a president who is serious, I hope and expect will be liked by the American people. But more than that, will do the kind of job that I'm elected to do, will do it with as much good humor as I can, but at the same time, will do it in a way which will achieve the goals we want for ourselves and our people. And I think we know what they are—

"Governor," interrupted Shaw.

"—a good strong future, a future in which there—"

"Your time has run out, sir," said Shaw.

"—is opportunity for all of our citizens," finished Dukakis.

Bush harped on Dukakis's one-time support for a bilateral freeze between the United States and the Soviet Union on nuclear weapons and his alleged support for "unilateral cuts" in defense spending. Using the debate to reinforce his basic campaign message that Dukakis, the advocate of change, was too risky to be commander-in-chief, he mentioned disarmament, the nuclear freeze, or unilateral cuts in seven answers. "You have to learn from experience that making unilateral cuts in the defense system is not the way that you enhance the peace," he said.

Margaret Warner asked about Bush's negative campaigning and quoted Senator Mark Hatfield of Oregon, who knew the vice president's late father, Senator Prescott Bush, as saying, "If his father were alive today I'm sure his father would see it as a shocking transformation."

"Well," said Bush, "I think my dad would be pretty proud of me, because I think we've come a long, long way." In the final weeks of the campaign, he often defended his campaign tactics as appropriate because they worked. He accused the Democrats of starting the negative campaign at the Democratic National Convention although he himself had begun the attacks more than a month earlier.

Dukakis also flubbed a question from ABC news correspondent Ann Compton seeking to find out whom he regarded as modern heroes by offering a meandering litany of public employees, by category, whereas Bush listed specific names ending with the hero of the hour, Ronald Reagan: "But look, I also think we ought to give a little credit to the president of the United States. He is the one that has gotten us that first arms-control agreement and the cynics abounded—

"Mr. Vice President," interrupted Shaw.

"—and he is leaving office with a popularity at an all time high—

"Mr. Vice President, your time has expired."

"—because American people say, he is our hero."

Bush was also a skilled emotional panderer, as when he partially deflected an abortion-related question by talking about losing his young daughter Robin to leukemia, an answer that he concluded with the bizarre observation that he was "very pleased indeed" that his daughter-in-law had not aborted his grandchild.

Dukakis matched the debating point, if not the tastelessness, mentioning that he and Kitty had also lost a child at infancy. He then gave the kind of convincing rebuttal he was unable to make for most of the remaining debate:

"But isn't the real question that we have to answer not how many exceptions we make—because the vice president himself is prepared to make exceptions—it's who makes the decision, who makes this very difficult, very wrenching decision. And I think it has to be the woman, in the exercise of her own conscience and religious beliefs, that makes that decision."

Dukakis occasionally struck back forcefully, but it was usually to make a defensive point. "I'm not keeping count," he said toward the end of the ninety-minute session, "but I think Mr. Bush has used the label 'liberal' at least ten times. If I had a dollar, George, for every time you used that label, I'd qualify for one of those tax breaks for the rich that you want to give away."

And he spoke several times of what he was supposed to speak about on September 25, the need for change, and preparing for the challenges of the future.

"The vice president is complacent," said the governor, "thinks we ought to stick with the status quo, doesn't think we ought to move ahead, thinks things are okay as they are. I don't. I think this is a great country because we've always wanted to do better, to make our country better, to make our lives better. We've always been a nation which was ambitious for America, and we move forward. And that's the kind of America I want; that's the kind of leadership I want to provide. . . let's stop labeling each other and let's get to the heart of the matter, which is the future of this country."

Toward the end, Dukakis seemed to get more pointed. "As we look at this nation's future—and we have two very different visions of this future—I want to move ahead. The vice president talks about a thousand points of light. I'm interested in 240 million citizens in this country who share in the American dream, all of them, in every part of this country. (Dukakis's focus-group polling had discovered that some voters inexplicably thought the "thousand points of light" referred to the nation's wealthiest citizens. Dukakis's use of the expression was a deliberate attempt to foster some "us-against-them" sentiment.)

But once again Bush was folksier, more approachable, more likable. "I get kidded by being a little old-fashioned on these things," he said in a just-between-us-guys voice, "but I do believe in public service. I believe that public service is honorable."

The hall was divided in two with Bush partisans on one side and Dukakis partisans on the other. When the debate ended, a throaty roar erupted from the Bush side as every supporter leapt to his feet. That response said it all.

Dukakis was scheduled for a rally in Beverly Hills almost immediately after the debate, but his hasty departure from the stage made it appear he was running from an accident scene.

As she headed from the staff room down a narrow walkway near the stage entrance to gamely face the press, Estrich almost collided with Dukakis as he returned from the stage. He kissed her, and then moved silently into the room; thirty paces behind the governor walked Kitty Dukakis. On the way to the rally, Nick Mitropoulos rode in the car with Dukakis and his wife; four months later he said it would not be appropriate to describe the scene or report what was said. Upstairs, back at the hotel, Victoria Rideout was one of the first senior staff members to return to the Bonaventure. Wandering by the suite where food and drinks were being served, she encountered Governor and Mrs. Dukakis. They were alone, and she stayed with them for nearly a half-hour before the rest of the Dukakis entourage started arriving. The governor, she told us later, was almost inconsolably depressed; Kitty Dukakis was the buoyant one, trying to revive his spirits.

By Thursday morning, he no longer had any time for tears, frustration, or gallows humor; Dukakis had to hit the road and keep running regardless of his private pain and disappointment at himself, and regardless of his campaign's pain and disappointment in him. His campaign now needed a straw to grasp, because not only was a fresh Bush surge in the polls a foregone conclusion within moments of the debate's end, the likelihood was also very strong that the surge would produce the first clear noises in the political community that Bush's election was now inevitable. The problem was, the campaign had no straws to grasp; the day after the debate, the first in a deluge of national and major state polls showing Bush with a double-digit lead appeared. CBS News reported a 54 to 43 percent Bush margin; the *Los Angeles Times* said it was 52 to 42 percent.

While the campaign labored behind the scenes to regain its composure and credibility, Dukakis had to labor in public, and his performance on the day after his debacle illustrated the larger plight afflicting his candidacy at this late stage. From southern California to Washington state and back, from barely dawn to nearly midnight, Dukakis offered not one message or theme for this critical day; he offered instead a pastiche of thematic confusion, dramatizing the trouble into which his debate performance had put him.

It all began in south-central Los Angeles, at a breakfast gathering of black community leaders featuring Mayor Thomas Bradley and Jesse Jackson; the applause at the lightly attended gathering was desultory, and although Jackson said not a discouraging word about Dukakis, he emphasized his own recent travels on behalf of the Democratic ticket, a clear Don't Blame Me message that made it evident to attentive observers that Jackson's thoughts and plans were already drifting past the election.

Still struggling with the last of his flu, and taking red lozenges for his hoarse voice, Dukakis began this important Friday gamely, primed to accomplish at least one part of the strategy he had failed to execute the night before: hit Bush hard on the issue of crime that had hurt him so badly.

"If your record on crime and drugs is as pathetic as his is, what do you do? you divert attention elsewhere," said the governor as he condemned Bush's use of the William Horton case, though this time with a surprising new twist.

"Last year," he said after repeating his standard references to the federal furlough program and to the program Ronald Reagan operated as governor of California, "in another tragedy, one of those drug pushers, on a weekend furlough from the federal prison system, raped and murdered a young mother of two."

That was as far as Dukakis went in his remarks: no names, no particulars, nothing more that might indicate just what it was he was trying to get across. He was dangling bait, a common political tactic designed to attract reporters' attention so that they would develop the story. It worked, and campaign officials were only too happy to supply details when the hoped-for inquiries came.

According to press secretary Dayton Duncan, who provided the basic facts en route to a late-morning rally in Sacramento, the story was about a prisoner in the federal system whose record made him the Southwest's very own William Horton. In and out of prison for parole violations after a drug conviction, Angel Medrano was on a weekend pass from a Phoenix halfway house on February 1, 1987, when he raped and murdered (with twenty-eight stab wounds) Patricia Pedrin, who was twenty-eight years old at the time, mother of two small children, and pregnant. Convicted by an Arizona court, Medrano was under a death sentence when Dukakis raised his case. Within a week, the pictures of Angel Medrano and Patricia Pedrin would be in a Dukakis television commercial, and the case would be at least one fat paragraph in the governor's stump rhetoric about crime from then on, raising several ironies: here was Dukakis, who said Bush's use of Horton was a cynical and hypocritical exploitation of an isolated incident with racial overtones, now using the case of a Hispanic convict roaming the countryside under the federal system's loose rules, to make the point that Bush's use of the Massachusetts case was intentionally insincere. Even though Dukakis always said in his speeches that he would never use the Medrano case, as he said Bush had used the Horton case, to accuse the vice president of being soft on crime, his commercial did falsely create the impression that Bush was somehow responsible for the system that made Medrano's temporary freedom possible. On this day, however, the political point seemed to be that the morning after not using the story of Angel Medrano in the debate, Dukakis was at least using it on the campaign trail as part of his larger effort to finally fight back.

Had Dukakis concentrated on it and developed his point, the Arizona case could have been a decent story for the day, a story he desperately needed to offset the larger political story about his crum-

For the final campaign frenzy, Sasso stuck close to his boss on the campaign plane using a portable telephone to keep in touch with headquarters. (Photo by James Steinberg)

bling prospects after the debate. One constant symptom of Dukakis's inability to rise to an unfamiliar general-election campaign, however, was his maddening inability at crucial moments to keep his message focused, and this Friday was no exception.

No sooner had Duncan finished providing details on the Medrano case when Kitty Dukakis came into the press section of the airplane. Normally, pleasantries with Mrs. Dukakis lasted several minutes before someone asked a newsy question, but on this tense day the conversation got down to political business almost at once, and naturally she was asked about the opening question in the debate; as ever, she responded directly, this time with a blast at Bernie Shaw.

"It was an outrageous question," she said of her hypothetical rape and murder. "How would you feel if someone asked you a question like that? Thank God I'm not the candidate; I don't know what I would have done."

Mrs. Dukakis added that she thought her husband felt the same way, and added one more adjective to her characterization of Shaw's question, "gross," before resuming her seat up front as the plane neared California's capital city. Now Angel Medrano was no longer the day's sole story line; now we had a blast at the debate's moderator and opening questioner by the nominee's deeply angry wife. And more was to come.

On the day's next flight, farther up the coast to Seattle, Dukakis himself wandered back to the press section briefly, and almost immediately was asked his own feelings about Shaw's question and whether he considered it appropriate. With hardly a pause, no emotion, and quite matter-of-factly, Dukakis answered, "Yes." Apprised of his wife's completely contradictory feelings, Dukakis hesitated, shrugged, and simply stated that here was another example of how he and she often disagreed. The story line for his campaign day now hopelessly muddled, Dukakis quickly retreated to his seat before any more questions could be asked of him.

A bit later in the flight to Seattle, U.S. House Majority Leader Thomas Foley, Spokane's congressman and a thoughtful man, this time was blunt and outspoken in making a more overtly political point.

"Dukakis should have hit Shaw's question right out of the park no matter what he thought of it," Foley said. "When it happened, I could hear myself saying that if I happened by my home when something like that happened, whoever did it wouldn't have left that house alive."

While the campaign was making confusing news in the air, Dukakis was unable to score at his one major crowd event of the day, a noon rally on the grounds of the state capitol in Sacramento. Dukakis awkwardly followed Lloyd Bentsen's game attempt at an enthusiastic introduction. ("Wasn't Michael Dukakis great last night? . . . It's a tough job debating George Bush, like eating Jell-O with a fork.")

Dukakis's one good line responded to his running mate's introduction, itself an uncomfortable reminder that he had failed to match Bentsen's October 5 performance: "I wonder if Mr. Bush can look the American people in the eye and say he picked the person who was best qualified."

The line, however, had not been written for a Friday-afternoon rally in Sacramento, California. It was supposed to have been one of Dukakis's major attention-getting moments in the debate itself, one more element in his game plan that the governor had left in his holding room.

In the early evening, though, Dukakis got at least one poignant reminder that some people would stick with him enthusiastically even in politically grim circumstances. Despite a steady rain and a mid-October chill, more than 10,000 people had filled a waterfront park in downtown Seattle; they spilled over onto Virginia Street across from the park and up a steep hill sloping away from the water. Set off brilliantly by well-placed television lights against the gathering darkness, Dukakis drew some strength from the outpouring of affection and gave it back for a change.

At the airport, political aide Donna Brazile had arranged for the governor to speak on a conference call to the NAACP board of directors in Washington, D.C. For ten minutes, the man who had decided two months before not to mention three of the civil-rights movement's martyred heroes during a speech before a nearly all-white audience in Philadelphia, Mississippi, talked eloquently about the life of Medgar Evers, another 1963 Mississippi martyr.

Flying back to Los Angeles, Dukakis's plane was barely airborne before Francis O'Brien walked up to the governor's seat, spoke to him briefly as he rose, and then gently guided him down the aisle, just past the first two rows of reporters, so that the press could crowd around him. O'Brien had explained to Dukakis that every writer on that plane was writing a story for his Sunday paper assessing the governor's debate performance and its presumably almost mortal effect on his sinking chances for winning the election. From the campaign's standpoint, no staff member could do for Dukakis what he had to do for himself—get into those stories and try to soften them with comments the reporters would need to use. Dukakis hardly needed the advice or prompting, and when O'Brien had delivered him as far as row 12, he broke away, sitting for the rest of the flight with actress Debra Winger, the day's traveling celebrity, while the governor answered questions. Aware that this was no routine press conference, Mrs. Dukakis urged daughter Kara up close behind her father, so that she could hear.

The last thing on earth to expect in a situation like this is that a politician will confess to a hideous debate performance in the clutch and call his cause nearly lost. Nonetheless, candor came out by implication and indirection during this thirty-minute exchange, which showed that Dukakis knew he had done poorly and knew that his odds had worsened, even as he vowed to fight on.

"We won the last one but it didn't move the polls . . . Debates don't win or lose elections," he said, which by implication was his admission that he had lost the debate.

And then: "One of the things I have to do is give people a better sense of who Mike Dukakis is," a poignant but mind-boggling acknowledgment of what he still had failed to accomplish after nineteen months on the road.

Dukakis was already more than twelve hours into it, but still his Longest Day wasn't over. From touchdown in Burbank, he was whisked to a meeting with a coalition of Los Angeles-area neighborhood organizations, and finally to a snazzy house in Brentwood, where he helped

"This is garbage," said the candidate as he inspected attack literature distributed by the state Republican Party in Quincy, Illinois, on October 20. (Photo by Paul Benoit)

observe Jesse Jackson's birthday. For those last outings, which kept him going almost to midnight, he earned some good will and some fresh material for the Los Angeles 11:00 news shows, but the Jackson party also provided one more unfortunate, if unintended metaphor for the grueling day. The entertainment at the party was provided by singer-actress Linda Hopkins, whom Dukakis had honored at the State House in Boston several years earlier. For her big number that Friday night, Hopkins sang Nobody Loves You When You're Down and Out; that made all the reporters' Sunday stories, too.

Dukakis had already been unsuccessful in his first outing against Bush, both in projecting a rounded, likable personality as well as in projecting the broad message he had agreed to before the debate about the need for a change in national direction. Fortunately for him, the damage had been contained by his continued improvement as a campaigner and by the perception that he was raising serious issues though Bush was not, as well as by Lloyd Bentsen's slaughter of Dan Quayle.

Then, in the second debate, he simply was unable to rise to the occasion.

In his Massachusetts campaigns, Dukakis was an experienced, skillful debater with sharp elbows, and he was magnificent in keeping cool and timing his thrusts for maximum advantage during the long Democratic primary season. But he was out of his league in the unique crucible of general-election debates; he had enough good moments to demonstrate his ability to play at this level, but he was a not-ready-for-prime-time player.

With hindsight, staff confidence in Dukakis's ability to perform may have been misplaced. He was quick, facile, and smart, but by late August it was also apparent that he was having severe difficulty making the quantum leap to a general-election figure of appropriate stature and demeanor, and his campaign was chaotic at the top as the agitation for and last-minute resistance to John Sasso's return continued without decisive resolution by the governor.

After the final debate Dukakis and his high command hunkered down to wait for the hop and the skip in Bush's polling numbers. It was not long in coming. On the evening of October 17, NBC News reported that from a national survey it had conducted over the three preceding days Bush had vaulted to a 55 to 36 percent lead. By a 74 to 14 percent margin, the respondents said they thought Bush would win the election, and in a hypothetical crisis requiring decisive action they said they'd rather have Bush as president by 62 to 32 percent. As for the climactic debate, the respondents thought Bush had done a better job by a 60 to 16 percent majority, and their approve-disapprove rating of Ronald Reagan was 59 to 35 percent favorable, nine points above the reported level in early summer.

It can't get much worse than that in a presidential election; the NBC numbers showed little more than a hard core of partisan Democratic support for Dukakis. As John Sasso read the results, the experienced politician in him knew that one of those watershed moments in a campaign had arrived when voters lean in for a last look at the expected loser, to see what his character is really made of. On Sky Pig, Dukakis, Mitropoulos, and Brountas talked for several minutes, not as campaign colleagues but as friends; Brountas told Dukakis it was time to reach down and make sure he ended the campaign with pride, mentioning Harry Truman's fighting spirit and observing that Bush might always make a whopper of a mistake and Dukakis had to be in position to capitalize if lightning struck. None of the three friends admitted to giving up the ghost, but their attitude was grimly realistic.

As they talked, the plans for the end game were already cooking in Sasso's brain. The day after the debate, he had flown back to Boston with Donilon. On the flight, they had agreed that Dukakis could make an effective stretch drive only by being disciplined enough to fire one positive and one negative salvo on each and every day that was left to him. They also resolved that the best way to try to establish that discipline was to head for the road themselves and guide the daily message strategy from Dukakis's side.

The basic message had been in Sasso's mind since the moment he had returned to the campaign at summer's end. The idea had been presented to him by a New York political consultant, Hank Morris, who had assisted the campaign since the primary season, and it consisted of nothing more complicated than adding up all the things Dukakis favored, linking them to the average American's interests and declaring that he was "on your side"; and the flip side was to focus on both Bush's economic proposals and his opposition to Dukakis's and declare that he was on "their" side.

At that time Sasso didn't press to have the message adopted as Dukakis's theme; instead, he thought he needed to first lay out his specific agenda before emphasizing its wrapping paper. Later, he wondered if he had erred; in introspective moments, he thought his instincts had been bad during the two months, that he had been rusty from his year away, and that he wasn't sure if he had ever hit his stride. To one campaign friend, he confided after the second debate that he thought he had been outsmarted by Bush's handlers all along.

The attempt at a comeback was launched as an attack on George Bush's campaign ethics. As a prop, the Dukakis campaign used leaflets printed by many state Republican parties for their direct-mail programs. They varied from state to state, but invariably they featured pictures of William Horton and a basic message that criminals like Horton all over the country were hoping for a Dukakis victory. The counterattack by the governor, which he rejected before the Republican convention in August, was finally scheduled for an October rally in Quincy, Illinois. As Dukakis's speech was being written, the word *lie* was very carefully put into the rhetoric about the Republican campaign material. To Kirk O'Donnell, calling the leaflets "lies" would be vital in trying to induce the media to do stories on Bush campaign commercials and direct-mail material that would help fuel the assault on his tactics. All the way in the motorcade with Dukakis to the Illinois event, O'Donnell repeated over and over again, "You've got to say lies, you've got to call them lies."

"My friends," Dukakis said minutes later, holding the Illinois leaflet aloft, "This is garbage, political garbage." He didn't say lie.

Even so, the speech fueled a week-long debate over Bush's campaign ethics, which gained impetus over the weekend when first Jesse Jackson and then Lloyd Bentsen—with Dukakis saying he agreed with him—charging that the emphasis on William Horton was racist.

Dukakis gave the preview for the homestretch in a jammed airplane hangar at Burbank airport on the evening of October 23, the last stop on another grueling cross-country day.

Dukakis seemed genuinely surprised that 2,000 people were screaming at him on a Sunday night. "You know," he said, "you're either all crazy or we're going to win this baby on November 8."

Of his opponent, he said, to a loud cheer, "He wants to help people who have it made. We want to help every American family make it in this country."

And then, the next morning, Dukakis gave the full version, appearing at the Scottish Rite Temple in Los Angeles, an imposing structure up Wilshire Boulevard, just inside the Hollywood line. A commercial video crew was there from Michael Kaye's firm, taping the speech for use in a highly effective California commercial.

His Illinois "garbage" forgotten, Dukakis didn't hold back this time:

> You know Mark Twain once said that a lie can travel half way around the world while the truth is still putting on its shoes. Mr. Bush must have read Mark Twain. Because he's running a campaign based on distortions and distractions—and outright lies. Why? Because he can't win an election where the real issues are discussed; the real challenges are faced; and the real differences are made known.
>
> Now it's not easy for the truth to catch up with the lies, but between now and November 8, I'm going to take my case directly to you; because this election isn't just about George Bush and Mike Dukakis; this election is about you. It's about the kind of life you're going to have for the next four years; and the kind of future we're going to build for our children and grandchildren.
>
> George Bush wants to help the people on Easy Street. I want to help the people on Main Street. He wants to help those who already have it made. I want to help every American make it. He's on their side; I'm on your side, because standing on your side is what I think being president of the United States is all about.

Attacking Bush's campaign was the first element in the attempted comeback; "on your side" was the second.

The third was accessibility. For the next ten days, Dukakis was on every television network news or interview program that would take him, and they all did; he also returned to his favorite format, the "town meeting," question-and-answer sessions with supporters. His specific performances were spotty: he was hideous on Ted Koppel's "Nightline," then excellent with Dan Rather on the CBS "Evening News." But that wasn't the point; the massive exposure showed the public a Dukakis who clashed with the caricature portrayed in Bush's attacks and television commercials, and gave Dukakis new credibility.

Whether this kind of campaign, had it begun in mid-August, could have won a winnable election is objectively unanswerable, though the commonest answer is no, on the grounds that the late Dukakis message did not have clear appeal beyond partisan Democrats. All that is known for certain is that the Dukakis campaign after the second debate brought Democratic-inclined voters home at the end, and cut the Bush polling lead in half.

For all the power in his end-game performance, however, Dukakis remained a far from flawless candidate. As had happened so many times before, his critical flaw was in not maintaining the discipline to stick to his message; his most harmful error involved the famous "L" word, and may have cost him grievously. On October 29, he taped an interview for the "MacNeil-Lehrer News Hour" on public television, to be broadcast two nights later. Toward the end of it coanchor Jim Lehrer asked him about the liberal label.

"Jim, I'm not a label," Dukakis replied. "I'm a guy that's been in public service for twenty-five years. I'm a liberal in the tradition of Franklin Roosevelt and Harry Truman and John Kennedy, while I'm fiscally a lot more conservative than George Bush."

That was the first time he had used the word to describe himself, and not using it had been campaign dogma from its inception. But the remark was made in a private taping, and for the moment caused no stir.

The next morning, however, it did. Just before his train pulled out of Bakersfield for the run up California's Central Valley, Dukakis addressed a raucous rally at the Amtrak station and brought up the subject of labels.

"I'm in the tradition," Dukakis said, and then paused very briefly and deliberately as if to take a breath before he bellowed, "Yes, the LIBERAL tradition of . . ."

The word was not in his text, no one had discussed using it, and the governor clearly had simply blurted it out in defiance. The crowd, most of it labor-union organized, went wild, but to John Sasso and Kirk O'Donnell it was clearly a gaffe that blocked out his populist message for the rest of the day. And on Monday, they felt obliged to have him say it again, if only because not saying it would produce a fresh round of stories that he had backed down. This sequence happened more than once down the stretch, and the gloating and crowing that Bush responded with gave the incident added power. Keeping in mind he lost such major states as Illinois, Pennsylvania, and Maryland by tiny margins, it was no small tactical goof, and a totally inexcusable one.

One of Dukakis's network interviews, on November 1, was with Bernard Shaw, who was as determined *not* to ask *the question* all over again, as Dukakis was to try to answer it. It was right after Dukakis had blurted out the statement that he was in the "liberal" tradition of past Democratic presidents, and Shaw began the interview mentioning that Bush had boasted that at last Dukakis had been smoked out of his liberal closet.

Instead of answering the question, Dukakis brought up the question he had been asked at the debate and delivered the response he would give if asked the question again.

"Well, Bernie," Dukakis said, dropping the Bernard of October 13, "let me begin by saying thank you to you for coming out and doing this interview. And can I say something at the beginning? Um, lots of people have asked me about that question that you asked me at the debate, and let me say that I thought it was a fair question, a reasonable one. I think it took me aback a little bit. And in thinking about it, had I had the chance to answer it again, let me just say this: Kitty is probably the most—is the most precious thing, she and my family, that I have in this world. And uh, obviously, if what happened to her was the kind of thing you described, I would have the same feelings as any loving husband and father."

"Would you kill him?" asked Shaw.

"I think I would have that kind of emotion. On the other hand, this is not a country where we glorify vengeance. We're a country that believes in the law and I believe very strongly in the law. But I'm a member of a family that has been victimized by crime and knows what it's like to feel the pain of crime. My dad practiced medicine for fifty-two years and was practicing when he was seventy-seven, when he was bound and gagged and beaten by an intruder who was looking for drugs in his office. My only brother lost his life in a hit-and-run accident where we've always assumed that the person who hit him was either drunk or on drugs. It's one of the reasons why I've worked so hard as governor of my state not only to get crime down, and we have, by more than any other industrial state in this country, but to reach out to victims. And I guess, had I had to do it over again, that's the kind of answer I would have given."

Shaw was flabbergasted. The governor had done the same thing in other interview formats in recent days. Shaw felt that Dukakis was making a personal statement to him. He wanted him to know he had feelings. Sasso, kneeling in the shadows just behind the cameras, hung on every word.

After the election, Sasso tried to deal with the question of how—

facing his last mass-media chance—Dukakis could have gone to all the trouble of preparing a plan and utterly failed to execute it. In an unnoticed section of a speech he gave to a Boston business group (which he discussed ahead of time with Dukakis) Sasso said: "Sitting with Mike Dukakis, alone, after the second debate with George Bush, was not to be with a man without emotions. He had prepared a plan to strike aggressively at Bush on abortion, on Dan Quayle, on the environment. For a lot of reasons, he decided to hold down the attack. Afterward, Mike knew he had been too reasonable. He was disappointed in himself. There, privately, he showed real and deep feelings."

In our last of several interviews with him, Sasso said Dukakis had not made a last-minute decision to play it safe out of mistaken belief that the race was closer than it really was; beyond that, he has told friends he cannot explain Dukakis's behavior. And Dukakis himself, though admitting that Shaw's question took him aback, has denied that his illness was a strong impediment to an effective performance. That, however, leaves deeper questions that only Dukakis can answer some day; until he does, the fact remains that he failed to rise to the two greatest challenges in the fall campaign.

12

Losing

The day after the 1988 presidential election, John Sasso visited his vanquished candidate at the Dukakis residence on Perry Street. A bustle of Secret Service agents, police cars and barricades, photographers, and curious spectators surrounded the brick duplex in this quiet residential neighborhood just as it had for six months. While the governor and Sasso talked, Dukakis signed a piece of paper that discharged the Secret Service of their responsibility to protect him.

He had never cared for security. As governor, he often traveled alone on the subway and rarely appeared at public events with more than one aide, a driver. In fact, he was the last serious presidential candidate in 1988 to accept protection by the Secret Service, and not until after an overly enthusiastic crowd of Greek-Americans in Astoria tried to take pieces of him home as souvenirs just before the New York primary.

When Sasso left the house about an hour later, he was startled to notice that the barricades, the police cars, Secret Service agents, hangers-on, and photographers were all gone. Perry Street was again quiet, back to normal. He found the normalcy jarring. It was as if nothing had happened.

The result of a presidential election is so final, the consequences of losing so absolute (not like parliamentary systems, in which the loser takes his place next day as functioning leader of the opposition), that

Election Day is almost like a public execution for the person who is defeated. The political culture—governmental and journalistic—moves on at once, with scarcely a backward glance, befitting a society that sees little value in history and tradition. In this total concentration on the winner, and in George Bush's case on his administration as well, the campaign either ceases to exist as a matter of current relevance, or it is seen as having inexorably produced an inevitable result, usually attributed to powerful forces like the state of the economy or international relations, or to such primal national moods as satisfaction with the status quo or fear of the future.

The facts about 1988 do not support that standard analysis. Neither the national nor the international landscape changed radically between July and August when Bush and Dukakis reversed positions in the polls. Instead, the change was political. By the end of August, voters had sharply different opinions about Dukakis and Bush than the first impressions recorded by pollsters in July. That shift came about because George Bush was repackaged, Michael Dukakis was eviscerated, and after his nomination Dukakis presented a face to the country that a great many people didn't like.

In the end, Michael Dukakis was beaten soundly; but before the voters thrashed him, they kept giving him third, fourth, and fifth chances to offer them a reason to break clear of their still-tentative, misgiving-filled inclination to vote for Bush. Dukakis's failure was especially exasperating for his partisans but a source of mild encouragement for the Democratic Party. Even after the second debate, Dukakis's campaign skirted credibility, survived a plunge in the polls, and then surged in several states during the race's last two weeks. He was moving fast enough to keep George Bush's handlers nervous well into the afternoon on Election Day.

Had Dukakis made his case in the second debate, his campaign was prepared for a stretch drive that had a credible scenario for victory in the Electoral College and in the popular vote. Less well known was an interesting plan for a long-shot Electoral College win with a minority in the popular vote, which had a brief life after that final debate.

Just hours before the governor lost the Los Angeles debate, field-operations director Charles Baker—the young bearded architect behind Dukakis's New Hampshire primary victory eight months before—outlined the plan: it assumed, after a strong debate, that Dukakis would hold on to nine voting jurisdictions with 91 electoral votes, in Oregon, Minnesota, Iowa, West Virginia, New York, Massachusetts, Rhode Island, Hawaii, and the District of Columbia; it also assumed Dukakis would break out of close races and take seven other states with 127 electoral votes, in California, Washington, Montana, Wisconsin, Michigan, Pennsylvania, and Maryland.

As Baker figured things, Dukakis would then have had to win 52 more electoral votes to be elected president. His target list had fourteen states with 148 votes: North Dakota, South Dakota, Colorado, New Mexico, Texas, Arkansas, North Carolina, Kentucky, Missouri, Illinois, Ohio, Delaware, Connecticut, and Vermont.

In other words, if Dukakis had followed the debate script to which he had agreed in advance, and if it had worked, he did have a way of getting elected president. Even in the states where the governor's chances were fanciful on the day of the debate—Arkansas, North Carolina, Kentucky, Ohio, Texas, and Delaware—a strong performance at UCLA that night could have brought him close enough to force Bush to spend significant amounts of money in those states on advertising in the final days, money that then would not have been available to the states where the election could have gone either way.

Even after losing the Los Angeles debate he still had a way of winning on paper, and this desperate, end-game strategy might have made the Electoral College result much closer had Dukakis snapped out of his post-debate funk sooner and started at once with his economic populism and nationalism themes, and then stuck with them every day. This minority president scenario had first surfaced back in September, with Washington pollster and consultant Paul Maslin (originally Paul Simon's adviser) as the public spokesman, though in private cahoots with Charlie Baker.

Ten days from the election, Maslin met with John Sasso late on a Sunday night in San Jose, California, following a stunning Dukakis journey by train up the state's pivotal Central Valley. Maslin was not sanguine, but on paper they could win the election with only 48 or 49 percent of the popular vote.

As later outlined by Sasso, the last scenario was built around California, New York, and Massachusetts, with 96 electoral votes. It then required at least Illinois, Pennsylvania, and Michigan, with 69 votes. And to win the election, Dukakis would have had to win 105 of the remaining 363 electoral votes.

It was fanciful in the extreme, but not technically impossible, and the real point in all these end-game scenarios was showing that Bush's hold on the country remained tenuous. The litany of Dukakis campaign horrors was endless in the fall campaign; but the continually amazing truth was that despite the errors and failures, Bush's grip on the election was constantly slipping just enough to give Dukakis a chance to survive, and more than enough to suggest that his election was anything but predestined by the stars of Reaganite peace and prosperity; it was more like a gift.

The problem for the Democrats in the campaign's final month was not a generic reaction to liberalism or some equally pejorative synonym, but a specific rebuff aimed at Michael Dukakis.

When America finally voted on November 8, the election results carried the same message. The Democratic Party made gains in both the House and the Senate, achieved a net gain of one governorship, and held big leads in state legislatures across the nation. In fact, in some places, the Democrats made unanticipated gains in state legislatures where the Dukakis-Bentsen organization brought extra people to the polls. In recent years voting for congressional offices has been increasingly skewed by the power inherent in incumbency, above all by incumbent's ability to scare away opposition by massive fund-raising. Nonetheless, though 54 percent of the voters were choosing George Bush, 58 percent of them were voting Democratic in contests for Senate and House of Representatives seats. What is more, one had to look hard to find any evidence of Republican presidential coattails in local and state races. Conversely, voters elected several Democrats ideologically similar to Dukakis in states that Bush won handily.

The two most vivid examples were Ohio and New Jersey. In Ohio, Senator Howard Metzenbaum, perhaps the most liberal member of the Senate, crunched his once highly touted Republican opponent, Cleveland Mayor George Voinovich, by much more than the ten percentage point margin by which Dukakis lost the state; and to the east, New Jersey Senator Frank Lautenberg was easily reelected over neophyte politician Pete Dawkins in a state that even more decisively rejected Dukakis. Both Dawkins and Voinovich were very weak campaigners, but both Lautenberg and Metzenbaum fought back ferociously when they encountered strenuous Republican efforts to portray them as leftist, outside-the-mainstream liberals. They not only matched their opponents' television advertisements, they also managed to turn the charges being made against them into liabilities for their opponents.

Interviews conducted by NBC News with 1,165 voters as they left the Ohio polls on Election Day dramatically illustrate the difference in the results. Metzenbaum beat the Cleveland mayor among men by twelve percentage points while Dukakis was getting clobbered among them by fourteen; and among women, Metzenbaum had an eighteen-point lead over Voinovich while Bush and Dukakis were battling to a statistical draw. Metzenbaum was narrowly ahead among whites while Dukakis was fully twenty percentage points behind; among blacks, the difference in outcome was not statistically significant, with each Democrat getting more than 90 percent of the black vote to less than 10 percent for the opponent.

In the political middle, moreover, where races are still won or lost, it was Metzenbaum by sixteen percentage points and Bush by twenty-four among Independents; and among Democrats who confessed straying to Ronald Reagan in 1984 it was Metzenbaum by three to one and Dukakis by three to two.

The same trend was apparent in the Ohio electorate, broken down by income and class. Voinovich was a two-to-one loser among voters with family incomes of less than $20,000; he was sixteen percentage points back among middle-income voters who earn between $20,000 and $50,000; and he was ten points up among the affluent making more than $50,000. By dramatic contrast, Bush held Dukakis to a three-to-two margin below $20,000, appeared to lead him slightly in the $20,000 to $50,000 world; and thumped the governor by 70 to 30 percent among the more affluent.

These results show that Bush was able to win or come close on turf that should have been Dukakis's, but he ran miles ahead on his own. According to another network "exit poll," conducted nationally for CBS News and the *New York Times*, Dukakis led Bush among the 61 percent of those surveyed who called themselves liberal (17 percent of voters) or moderate (44 percent). By nearly tying Dukakis among moderates, however, Bush could parlay into victory his four-to-one margin among the 33 percent of the poll's sample who called themselves conservative.

But on Election Night, very little of this complexity was apparent as national television catalogued the one-sided Bush march to triumph through the Electoral College, and as he steadily built a decisive margin in the popular vote.

State after state lit up for Bush on the television networks' color-coded maps on the evening of November 8 with monotonous regularity, giving the victory more inevitability than it deserved. Dan Rather gave the election to Bush on CBS before 9:30 P.M. Eastern Standard Time, a full two and half hours before the polls would close on the West Coast, and NBC and ABC called the election less than an hour later. The task of certifying the Bush victory seemed humdrum, an exercise in simple addition.

Actually, the end was more complicated than that; indeed, the election results were closer than the tote boards indicated. At the twin bottom lines—53.4 percent for Bush to 45.6 percent for Dukakis in the popular vote and 426 to 111 in the Electoral College (one perverse West Virginian elector voted for Lloyd Bentsen for president and Dukakis for vice president)—Bush was every bit the winner of the "decisive victory" for which Dukakis congratulated him in his press conference the next day. The makeup of the victory, though, was one reason Bush's election has not been considered particularly decisive in its meaning for his infant government, and for the Democratic Party. The results depict a far more decisive Dukakis defeat than a decisive Bush victory.

To begin with, the Bush victory numbers were far from uniform. At the core of his political base were fourteen states with 103 electoral votes, where Bush won by the crushing margin of twenty percentage points or more: Florida, Georgia, Mississippi, South Carolina, and Virginia in the South; Alaska, Arizona, Idaho, Utah, and Wyoming in the West; Dan Quayle's loyal Indiana and Nebraska in the Midwest; and tax-hating, Massachusetts-loathing New Hampshire in the Northeast. Within those states, Bush's popular-vote margin over Dukakis was more than 3.5 million votes, or slightly more than half his overall margin.

Beyond the rock-solid fourteen states, Bush carried fourteen others with 151 electoral votes by margins of roughly 10 to 20 percentage points: Alabama, Arkansas, Kentucky, Louisiana, North Carolina, and Tennessee to the South; Texas and Oklahoma to the Southwest; Kansas, North Dakota, and Ohio to the Midwest; and Delaware, Maine, and New Jersey to the Northeast. These states provided Bush with a popular-vote margin of another 3.3 million votes.

Against this Bush base must be placed the Dukakis victories, in all but a few places by far smaller margins, in eleven electoral jurisdictions: Massachusetts, Rhode Island, New York, District of Columbia, and West Virginia in the Northeast; Wisconsin, Minnesota, and Iowa in the Midwest; and Oregon, Washington, and Hawaii in the West. Dukakis built a margin of roughly 1.2 million votes over the vice president in those places.

For all Bush's complete domination in fully twenty-eight states, though, they added up to only 254 electoral votes, sixteen short of victory.

Symbolically as well as literally, for the state was a key Dukakis target and the critical judgment call for the television networks on Election Night, it was the governor's loss of Michigan's twenty electoral votes by not quite eight percentage points that effectively put Bush over the top. Another major Dukakis target from the not-too-distant past, Colorado, also roughly matched Bush's eight-point margin nationally in the popular vote.

Thus, thirty states provided 282 electoral votes for the Republican ticket in convincing fashion. In varying ways, they reflected the Republican Party's strong geographic base in an increasingly conservative era in presidential politics that began with Richard Nixon's election on his second try twenty years before; but they also reflected failures by the Dukakis campaign and its candidate dating from late spring and continuing past Labor Day through the two debates. A Dukakis campaign that lived up to the promise reflected by its post-Atlanta "bounce" in the polls could have been a contender at least in Arkansas, Kentucky, Louisiana, Maine, North Dakota, New Jersey, and Ohio. The requiem for this not-quite heavyweight was therefore not inevitable; or, as Dukakis said ruefully in his next-day press conference, "It was winnable."

Once the networks had made their projections and Dukakis and Bush had made their concession and victory statements, Bush's Electoral College total still had to be determined in the early morning hours.

In six states with 78 electoral votes—all having given Dukakis the lead in state polls during the summer—Bush ended up the winner by four to six percentage points: Connecticut, Missouri, Montana, South Dakota, California, and New Mexico. And in four others with 62 electoral votes, the governor lost by zero to two percentage points: Illinois, Pennsylvania, Maryland, and Vermont.

Counting the pivotal results from Michigan and Colorado, it is fair to say that twelve states with 168 electoral votes supplied the margin of victory in the 1988 presidential election. Dukakis had led in all these at the time of the Republican convention in mid-August, was in position to regain his advantage at the time of the first debate on September 25, was not out of contention at the time of the second one on October 13, and was moving in all of them down the homestretch in the campaign. In the end, Bush won them all in popular votes by the cumulative total of 15.4 million votes to 14.2 million for Dukakis. In this election within the election, the Bush margin was just short of 52 to 48 percent in a universe where 29.6 million votes, almost exactly one-third of the total, were cast.

This is the election that could have gone just as decisively the other way, at least as late as the end of September, had Dukakis developed and stuck with a cogent campaign theme, and had he done what he was capable of doing, and indeed what he had agreed to do, in the two debates.

Defeat is defeat, but for the Democratic Party's future at the presidential level it is of more than idle historical interest whether Dukakis's defeat was preordained on the larger tableau of the 1980s megatrends in politics and economics, or whether it was a product of the 1988 campaign itself and of Dukakis himself.

Going into 1988, one supposed given in the landscape was a Republican "lock" on the modern Electoral College: twenty-three states, offering 202 electoral votes, which had voted for the Republican nominee in each election from 1968 through 1984. On one level, Dukakis was the first Democratic nominee in twenty years to break that lock with his victories in Iowa and Oregon, and his narrow misses in California, Illinois, New Mexico, South Dakota, and Vermont; but on another level, he showed most clearly how the lock can be obliterated by building—before his fall—double-digit polling leads not only in those states, but in Colorado and New Jersey as well.

Even after he had squandered the summer and much of September as well, the fact remains—vexing in the extreme for Dukakis but encouraging for his party—that twenty-three states with 280 electoral votes remained in play at least through the first debate and quite possibly even after the second one; in those states, moreover, Dukakis was in fact surging after he finally hit his thematic stride in the campaign's final three weeks.

For the electorate itself, the profile sketched by the networks' exit polls on Election Day appears to be very hostile not only to Dukakis but also to any Democrat seeking the presidency. Closer inspection, however, shows that this was potentially a much closer election, and in fact was closer than the national data suggest.

According to the CBS News-*New York Times* survey of 11,645 voters who filled out questionnaires as they left polling places around the country, four Bush-Dukakis gaps stand out starkly: Among men, Bush was the winner by 57 to 41 percent; among whites, it was Bush by 59 to 40 percent; among married people (69 percent of this huge sample), the vice president dominated, 57 to 42 percent; and among professional or managerial workers (31 percent of the sample), Bush beat Dukakis by 59 to 40 percent.

The polling data, however, were, like the results themselves, profoundly skewed by Bush's overwhelming dominance and Dukakis's manifest failure among southerners. According to the CBS-*New York Times* survey, Bush beat Dukakis by seventeen points, 58 to 41 percent, among the 28 percent of the survey's respondents who voted in the South; by significant contrast, he had little advantage in the East and was ahead by five and six percentage points respectively in the Midwest and West.

In actual votes, the geopolitical split was equally pronounced. In eleven southern states that gave Bush 138 electoral votes for sweeping them, the vice president beat Dukakis by roughly 58.7 to 41.3 percent; his margin in the states was more than 3.9 million out of more than 22.8 million votes cast in the eleven southern states, comprising slightly more than one-fourth of votes nationally, and more than half his popular-vote margin.

The Bush southern sweep, marginally less overwhelming than Ronald Reagan's in 1984, reflected the region's more pronounced conservatism, its greater devotion to national-defense issues and to anticommunism, and its more widespread view of Michael Dukakis as an out-of-the-mainstream liberal. The Bush margin in the South, however, also reflected Dukakis's essentially writing off the region after Labor Day and restricting his appearances almost exclusively to the border states and to Texas, while pulling most paid workers out of Deep South states and making no significant purchases of television time in southern markets.

Under different circumstances—above all a clearly tight national race—Dukakis might have had a shot at, and indeed had originally targeted, the six states in the so-called Outer South: Tennessee, North Carolina, Georgia, Arkansas, Louisiana, and Texas. And indeed, in one of these, Arkansas, campaign pollster Tubby Harrison tested in September a version of the later Dukakis message on economic populism and nationalism in the campaign's closing weeks.

The reality in fall 1988, though, was a Democratic candidate bereft of fight, message, and effective television advertising; the South was as good as lost by Labor Day, and Dukakis's dim chances on its fringe probably were gone after his performance in the first debate failed to change the political landscape.

The rest of the country proved more durably competitive. In the forty other jurisdictions offering 400 electoral votes that voted on November 8—including several midwestern and western states that Bush carried by hefty margins—the vice president's margin while taking twenty-nine of them was not quite three million out of more than 66 million votes cast, or 52.2 to 47.8 percent; that election was close, and Dukakis's defeat is attributable primarily to his deficiencies and mistakes as the nominee.

Dukakis's defeat is not at all attributable, moreover, to a fantasy favorite among Democrats in general and some liberals in particular, that if only a person on a galloping stallion of charisma would appear some day the party could mobilize an overwhelming majority among the roughly half of the eligible adults who sat out the 1988 presidential election. The numbers are indeed tantalizing, but the evidence strongly suggests that the view from the sidelines was not appreciably different from the voting-booth view.

According to a survey by CBS News and the *New York Times* of about 400 interviews with nonvoters contacted a week after the election, Bush's margin over Dukakis would have been 50 to 34 percent had they voted; even allowing for error and bandwagon mentality, the suggestion is that no Dukakis tide was lurking offshore.

Overall, according to the best chronicler of this information, the nonpartisan Committee for the Study of the American Electorate in Washington, voter registration was down in 1988, the 2.2 percent decline erasing most of the slight gain of 3.2 percent registered by the considerable Republican and Democratic activity in 1984. This decline was a definite benefit for the Republican Party, whose registration total in sixteen states studied by the committee was up 2.1 points, roughly equal to the Democrats' dip of 2.1 points.

Even before the numbers began to flow out of election departments around the country, intimations were seen that despite the first presidential election in twenty years without an incumbent on the ballot, voting would continue its thirty-year decline. Viewers' ratings for the television networks' scaled-back coverage of the national conventions, for example, slipped extensively, and displeasure with both parties' nominees was an almost constant leitmotif in the general election. The committee reported that the Gallup Organization's plague-on-both-your-houses sentiment was matched in modern times only by public reaction to Jimmy Carter versus Ronald Reagan in 1980, a year with a quasi-credible alternative in John Anderson's independent candidacy.

As it was, the 91.3 million Americans who trooped to the polls on November 8—half of the eligible electorate—were part of the lowest turnout since the nation was offered the unappetizing choice between Calvin Coolidge and John Davis in 1924. Indeed, according to one of the committee's board members, Professor Walter Dean Burnham of the University of Texas at Austin, the voter turnout outside the South was the lowest since John Quincy Adams's election in 1824.

Despite the Republicans' slight gain in registration as compared to the Democrats' efforts, Republican voter turnout was off 5 percent nationally from 1984, and declined in every state. On the other hand, the committee found that participation by Democrats was slightly up (by just less than one point), rising in thirty-eight jurisdictions and dipping in thirteen.

It is impossible to know with objective confidence how much of this Republican dip stemmed from the almost universal, media-fed view by Election Day that George Bush couldn't lose, though the question seems valid. It is also probably fair to observe that Bush had a more difficult task as the Republican nominee running as the representative of continuity after two terms under a far more beloved president; and it is similarly fair to observe that most of his message to the voters was grossly negative, and was seen thus by clear majorities in most preelection polls.

Dukakis, however, must bear the responsibility for not being more successful in giving Democrats compelling reasons to support him. Leading the out party with a clear shot at the White House, he not only failed to articulate a case for a new direction in national policy, he also failed to make a consistently compelling case except at the very end to the working class, modest-income core of his party. And some evidence says that this failure, particularly with black voters, cost him a few vital states.

Detailed evidence about racial voting patterns comes out slowly, but the data suggest that he won at worst only a slightly smaller percentage of the black vote than Walter Mondale received in 1984. According to CBS News exit polling on Election Day, Dukakis's share of the black vote was 86 percent, compared to 89 percent for Mondale. This difference amounts to a statistical dead heat because it is within the 3 percent margin of error for the sample of about 1,500 blacks in the poll.

Other data in the CBS survey indicate, however, that turnout by blacks was down along with overall turnout, though for blacks the apparent decline reverses the notable increases since 1980. In a post-election analysis done at the Joint Center for Political Studies, Dr. Linda F. Williams, associate director of research, focused on data from seven states with 146 electoral votes, all won by Bush: California, Illinois, Maryland, Michigan, Mississippi, North Carolina, and Pennsylvania. In each, judging by CBS exit polls in those states, Bush's margin of victory appears to have been exceeded by an admittedly rough estimate of the number of blacks who did not vote.

We feel that the results in North Carolina and Mississippi could not have been reversed without unreasonably large black voter turnouts; moreover, in Michigan, the CBS exit poll suggests a sizable jump in black turnout over 1984 that still left Dukakis nearly 300,000 votes short of victory.

In the other four states, though, the numbers are more interesting. In California, where black turnout appeared to have dropped, Bush's margin of 308,000 votes compares to a nonvoting black adult population of possibly 840,000; in Illinois, the Bush margin was 117,000, and 541,000 blacks appear not to have voted; in Maryland, the most dramatic example, the tiny Bush edge of 40,000 votes is dwarfed by the estimated 588,000 blacks who didn't vote; and in Pennsylvania, Bush won by 107,000 votes, and more than 380,000 voting-age blacks stayed away from the polls.

Dukakis neglected black voters in the general election. The problem was not his side of the relationship with Jesse Jackson after the Democratic convention, nor was it Jackson's side of the relationship. The problem was symbolized by Dukakis's decision in August—on last-minute advice from a white Mississippi politician—not to mention the anniversary of the murders of three civil-rights workers when he visited the Neshoba County Fair. Until the very end of the campaign, the governor did not reach out to black communities in America, didn't campaign in them early enough in the day for his appearances to make the network news shows, didn't emphasize his very real commitment to justice, didn't utter the magic words "I need your help," and didn't visibly target significant campaign resources. The Dukakis campaign's focus on the Democrats who had supported Ronald Reagan in the 1980s was not misplaced, but it never required slighting black Democrats to be effective; a great many black Americans got the message loud and clear.

It should be frustrating for Dukakis to know that he did not pay enough attention to his party's base of support in the general election; neglecting your base breaks the first rule of politics. Nothing can be more vexing, however, than knowing that the electorate that chose George Bush to be the country's forty-first president was more inclined to see the country through Dukakis's eyes than Bush's; his failure in fall 1988 was clearly personal, both in perceived lack of presidential stature and equally perceived lack of commitment to values that matter to a great many voters—especially patriotism, strength, and being tough on criminals.

On November 21 and 22, 1,010 adults who voted in the election were surveyed by Peter D. Hart Research Associates for the American Federation of State, County and Municipal Employees.

Hart's report, like the election results in detail, provides almost no comfort to conservatives and to the positions Bush took during the campaign.

Asked what bothered them most about Dukakis's perceived positions, only 12 percent cited his refusal to rule out a tax increase, and his proposal to increase spending on education and health care was cited by only 10 percent. Hart wrote that "The voters may have read George Bush's lips on no new taxes, but they did not cast their vote on this basis. . . . In terms of dealing with the deficit, voters appear to be significantly more concerned about avoiding cuts in domestic programs and investing in key domestic needs than about protecting the defense budget and avoiding new taxes."

Specifically, two-thirds of Hart's respondents said they would be willing to see their taxes raised to pay for more long-term health care for the elderly and disabled (including 57 percent of the Bush voters); and half would be willing to see their taxes rise to pay for more financial aid to college students from middle-income families and to make housing costs and mortgages affordable for young families and first-time home buyers.

Hart also offered his respondents two alternative national strategies that expressed the alternatives facing the nation in a harsh environment filled with fiscal red ink and conflicts among national goals.

His first choice was the conservative one: "We should insist that defense programs be fully funded and reject any attempt to raise taxes, even if this means that many domestic programs will only receive limited funding until the deficit is under control."

The other choice went toward the liberal: "We should avoid cuts in domestic programs and allow for new spending on education and health care, even if this means no increases in defense spending and increased taxes."

Combining those who strongly supported each position with the less strong supporters and the leaners left a crunching victory for the less conservative statement, by 56 to 33 percent.

"Dukakis's advantages in this race," Hart summed up, "were perceptions that he was more likely to help the middle class and working people and more willing to invest in important domestic needs such as education and health care. By two to one, voters say they preferred Dukakis's approach over Bush's on helping the middle class and working people. What voters liked best about Dukakis in general was greater willingness to spend money on education and health care."

Why then did a clear majority vote for Bush? The answers vary, but they can be grouped into two areas: presidential stature and "social issues," especially crime and law enforcement, but also perceptions about each candidate's ideology in a relatively conservative age.

Peter Hart didn't mince words: "Bush won this election first and foremost on experience. He also established a clear advantage over Dukakis on national defense and military issues and on crime and law enforcement issues. Ideological labeling and the social issues took some toll on Dukakis as well."

Similar results showed up in another major postelection voter survey, a poll of more than 2,000 registered voters nationwide that the Gallup Organization conducted for the Times Mirror newspapers on November 9 and 10. Asked to pick from a list of voting reasons, more Bush voters than Dukakis voters chose these four topics: Dukakis's liberalism (very important to 50 percent of the Bush voters, compared to 23 percent of Dukakis's); Bush's conservatism (47 percent of Bush's suporters mentioned it versus 28 percent of Dukakis's); the Pledge of Allegiance controversy (a 39 to 20 percent margin for the Bush voters); and the Massachusetts furlough program controversy (a 37 to 14 percent edge to Bush's voters).

Two issues were significantly more important to Bush's supporters than to Dukakis's: strengthening the country's defenses (72 to 37 percent), and the death penalty (57 to 38 percent).

Behind these numbers we see first a phenomenon picked up in the television networks' exit polls on Election Night: Dukakis led Bush among the clear majority of voters (about 60 percent) who described themselves as liberals or moderates; however, Bush not only had a viselike grip on conservatives but was able to nearly tie Dukakis among more moderate voters, thus producing his majority. His skillful campaign was maternal in nurturing the right by favoring the death penalty, every new weapons system worth a drawing board, no new taxes, a ban on abortion and lower capital-gains taxes; but it also assiduously made inroads in the center with its "kinder, gentler" imagery: the education president, born-again environmentalist, tax breaks for child care, and ethics. And, taking some of the Reaganite ideological edge off Bush, his campaign also had strong support from the Ronald Reagan White House, which in a summer of flip-flops accepted previously opposed legislation: requiring public notification of business closing plans, beginning catastrophic health insurance, toughening foreign-trade rules, and reforming welfare; got rid of Attorney General Edwin Meese; and postponed controversial steps until after the election, including farm-foreclosure notices and new rules permitting piecework labor in the home.

A final factor in the postelection polls cannot be overlooked, but that can be overemphasized, is foreign policy and national defense. Long before the general-election battle was joined, Boston political consultant John Marttila, Tom Kiley's partner, called a candidate's success in showing strength on national security issues the "price of admission" to winning the presidency. Marttila did not necessarily mean that foreign policy was the most important, or even a major issue for American voters in the 1988 election; if a candidate's credentials on a topic that always lurks in the background in this nuclear age are not seen as legitimate, he will not make it to the White House because voters realize that clear incompetence in foreign policy is the most intolerable of all unacceptable attributes of a presidential candidate.

Martilla began the 1988 cycle as one of Joe Biden's top advisers, and after the senator's withdrawal he teamed with three other polling organizations (two of which eschew partisan political work, and the other is Republican oriented), got some foundation support, and proceeded to help with some of the most profound research into American attitudes about foreign policy and national security issues that has ever been done. For our purposes, two surveys done in early October and just before the election by the Daniel Yankelovich Group provide some food for thought.

As the election year began, the broad political consensus in both parties was that because President Reagan and Soviet President Mikhail Gorbachev had taken strides toward a new, less confrontational relationship, foreign policy was not likely to be a major issue in the long campaign. By Election Day, that agreement was no longer a matter of clear consensus. The Yankelovich report summarized its findings:

Our investigation of the role played by national security issues in voter decision-making in the 1988 election suggests that the power of national security issues should not be underestimated in presidential politics. While it is true that early survey results, including our own data, showed that voters were significantly more focused on economic and social issues and truly played down national security issues, in the end national security issues may well have made the difference for George Bush.

The polls on which this and other judgments were based sampled slightly more than 1,000 registered voters between September 30 and October 4, and November 4 to 7. In general both foreign-policy concerns and the Bush advantage increased between the two surveys.

As shown in the other polls, the Bush voters generally cared much more deeply about foreign policy and defense issues, 43 percent of them calling these the most important topic, whereas 37 percent chose economic issues. By contrast, foreign policy was the lowest priority for Dukakis supporters; only 24 percent cited it as extremely important just before the election, below the environment and personal qualities, and well below economic and social issues.

Among the electorate as a whole, acknowledgment of Bush as likely to do a better job in specific foreign-policy areas was overwhelming. He had a 67 to 22 percent advantage over Dukakis on handling relations with the Soviet Union, a 64 to 22 percent margin on negotiating arms-control agreements, a 62 to 24 percent advantage on guarding against Soviet aggression, a 53 to 26 percent edge on solving the Arab-Israeli conflict, and a 57 to 28 percent margin on dealing with Central America. And on the basic question of who would strengthen and who would weaken United States national security, the preelection poll found Bush chosen as more likely to strengthen it by 25 to 15 percent, and more important, Dukakis more likely to weaken it by fully 37 to 8 percent.

Back in June, during an interview, Tom Kiley voiced to us his worry that a perception of not being tough enough on foreign-policy issues would be a major liability for Dukakis if it ever became widely held, a view that Tubby Harrison also held long before the general-election battle. In fact, late one night in summer 1987, as he labored over a message for the fledgling candidacy, Paul Tully looked up in dismay and growled, "I think we've got another George McGovern," whose losing candidacy Tully had slaved for in 1972. Moreover, making sure that Dukakis was accepted by most voters as fundamentally qualified to run the nation's foreign policy had been a constant intent among the governor's small group of foreign-policy advisers, led by Georgetown University Professor Madeleine Albright, assisted later by former Edward Kennedy aide James Steinberg, from the campaign's earliest days.

They did not always have a cooperative candidate, however. Although he was generally well informed, Dukakis had an annoying habit of misspeaking slightly throughout the campaign, reinforcing the impression of a novice and giving his Democratic and Republican opponents a constant supply of ammunition, whether on the United States commitment to South Korea; the NATO doctrine of early, first use of nuclear weapons in the event of Soviet aggression in Europe; his opposition to many new strategic weapons systems; and his long insistence that the Reagan military buildup had nothing to do with the Soviet Union's willingness to resume arms-reduction negotiations.

Moreover, once the general-election campaign was under way in earnest, he used little foreign-policy material in his campaigning after mid-September speeches, leaving the field both to a constant stream of Bush attacks on his alleged weakness and willingness to unilaterally disarm and of Bush claims to significant foreign-policy experience during his career.

Dukakis did not make the substantive merit in the attacks an issue until just before the election, after they had already worked; the thin record behind Bush's claims was never consistently highlighted; and the governor never advanced his own ideas with enough frequency or cogency to make them part of the political mix. He lost the foreign-policy battle by default, not because his views were rejected.

Moreover, he also failed in the one foreign-policy area that Americans consider just as serious as the more standard topics of diplomacy and weaponry—economics—in an era when the United States has become the largest debtor nation in the world, has had a hemorrhaging trade deficit almost all the way through the 1980s, and has become deeply dependent on foreign capital to finance its public and private business debt.

According to the preelection Yankelovich poll, 72 percent of the registered voters surveyed strongly approved of the statement that the government should pay as much attention to America's economic strength as to its military strength. That proposition received more approval than any other. Moreover, among probable voters, this view was identified as a Dukakis position by a 50 to 36 percent majority.

Nonetheless, the poll gave dramatic evidence of Dukakis's complete failure to communicate his position. By 38 to 33 percent, more Bush than Dukakis supporters called it extremely important to make the United States more competitive in the world economy. And much, much worse were these additional findings: by 52 to 37 percent, voters said Bush would do a better job in making the country more competitive;

and by 44 to 39 percent he was preferred as the person to stand up to nations using unfair trade practices.

In the 1988 election, foreign policy, broadly defined, was far more than than a collection of positions on major questions of the day; the situation was quite different politically from the one that prevailed when Ronald Reagan was first elected in 1980, in part because of his very specific views about the alleged decline of American military might and its will. In 1988, foreign policy was a metaphor for the personal qualities Americans want their presidents to radiate—stature, readiness, and strength; the verdict Dukakis lost had far more to do with his general election campaign's failure at every critical juncture to project lack of stature, lack of readiness, and his weakness, defined as unwillingness to fight back. His tragedy is that he lost the verdict to a man whose own campaign consisted primarily (Jack Corrigan's old phrase about Gary Hart) of Dukakis antimatter.

His tragedy is compounded because the dangers, the pitfalls, the needs, and the best solutions were all laid out for him: from the earliest stirrings of his candidacy (when John Sasso emphasized drawing contrasts with opponents and not being bashful about rhetorical hyperbole); through his clinching primary victories (when Tubby Harrison warned about the lurking danger in a liberal image and began urging the twin messages of middle-class security and American economic primacy); through April (when Dukakis was first urged by his closest advisers to bring in fresh talent for the general election, beginning with John Sasso); through May (when his party's sharpest minds showed precisely why scarce resources had to be carefully targeted on the states with the best chance of producing an Electoral-College majority); through June (when Tom Kiley recommended a strategy for combining political know-how with advertising creativity to get Dukakis on the air quickly and with power); through the summer (when Susan Estrich urged Dukakis not to sit tight in Massachusetts and to vigorously counter Bush's assaults with offensives of his own); and through two high-stakes debates (when Tom Donilon provided Dukakis with enough material to win decisively).

Against all this advice, above all during August when he lost his momentum, his direction, his confidence, and his lead, all these people and more recall vividly Dukakis's clipped phrases and self-assuredness in meetings: you're pressing me to go too hard too soon; the voters don't care what Bush and I think of each other; nobody pays attention in August; I need to lay out my specific ideas first before I go on the attack because people don't know me well enough.

No one agreed with him. The collective failure of Dukakis's campaign lay in its high command's failure to batter down the candidate's certainty about things he didn't know. This candidate had a right to far more candor and face-to-face bluntness than he got.

With Sasso's departure in September 1987, Dukakis halted the most important process in presidential politics—growth. He was in most respects an ideal candidate for the long grind in the primaries: disciplined, steady, the safest of bets. Dukakis failed to realize that in presidential politics the hurdles get higher as you go down the track. Trapped within his self-sufficiency, he never prepared himself to clear them. The governor himself has often commented about how shocked he was by the difference between the frenzy of general-election life and the primary grind. With the hopes of millions of Americans riding on him by then, however, he had no right not to be ready for that frenzy, no right especially after having been told what he would face.

His defeat in Massachusetts in 1978 and his comeback four years later was understandably a defining experience in his public career. Nothing about his conduct in 1988, however, indicates that he learned from the experience; George Bush's potential and his punches were telegraphed far more clearly than those of Ed King. It is understandable that Dukakis loved the story of Aristides the Just—banished and then called back by a chastened Athenian citizenry—as it was told in the volume Peter McCarthy gave him after his 1978 defeat. The allegory here is the immutable, well-formed leader, and the people who eventually see his worth. In that concept is the sense of one's own adequacy that the Greeks call *hubris*, the excessive pride that Americans saw as arrogance in 1988.

Rather than chuckle over the Aristides story, Dukakis might have been better advised to ponder a character from Greek tragedy who also had a tic to Dukakis family lore: Euripides' Hippolytus. The governor's father had been in a college theatrical group and played the famed character when he met his future wife.

The play is about the demise of a fundamentally good man consumed by the virtue in his chaste love for the virgin goddess of the hunt, Artemis. His contempt for profane love, for passion, infuriates the goddess of love, Aphrodite, who plots his ruin and succeeds partly because Hippolytus is much too disdainful to notice the attacks being readied on his life. His servant warns him of "an old law laid down for mortal men": "Abhor pride and avoid exclusiveness." But of Aphrodite, Hippolytus says, "I greet her from a distance. My body is pure."

Nothing is inevitable, but a more than haunting beauty lies in this observation by Professor J. Peter Euben of the University of California at Santa Cruz in a collection of essays on Greek tragedy and political theory: "Somewhere Goethe writes of classical Greece as a magic mirror

in which, when living men and women gaze seeking the image of a
culture long dead, they see not unreturning ghosts but the half-veiled
face of their own destiny."

Michael Dukakis in 1988 failed as a politician to offer a token to the
Aphrodite in our culture. He is a passionate husband, a magnificent
father, his closest friends have loved him since adolescence, and his most
intimate political associates have been ardent supporters for years. In the
final phase of a presidential election, however, there is no time for
retailing; you either make the grand gesture, you either fight for the
prize, or you are almost certain to lose, especially to the determined
cynicism in a crusade of vilification. We believe that when the crunch
came, Dukakis was overwhelmed.

We do not, however, share the prevailing view that Dukakis's
failure was a legitimate clue that he would have been a bad president.
To us, that is the necessary irony in this tragedy. Dukakis thinks big,
not small. More than a dozen interviews with him over the twenty
months he was a candidate, like dozens of other conversations since he
first ran for governor in 1974, depict a man as ready for the challenge
of national governance as he was unready to meet the challenge of the
general election.

As he put it often in automobiles, airplanes, hotel suites, and his
State House office, we had a chance at last to break the stalemate that
has gripped domestic policy since the Reagan revolution ran out of
gas during the 1982 recession. A president, he said, who took
advantage of a remarkable bipartisan consensus in Congress, instead
of standing in its way, could make major policy breakthroughs; could
begin extending health-care protection to the tens of millions of
people who lack it; could help young people finance the higher
education that is critical to our economic future; could make home
ownership possible for young families of average means. He also
sensed the power of the bipartisan consensus already held in Congress
for achieving steady progress in lowering the federal deficit, if a
president would support instead of block it with blind ideological
inflexibility. And unlike his opponent, he had already thought
through the obvious incompatibility between Ronald Reagan's and
George Bush's appetites for weaponry and budgetary reality, and had
made the choices that neither of them would face. And finally, for all
his supposed arrogance, he was acutely conscious of his status as
Washington outsider and spoke often about his most helpful advisers
being the leaders of Congress; within days, he knew that his choice of
Lloyd Bentsen was even more inspired for its potential for governance
than its political benefits. As a politician, he almost perfectly fits the
model of a successful president designed by presidential scholar

James David Barber of Duke University: intensely active and activist about challenges, and positive in his attitude toward tough work.

The last conversation we had was six days before the election, in a car ride from downtown Pittsburgh to the airport. "I think there is a very broad consensus behind a great many things in this country," he said. "One of the things you've got to do as president is to decide what the most important priorities are, because as we know you've got to focus in on the most important, and secondly build the kind of support using the platform of the office, the strength of the office, as well as the political skills that you have to have to involve the Congress in what you're doing. You can sit up there on Olympus and talk all you want."

The experience that is so maddeningly mystifying is seeing all this in a reporter's notebook and rarely hearing it in a speech.

Dukakis knew that is what we were thinking that night as he rattled on: "You know a lot of people have said it should have happened months ago, and we'll find out on the eighth of November."

He did.

Index

J

K

L